Chocolate
Coffee
Peanut
Chicken
Pork
Black Pudding
Liver
Beef
Lamb
Goat's Cheese
Washed-rind Cheese
Blue Cheese
Hard Cheese
Soft Cheese
Mushroom
Aubergine
Cumin
Beetroot
Potato
Celery
Watercress
Caper
Horseradish
Onion
Garlic
Truffle
Cabbage
Swede
Cauliflower
Broccoli
Globe Artichoke
Asparagus
Egg
Shellfish
White Fish
Oyster
Caviar
Oily Fish
Anchovy
Smoked Fish
Bacon
Prosciutto
Olive
Saffron
Anise
Cucumber
Dill
Parsley
Coriander Leaf

Roasted

Meaty

Earthy

Mustardy

Sulphurous

Marine

Brine & Salt

Green & Grassy

THE *flavour* THESAURUS

THE *flavour* THESAURUS

Pairings, recipes and ideas for the creative cook

NIKI SEGNIT

B L O O M S B U R Y

LONDON · BERLIN · NEW YORK · SYDNEY

It seems fitting to dedicate this book to a pair:
my cooking advisor and mother, Marian Stevens,
and my writing advisor and husband, Nat Segnit.

Contents

'... lamb and apricots are one of those combinations which exist together in a relation that is not just complementary but that seems to partake of a higher order of inevitability – a taste which exists in the mind of God. These combinations have the quality of a logical discovery: bacon and eggs, rice and soy sauce, Sauternes and *foie gras*, white truffles and pasta, *steak-frites*, strawberries and cream, lamb and garlic, Armagnac and prunes, port and Stilton, fish soup and *rouille*, chicken and mushrooms; to the committed explorer of the senses, the first experience of any of them will have an impact comparable with an astronomer's discovery of a new planet.'

John Lanchester, *The Debt to Pleasure*

Introduction

I hadn't realised the depth of my dependence on cookery books until I noticed that my copy of Elizabeth David's *French Provincial Cooking* had fingernail marks running below the recipes. Here was stark evidence of my timidity, an insistence on clinging to a set of instructions, like a handrail in the dark, when after 20 years of cooking I should surely have been well enough versed in the basics to let go and trust my instincts. Had I ever really learnt to cook? Or was I just reasonably adept at following instructions? My mother, like her mother before her, is an excellent cook, but owns only two recipe books and a scrapbook of clippings, and rarely consults even those. I began to suspect that the dozens of books I owned were both a symptom and a cause of my lack of kitchen confidence.

It was at a dinner around the same time that a friend served a dish using two ingredients it would never have occurred to me to pair. How, I wondered, did she know *that* would work? There was something in the air about surprising flavour matches, the kind of audacious combinations pioneered by chefs like Heston Blumenthal, Ferran Adrià and Grant Achatz. What lay at the heart of their approach to food was, as far as I could see, a deeper understanding of the links between flavours. Being an ordinary, if slightly obsessive, home cook, I didn't have the equipment or resources to research these; what I needed was a manual, a primer to help me understand how and why one flavour might go with another, their points in common and their differences. Something like a thesaurus of flavours. But no such book existed and so, with what turned out in hindsight to be almost touching naivety, I thought I might try to compile one myself.

My first task was to draw up the list of flavours. Stopping at 99 was to some extent arbitrary. Nonetheless, a flavour thesaurus that accounted for every single flavour would be as impractical as it would be uncomfortable on the lap. Other than potatoes, the staple carbohydrates have been omitted. The same goes for most common condiments. There are, of course, plenty of interesting things to say about the flavours of rice, pasta, black pepper, vinegar and salt, but their flavour affinities are so wide as to exclude themselves by virtue of sheer compatibility. Other omissions, like courgette, might strike you as odd: all I can say to the courgette fan is a) sorry, and b) this book makes no claims to be the last word on the subject. Any book on flavour is going to be at least in part subjective and, in writing about the pairings I find most interesting, or like to eat the most, I will inevitably have left gaps that come down to nothing other than a matter of taste.

The majority of flavours appear under their own heading. In a few instances, where it seemed to make sense, some very similarly flavoured ingredients share a heading. Anise, for example, covers anise seeds, fennel, tarragon, liquorice and pastis. Similarly, neither bacon and ham nor Brussels sprouts and cabbage could easily be separated, so they labour slightly uncomfortably under composite categories. When it came to a choice between untidiness and boring the reader with repetitions, I chose untidiness every time.

Then I sorted the flavours into categories. Most of us are familiar with the concept of flavour families, whether we know it or not. Floral, citrus, herbaceous: the sort of descriptors you might encounter on the back of a wine bottle, to help conjure an idea of how something might taste. And it's into these, or adjectival headings like them, that the flavours are divided. The flavours in each family have certain qualities in common; in turn, each family is linked in some way to the one adjacent to it, so that, in sum, they comprise a sort of 360° spectrum, represented opposite as a 'flavour wheel'.

Take the Citrussy family, for example. This covers zesty, citric flavours like orange, lemon and cardamom. Cardamom, in turn, has flavour compounds in common with rosemary, which is the first flavour in the next flavour family, Bramble & Hedge. At the other end of Bramble & Hedge, blackberry leads to the first flavour in the Floral Fruity family: raspberry. And so on round the wheel, flavour leading to flavour, family to family, in a developing sequence of relations you might enter at lemon and leave at blue cheese.

I acknowledge that this methodology has its limitations. Some flavours resisted easy categorisation: coriander seed, for instance, ended up under Floral Fruity, but might as easily have sat in Citrussy or Spicy. And how an ingredient is prepared can make all the difference to its character. The flavour of cabbage, for example, is mustardy when raw, sulphurous cooked. The flavour wheel, in short, is by no means intended to be an inarguable, objective framework for understanding flavour – but it does provide a stimulating and intriguing means of navigating your way around the subject.

Next came the pairings. Clearly, dishes often have more than two primary ingredients, but a couple of considerations led me to make pairs of flavours the organising principle of my *Flavour Thesaurus*. First, sanity (mine). Even restricting myself to 99 flavours, if I had set out to write about flavour *trios* I would have been faced with 156,849 possible combinations; 4,851 possible pairings seemed more to scale with the sort of book it would be both possible to write and pleasurable to read. Second, clarity. To assess, in the mind's palate, the compatibility of two flavours is exponentially easier than imagining the interplay of three or more. Necessarily, I often discuss a flavour combination in the context of a dish that contains other ingredients (for example, parsley and mint in tabbouleh), but the emphasis is always on the main flavour pairing under discussion.

The entries elaborate on each of these pairings, drawing promiscuously on flavour science, history, culture, chefs' wisdom and personal prejudice – anything that might shed light on why certain flavours work together, what

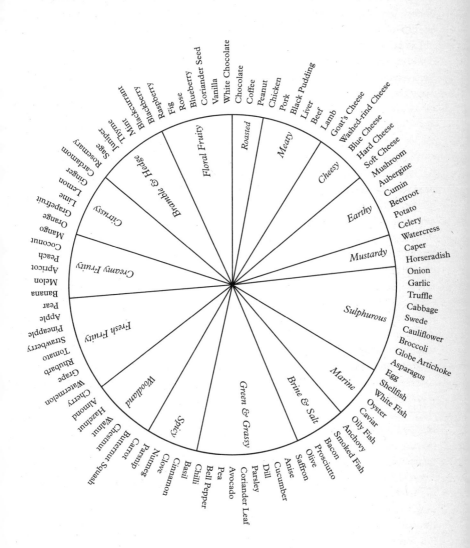

9

they bring out in each other, how the same flavour pairings are expressed in different cuisines and so on. I've given any recipes in the briefest possible terms, rather in the manner of Victorian cookbooks – compressed in the expectation that you have some experience in the kitchen. If you're tempted to cook anything in the pages that follow, it's best to read the recipe through before you start (see Beetroot & Pork, page 87, if you need convincing). I've assumed you know that you usually need to add salt to savoury dishes, taste them and adjust before you serve, turn off the cooker when you're finished, and fish out any ingredients that might choke your loved ones. If something in a recipe isn't clear – stop, think, and if the solution still isn't forthcoming, find a similar recipe and see if that sheds any light.

Most often, I guarantee, the answer will just dawn on you. One of the great satisfactions of discovering more about flavour combinations is the confidence it gives you to strike out on your own. Following the instructions in a recipe is like parroting pre-formed sentences from a phrasebook. Forming an understanding of how flavours work together, on the other hand, is like learning the language: it allows you to express yourself freely, to improvise, to find appropriate substitutions for ingredients, to cook a dish the way you fancy cooking it. You'll be surprised how rarely things go seriously wrong. Although the author takes absolutely no responsibility for anything that ends up in the bin.

Flavour is, of course, notoriously subjective and hard to describe. Still, there are a few things worth noting before you try. As anyone who has been on a wine course will tell you, flavour is not the same as taste. Taste is restricted to five qualities detectable on the tongue and elsewhere in the mouth: sweetness, saltiness, sourness, bitterness and 'umami' (or savouriness). Flavour, on the other hand, is detected mainly thanks to our sense of smell, by the olfactory bulb and, to a lesser extent, orally. Pinch your nose and you can tell if an ingredient is sweet or salty, but not what its flavour is. Your sense of taste gives you a back-of-an-envelope sketch of what a particular foodstuff is like: flavour fills in the details. Nonetheless, in its general, broadest use, the term 'flavour' tends to incorporate taste, as well as the 'trigeminal' qualities of ingredients – that is, the sensation of heat from chilli, pepper and mustard, the cooling properties of menthol and the drawstring pucker of tannins in red wine and tea.

Beyond the basic taste elements, to characterise a flavour can be as elusive a task as describing any other sort of feeling. Inasmuch as the flavour of an ingredient is attributable to the chemical compounds it contains, we might with some degree of objectivity observe that two ingredients that share a compound have similar flavours. Holy basil and clove, for instance, both contain a compound called eugenol – and holy basil has a clove-like flavour. But what do we mean by a clove-like flavour? To me, it's a bit like sucking on a sweet, rusty nail. However, no person's taste buds, or olfactory systems, are quite the same, and neither are their faculties for converting sensory input into words.

Where you come from and what you're accustomed to eating are also important determinants of how you sense and describe flavour, and of which flavours you tend to pair with others. I've used expert opinions to lend to my own judgements as robust an edge of objectivity as possible. But there's no escaping the fact everyone's flavour thesaurus would to some extent be different. Flavour is, among other things, a repository of feeling and memory: just as smell is said to be the most redolent sense, so the flavour of a certain dish can transport us back instantaneously to the time and place we first experienced it, or experienced it most memorably. *The Flavour Thesaurus* may look like, and even sometimes read like, a reference book, but for all its factual content it's an inescapably subjective one.

Writing *The Flavour Thesaurus* has taught me many things, not least to take a more open-minded approach to combinations that other cooks, in other cultures, take for granted. But as a naturally untidy person, I'm always looking for patterns, some means of imposing order on unruly reality. And in part I suppose I expected the book to add up, over its length, to something along these lines, a Grand Unifying Flavour Theory that would reconcile the science with the poetry and my mother's thoughts on jam.

It didn't. Or not quite. I did learn some broadly applicable principles, like how to use one flavour to disguise, bolster, temper or enliven another. And I'm now far more alert to the importance of balancing tastes – salt, sweet, bitter, sour and umami – and making the most of contrasting textures and temperatures. But what *The Flavour Thesaurus* does add up to, in the end, is a patchwork of facts, connections, impressions and recollections, designed less to tell you exactly what to do than to provide the spark for your own recipe or adaptation. It's there, in short, to get the juices flowing.

Niki Segnit
London, March 2010

ROASTED

Chocolate

Coffee

Peanut

Chocolate

The complex processing undergone by most chocolate explains the huge variation in flavour. The untreated beans are astringent and bitter but fermentation gives rise to fruity, wine-like or sherry flavours, and the roasting process can introduce a near-infinite variety of nutty, earthy, woody, flowery and spicy notes. The flavour of good-quality chocolate is best appreciated by pushing a piece to the roof of your mouth and letting it melt. The more sweetened the chocolate, the quicker it will reveal its flavour. As you work your way up the cocoa percentages you'll notice that it takes longer for the flavour to develop, and that there's an increase in bitterness and length – the time the flavour lingers in your mouth. When you get to 99 or 100 per cent cocoa content, you may also note that the experience is like running your tongue along the main London–Edinburgh railway line. In this section, 'chocolate' is taken to cover dark chocolate, milk chocolate and cocoa. White chocolate is dealt with separately (see page 351).

Chocolate & Almond: What does parental guilt taste like? Chocolate and almond, the ingredients in the Toblerone your dad grabbed at the airport instead of a pair of maracas or a genuine bear's paw. The secret of its success must have something to do with the genial compatibility of chocolate and almond. A wealth of nutty flavour notes is formed when cocoa beans are roasted during the chocolate-making process. Similarly, the flavour of almonds is intensified by toasting, which helps them stand up to chocolate's strength of flavour. Put this to the test in Christopher Tan's chocolate soup with salted almonds. Melt 1 tbsp unsalted butter in a frying pan over a medium-low heat, add 45g flaked almonds and sauté them with care for 4–5 minutes, until they are golden brown. Set aside. Whisk 250ml water, 100ml whipping cream, 25g caster sugar and 40g sifted cocoa powder in a saucepan over a medium-low heat until the sugar has dissolved. Let the mixture bubble gently for 2–3 minutes, then add 100g chopped dark chocolate containing at least 60 per cent cocoa solids. Stir with the whisk until smooth, then pour into little bowls, top with the almonds and sprinkle over a few grains of *fleur de sel*. Divide between 4–6 bowls and serve straight away.

Chocolate & Anise: See *Anise & Chocolate, page 182*
Chocolate & Apricot: See *Apricot & Chocolate, page 281*
Chocolate & Avocado: See *Avocado & Chocolate, page 198*

Chocolate & Bacon: Chocolatier Katrina Markoff, founder of Vosges Haut-Chocolat, combines applewood-smoked bacon and smoked salt with a dark milk chocolate in her Mo's Bacon Bar. She says she was inspired by eating choc-chip pancakes with maple syrup and bacon when she was six. You might see how the classic combination of savoury and sweet would work and be made that bit more unusual by the smoky element in the bacon. Taking the combination a step further, Tee and Cakes in Boulder, Colorado, makes maple-flavoured cupcakes topped with a slightly salted dark chocolate ganache and a sprinkle of chopped-up rashers.

Chocolate & Banana: *See Banana & Chocolate, page 278*
Chocolate & Beetroot: *See Beetroot & Chocolate, page 86*

Chocolate & Blackcurrant: Dark and heavy as Finnish Goth poetry. But not quite as popular. A fair few famous brand names (Matchmakers, Jaffa Cakes) have given the pair a whirl, announcing them with a fanfare before ushering them silently out of the back door. The combination is more likely to work with the soothing influence of dairy – say, in a blackcurrant mousse or fool with a chocolate sauce, or a chocolate gâteau with fresh cream and a blackcurrant filling.

Chocolate & Black Pudding: *See Black Pudding & Chocolate, page 38*

Chocolate & Cardamom: Like a puppeteer's black velvet curtain, dark chocolate is the perfect smooth background for cardamom to show off its colours. Use the cardamom in sufficient quantities and you can pick out its enigmatic citrus, eucalyptus and warm, woody-floral qualities. I find adding a pinch of ground cardamom can make even the most ordinary dark chocolate taste expensive. This tart is spectacularly delicious and very quick to make but needs a couple of hours in the fridge to set. Prepare and bake a 23cm sweet pastry case. Slit open 10 cardamom pods, grind up the contents with a mortar and pestle, add to 300ml double cream in a pan and scald. Remove from the heat and add 200g dark chocolate, broken into pieces, and 25g unsalted butter. Stir until melted and well mixed. When cooled a little (don't let it set), pour into the pastry case and place in the fridge for two or three hours. When it has hardened, sift a little cocoa powder over it and serve with a modest dollop of crème fraîche.

Chocolate & Cauliflower: *See Cauliflower & Chocolate, page 122*
Chocolate & Cherry: *See Cherry & Chocolate, page 247*

Chocolate & Chestnut: Charles Ranhofer, chef at Delmonico's restaurant in New York in the nineteenth century, used to fashion potatoes out of chestnut ice cream, with almond slivers for eyes, and the whole rolled in grated chocolate for an authentic muddy look. Tempting, perhaps, to make these and bury them in a deep soil of finely grated chocolate, then let your guests dig for the potatoes with spoons. For fear of friends thinking you've lost it completely, a chocolate sauce on a chestnut ice cream would be tasty, if less fun. If you're on a chestnut bender, use the egg whites left over from making the ice cream to make a Mont Blanc, the classic dessert of meringue topped with a mound of sweetened chestnut purée, a summit of whipped cream and a light dusting of icing sugar.

Chocolate & Chilli: One of the original 'wow' flavour pairings to have made its way around the world. As chillies turn red, they develop a sweet, fruity flavour that combines harmoniously with bitter chocolate – even more so when the chilli is dried and has taken on still sweeter, raisiny, leathery notes. Look out for mulato and ancho dried chillies, which are considered inherently chocolatey themselves. Besides flavour compatibility, the fattiness of chocolate offsets some of the chilli heat, as in a chilli-rich Mexican *mole*. *Mole* simply means 'sauce', and there are many different types. Most of them contain dried chillies, but as a rule chocolate turns up only in 'red' or 'black' *moles*. As well as chilli and chocolate, these contain various dried fruits, bread, nuts, tomato, onion, garlic, seeds, dried and fresh herbs, spices, oil, lard and stock. As you might imagine, the result is a complex, sweet-piquant sauce that requires much pounding, grinding and toasting to prepare. Incidentally, the meat is either browned and added to the sauce to finish cooking, or cooked (usually roasted) separately and served with the sauce draped over it. Fresh *moles* are primarily confined to special occasions. If you fancy making one to an authentic recipe but don't have Mexican chocolate (which is coarse, dark and often blended with cinnamon and vanilla), cookery writer Rick Bayless suggests using a third as much unsweetened cocoa powder instead. Aside from *moles*, American spice shops sell prepared blends of cocoa, chipotle and paprika to add to chilli con carne, stews or even cakes and brownies. You might also try adding a few pinches of dried red chilli flakes to chocolate cornflake clusters – I call these mini Krakatoa cakes. The corn flavour is very harmonious with the chilli and chocolate, and the crunchy texture adds to the fun. Get the basic recipe from a five-year-old. But best not to serve him or her the results.

Chocolate & Cinnamon: *See Cinnamon & Chocolate, page 217*

Chocolate & Coconut: Just as government health departments warn that using marijuana can lead to harder drugs, so sweet tobacco led to my addiction to cigarettes. You could, with rice paper, make a rollie out of the strands of cocoa-flavoured coconut. 'Don't let's ask for the moon,' I puffed at the dog, *à la* Bette Davis. From there it was only a few fake hacking coughs to the truly rank taste of real fags. Crikey, I thought, as I inhaled my first. These are *terrible*. If, as I'd been led to believe, the cigarette companies were so dastardly, why didn't they learn something from the confectionery companies and make their products irresistible? I soon learnt that they had, but it had nothing to do with the taste. Years later, I was back on the confectionery again, this time in the form of fancy chocolate with notes of tobacco and smoke. If you're looking for a hit, try Pralus's Tanzanie (tobacco, treacle, raisin) or their Vanuatu (smoke, spice, liquorice). For a chocolate with notes of tobacco and coconut, try Michel Cluizel's Mangaro Lait 50%, a milk chocolate that, as the name suggests, contains a whopping 50 per cent cocoa.

Chocolate & Coffee: *See Coffee & Chocolate, page 20*
Chocolate & Fig: *See Fig & Chocolate, page 340*
Chocolate & Ginger: *See Ginger & Chocolate, page 310*
Chocolate & Goat's Cheese: *See Goat's Cheese & Chocolate, page 56*

Chocolate & Hazelnut: We have the scarcity of cocoa in late-nineteenth-century Piedmont to thank for the popularity of this heavenly combination. The bulking out of chocolate with ground hazelnuts led (eventually) to the invention of Nutella, although it was originally sold as a solid loaf and called *pasta gianduja*. *Gianduja*, which means something along the lines of 'John the pottering man', is a carnival character representing the typical Piedmontese, and still the generic term for the sweet paste made from chocolate and hazelnut. In the 1940s mothers would cut a slice off the loaf, put it between slices of bread and give it to their children, who were smart enough to throw away the bread and just eat the chocolate. Piedmontese ducks must have been fantastically plump mid-century. In 1951 a technique was developed to soften the mixture, and the product was renamed *Supercrema Gianduja* and sold by the jar. Finally, in 1964, its name was changed to the more internationally pronounceable Nutella, and today it outsells peanut butter worldwide. If you find Nutella too sweet, you might like to get your *gianduja* fix from a Ferrero Rocher or from Baci – or, if you prefer something a little more unusual, try Valrhona's Caraibe Noisettes or Amedei's milk chocolate with Piedmont hazelnuts. See also Nutmeg & Walnut, page 223.

Chocolate & Lemon: *See Lemon & Chocolate, page 304*

Chocolate & Lime: Chocolate limes are a classic British sweet. In your mouth, the lime candy falls away in sharp, slatey layers to reveal a dry, crumbly chocolate centre. Sadly the combination rarely crops up in other forms, although I once ate a spectacular dark chocolate tart with a sharp lime sorbet at one of Terence Conran's restaurants.

Chocolate & Mint: *See Mint & Chocolate, page 330*

Chocolate & Nutmeg: Few recipes call for milk chocolate. It's more difficult to work with than dark chocolate, usually doesn't have as much cocoa flavour and is, in most cases, quite sickly. If you genuinely can't bear dark chocolate, consider a milk chocolate and nutmeg tart. The nutmeg boosts the flavour of the chocolate and freshens its cloying sweetness (nutmeg has a similar effect in creamy custard tarts and eggnog – see Egg & Nutmeg, page 135). The milk chocolate needs to be at least 30 per cent cocoa solids. Follow the recipe in Chocolate & Cardamom, page 14, but scald the cream with ¼ of a whole nutmeg grated into it instead of the cardamom. Cool the chocolate a little before grating in a further ¼ nutmeg. Taste for strength, then pour into the pastry case and leave to set in the fridge. Grate over a little more nutmeg before serving.

Chocolate & Orange: *See Orange & Chocolate, page 294*

Chocolate & Peanut: According to Alexandre Dumas, the Spanish called peanuts *cacohuette* because of their resemblance in flavour to cocoa. He goes on to note that they took advantage of this flavour harmony by mixing small amounts of expensive cocoa into a peanut mixture to make a sort of cheap chocolate. Fifty years later, in 1912, the Goo Goo Cluster, a mixture of chocolate, peanuts, caramel and marshmallow, became the first combination chocolate bar in the US. By the close of the 1920s, Reese's and Mars had respectively launched Peanut Butter Cups and Snickers, the latter becoming America's favourite chocolate bar, a position it holds to this day. Unroasted peanuts actually don't taste too nice with chocolate, since (being legumes) they have a greenish, vegetal taste; the success of most peanut-chocolate combinations is down to the formation of pyrazines during the roasting process, which are harmonious with roasted notes in the chocolate. Use the combination at home for diner-style treats like a sundae made with vanilla ice cream topped with chopped, roasted peanuts and chocolate sauce, or a milkshake made with liquidised peanut butter and chocolate ice cream. Chef Paul Heathcote uses dark chocolate instead of the usual milk in his salty chocolate, caramel and peanut tart.

Chocolate & Pear: A little chocolate will highlight pear's sweetness; too much and you swamp the fruit's flavour. *Poires Belle Hélène* – poached pears with chocolate sauce – is frequently a case in point. Too often a thick blanket of chocolate overpowers the dish, so use it sparingly and be sure to poach the pears in vanilla syrup to create a connection between the two flavours. Nuts fulfil a similar bridging role; pear and chocolate both love hazelnut, and the trio make a great cake. Or follow Nigel Slater's decadent tip of stirring broken-up florentines into whipped cream and spooning it into the cored cavities of poached pears. Use bought florentines or the recipe in Ginger & Chocolate, page 310.

Chocolate & Pineapple: *See Pineapple & Chocolate, page 266*

Chocolate & Raspberry: Raspberry is a reflex pairing for chocolate tarts and puddings. Too often, in my humble opinion, berries are strewn on a chocolate dessert plate for no better reason than to pretty it up. All very well if there's enough cream to smooth the transition between the two, but if there's not, or if the raspberries aren't perfectly ripe, the combination is like being offered a soothing cuddle only to be pinched hard on the fleshy underside of your arm. A more balanced chocolate–raspberry experience is to be had in chocolate with strong raspberry notes, such as Valrhona's gorgeous Manjari or Amano's Madagascar.

Chocolate & Rose: *See Rose & Chocolate, page 342*
Chocolate & Rosemary: *See Rosemary & Chocolate, page 317*

Chocolate & Strawberry: Not all it's cracked up to be. Strawberry's heart-like shape and colour have seen it unimaginatively match-made with that default love token, chocolate. But doesn't a strawberry dipped in chocolate just look like a fruit wearing big knickers? And aren't they the sort of thing asset-strippers feed to call girls in cream-coloured hotel rooms? I'd take chocolate and hazelnut over these two any day.

Chocolate & Thyme: *See Thyme & Chocolate, page 326*

Chocolate & Tomato: A hint of chocolate flavour in spicy tomato recipes such as chilli con carne, caponata, ketchup or meatballs is recommended by the American food historian, Alice Arndt. Mexican cooks think of cocoa/dark chocolate as spices as well as confectionery ingredients; for them, chocolate is a flavouring that, used in moderation, adds richness and depth to savoury dishes and smooths the raw edges of sharp ingredients such as tomato.

Chocolate & Vanilla: *See Vanilla & Chocolate, page 348*

Chocolate & Walnut: A classic in brownies. It's also worth throwing a handful of walnuts into a chocolate bread and butter pudding. Or add caramel to chocolate and walnuts to make what is sometimes called 'turtle' flavour. Turtles are a popular confectionery in Canada. The name comes from the shape: a small pile of nuts (usually pecan or walnut) is held together with caramel and covered with a smooth shell of chocolate under which some of the nuts stick out like the head and legs of a turtle. Add a swirl of caramel to the recipe in Chocolate & Almond (see page 13) and you might call it turtle soup.

Chocolate & Watermelon: *See Watermelon & Chocolate, page 249*
Chocolate & White Chocolate: *See White Chocolate & Chocolate, page 352*

Coffee

Like chocolate, coffee goes through multiple stages before it reaches the cup, which accounts for its complexity. More than 800 aroma compounds have been identified in the roasted bean. Raw, the green seed is a relatively unfragrant little thing. Roasting expands it by 50–100 per cent and, in turning it brown, releases its flavour. As a rule, lighter-brown beans (roasted for 9–11 minutes) are truer to their origins – i.e. they reveal more about the variety of bean and its growing conditions. When a coffee is darker (12–13 minutes' roasting time) and oily on its surface, roasted flavours will have begun to dominate, and it'll be spicier and more chocolatey. Coffee might contain notes of blackcurrant, coriander seed, clove, vanilla, chocolate and nuts, all of which make harmonious matches, and are used to flavour the kinds of syrup you find in coffee bars. Tia Maria and Kahlua are both coffee-flavoured liqueurs but have markedly different characters.

Coffee & Almond: Once roasted, coffee is one of the most complex of all flavours, and one of its most desirable characteristics is 'nutty' – which might explain why it's so frequently paired with nuts. Walnut (see Coffee & Walnut, page 22) is the most common nut note identified in coffee but almond (or marzipan) is also typical. Even if you don't detect almonds in your cup of joe, it'll still work a treat with a plump almond croissant covered with a generous dusting of icing sugar. French women seem to be able to eat these without looking as if they've been caught in a snowstorm. I can't.

Coffee & Avocado: *See Avocado & Coffee, page 199*
Coffee & Banana: *See Banana & Coffee, page 278*

Coffee & Beef: Caffeinated red meat. Something to serve your most militantly health-conscious friends. Why not add a garnish of lit cigarettes? Coffee is used in the American South as a marinade or rub for meat. It's also been spotted in fancier restaurants, perhaps because there's a well-reported flavour overlap between roasted coffee and cooked beef. But my experience suggests it's a shotgun wedding. I tried a coffee marinade on a steak and found it gave the meat an overpoweringly gamy flavour. Best to keep these at least one course apart at dinner.

Coffee & Blackcurrant: A mysteriously good pairing that often crops up in wine tasting notes. Once vinified, the rare Lagrein black grape, native to the Italian Alps, captures both flavours. I encountered them just over the border in Haute-Savoie in a heavenly *vacherin glace*: layers of meringue, blackcurrant sorbet, whipped cream and coffee ice cream with a sprinkling of toasted almonds. It's in the running for the most delicious sweet thing I have ever put in my mouth. The coffee flavour had the fresh fragrance of just-ground beans and the blackcurrant that hint of muskiness that processed fruit can't help but lose by oversweetening. Worth trying in a variant of pavlova (coffee-flavoured meringue with cream and a just-sweet-enough blackcurrant compote), or even blackcurrant jam in a coffee gâteau.

Coffee & Cardamom: The Bedouin way of preparing Arabic coffee. In Morocco, Algeria, or the Algerian Coffee Stores in Soho for that matter, they'll grind together coffee beans and cardamom in equal measure (although obviously adjust proportions according to your preference). Drunk in tiny cups with or without sugar, maybe with a drop or two of orange-flower water, the aromatic spice rounds out the tartness of the coffee. I pair the flavours in this coffee-iced cardamom cake. The cardamom makes for a soft, fragrant sponge, while coffee icing lends a zingy contrast. Put 175g each of sugar and self-raising flour, 100g softened butter, the seeds of 12 cardamom pods, ground to a powder, 1 tsp baking powder, 4 tbsp milk and 2 eggs in a large bowl and beat well for 2–3 minutes. Transfer to a greased and lined round 20cm springform cake tin and bake at 180°C/Gas Mark 4 for 50–60 minutes. Remove and leave to cool. Dissolve 2 tsp instant coffee in 2 tbsp hot water with a few drops of vanilla extract. Mix into 125g icing sugar. The icing should be translucently thin, so add the liquid drop by drop until you've achieved an easily spreadable consistency. Spread the icing over the cooled cake. Note that the cardamom tastes stronger the next day.

Coffee & Cherry: While the world fretted over who killed Laura Palmer in David Lynch's *Twin Peaks*, all I wanted was to slide up and join Agent Cooper in the Double R Diner for damn fine coffee and a slice of cherry pie.

Coffee & Chocolate: Matari, or mocha, coffee beans come from the Yemeni city of Moka. They have a rich, mellow chocolate aftertaste and have lent their name to the various concoctions that attempt to reproduce their flavour by adding chocolate to less exotic coffees. Commonly this involves a shot of espresso in a cup of steamed milk and cocoa. Personally, I don't like this pairing in drinks. Part of the pleasure of coffee is feeling the sort of new-dawn determination I associate with Melanie Griffith taking the streets of Manhattan in her stride in the opening titles of *Working Girl*. Whereas hot chocolate I associate with Meg Ryan, in an over-size sweater, clutching a massive mug with both hands as if in supplication. You can't be determined *and* vulnerable. Forget hot drinks. Coffee and chocolate work much better together in mousses, truffles and cakes. Or use them as uncredited flavour boosters. A little coffee flavour in chocolate dishes can make them taste more chocolatey, and vice versa.

Coffee & Cinnamon: Cinnamon has the strength and sweetness to round out coffee flavour in baking. In cafés in Mexico they sometimes give you a stick of cinnamon to stir your coffee. Tastes good and saves on the washing up. One of Thomas Keller's more famous dishes pairs doughnuts dusted in cinnamon sugar with a coffee cup of cappuccino-flavoured semifreddo.

Coffee & Clove: *See Clove & Coffee, page 220*
Coffee & Coriander Seed: *See Coriander Seed & Coffee, page 345*

Coffee & Ginger: In the late seventeenth century, English coffee houses served their brews black with optional additions of ginger, clove, cinnamon or spearmint. To this day in the Yemen, ginger is a popular flavouring for a tea brewed with coffee husks. The combination is called *qishr*, and is short and golden, with a bite to make you wince over your *bint al sahn*, or honey cake. An espresso lover's alternative to the milky gingerbread concoctions the coffee chains serve at Christmas time. See Ginger & Cinnamon, page 310.

Coffee & Goat's Cheese: *See Goat's Cheese & Coffee, page 56*

Coffee & Hazelnut: If you find yourself at a good-quality ice cream parlour in France or Italy and you suffer an attack of selection anxiety, remember this: coffee and hazelnut, coffee and hazelnut, coffee and hazelnut.

Coffee & Orange: Breakfast companions. If you can find it, San Matteo of Sicily makes a heavenly orange and coffee marmalade. I once had burnt orange and coffee ice cream, bitter as a custody battle, but resolved by the sweetness of the cream. Orange and coffee tiramisu is also nicer than it sounds. You could even make it with this orange and coffee-bean liqueur. The recipe is adapted from one by Patricia Wells, who originally used eau de vie. I rather like the way, with marvellously arbitrary bossiness, it calls for 44 coffee beans, no more and no less. Take a large orange and make 44 slits in it. Put a coffee bean in each. It will now look like a medieval weapon or tribal fetish. Put 44 sugar cubes in a jar. Position the orange on top and pour over 500ml brandy, rum or vodka. Leave it to steep for 44 days, then squeeze the juice out of the orange, mix it back into the alcohol, strain and pour into a sterilised bottle. Alternatively, put it somewhere dark and cool, forget about it completely, find it covered in dust something like 444 days later, try it sceptically, and realise on your second sip that it's absolutely delicious without the addition of the juice. Perfectly balanced, not too sweet, and with a complex lingering coffee/orange flavour that proves to be as good at rounding off a day as it is at starting one.

Coffee & Rose: Bitter flavours can be used as an antidote to the overpowering sweetness of florals such as rose. I wouldn't normally relish a Turkish coffee, as thick and black as liquid tarmac, but a cube of rose-flavoured Turkish Delight brings it into balance.

Coffee & Vanilla: *See Vanilla & Coffee, page 349*

Coffee & Walnut: I've always thought that walnuts had a slightly nicotine character, which might explain why coffee and walnut is such a natural combination. Barring a ban on eating walnuts in public places – someone with a nut allergy might be nearby, after all – a partial substitute for a cigarette and coffee is a large slice of coffee and walnut cake. But it's hard to find a good one. The coffee sponge must be moist, the icing not too sweet, and the walnuts plenteous.

Coffee & White Chocolate: *See White Chocolate & Coffee, page 352*

Peanut

Raw peanuts taste beany. Roasted or fried, they take on a sweet flavour, with hints of chocolate and meat, plus a vegetal undertone. It's a highly complex and satisfying flavour experience that works well with rich meats, sweet shellfish and sharp fruits such as apple and lime. Ground into peanut butter, the flavour becomes sweeter and saltier with a pleasing edge of bitterness. Some say bacon goes with everything, but peanut is surely even more marriageable and, unlike bacon, it has huge international and cross-cultural appeal.

Peanut & Apple: An apple grated or sliced into a peanut butter sandwich is the worthy parent's alternative to jam or jelly. Righteousness aside, a sharp Granny Smith can provide a more refreshing contrast than sugary jam. Apple is particularly good with the cinnamon-raisin swirl peanut butter made by Peanut Butter & Co, and not at all bad with their maple-syrup-flavoured one either. You can buy it in a jar, or try it at their peanut butter café in Greenwich Village, New York.

Peanut & Asparagus: *See Asparagus & Peanut, page 131*
Peanut & Banana: *See Banana & Peanut, page 278*

Peanut & Beef: In common with Indonesian satay, in Peru the term *anticucho* refers to the process of cooking skewered meat over a grill rather than to the ingredients used. That said, ox heart is the usual meat of choice, although beef is becoming more prevalent. Either way, the meat is marinated in vinegar, garlic, chilli, cumin and oregano, as it is in Bolivian *anticuchos*, but with the addition of thick peanut and chilli sauce on the side. In both versions there may also be a few baby potatoes threaded on to the skewer. The combination of beef, peanut and potatoes may put you in mind of Thai *mussaman* curry. David Thompson says that this peanut-enriched sauce, thick with potatoes and meat (not always beef – lamb and duck are frequent alternatives), is the most laborious of all the Thai curries – and the most delicious.

Peanut & Blackcurrant: *See Blackcurrant & Peanut, page 333*

Peanut & Broccoli: Crunchy peanut butter was made for broccoli, which catches the kernel crumbs in its unopened flowers. Put this to the test in a salad dressed like the one in Peanut & Coconut on page 24. Or, if you're good at chopping the florets into neat pieces, give them the *kung pao* treatment – see Peanut & Chicken, below.

Peanut & Carrot: Nigella Lawson gives a recipe for 'The Rainbow Room's Carrot and Peanut Salad', named in honour of the restaurant where her mother ate something similar. The mix of ingredients might, she admits, sound odd, but it works, particularly if you're brave with the vinegar: its astringency cuts through the oiliness of the nuts and, in combination with sweet carrot, gives the whole thing a mouthwatering quality that I associate with lime-juicy Asian salads. Coarsely grate 4 carrots and mix them with 75g salted peanuts, 2 tbsp red wine vinegar, 2 tbsp groundnut oil and a few drops of sesame oil. Eat immediately.

Peanut & Celery: *See Celery & Peanut, page 96*

Peanut & Chicken: The obsessively tidy may find comfort in the Sichuan dish of *kung pao* chicken, in which peanuts are paired with chicken, chillies and spring onion cut into peanut-sized pieces. Stir-fried, everything bar the chillies takes on a uniform golden colour, belying the contrast in the mouth of bland, soft chicken against crunchy, rich nuts in their spicy sauce. Cut 2 chicken breasts into 1cm squares and place in a mixture of 1 tbsp light soy sauce, 2 tsp Shaoxing wine, 2 tsp cornflour and ½ tsp salt. Leave to marinate while you slice the white parts of 6 spring onions into 1cm pieces, then do the same for 6 dried chillies (removing the seeds if you want to contain the heat). Combine 1 tbsp sugar, 1 tbsp black rice vinegar, 2 tbsp water, 1 tsp cornflour, 1 tsp light soy sauce, 1 tsp oyster sauce and 1 tsp sesame oil, then set aside. Heat some groundnut oil in a wok and add the chillies, taking care not to burn them. Add the chicken, brown it, then add 2 sliced garlic cloves, a 2cm piece of fresh ginger, finely chopped, and the spring onions. Fry until the chicken is cooked through. Add the sauce and cook until thick and shiny. Then add a generous handful of unsalted roasted peanuts, give a quick stir and serve. You could use cashews instead, but peanuts are the more authentic choice. Chicken and cashew nuts has a special place in my heart – it was the first Chinese food I ever ate. When I came to describe it to my mother, my nine-year-old mind struggled to evoke the sheer unfamiliarity of it. How to describe a beansprout? Or a water chestnut, with its odd, raw-potato crispness? Or the soft, salty gloop they came in? I'd never seen these things before. I *still* hadn't seen them, in fact, as we'd eaten our takeaway in a car, in a car park, after dark, the windows steamed up with egg-fried mist. 'The rice had peas in it,' I managed. See also Peanut & Lamb, page 24.

Peanut & Chilli: *See Chilli & Peanut, page 210*
Peanut & Chocolate: *See Chocolate & Peanut, page 17*

Peanut & Cinnamon: Castries Crème is a peanut liqueur with a strong peanut-butter start, according to its maker, giving way to subtle notes of spicy cinnamon and brown sugar. See also Peanut & Apple, page 22.

Peanut & Coconut: Frequently paired in Indonesian cooking. Used to pep up rice dishes, *seroendeng* is toasted grated coconut cooked with onion, garlic and spices, then mixed with peanuts. *Rempeyek kacang* is a deep-fried snack made with chopped peanuts folded into a spicy coconut milk and rice flour batter. Most famously, peanuts and coconut are combined in a sauce for satay, and in the dressing for *gado gado*, the classic Indonesian salad. Not to undervalue *gado gado* in any way, but it's a great recipe to have up your sleeve when you have vegetable odds and ends to use up. Roast 200g skinned peanuts in the oven at 190°C/Gas Mark 5 for 6–8 minutes. Cool, then whiz in a food processor until finely ground. Add 50ml soy sauce, 2 tbsp palm sugar (or brown sugar), the juice of ½ lime, a couple of crushed garlic cloves (fried with 2–3 chopped shallots) and chilli to taste. Whiz until smooth, add 400ml coconut milk and whiz again until all is well combined. Use this to dress a combination of cooked, blanched and raw vegetables. Cooled cooked potato, blanched green beans and raw beansprouts are a common combination, variously supplemented with carrot, spring onions, cabbage, cucumber or lettuce. Boiled eggs, prawn crackers, fried onion or tofu are used as a garnish.

Peanut & Coriander Leaf: *See Coriander Leaf & Peanut, page 197*

Peanut & Cucumber: In India, *khamang kakadi* combines peeled, diced cucumber, roasted crushed peanuts, finely chopped fresh green chilli and grated coconut. It's dressed with lemon juice, salt, sugar and cumin, or sometimes an oil containing mustard seeds that's been heated until the seeds pop and release their flavour. Serve as a chutney.

Peanut & Grape: *See Grape & Peanut, page 252*

Peanut & Lamb: In Bolivia they pair lamb with peanut in a soup or stew. In West Africa peanut and lamb might turn up in a *mafe* (see Peanut & Tomato, page 25) and in Thailand in a *mussaman* curry (see Peanut & Beef, page 22). Small pieces of lamb might be threaded on to a skewer, grilled and served with a peanut sauce in a Southeast Asian satay. The term satay refers to the technique of cooking food on a stick over charcoal, and doesn't imply any particular flavour combination. In the West, we have come to expect satay accompanied by a peanut sauce, but in Indonesia it might come served with *kecap manis* or a mixture of tomato and chilli. As to the satay itself, anything goes: lamb, goat, chicken, beef, seafood, minced duck, ox offal, water buffalo, turtle, tofu, or pretty much anything you can thread on a stick.

Peanut & Lime: Packets of peanuts flavoured with lime, or lime and chilli, are popular in Mexico, where you can also buy them fresh from a street vendor, fried in their skins in pork fat and scooped still hot into a cup with a squeeze of lime juice. Peanut and lime is also a very common pairing in Thailand and Vietnam, where both are used to garnish noodle dishes, soups and salads. Like the vinegar in Nigella Lawson's 'Rainbow Room' salad (see Peanut & Carrot, page 23), the astringent juice provides a great counterpoint to the fattiness of the nuts.

Peanut & Mint: *See Mint & Peanut, page 331*
Peanut & Pork: *See Pork & Peanut, page 36*
Peanut & Potato: *See Potato & Peanut, page 92*

Peanut & Shellfish: Satay sauce can turn a skewer of lean mussels or prawns into a rich treat. In the intensely flavoured, hearty Brazilian dish, *vatapá*, shellfish is stewed in a peanut and coconut sauce thickened with bread. When combined, the prawns and peanuts share a nutty sweetness that sits just on the satisfying side of sickly.

Peanut & Tomato: Combined in the popular West African stew, *mafe*. A *mafe* might be made with chicken, goat or beef, and a variety of vegetables, but the peanut and tomato sauce is a constant. The following is more of a rough guide than a recipe, but you'll get the idea. Cook a chopped large onion in oil until softened, then throw in a couple of finely chopped garlic cloves and some chopped red chillies. Add about 1kg meat, jointed or cut into chunks, and allow to brown. Empty in a tin of tomatoes, 2 tbsp tomato purée, a bay leaf, and 125g peanut butter whisked into 500ml hot water or stock. Simmer for about an hour, then add a green bell pepper and some root vegetables (carrot, sweet potato, squash, yam – say about 4 large carrots' worth), chopped into bite-sized pieces. Continue to simmer until they're just tender. Give it a good stir and serve on rice, couscous or millet.

Peanut & Vanilla: I had a happy childhood but it might have been a deal happier if snow-white, vanilla-flavoured Marshmallow Fluff had been available in Hampshire. I could have demanded, or even made, fluffernutter sandwiches. One slice of (white) bread is spread with the fluff, the other with peanut butter, before they're pressed together and sliced. In season four of *The Sopranos*, Christopher Moltisanti asks his mother to make one and she refuses. Look how *he* ends up.

MEATY

Chicken

Pork

Black Pudding

Liver

Beef

Lamb

Chicken

Chicken has a reputation for being bland – the magnolia of foods – and yet standing up to 40 cloves of garlic (see Garlic & Chicken, page 112), or to big flavours like rosemary, thyme and lemon, takes some serious meatiness. The well-exercised joints – legs, thighs – are the tastiest, even more so when cooked skin-on and bone-in. It's the skinless, boneless breast meat, especially from intensively farmed birds, that has earned chicken its pale reputation. It's like a sort of dry tofu for carnivores. The best that can be said of it is that it adds bite to dishes, and doesn't get in the way of more interesting flavours in a sauce – salty, sweet, nutty, fruity, spicy, even fishy. This chapter also touches on turkey, goose, quail and the odd game bird. And swan.

Chicken & Almond: *See Almond & Chicken, page 242*
Chicken & Anise: *See Anise & Chicken, page 182*

Chicken & Avocado: Good together, if a little blandly healthy, like those smug couples you see jogging in the park. Give the chicken a smoke and things could start to look up. Or throw them some toasted pine nuts and a handful of raisins, toss through some leaves and dress with something sharp.

Chicken & Bacon: *See Bacon & Chicken, page 168*
Chicken & Banana: *See Banana & Chicken, page 277*
Chicken & Basil: *See Basil & Chicken, page 213*

Chicken & Bell Pepper: One of the easiest, most foolproof combinations in this book. Deseed 6–8 peppers (red, yellow or orange, not green), chop them into generous chunks and put in a large non-stick saucepan with 8 chicken thighs, skin-on and preferably bone-in too. Leave over a medium heat. Keep an eye on it for the first ten minutes, giving it the odd stir to prevent it sticking. Then all of a sudden the peppers release their juices and you can leave it alone. Put a lid on and cook over a low-medium heat for 30 minutes, or until the pan is half-full of sweet, oily, autumn-coloured stock. It's a bit of a miracle, this – you can hardly believe the rich complexity of the sauce comes from just two ingredients. Season and serve with rice, couscous or French bread, whichever you prefer to mop up with.

Chicken & Blue Cheese: *See Blue Cheese & Chicken, page 62*
Chicken & Cabbage: *See Cabbage & Chicken, page 119*

Chicken & Caviar: In Sylvia Plath's *The Bell Jar*, Esther Greenwood attends a smart luncheon where she hatches a plan to monopolise an entire bowl of caviar. If, she observes, you carry yourself with a certain arrogance when you do something incorrect at the table, people will think you're original rather than bad-mannered: 'Under cover of the clinking of water goblets and silver-ware and bone china, I paved my plate with chicken slices. Then I covered the chicken slices with caviar thickly as if I were spreading peanut-butter on a piece of bread. Then I picked up the chicken slices in my fingers one by one, rolled them so the caviar wouldn't ooze off and ate them.'

Chicken & Celery: *See Celery & Chicken, page 96*
Chicken & Chestnut: *See Chestnut & Chicken, page 233*

Chicken & Chilli: The Portuguese went to Mozambique and came back with chicken peri peri (or piri piri), a simple dish of flame-grilled chicken marinated in oil, chilli, salt and citrus juice. *Peri peri* is a generic African word for chilli, but usually refers to the hot, simply flavoured bird's eye variety. Having taken to the dish themselves, the Portuguese exported it to their colonies, including Goa, where it's particularly popular. The peri peri diaspora has been accelerated in recent years by the South African chain, Nando's, which, spotting the mass-market appeal of chicken that can make tears run down your cheeks, has opened restaurants in five continents since 1987. See also Ginger & Chilli, page 309, and Peanut & Chicken, page 23.

Chicken & Coconut: *See Coconut & Chicken, page 287*

Chicken & Coriander Leaf: Coriander leaf is widely used in Thai chicken dishes such as green curry, and in Vietnam, *rau ram*, or 'hot mint', is included in chicken salads and summer rolls. Unrelated botanically to coriander, *rau ram* nonetheless has a similar, if slightly more peppery, citrussy flavour. In Malaysia it's known as the 'laksa herb', after the noodle soup, called *laksa lemak*, that it's often used to garnish.

Chicken & Egg: *See Egg & Chicken, page 134*
Chicken & Garlic: *See Garlic & Chicken, page 112*
Chicken & Grape: *See Grape & Chicken, page 252*

Chicken & Hard Cheese: In the 1980s there was something of a vogue for chicken Cordon Bleu, a somewhat unbalanced dish of skinless, boneless chicken breasts stuffed with slices of Gruyère and ham. This recipe for *poulet au Comté* is an improvement, not least because the skin-on, bone-in roasted chicken has enough character to take on the weight and fruity, nutty, caramelised flavours of the cheese. Joint a chicken into 4 pieces and lightly dust with seasoned flour. Brown the pieces in butter, remove from the pan and keep warm. Deglaze the pan with 300ml dry white wine and 2 tbsp strong mustard. Pour this sauce over the chicken in an ovenproof dish and bake for 40 minutes at 200°C/Gas Mark 6, turning a few times. Sprinkle with 100g finely grated Comté and put back in the oven for about 5 minutes, until the cheese starts to brown. Serve with boiled potatoes or rice.

Chicken & Hazelnut: *See Hazelnut & Chicken, page 239*
Chicken & Lemon: *See Lemon & Chicken, page 304*

Chicken & Lime: Citrus fruits are paired with chicken in cuisines the world over. I love the tang of lime juice in spicy chicken soups such as the famous *sopa de lima* of the Yucatán peninsula. Shredded chicken, chilli and strips of tortilla are served in a chicken and tomato broth seasoned with cinnamon, garlic, allspice, and black peppercorns and finished with a generous squeeze of lime and some coriander leaf.

Chicken & Mushroom: *Grifola frondosa*, or hen of the woods, is a species of mushroom named for its resemblance to a chicken ruffling its feathers. Chicken of the woods, *Laetiporus sulphureus*, which looks more like a flattened chicken nugget than anything, is perhaps the closest to actual chicken in texture, but opinion is divided as to whether the flavour bears much comparison. Add a handful or two of mushrooms to the pot with your chicken and they will contribute a gamy flavour that makes the bird taste as if it really did come from the woods, as opposed to the middle shelf of your refrigerator. Add them to a braising pheasant or partridge and you'll almost be able to hear the twigs snap underfoot. The pairing of morels with chicken in a cream sauce is altogether less rustic; morels are often said to be closer to truffles in their complexity and refinement of flavour. Like truffles, they come in 'white' and black forms, both of which the late American food writer, Richard Olney, thought were 'exquisite'. He added that while dried morels have their uses in sauces and terrines, they can never quite measure up to fresh. The general feeling is that the drying process robs morels of some of their honeyed sweetness. Fresh or dried, black or white, morels must be cooked.

Chicken & Onion: Brillat-Savarin wrote that 'poultry is to the kitchen what canvas is to the artist'. In its neutrality, the chicken finds common ground with the leek, a native not of Wales but, appropriately enough, of Switzerland, according to the *Encyclopaedia of Domestic Economy* (1855). Offend no one (but the vegetarians) with a cock-a-leekie soup – a traditional Scottish preparation of leeks, prunes and chicken stock.

Chicken & Oyster: *See Oyster & Chicken, page 151*

Chicken & Parsnip: Roast parsnips make a welcome side dish to roast chicken, and they're essential with the roast turkey at Christmas. Some cooks swear by the use of parsnip to flavour a really good chicken broth, although if you don't have a parsnip to hand, chef Robert Reid says a pinch of curry powder will improve your stock at a subliminal level, while some mushroom peelings will give it a meatier quality. As will chicken's feet, which also give the finished article a pleasantly gelatinous texture. Easy and cheap to put to the test if you have a Chinese supermarket nearby.

Chicken & Pea: *See Pea & Chicken, page 202*
Chicken & Peanut: *See Peanut & Chicken, page 23*

Chicken & Pear: Chicken and pear might not sound like much to sing about, but when braised together in good stock with bacon and shallots, partridge and pear is. The pear pieces absorb the rich cooking liquid but retain their subtle, fruity sweetness. For a Christmas-time dinner, heat 1 tbsp oil in a hefty casserole and brown 4 small partridges. Set the birds aside and in the same pan cook 150g chopped smoked bacon with 25g butter, 20 peeled whole shallots, 4 peeled, cored and quartered pears and a chopped garlic clove. When the shallots are golden and softened, return the partridges to the pan and pour over 150ml hot chicken stock. Season, cover, and cook in the oven at 160°C/Gas Mark 3 for 20–25 minutes. You can serve this straight from the pot but it's better to remove the partridges and rest them under foil while you put the casserole back on the hob and stir in 200g cooked, peeled chestnuts until they're warmed through. Five gold rings in the form of hot apple fritters would make the perfect pudding – see Vanilla & Apple, page 347.

Chicken & Potato: In Antibes, on the Côte d'Azur, I lost my heart not to a lifeguard in a stripy swimsuit but to a humble, free-standing rôtisserie. Strolling along the rue Aubernon, I was stopped in my tracks by a bizarrely beautiful contraption of black iron and brass, like one of Jean Tinguely's creaking kinetic sculptures, except it smelled of roast chicken. Rows of birds levitated in different stages of readiness, goosebump-raw to bronzed, reaching the top of their elliptical cycle before gravity turned the skewer and the birds adjusted to the downward part of their journey, with a judder that shook free molten droplets of fat. The machine had a similarly hypnotic effect to the Penny Falls in amusement arcades, as if by pushing a raw chicken into a slot at the top a cooked one might be displaced into the tray at the bottom. In fact the tray at the bottom was full of crisps. Could there be anything more delicious in the world? Chicken and roast potatoes, maybe, or Portuguese-style chicken and chips, but there was something particularly irresistible about the crisps from the bottom of the rôtisserie, chewy and glisteningly coated in the fat dripping from the chickens above.

Chicken & Rose: Chicken served with rose petals, or rosewater, was popular in Moghul, Moorish and medieval English kitchens. In Laura Esquivel's novel *Like Water for Chocolate*, the heroine, Tita, brings her sister, Gertrudis, to an orgasmic boiling point with a dish made from rose petals and quail. Brillat-Savarin would *not* have approved. In his opinion, the flavour of quail was the most exquisite, but the most fugitive, of all game, and therefore to serve it any way other than plainly roasted or *en papillote* was nothing short of barbaric. If you subscribe to this view, you might find chicken an acceptable substitute in quail dishes that call for sauce; many cooks do. The psychologists Hollingworth and Poffenberger claim that with 'tactual' qualities eliminated, most people fail to distinguish between the flavours of chicken, turkey and quail. But tactual qualities are not to be sniffed at. Would Gertrudis have had such a good time chomping through a skinless chicken breast as gnawing on a sticky little quail's leg?

Chicken & Saffron: *See Saffron & Chicken, page 180*

Chicken & Sage: Sage, usually paired with onion in a stuffing or a sauce, bolsters the savoury quality of chicken, although gamier turkey is better able to roll with the pungent herb's punches. Sage is also good with goose, as the bird has more fat, something with which sage has a particular affinity, as Harold McGee points out. Goose stuffed with sage and onion and served with apple sauce was the classic Christmas dish in the UK from the reign of Elizabeth I to the Second World War, although by the end of the Victorian era most people, particularly in the south of England, had switched to turkey. Victoria herself didn't care for either bird, preferring beef or a bit of roast swan. If you're curious, Peter Gladwin, once chef to Elizabeth II, compares swan's dark, tough meat to undernourished goose.

Chicken & Shellfish: *See Shellfish & Chicken, page 140*

Chicken & Thyme: Thyme is often used to flavour roast chicken, pushed under the skin or into the cavity. Brining a chicken before roasting it, however, makes the meat juicier and lend an extra intensity of flavour, not only because the salt penetrates the meat but because the brine can be flavoured with herbs, spices and/or vegetables. Put 70g sea salt and 4 tbsp sugar in a pan with 500ml water and a dozen sprigs of thyme (or 1 tbsp dried thyme), heat gently till dissolved, then leave to cool. Add 1.5 litres cold water to the salt water and refrigerate. When the brine is good and cold, wash the chicken and put it in a large roasting bag, big enough both to hold it and to immerse it totally in brine. Pour in the brine, then seal the bag, smoothing out as much of the air as possible. Leave in the fridge for 4–8 hours, moving it around from time to time. Give the chicken a thorough rinse in cold water before patting it dry. It can then be roasted as normal, immediately or after a day or two left covered in the fridge.

Chicken & Tomato: Hard to get that excited about, once you've grown out of drenching your dinosaur-shaped chicken bites in tomato ketchup. Tomato and chicken are the controlling partnership in chicken tikka masala and in chicken cacciatore, or hunter's stew – which is not, sadly, the invention of pockmarked Sicilian peasants, returning home with a brace of feral chickens slung over their waistcoats, but an English recipe from the 1950s, taught to nice girls by their mothers in the hope they'd bag the sort of chap who'd be neither too unadventurous nor too suspiciously cosmopolitan to object to a lightly herbed slop of chicken in tomato sauce.

Chicken & Truffle: *See Truffle & Chicken, page 116*

Chicken & Walnut: Ground nuts make an excellent basis on which to build a stew, contributing their own light, buttery background flavour as well as absorbing the rich flavours of meat and spice to make a thick, luxurious sauce. The popular kormas of northern India (and every curry house in the world) are based on ground almonds, cashews or coconut, an idea dating from Moghul times. The same principle applies to the Turkish dish of Circassian chicken. Poached chicken is shredded and served at room temperature in a sauce made with onions, garlic, ground walnuts, soaked bread and maybe some ground coriander or cinnamon. In Georgia, *satsivi* is made with chicken, fish or vegetables cooked in a mixture of walnuts and a long list of spices, including cinnamon, cloves, coriander, paprika and cayenne. Unlike Circassian chicken, no bread is used to supplement the nuts, but a sour flavouring such as vinegar or pomegranate juice will be added for balance – as it is in Iranian *fesenjan*, sometimes made with chicken but more often with duck. The combined tannic punch of walnut and pomegranate counters duck's fattiness deliciously. See also Almond & Chicken, page 242.

Chicken & Watercress: *See Watercress & Chicken, page 99*

Pork

Despite its prohibition by two of the major religions, pork is the world's most consumed meat. It tastes less salty and somewhat sweeter than beef. When roasted, good pork contains a tantalising combination of woodland and farmyard flavours, which can be emphasised with garlic, mushrooms, cabbage, potatoes and robust herbs or contrasted with the sharp flavour of apple. Sweet anise, white pepper and cooked onions all tease out its savoury meatiness. Remember that the colour of meat is an indicator of how much exercise the animal has been allowed; when raw, fully flavoured pork will therefore be a healthy rose pink. If it's the colour of a student's dishcloth, it will undoubtedly have seen as much action.

Pork & Anise: How long have you got? Three hours? Braise a 2kg piece of pork belly in the aromatic stock ingredients given in Anise & White Fish, page 185: put the pork (in one piece) in an ovenproof pot with a tight-fitting lid, add 2 litres of water, bring slowly to the boil and, at a low simmer, skim the scum until it desists. Stir in all the other ingredients, cover and transfer to the oven. Cook at 130°C/Gas Mark 1 for 2–3 hours. It is ready when the meat yields easily to a skewer. Set the meat aside while you simmer the sauce on the hob to reduce it. Serve the meat in pieces with white rice, the sauce and some sort of freshening garnish like shredded spring onions or coriander leaves. One hour? Stud a pork tenderloin with garlic, brush with olive oil, sprinkle over 1 tsp crushed fennel seeds and roast in the oven at 220°C/Gas Mark 7 for about 30 minutes, maybe with some sliced fennel bulb underneath the meat. Half an hour? Make a pasta sauce of delicious sweet Italian sausages – see Pork & Tomato, page 37. Five minutes? Unwrap the lacy, rose-pink slices of fennel-dotted *finocchiona* that you bought to lay on homemade pizza and fold them into different shapes as you eat them all, one by one.

Pork & Apple: *See Apple & Pork, page 272*
Pork & Apricot: *See Apricot & Pork, page 282*

Pork & Bacon: Bacon is like pork's older, more experienced brother. They team up in the full English breakfast (bacon, sausage), in French *choucroute garnie* (back bacon, pork knuckle, pork shoulder, salt pork and Frankfurt, Strasbourg and Montbéliard sausages) and in the astonishingly delicious Asturian bean stew, *fabada* – see Black Pudding & Pork, page 39. Ruddy-faced bacon lends pale pork colour, as well as a salty, brothy flavour. The pork in your pork pie would have a rather insipid city-dweller complexion if it wasn't mixed with bacon to give it its rosy flush: 1 part bacon to 3 parts pork shoulder works well. See also Pork & Egg, page 35.

Pork & Beef: In *Goodfellas*, Vinnie tells us that for authentic meatballs three different types of ground meat are needed. 'You got to have pork. That's the flavour.' But beef's the flavour too, albeit a darker, ferrous note against the lighter, sweeter background of pork. Veal is there for texture. In the US, you can buy the trio pre-mixed, often in equal measures, in the form of meatloaf or meatball mix. The flavour and texture of a beef stew can be enriched by the addition of pork rind – hold a little back when you're roasting a pork joint, even if that means less crackling. And pork lard is hard to beat when it comes to browning meat for a pot roast.

Pork & Beetroot: *See Beetroot & Pork, page 87*
Pork & Black Pudding: *See Black Pudding & Pork, page 39*

Pork & Broccoli: Broccoli raab, the broccoli lover's broccoli, is hugely popular in southern Italy. Some people say it's more mustardy and spicy than standard broccoli; I'd add that it has a ferrous tang and a salty hint of liquorice. And with those hot and anise-like qualities, it's just perfect with Italian pork sausages (often flavoured with chilli and fennel seeds themselves). There are several ways to cook this dish. Sometimes the broccoli is cooked with the pasta, or everything is thrown into the same pan together. Some recipes stipulate that the sausages should be kept whole, others that the meat should be liberated from the casings, others still that the sausages be sliced into bite-sized pieces. I favour the last method, cooking the pieces slowly in olive oil. When some of the fat has rendered, I add chopped broccoli and cook it with the sausage pieces for 15–20 minutes. A tablespoon of hot pasta cooking water can be added to the sauce now and then to create a brothy juice that's soaked up by the florets. Serve with orecchiette pasta, so that, properly mixed into the sauce, the 'little ears' of pasta fill up with the broccoli's tiny green flower buds like miniature salad bowls.

Pork & Butternut Squash: *See Butternut Squash & Pork, page 231*
Pork & Cabbage: *See Cabbage & Pork, page 119*

Pork & Celery: Some people detect an anise or fennel quality in celery, and it certainly shares those flavours' affinity for pork. Celery seed is used extensively in charcuterie, liver sausages and meatloaf. The stalks of celery are braised with cubed pork, onion, white wine and stock, and thickened by *avgolémono* (see Egg & Lemon, page 134) in the simple, savoury Greek stew, *hoirino me selino*. See also Prosciutto & Celery, page 171.

Pork & Chestnut: *See Chestnut & Pork, page 233*
Pork & Chilli: *See Chilli & Pork, page 210*
Pork & Cinnamon: *See Cinnamon & Pork, page 218*
Pork & Clove: *See Clove & Pork, page 220*

Pork & Coconut: The Vietnamese dish *thit heo kho tieu* consists of caramelised pork slow-cooked in coconut water (not milk) and fish sauce. Boiled eggs are added towards the end. Melbourne chef Raymond Capaldi offers a less rustic take on the combination – cold coconut noodles served with a neat brick of hot, gelatinous pork belly. The noodles aren't rice noodles cooked in coconut milk, as you might expect, but are *made* of coconut milk, chilli oil and palm sugar, set with agar-agar. They're as thick as liquorice bootlaces and white as fresh paint. The dish is garnished with typically Vietnamese herbs such as mint and coriander and served with a *laksa* vinaigrette.

Pork & Coriander Leaf: In Portugal, coriander is the most widely used herb, and the word *coentrada* on the menu means that the dish has been cooked with lots of the stuff. A popular recipe is pig's ears with coriander and garlic, tossed in oil and vinegar and served cold. If pig's ears sound a little on the chewy side, consider coriander's knack of cutting through fatty Asian dishes such as *roujiamo*, a Chinese hot meat sandwich usually served as a street snack. Originally from Shaanxi Province, it can involve various ingredients, but a common combination is braised pork stuffed into wheat flatbread with lots of coriander leaf and some bell pepper.

Pork & Coriander Seed: *See Coriander Seed & Pork, page 346*
Pork & Cucumber: *See Cucumber & Pork, page 187*

Pork & Cumin: As lamb is often suited to flavours redolent of its habitat – grassy, herbal, *maquis* – so pork is complemented by the earthy flavour of cumin. Sprinkle ground cumin on an oiled pork tenderloin or chops before cooking, or let them bask in this glorious marinade. Mix 1 tbsp honey, 2 tsp ground cumin, 5 tbsp red wine, 2 tbsp olive oil and 1 tbsp red wine vinegar in a medium-sized freezer bag. Add the pork and muddle it around, then seal it and leave to rest in the fridge for a few hours before removing and cooking.

Pork & Dill: *See Dill & Pork, page 190*

Pork & Egg: Come together in a fry-up or a Sausage McMuffin, neither of which is a patch, visually speaking, on a slice of gala pie. That slender key-line of hot-water pastry enclosing another of shimmering aspic, the mottled-pink rectangle of minced pork and bacon, the ovoid cross-section of boiled egg white, the yellow circle of yolk. Maybe it's the Pop Art neatness that appeals, as I feel the same way about Scotch eggs. Good examples of either are hard to find. Best to make your own. For 4 Scotch eggs, mince together 200g pork shoulder and 75g unsmoked streaky bacon and season. Divide into 4 and, with wet hands, form into balls and then into cups. Dust 4 peeled boiled eggs with flour and sit the fat end of each in a 'cup'. Work the meat around the egg, making sure there are no holes. Dip in beaten egg, then breadcrumbs and deep-fry for 7–8 minutes, turning a few times for even colour. Little Scotch quail's eggs are a brilliant variation, but only if someone else is peeling the shells off. See also Black Pudding & Egg, page 38.

Pork & Garlic: Pair pork with shameless amounts of garlic: they're made for each other. *Adobo*, a Filipino stew that has a claim to be the national dish, combines loads of garlic with meat – usually fatty pork – vinegar, soy sauce, bay leaves and peppercorns. You can make a quick, no-fuss *adobo* by piling all the ingredients into a pot, bringing to the boil, and simmering, covered, until the meat is tender – about 1½ hours. The following method involves a little more work but the results will be considerably more flavourful. Marinate, for anything between a few and 24 hours, 500g pork shoulder or belly, cut into chunks, all but 4 cloves of a garlic bulb, crushed, 4 tbsp soy sauce, 125ml rice vinegar, 1 bay leaf and 1 tsp freshly ground black pepper (for a slightly different but still delicious flavour, you can use inexpensive balsamic or Chinese black vinegar instead of the rice vinegar). Transfer to a pan, add enough water to cover, then bring to the boil, cover and simmer until the meat is tender. Strain, pour the broth back into the pan and boil until reduced to a thick gravy. Meanwhile, heat some groundnut oil in a frying pan and fry the pork pieces, adding them back to the broth when they're crisp. Finally, crush the remaining 4 cloves of garlic, fry them until golden and add to the pot. Simmer for a few minutes, then serve with rice or, even better, *sinagong* – garlic fried rice. Simply fry cold cooked rice with crushed garlic, finely chopped shallots and a little soy sauce.

Pork & Ginger: *See Ginger & Pork, page 312*
Pork & Globe Artichoke: *See Globe Artichoke & Pork, page 128*
Pork & Grape: *See Grape & Pork, page 253*

Pork & Grapefruit: Some years ago I was lying on the beach in Antigua irritated at the sunshine, the cool breeze in the palms, the white sand fine as caster sugar, and the volcano on distant Montserrat, still puffing after its eruption six months earlier, for the expectation they embodied that I was in paradise. And then a waft of jerk pork drifted over and I was. I turned on to my stomach, partly to stop it rumbling. A woman had set up an oil-drum barbecue in the shade of the beach's fringe of trees. Twenty minutes later I had a fresh roti in one hand, stuffed with hot pork fiery with allspice and Scotch bonnet peppers, and a can of ice-cold grapefruit Ting in the other.

Pork & Juniper: *See Juniper & Pork, page 325*
Pork & Mushroom: *See Mushroom & Pork, page 79*

Pork & Oily Fish: 'The eel goes very well with pork, because it is among fish what the pig is among quadrupeds,' writes Norman Douglas in *Venus in the Kitchen, or Love's Cookery Book*, before giving a recipe for suckling pig stuffed with eels. As preparing a romantic dinner goes, wrestling an eel into a piglet has to give Annie Hall and Alvy's lobsters a run for their money. Douglas suggests stuffing a gutted 10–15-day-old suckling pig with thick pieces of boned, vinegar-washed eel, peppercorns, cloves and sage.

Pork & Onion: *See Onion & Pork, page 110*
Pork & Oyster: *See Oyster & Pork, page 153*
Pork & Parsnip: *See Parsnip & Pork, page 225*
Pork & Pea: *See Pea & Pork, page 203*

Pork & Peanut: Peanut and pork are often combined to make the American take on *dan dan* noodles, but peanut's not part of the authentic Sichuan version. Mine is an inauthentic version of the inauthentic version, so should probably be called spicy pork and peanut noodles. Roughly chop 100g salted roasted peanuts. Heat 1 tbsp groundnut oil in a frying pan and fry sliced dried red chillies to taste. Don't let them burn. Add 300g minced pork, mixed with 1 crushed garlic clove, and fry slowly until browned and cooked through. Drain off any fat and, back on the heat, sprinkle over 2 tbsp light brown sugar and 1 tbsp soy sauce. Stir in most of the chopped peanuts. In a separate pan, cook 4 sheets of fine or medium egg noodles in 700ml chicken stock laced with 2 tbsp soy sauce and 1 tsp sesame oil. Put a little chilli oil in the bottom of 4 soup bowls. Using a slotted spoon, divide the noodles between them, add a few tablespoons each of stock and top with the pork mixture. Garnish with the rest of the crushed peanuts and some rings of fresh red chilli.

Pork & Pear: *See Pear & Pork, page 274*
Pork & Pineapple: *See Pineapple & Pork, page 267*

Pork & Potato: A salty, earthy pairing that gives us sausages and mash, frankfurters with potato salad, and a hearty Tuscan roast – see Rosemary & Pork, page 319. In Peru, they meet in *carapulcra*, a stew made with dried potato, chillies and peanuts. And in Korea, a soup called *gamjatang* combines pork backbone with potatoes and lots of spice, and is often served as a late-night corrective to a few too many beers.

Pork & Rhubarb: Rhubarb chutney is a familiar accompaniment to pork chops but more recently the pair has been turning up in barbecue and Asian-style recipes. Rhubarb's sour fruitiness is apt to absorb complex spice mixtures, and can cut through sweet, salty sauces.

Pork & Rosemary: *See Rosemary & Pork, page 319*
Pork & Sage: *See Sage & Pork, page 322*
Pork & Shellfish: *See Shellfish & Pork, page 144*

Pork & Swede: Swede makes most sense mashed under a hunk of braised or roasted meat steeped in gravy. There's no point trying to make this dish refined; it's as coarse as a farmer cursing in his long-johns. Try it with a hand of pork (the fatty shoulder – sweeter than the leg) or the pig's cheeks. Both are usually used for making sausages but also reward a long braising.

Pork & Thyme: *See Thyme & Pork, page 327*

Pork & Tomato: The acidity of tomato makes a delicious contrast to pork's fatty sweetness. Cut into pieces and cooked in tomato, good Italian sausages (with fennel, if you can get them) will disintegrate into the liquid, giving you a *ragù* of a richness and depth you normally have to drum your fingers for two hours to achieve. Soften a little garlic in olive oil, then add 4 sliced sausages, allowing them to brown a little before adding a can of peeled plum tomatoes. Break the tomatoes up with a spoon and, while you're at it, use the tomato liquid to help scrape off the tasty bits of pork stuck to the bottom of the pan. Season and allow to simmer for about 20 minutes. Serve with pasta, polenta, bread or rice. In Thailand, tomatoes add a sweet element to *nam prik ong*, a cooked dip made with a fried paste of chilli, lemongrass, shallot, garlic, shrimp paste, coarsely chopped tomato and minced pork, seasoned with fish sauce and palm sugar. It's eaten with raw or boiled vegetables, steamed rice or fried pork skin.

Pork & Truffle: *See Truffle & Pork, page 117*
Pork & Watercress: *See Watercress & Pork, page 100*
Pork & Watermelon: *See Watermelon & Pork, page 250*

Black Pudding

A good black pudding will have a velvety texture and a rich, mellow sweetness that should please fans of foie gras. Black pudding from Britain, *boudin noir* from France, *morcilla* from Spain or Argentina, *sanguinaccio* from Italy, *Rotwurst* from Germany and *kishka* from Eastern Europe may all be made with fresh blood but the additional ingredients can vary from country to country, region to region, sausage maker to sausage maker. The blood in question is often pig's, which has a particularly fine flavour, but lamb's blood is also used, and in *The Odyssey* a feast is prepared of she-goat blood cooked in the animal's intestine. Oats, barley, cubed fat, rice, pine nuts, chestnuts, almonds, cream and combinations thereof are used to thicken blood puddings, and a blood sausage may also include meat or offal. The mixture is seasoned according to the sausage maker's blend of choice, stuffed into lengths of intestine or synthetic casings, then poached. Black pudding rubs along particularly well with autumnal flavours such as apple and sweet root vegetables, and is good used as a seasoning ingredient, enhancing the flavour of meat dishes.

Black Pudding & Apple: *See Apple & Black Pudding, page 269*

Black Pudding & Bacon: There's more to the partnership of bacon and black pudding than their contribution to a breakfast fry-up. They can be used in a salad or a pilaf, or combined with pork in a pie or stew. See also Black Pudding & Pork, page 39.

Black Pudding & Chocolate: A mixture of chocolate and cream is combined with blood to make the Italian black pudding, *sanguinaccio*. If that doesn't sound rich enough to begin with, it's often embellished with sugar, candied fruit, cinnamon or vanilla. *Sanguinaccio* is sometimes made into a sausage form, like other black puddings, but is also eaten (or drunk) while still in its creamier liquid state. This may bring to mind recipes for jugged hare, in which the animal is cooked in its own blood with dark chocolate.

Black Pudding & Egg: Terence Stamp and Julie Christie. Very English. And, like Terry, black pudding consorts with the best of them these days, having left the confines of the greasy spoon for the swank expanses of Michelin-starred restaurants, where it hangs out with scallops and fancy salad leaves. If you're in a mood to make something fiddly, it's fun to fill ravioli with black pudding and a soft egg yolk that breaks when you cut into it. Serve with sage butter. For a more down-to-earth take on the combination, mix 1 part black pudding with 2 parts sausage meat for deliciously dark Scotch eggs. See Pork & Egg, page 35, for the Scotch egg recipe.

Black Pudding & Lamb: A handsome, unpretentious dinner-party dish. Unroll a 750g boned loin of lamb. Uncase a black pudding and carefully lay it the length of the meat, as if it were Cleopatra rolling herself up in a carpet. Roll it up, tie with string and present to Caesar. Or season and roast at 180°C/Gas Mark 4 for approximately 1 hour. Worth trying with pork too.

Black Pudding & Liver: Grilled black pudding with foie gras has been on the menu at Andrew Pern's The Star in Yorkshire for over a decade. The foie gras is sandwiched between two slices of black pudding, topped with a slice of caramelised apple and served with a salad of watercress, apple and vanilla chutney and a scrumpy reduction. Pern named his 2008 book after the best-selling combination.

Black Pudding & Mint: A few years ago I decided I'd learn more about cooking if I concentrated on the cuisine of one country a month. Breakfast, lunch and dinner, I'd cook nothing but Indian, or French, or Japanese food. Spain came first and *The Moro Cookbook* by Sam and Sam Clark saw me through most of a hot but cloudy June – weather that found its perfect match in *habas con morcilla*, broad beans with blood pudding. I associate black pudding with cold weather and hearty dishes, perky broad beans with bright, summery sweetness. Fresh mint has a foot in both camps. It's a summery herb that yearns for the cold; the flavour of shade. Fry 200g *morcilla*, cut into thick rounds, in 3 tbsp olive oil over a medium heat, until the contents burst from their casings like biceps from a body-builder's T-shirt. Set them aside and, in the same pan, cook a couple of thinly sliced garlic cloves and ½ tsp fennel seeds. When the garlic starts to turn golden, add 500g broad beans and 100ml water. Cook for 3–5 minutes, until the beans are tender. Finally, return the *morcilla* to the pan to reheat and add a good handful of roughly chopped mint. Season and serve on toast.

Black Pudding & Onion: Combined with potato, black pudding and leek make delicious patties. Boil 4 large potatoes until soft, then drain and mash them with seasoning but no butter or cream. While the potatoes are cooking, soften 3 or 4 thinly sliced leeks in butter. Fold the leeks into the potato with a generous pinch of mustard powder and a shake of white pepper. Finally mix in about 150g crumbled black pudding. Wet your hands and shape the mixture into 6–8 patties. If there's time, it's best to let them rest in the fridge for at least half an hour – this stops them breaking up in the pan. Lightly dust the patties with flour, then shallow-fry till they are thoroughly heated through (the pudding is already cooked) and tantalisingly browned on each side. Serve with spinach salad in a mustardy dressing, plus a glass of ale.

Black Pudding & Pork: The next time a friend goes to Spain, tell them to forget about the straw donkey and bring you back a bag of *fabes*. *Fabes* are big white beans – bigger than butter or lima beans. Bigger, in fact, than a woodsman's thumbs. They're heaven, each a perfect mouthful of soft, beany purée flavoured with whatever rich stock they've been cooked in. If your friend forgets, butterbeans or limas will do fine for this Asturian dish called *fabada*. Soak 500g large dried white beans in cold water overnight. The next day, put them in a roomy pan with a sliced Spanish onion and 3 chopped garlic cloves, cover with water and bring to the boil, skimming as necessary. Then add 200g whole *morcilla* and 200g cooking chorizo sausages (having pricked them a few times to prevent them bursting), 250g pork belly slices and 3 smoked bacon rashers. Pour in extra boiling water to cover and, once it starts bubbling, reduce to a low heat and simmer for about 3 hours. Top up the water if it drops below the ingredient-line (which it will: this is a thirsty stew). Agitate the pan now and then to stop things sticking – stirring will break up your precious ingredients. They'll break up anyway, to an extent, but you don't want this too mushy. In the last hour, taste from time to time and add salt if necessary. Cut the meat into bite-sized portions and serve.

Black Pudding & Potato: In Ireland you might eat black pudding with potato pancakes or with champ, a dish of buttery mashed potatoes and spring onions. In a similar vein, German *Himmel und Erde* ('heaven and earth'), a combination of apple and potato, sometimes mashed, sometimes in pieces, is often served with black pudding. See also Black Pudding & Onion, page 39.

Black Pudding & Rhubarb: Like apple, rhubarb's sharpness can cut through the richness of black pudding. A tart, quick-to-make rhubarb chutney is a case in point – see the recipe at Rhubarb & Oily Fish, page 255. Try this in a *morcipan*, grilled *morcilla* served in a roll, as sold from street carts in Argentina.

Black Pudding & Shellfish: A modern classic. In fancy restaurants, pale scallop is often found perched, trembling like an ingénue, on filthy old black pudding's knee.

Liver

Liver has a recognisable flavour across animal species. Both its intensity of flavour and its level of tenderness or toughness depend to some extent on the animal's age, which is why calf's and lamb's liver are generally favoured over ox liver. That said, a well-reared, grass-fed cow will usually furnish superior liver to that of an ill-kept calf pumped full of antibiotics. The liver is the clearing house for the body's toxins, and an animal that has experienced a lot of stress will have had to metabolise more compounds that detract from the ultimate eating quality of the meat.

Liver & Apple: It's blood that gives liver its characteristic flavour. The liver is one of the few places in a mammal's or bird's body where a large amount of liquid blood collects. So it's perhaps not surprising that apple, which goes so well with rich, delicate blood sausage, should go well with liver too. In mainland Europe, poultry liver and apple are combined in mousses, pâtés and terrines.

Liver & Bacon: I wonder if the key to this classic combination might be that liver is low in fat while bacon often has some to spare. Fry your slices of bacon until crisp and set them aside somewhere hot while you quickly fry the liver in the bacon fat. Calf's liver is often served with bacon in restaurants but lamb's liver can be excellent too. If you're worried that the liver might be too strongly flavoured, you can soak it in milk (as some do with anchovies) for an hour or so before cooking, remembering to pat it dry. And bear in mind that, like cabbage and eggs, liver's flavour intensifies with longer cooking.

Liver & Beef: *See Beef & Liver, page 45*

Liver & Beetroot: Nutritionists say that beetroot is good for your liver. I say it's even better for the liver on your plate. Fergus Henderson notes that when he first tried venison liver he had expected it to be rather bitter and taste strongly of iron. In fact, he found it particularly sweet and delicate and suggests it as a great match for roast beetroot.

Liver & Black Pudding: *See Black Pudding & Liver, page 39*

Liver & Chilli: Liver needs robust partners to set off its bold iron flavour. Try marinating chicken livers in an Indian sauce of hot paprika, mustard oil and yogurt, then grilling them over charcoal. Chef and writer Mridula Baljekar notes that while it's rare to find liver on the menus of Indian restaurants, it's frequently cooked in Indian homes. She coats chicken livers in a mixture of flour, chilli, cumin and garam masala, then fries them with garlic in oil, serving them with browned fried onions and a tomato and coriander sauce.

Liver & Fig: *See Fig & Liver, page 340*

Liver & Garlic: As every parent knows, children are inherently conservative. As a kid, I implored my mother not to put egg sandwiches in my packed lunch, in order to avoid the merciless mime festival of pinched noses and dry retching that attended the release of their sulphurous odour, intensified after a morning brooding eggily in a plastic lunchbox. Okay: no egg sandwiches. Then, one day, I suppose after my parents had had a dinner party, I peeled back the corner of the lunchbox and filled the classroom with a heady mix of chicken liver, garlic, brandy and thyme, as if a gourmet giant had galumphed in and belched. I nibbled my sandwiches amid howls of derision from my classmates.

Liver & Oily Fish: Red mullet is sometimes known as the 'woodcock of the sea' as, like the woodcock, its liver is highly prized. It might be served separately as a pâté or pounded up into a sauce to accompany the fish. In Provence, it's sometimes used in the saffron and garlic rouille that accompanies a bouillabaisse. *Ankimo*, or monkfish liver, is one of the most revered *chinmi*, or rare delicacies, of Japan. Its velvety, creamy texture has a greater claim than even red mullet liver to be the foie gras of the sea.

Liver & Onion: The sweetness of onion contrasts with liver's bitter, savoury flavour. The combination is a classic all over the world. In Poland they fry pig's liver in breadcrumbed strips and serve them on a bed of fried onion. In the Philippines pig's liver is commonly fried with garlic, onions and a little pork. The English sauté lamb's liver with onions, or braise ox liver in a rich, mahogany-coloured stew. The Indian dish of tandoori chicken livers, cooked on a skewer and served on a sizzling plate of onions, is in contention for the best take on the pairing, but for me the finest liver and onion dish of all is the Venetian *fegato alla veneziana* – lightly fried strips of calf's liver and meltingly soft slow-cooked onions, served with polenta or rice.

Liver & Sage: *See Sage & Liver, page 322*
Liver & Truffle: *See Truffle & Liver, page 117*

Beef

The taste of beef is predominantly salty and umami-ish, with some sweetness and sourness (and bitterness if the meat is rare). Its flavour is clean, yeasty and meaty, with a slight metallic edge, and little of the animalic character so apparent in most pork and lamb. As with all meat, the flavour will to some extent depend on the species, how the animal has been reared, the cut and the cooking method. Grass-fed beef is fuller flavoured than grain-fed. Most beef benefits from hanging, which gives it a deeper, gamier flavour. Beef works well with vegetables and shellfish, as do other meats, but it has a particular affinity for sharp flavours, notably horseradish and mustard.

Beef & Anchovy: *See Anchovy & Beef, page 161*
Beef & Anise: *See Anise & Beef, page 182*

Beef & Bacon: Even bullish beef can benefit from the bolstering flavour of bacon. Cured meat brings a generic meatiness to a dish, not to mention some very welcome fat. The leanness of many beef cuts has always invited a good larding, and in French butcher's shops you can still see cuts of meat with the fat neatly stitched on to them. Roughly the same principle obtains when pancetta is added to spaghetti bolognese, or lardons to beef bourguignon. In Germany, bacon is rolled between thin slices of beef with mustard and pickles to make *Rouladen*. Similarly, in Italy *saltimbocca* is made by laying prosciutto and sage leaves on very lean veal before cooking.

Beef & Beetroot: In New England, red flannel hash is prepared with beet-root, corned beef, onion and cooked potatoes (diced or mashed). Fry it up for breakfast, with a fried or poached egg on top. Add a pickled gherkin on the side and you could call it *labskaus*, a dish that in various guises was common to northern European port cities such as Hamburg and Liverpool. In Hamburg, the dish might have salted herring mashed into it too, or come served with a rollmop as a garnish along with the egg and pickles. The related British dish, lobscouse, is more of a simple meat and potato stew than a hash, and piquant additions like pickled beetroot, red cabbage or onions are served on the side. See also Caper & Beetroot, page 102.

Beef & Bell Pepper: *See Bell Pepper & Beef, page 205*
Beef & Blackberry: *See Blackberry & Beef, page 335*
Beef & Blue Cheese: *See Blue Cheese & Beef, page 61*
Beef & Broccoli: *See Broccoli & Beef, page 125*
Beef & Cabbage: *See Cabbage & Beef, page 118*

Beef & Caper: Unsurprising that beef should have an affinity for caper, as the latter is a tropical relative of the mustard family and contains isothiocyanate, or mustard oil. Capers are known as *mostacilla* (little mustard) in Cuba, and *jeerba* (herb) mustard in Aruba and Curaçao. Make a dressing of olive oil, lemon juice, chopped parsley and drained rinsed capers for cold roast beef. See also Beef & Egg, page 44.

Beef & Carrot: In the nineteenth century the English upper classes ate their carrots with rib of roast beef. The working classes made do with cheaper beef cuts such as brisket, which they ate salted and boiled. Carrots were thrown into the pot towards the end of the lengthy cooking process. A similar Jewish dish, sweetened with honey, syrup or dried fruit, is called *tsimmes*. In the 1850s, Thackeray acknowledged both the deliciousness and the popularity of the combination in his essay 'Great and Little Dinners'. Sixty years later, it was still popular enough to merit a music-hall song, 'Boiled Beef and Carrots' by Harry Champion.

Beef & Celery: *See Celery & Beef, page 95*

Beef & Chilli: The *carne* in chilli con carne is usually beef, although a combination of pork and beef is common too. The dish is said to have originated in San Antonio, Texas, in the late nineteenth century, when it was sold from cauldrons under lamplight by the famous 'chilli queens'. Health and

Safety did for them in the 1940s, but at heart chilli (or at least a 'bowl of red') still belongs to Texas. There is a predictably high level of debate about what constitutes an authentic chilli, but most recipes are agreed on a spice mix of dried powdered chilli, cumin and oregano. The pepper of choice is the smoky, dried ancho, with a blast of extra heat supplied by the infernal cayenne. An altogether different take on this pairing comes in the form of weeping tiger salad from Thailand, in which seared beef steak is served on a crisp salad with a chilli, lime and fish sauce dressing.

Beef & Cinnamon: Cinnamon, which is used in a lot of Greek meat dishes, is a key ingredient in *pastitsio*, a pasta dish somewhere between moussaka and *lasagne al forno*. Layers of macaroni are alternated with a spiced meat and tomato sauce, then topped with a thick béchamel. In Italy the term *pasticcio*, which translates (like *pastitsio*) as 'mess', or 'muddle', is used to describe any pie that contains a mixture of sweet and savoury ingredients. Elizabeth David gives a recipe for *pasticcio* in which cooked spaghetti is layered with a beef ragù flavoured with orange zest and cinnamon, then baked in a double crust of sweet pastry (the use of sweet dough isn't that unusual for savoury pies in southern Italy). The Italian practice of spicing beef with cinnamon goes back to Roman times, and to this day is a feature of braised oxtail, *brasata di coda di bue*. They might put a little chocolate in it too.

Beef & Clove: *See Clove & Beef, page 220*

Beef & Coconut: The Blue Elephant's *beef penang* was unforgettable, but The Fatty Crab's *beef rendang* knocked me sideways. Beef *penang* and *rendang* are both salty, sweet, slow-cooked coconut-based stews from Southeast Asia. *Rendang*, from Indonesia, is the more concentrated, all the water in the coconut milk having been evaporated until the meat is left to fry in the residual coconut oil, which makes the dish very intensely flavoured. If cooking is halted while the dish is still wet, it's called *kalio*. This makes it more like the *penang*, which is a curry with plenty of sauce. Both dishes include shallots, garlic, ginger or galangal, chilli and lemongrass, to which the *penang* adds lime leaves, coriander root, fish sauce and lots of peanuts.

Beef & Coffee: *See Coffee & Beef, page 19*
Beef & Dill: *See Dill & Beef, page 189*

Beef & Egg: Pending the inevitable advent of European Health & Safety Directive 9/24675(F): Beef Tartare (Severe Danger of Death), you must order one *now*, this minute, before it's too late. Raw beef has a mild ammonia flavour with a hint of pepperiness and the gentlest hint of fish, as if at some point in its life the cow had yearned for the sea. The raw egg yolk beautifully emphasises the meat flavour. How exposed your palate will be to these flavours will depend on the amounts and relative proportions of chopped anchovy, caper, shallot, parsley and mustard you choose to mix in. Even if you don't quite fancy the idea, it'll be something to tell the grandchildren, along with the one about driving without seatbelts and smoking in pubs.

Beef & Garlic: Garlic brings out the butch character in beef. Pair a rib-sticking roast beef with garlicky mashed potatoes, or make a sauce for thin slices of teriyaki beef by softening a fistful of peeled garlic cloves in beef stock and then puréeing it. Or simply push slivers into the nicks you've made in a joint, very much like an inverse of the game, Operation, without the burden of that pesky rubber band.

Beef & Ginger: *See Ginger & Beef, page 308*
Beef & Hard Cheese: *See Hard Cheese & Beef, page 66*

Beef & Horseradish: This most English of combinations may well have originated in Germany. In sixteenth-century England, horseradish was used for medicinal but not culinary purposes, although the contemporary botanist John Gerard noted that in Germany the root was used to accompany fish and meat dishes in the way that the English used mustard. The beef-on-weck sandwich, a speciality of Buffalo, New York, also has German roots – *Weck* is a German dialect word for 'roll', and the specific type used is called *Kummelweck*, topped with a mixture of kosher salt and caraway seeds. The roll is stuffed with thin slices of rare roast beef and horseradish. Horseradish and beef can also be combined in a stew. Horseradish loses its pungency when cooked, so is added towards the end; used in the form of a creamed sauce, it gives a stroganoff-like effect, its sharp, slightly sour bite giving an edge to the rich beef sauce.

Beef & Juniper: The Corsican dish, *premonata* (or *prebonata*), involves beef, kid or goat served in a rich braised sauce of wine, tomatoes, peppers and juniper berries. As sinister as the backstreets of Calvi at midnight.

Beef & Lemon: *See Lemon & Beef, page 304*
Beef & Lime: *See Lime & Beef, page 300*

Beef & Liver: Less fancy versions of beef Wellington prevail, but the real deal is fillet steak slathered in *pâté de foie gras* and shavings of fresh truffle, then wrapped in puff pastry. Putting it together is simple, cooking it less so. Left in the oven for too long, the meat begins to steam and shrink. Lose your nerve and take it out too soon and you'll have soggy pastry and under-cooked beef; exactly what happens to Doris Scheldt in Saul Bellow's *Humboldt's Gift*, when she makes beef Wellington for her boyfriend, Charlie Citrine. Charlie's next girlfriend, Renata, plays it safe and sticks to serving champagne cocktails while wearing feathers and a G-string. Worth bearing in mind if you're having an off day in the kitchen.

Beef & Mint: *See Mint & Beef, page 329*

Beef & Mushroom: A garnish of mushrooms is a steakhouse standard. Beef and mushroom are also paired in a stroganoff, or in a pie with a thick, booze-laced gravy. A few years ago, at the Fence Gate Inn in Burnley, Lancashire, the chef, Spencer Burge, caused a fuss by making a beef and mushroom pie that cost £1,000 a slice. It consisted of 2.5kg wagyu beef, 1.5kg rare, cinnamon-scented Japanese *matsutake* mushrooms (so precious they were picked under the protection of an armed guard), black truffle, and that favourite ingredient of the honest British pie, gold leaf. Most connoisseurs recommend eating wagyu raw or rare truly to appreciate its quality. If stuffing it in a pie isn't enough to make them weep, the two bottles of Château Mouton Rothschild '82, reduced to half their volume for the sauce, should do it.

Beef & Oily Fish: The famous Italian summer dish, *vitello tonnato*, consists of thin slices of cold cooked veal served with a tuna mayonnaise sauce. Marcella Hazan sounds a warning note: tinned tuna is essential; fresh won't work. Chicken can be substituted for veal – Elizabeth David gives a recipe for *pollo tonnato*, so that makes it okay. The chicken might seem like a compromise but in flavour terms it has a strong harmony with tinned tuna, as does cooked beef. According to *Sensory-Directed Flavor Analysis* by Ray Marsili, 2-methyl-3-furanthiol has one of the meatiest characters of all flavour compounds, and is very pronounced in cooked beef, chicken broth and tinned tuna.

Beef & Olive: *See Olive & Beef, page 175*

Beef & Onion: The original Philly cheesesteak sandwich, which was devised by Philadelphians Pat and Harry Olivieri as something a little different to offer on their hotdog cart, consisted of just finely sliced steak and onions in a soft white roll. The addition of provolone cheese came some years later. In the Japanese *gyudon*, steak and onions are likewise thinly sliced and fried, then a little soy, mirin and water are thrown in to deglaze the pan and provide a sauce. It's served on rice. In the Lyonnaise dish of *grillade des mariniers*, thinly sliced rump steak is marinated in olive oil, red wine vinegar, bay leaf, orange rind and cloves. When it's had time to infuse, the meat is layered in a heavy pot with oodles of sliced onions and garlic, sprinkled with the marinade and braised for hours. To lend piquancy, a little anchovy and garlic, mixed to a paste with some of the cooking juices, is sometimes added in the last 15 minutes of cooking. And if you've ever tasted French onion soup made with veal stock, you'll never want it any other way.

Beef & Orange: *See Orange & Beef, page 294*
Beef & Oyster: *See Oyster & Beef, page 151*

Beef & Parsley: St John restaurant in London is famous for its dish of marrowbone with parsley salad. Middle veal marrowbone is roasted until the marrow is loose but not melted away, then served with a salad made with lots of parsley, a little sliced shallot and some tiny capers, dressed with olive oil and lemon. They give you some toast and a hillock of sea salt too. I once had a first date with a guy who ordered it. I quite fancied him to begin with, but the sight of him frowning at a bone, turning it over, and then over again, picking at it, smearing it on toast and adding pinches of salt like a geriatric pharmacist cast an irreversible pall over the evening. We might have been better off eating Argentinian: charred steak with *chimichurri* sauce is not only delicious but can be eaten with a knife and fork, and is a cinch to make at home. Finely chop a large bunch of flat-leaf parsley and mix it with 5 tbsp olive oil, 2 tbsp red wine vinegar, a crushed garlic clove (or two) and some seasoning. Serve on the side of a steak cooked as you like it.

Beef & Parsnip: *See Parsnip & Beef, page 224*
Beef & Pea: *See Pea & Beef, page 201*
Beef & Peanut: *See Peanut & Beef, page 22*

Beef & Pear: Nashi pear and beef are combined in two popular Korean dishes, one with raw beef and one with cooked. *Yuk hwe* is a special-occasion dish of finely sliced raw beef tenderloin marinated in soy, sesame, garlic, spring onion and chilli, served with shredded Asian pear and maybe some pine nuts. As in beef tartare, a raw egg yolk might be stirred into the beef. *Pulgogi* consists of thin strips of beef marinated in grated Nashi pear, lemon juice, rice wine, sesame oil, sesame seeds, garlic, soy and sugar for a few hours and then fried quickly. It's eaten wrapped in small, crisp lettuce leaves with raw vegetables such as carrot, cucumber and radish.

Beef & Pork: *See Pork & Beef, page 33*
Beef & Potato: *See Potato & Beef, page 88*
Beef & Shellfish: *See Shellfish & Beef, page 140*

Beef & Swede: One wintry afternoon we inserted the car into the herringbone pattern of lorries and made our way under the low lintel to the striplit interior of the building. At high, Formica-topped tables drivers sat hunkered over their food, staring at us like dogs drowsily protective of their bones. There was no menu, and as the staff didn't seem to speak much English – or speak much at all – there was nothing for it but to point at what we wanted. It wasn't long before we, too, were hunched over our food, just as jealous of it as the wordless *routiers* patting flakes of pastry off their stomachs. Thin layers of swede, turnip and potato lined the bottom of the casing; above that, a generous pile of tender beef, seasoned as it should be with white pepper. And just below the pastry lid lay a seam of soft onions, whose juice had seeped through the meat, tenderising it right through to the strata of vegetables, so the whole pie was steeped in a tangy, earthy sweetness that set off the robust savouriness of the meat. So simple, yet so sensitive to the ingredients. Were we at a simply wonderful, if (thankfully!) little-known, Relais Routiers somewhere between Normandy and Burgundy? No, we were in a petrol station off the A390 in Cornwall. We followed our pasties with the most marvellous pouch of Maltesers.

Beef & Thyme: *See Thyme & Beef, page 325*

Beef & Tomato: With a keen fisherman for a father, a great cook for a mother, a granny with her own miniature fruit orchard, and the cold hands of natural pastry makers, it was inevitable that my sister and I should be filled with lust for processed food. We nagged for orange-crumbed fish fingers, level as mantelpieces, and sawdusty cakes in lurid icing. When the Pot Noodle (like Cup Noodles in the US) launched in the 1970s, I pestered and pestered until my mother gave in. One Beef and Tomato Pot Noodle was procured from the corner shop and the entire family huddled round, as a generation back they might have round an early television, to peer into the cup and witness the alchemical transformation from fish food into a hot meal. Mixing up the noodles, soy-based meat substitute, freeze-dried vegetables and bouillon powder with a sachet of tomato ketchup beat my mother's spaghetti bolognese hands down for entertainment value but offered an eating experience whose weirdly one-dimensional inauthenticity I dimly understood was half the point: a sort of slippery soup that tasted of barbecue-beef-flavour crisps.

Beef & Truffle: The French and Italian ways of serving truffles with beef say a lot about their respective cuisines. Tournedos Rossini calls for perfectly cooked steak and a slice of foie gras, served on a croûton with Madeira sauce. Black truffle is shaved over the top and usually added to the sauce too. The Italians might shave a little white truffle – which doesn't tolerate being cooked – over a plate of carpaccio. No frills or furbelows: they just let the ingredients speak for themselves.

Beef & Walnut: Pickled walnuts became fashionable in England in the eighteenth century. They're preserved in vinegar when the nut is still green, before the shell has formed. If you're making your own, this means gathering the nuts in summer. They're lovely things: black as crude oil, with a slight beetroot-like resistance to the teeth, a mild piquancy and a flavour only subtly reminiscent of unpickled walnuts. They're frequently paired with Christmas foods – cold roast beef, Stilton or leftover turkey. Chef Fergus Henderson makes a beef stew with pickled walnuts, cooked in red wine with lots of red onion, garlic, herbs and rich stock.

Beef & Watercress: *See Watercress & Beef, page 99*

Lamb

In the US, lamb comes bottom of the flavour-preference table, behind beef, chicken, fish, pork, turkey and veal. Per-capita consumption is only 1 per cent that of beef or chicken. The flavour, even of young lamb, is considered by many to be too sheepy and gamy, and the use of flavour descriptors like 'sweaty-sour' is enough to make anyone pause before taking a fork to a heavenly, subsiding lamb shank. The characteristic flavour is primarily in the fat – in blind tastings, many people find it hard to distinguish the flavours of very lean lamb and beef – and improves with hanging, even in the case of young lamb. Mutton, for its part, not only develops a deeper flavour when hung for two or three weeks but becomes tender enough to roast. One of the great pleasures of full-flavoured lamb is its ability to stand up to other strong flavours – robust herbs such as rosemary, for example, or bold spices in curries and stews.

Lamb & Almond: A luxurious pairing, fit for a feast, or a delicious meal for two. Scale down the Moroccan tradition of stuffing whole lambs with rice, spices and almonds to your humbler requirements by using a boned shoulder of lamb. Alternatively, pair lamb and almonds in a slow-cooked tagine. Or try my Moroccan-style lamb meatballs, cooked with spiced rice and garnished with toasted almonds, which boasts similarly fine flavours to a tagine but can be made in minutes rather than hours. Slowly soften an onion in oil and a little butter with a cinnamon stick. Meanwhile, mix 2 tsp allspice into 500g minced lamb. Season and form into walnut-sized balls. Steep a pinch of saffron threads in hot water. When the onion is soft, add 750ml hot water, 2 tsp honey, 2 tsp pomegranate molasses, 2 tsp allspice, 1 tsp salt and the saffron water, then bring to the boil. Add the meatballs. When the water starts to bubble again, add 200g basmati rice, stir and simmer, covered, for 10 minutes. Check for seasoning and the rice's texture – you don't want it to turn mushy. When the rice is just cooked, stir in 6 tbsp chopped parsley, 3 tbsp chopped mint and a drained tin of chickpeas. Heat through and serve with lots of toasted almond flakes and a little more chopped parsley or mint. This is, in essence, a thick soup, so needs no other accompaniment.

Lamb & Anchovy: This has to be one of my favourite combinations. Anchovy works as a flavour enhancer for the meat. All you have to do is stick a knife into a shoulder or leg joint at various intervals, then push drained salted anchovies into the slits. I tend to use 8–12 anchovies for a 2kg joint. You can always make more slits and press in some garlic and/or rosemary too – all feisty flavours that rub along very nicely together. Roast the lamb in the usual way. The anchovy melts into the meat and intensifies the flavour with a mouthwateringly rich, savoury saltiness, and the gravy should be terrific.

Lamb & Anise: Although the tarragon-sharpened flavour of Béarnaise sauce is most strongly associated with beef, it's perfectly suited to roast and grilled lamb too. And Pernod gives a warm breeze of anise to this summery lamb dish. Soften a diced onion and a little garlic in olive oil. Add 8 lamb loin chops dusted with seasoned flour and cook until browned. Add 45ml Pernod and allow to cook over a high heat for 1 minute. Then add 3 small courgettes, cut into coins, and a can of peeled plum tomatoes, chopping them up in the pan with a spoon. Stir in some seasoning, 1 tsp herbes de Provence and 1 tbsp tomato purée. Bring to the boil, then simmer, covered, for 45 minutes, giving the odd stir. Serve with saffron rice or couscous.

Lamb & Apricot: Go way back. *The Baghdad Cookery Book*, dating from the thirteenth century, features a slow-cooked lamb and apricot tagine called *mishmishiya*, which means 'apricoty'. Lamb and apricot both have an affinity with sweet spices, and while their sharpness cuts through the lamb's fattiness, the intense sweetness of the dried apricots throws the lamb, spices and almonds, all very sweet themselves, into a far more savoury light, making the meat taste meatier. Meanwhile, the musky, rich apricots plump up with lamb stock, cinnamon, coriander and cumin, so by the time the dish is served they're neither too cloying nor too fruity. You might also pair apricot with lamb in a similarly spiced pilaf, or stuff lamb with a mixture of chopped dried apricots, onion, almonds and rice or couscous.

Lamb & Aubergine: Aubergine was, I can only imagine, designed with lamb in mind. Its kitchen-towel propensity to soak up fat and juices suggests as much. Moussaka is the most obvious application, but there's also *hukar begendi*, a Turkish dish of cubed lamb served with an aubergine purée, and *patlican kebab*, wherein lamb and aubergine are simply cubed, threaded on to sticks and cooked over the chargrill – or, if you're lucky, whole aubergines are stuffed with minced lamb, cooked until the skin is wrinkled and the flesh yieldingly soft, then served in slices with thick white yogurt on the side.

Lamb & Black Pudding: *See Black Pudding & Lamb, page 39*

Lamb & Cabbage: *Farikal* is a popular Norwegian dish traditionally eaten around September to mark the passing of summer. It's simply mutton (or lamb) on the bone, simmered with cabbage, served with boiled potatoes and washed down with beer or aquavit. If this sounds stark, remember that lamb and mutton make boldly flavoured, fatty stock. In Venice a (slightly) more festive combination of salted, smoked mutton and Savoy cabbage is called *castradina*. It's served on 21 November to celebrate the *Festa Madonna della Salute*, when locals offer up thanks for their health. The lamb and cabbage stand for the food sent across the Adriatic by their Dalmatian neighbours when its isolation during the plague threatened the city with starvation.

Lamb & Caper: *See Caper & Lamb, page 102*
Lamb & Cardamom: *See Cardamom & Lamb, page 314*
Lamb & Celery: *See Celery & Lamb, page 96*

Lamb & Cherry: Broadly speaking, cherry flavour divides into two groups: sweet and sour. The sour cherry is too sharp to eat from the tree but has more flavour than the sweet variety, making it better for cooking. Morello (called *griottes* in France) and Montmorency are famous sour cherries, cropping up in lots of Middle Eastern, Russian and Eastern European dishes. Claudia Roden gives a recipe for shoulder of lamb with rice stuffing and sour cherry sauce, remarking that in the West the cherry has yet to become as popular a pairing for lamb as apricot. A rich mutton and potato stew with sour cherries is made in Azerbaijan, while in Turkey you might find sour cherries and lamb in a pilaf accompanied by any combination of onions, saffron, almonds, pomegranate, feta, mint, parsley and pistachios.

Lamb & Chestnut: *See Chestnut & Lamb, page 233*
Lamb & Cinnamon: *See Cinnamon & Lamb, page 218*
Lamb & Coriander Leaf: *See Coriander Leaf & Lamb, page 195*

Lamb & Cumin: In *Shark's Fin and Sichuan Pepper*, Fuchsia Dunlop writes about the Uighur migrants of Chengdu in southwestern China, who sell salty lamb kebabs flavoured with chilli and cumin, cooked on portable grills they set up on the street. They sell hash, too, and you could tell when the police were having a crackdown, she recalls, because the fragrance of sizzling lamb and cumin was abruptly conspicuous by its absence from the streets.

Lamb & Dill: *See Dill & Lamb, page 190*
Lamb & Garlic: *See Garlic & Lamb, page 113*
Lamb & Globe Artichoke: *See Globe Artichoke & Lamb, page 128*

Lamb & Goat's Cheese: Goat's cheese and lamb have, unsurprisingly perhaps, a great flavour affinity, and have defied what might seem their unfashionable level of richness to become an increasingly popular combination. They're paired in warm flatbread wraps and two-bite filo pastry parcels. Goat's cheese and feta are crumbled over lamb pasta sauces and pushed inside lamb burgers. And moussaka made with a goat's cheese béchamel is a rich treat, although for light relief you might serve it with baby spinach leaves tossed in a lemony dressing.

Lamb & Lemon: *See Lemon & Lamb, page 306*

Lamb & Mint: The French say *bof* to the Brits' love of mint with lamb, and they might have a point when it comes to the brutally vinegary strains of mint sauce. In 1747 Hannah Glasse wrote that a roasted, skinned hindquarter of pork will eat like lamb if served with mint sauce, which must have more to do with the overpowering nature of the sauce than any true similarity between the meats. But mint as a partner for lamb should not be dismissed wholesale. Lamb has a natural affinity for herbal flavours and, like citrus, mint's cleansing properties serve the useful purpose of deodorising some of lamb's funkier notes. Consider, for example, the lamb and mint ravioli served at Mario Batali's Babbo restaurant in New York. Or *sauce paloise*, which is like Béarnaise but swaps the tarragon for mint and is served with roast or grilled lamb. And in Azerbaijan a minted soup called *dusbara* is served with teeny lamb-filled tortellini bobbing in it. It's most often garnished with soured cream and garlic, although some prefer vinegar and garlic, which sort of takes us back to where we started.

Lamb & Nutmeg: *See Nutmeg & Lamb, page 222*
Lamb & Onion: *See Onion & Lamb, page 109*

Lamb & Pea: Peas act as apt reminders that lamb, not yet at its best by Easter, starts to develop its true lamby flavour in early summer, when the peas will be straining from their pods like glimpses of belly in an undersize shirt. Lamb and fresh peas, grassy as the fields the lambs have nibbled, are a gorgeous combination, whether you roast the lamb and boil the peas with earthy new potatoes or make *agnello alla romagnola*, lamb cut into pieces and stewed in butter with pancetta, tomato and peas, Emilia Romagna style. For minced lamb, try a spicy, aromatic Indian *keema* curry, polka-dotted with peas and served with rice or chapatis.

Lamb & Peanut: *See Peanut & Lamb, page 24*
Lamb & Potato: *See Potato & Lamb, page 91*
Lamb & Rhubarb: *See Rhubarb & Lamb, page 255*
Lamb & Rosemary: *See Rosemary & Lamb, page 318*

Lamb & Saffron: Iranian saffron is sweeter in character than the Spanish variety. Iran is the world's biggest producer of saffron by some way, and so it's no wonder that its national dish, *chelow kebab*, consists of lamb or chicken kebabs and saffron rice, sometimes accompanied by charred tomatoes and maybe a raw egg yolk and a sprinkle of citrussy sumac. The steaming, fragrant rice is usually flavoured with a pat of saffron butter that melts into it like solid sunlight. Make some by grinding 30 saffron threads with a mortar and pestle, then adding it to 1 tsp hot water and putting it aside while you zest a lemon. Mix the lemon zest, saffron water and a little lemon juice to taste with 100g soft butter. Shape into a log, wrap in cling film, place in the fridge and use in slices as and when needed.

Lamb & Shellfish: *See Shellfish & Lamb, page 142*

Lamb & Swede: Walk into a room where a haggis is being cooked and the first thing to hit you will be the aroma of lamb. Of all meats, lamb is the easiest to identify by cooking fragrance alone, as the meat contains chains of fatty acids not found in chicken, beef or pork. And haggis is intensely lamby. It's made from the 'pluck' – the animal's liver, heart and lungs – mixed with oatmeal, suet, pepper, allspice, clove and nutmeg. Neeps (swede) and tatties (mashed potatoes) are the essential side dish. The peppery sweetness of the neeps chimes with the haggis's own spiciness, and makes the meal worthy of its arrival to a flourish of bagpipes. See also Potato & Swede, page 93.

Lamb & Thyme: *See Thyme & Lamb, page 326*
Lamb & Tomato: *See Tomato & Lamb, page 260*

CHEESY

Goat's Cheese

Washed-rind Cheese

Blue Cheese

Hard Cheese

Soft Cheese

Goat's Cheese

The flavours in goat's cheese range from the lightest and most citric to the fullest Billy Goat Gruff. Its sharpness works well with sweet, dense ingredients like beetroot, butternut squash, good bread and honey. Traditionally feta and halloumi are made with sheep's milk, or a combination of sheep and goat's. They are included in this chapter because they share many flavour affinities with goat's cheese. Like all cheeses, the flavour of goat's cheese is markedly influenced by what the animal has eaten. In a sensory evaluation study conducted in 2001, over two-thirds of the tasting panel correctly identified which one-day-old goat's cheese had come from pasture-grazed goats and which from animals fed on hay and concentrate. For the 20-day-old cheese, the figure rose to 100 per cent.

Goat's Cheese & Anise: *See Anise & Goat's Cheese, page 183*

Goat's Cheese & Apricot: A great stand-up kitchen snack. Stuff a plump dried apricot with a modestly pungent goat's cheese and note just how meaty the combination is. The sweet, perfumed fruitiness of apricot emphasises the savouriness of the cheese, and the whole somehow recalls lamb. Goat's cheese, in common with cooked lamb and mutton, contains caprylic acid, which may account for the similarity in flavour.

Goat's Cheese & Basil: *See Basil & Goat's Cheese, page 214*
Goat's Cheese & Beetroot: *See Beetroot & Goat's Cheese, page 86*

Goat's Cheese & Blackberry: *Banon*, or *banon à la feuille*, is a French goat's cheese that's dipped in eau de vie before being wrapped in chestnut leaves. Once it's wrapped, it will be ready to eat in about three weeks, but leave it a little longer and it will develop rich, fruity, woody notes that complement blackberry right down to the hairs between its drupelets.

Goat's Cheese & Butternut Squash: *See Butternut Squash & Goat's Cheese, page 231*

Goat's Cheese & Caper: Australian agricultural writer E. A. Weiss writes that the flavour of caper is mainly attributable to capric acid, which develops after the buds are pickled. In its pure form, capric acid is pungently goaty, but the tiny amount in capers is modified by the pickling process. Capric acid also makes a significant contribution to the flavour of goat's cheese, and a soft goat's cheese will work well in the recipe suggestion under Caper & Soft Cheese, page 103.

Goat's Cheese & Cherry: *See Cherry & Goat's Cheese, page 248*

Goat's Cheese & Chilli: The Spanish habit of giving everything a liberal dusting of heat extends to the Canary Islands, where one of the three versions of the local Majorero cheese comes rubbed with *pimentón*. Texturally similar to Manchego (the popular Spanish ewe's milk cheese from La Mancha), Majorero is a firm, white cheese made with fatty goat's milk from Fuerteventura. Arico, from neighbouring Tenerife, is rubbed with a combination of *pimentón* and *gofio*, a toasted cereal, and was declared supreme champion at the World Cheese Awards in 2008.

Goat's Cheese & Chocolate: At a tasting of cheese and chocolate pairings held by chocolatier Paul A. Young, we kicked off with a ten-day-old Cerney, a goat's cheese from Gloucestershire, paired with an Amedei 63 per cent cocoa dark chocolate, moving on to a matured version of the same cheese with a 64 per cent Valrhona Madagascan Manjari. Chocolate with cheese may sound an unlikely, even offputting, proposition, until it strikes you how comparable it is to chocolate and milk (or cream) and, further, how the flavour notes in some good chocolate – spicy berry fruits, dried fruits, caramels – are natural partners for cheese. We also tried Colston Bassett Stilton with Valrhona 70 per cent, following the precedent of Young's Stilton and port truffles, which were originally conceived as a seasonal special but proved so popular that they're now on the menu year-round. But the revelation of the night was the pairing of Milleen's, a deliciously piquant, floral washed-rind Irish cheese made from cow's milk, first rind-on with an 85 per cent Valrhona African, then rind-off with a Valrhona 40 per cent Java milk chocolate. Try adding a few types of chocolate to your cheeseboard at the end of a meal – if your guests really can't face combining chocolate and cheese, they can always eat them separately. And both will work with port.

Goat's Cheese & Coffee: Coffee with cheese might sound even less promising than chocolate and cheese; but then Norwegian *ekte gjetost* is only cheese in a manner of speaking. It's made with whey left over from the cheese-making process, cooked until the lactose caramelises, then poured into rectangular moulds. Left to cool, the smooth, sweet, fudge-coloured, caramel-flavoured results are eaten in thin slices on toast or crispbread with morning coffee. It's also served with fruitcake or used in a sauce for game. A cow's-milk *gjetost* is popular too, but goat's is the more traditional version.

Goat's Cheese & Coriander Leaf: In Mexico the fresh, citrussy flavour of coriander leaves helps to cut through the fattiness of cheese in the ubiquitous enchiladas and quesadillas. Mexican cheeses are hard to find beyond the Americas, but Rick Bayless says that *queso fresco* is not unlike fresh goat's cheese, if a little drier, saltier and crumblier. Parmesan or (even better) pecorino romano can be substituted for *queso añejo*. And for the Chihuahua (the cheese, not the dog) that's used in quesadillas, try mild Cheddar or a Monterey Jack. Or you could follow Bayless's suggestion and mix cream cheese with goat's cheese, spring onion, a little salsa and chopped coriander, and spread it on bread with some sliced tomatoes.

Goat's Cheese & Coriander Seed: *See Coriander Seed & Goat's Cheese, page 346*
Goat's Cheese & Cucumber: *See Cucumber & Goat's Cheese, page 187*
Goat's Cheese & Fig: *See Fig & Goat's Cheese, page 340*

Goat's Cheese & Garlic: A goat's cheese and garlic pizza has been on the menu at London's Orso restaurant for over 20 years. The sweet flavour of the garlic takes the edge off the sharpness of the cheese. It's quite a mouthful, but the pizza base is light and crisp and the whole thing small enough not entirely to preclude a *secondo*. Make something similar by spreading a small amount of the tomato sauce in Garlic & Basil, page 112, on a pizza base and decorating it with thin slices of goat's cheese. While the oven is warming up, put some unpeeled garlic cloves in it on a roasting tray; by the time the oven is hot, they'll be lightly cooked. Scatter them on the pizza and bake it at 230°C/Gas Mark 8 for 10 minutes. If your tolerance for outlandishly pungent flavours is high, you may enjoy *Foudjou*, a potted French combination of fresh and older grated goat's cheese with garlic, herbs, brandy and olive oil. It's kept in a crockery pot and left to mature for a few months, after which it's eaten spread on French bread or baked potatoes.

Goat's Cheese & Lamb: *See Lamb & Goat's Cheese, page 51*
Goat's Cheese & Lemon: *See Lemon & Goat's Cheese, page 306*

Goat's Cheese & Mint: Authentic halloumi cheese is made from a mixture of goat's and sheep's milk. Mint is often added at the dry-salting stage; you may taste a hint of it, in addition to a citrussy flavour, in the end result. Like halloumi, feta is a brined cheese, whose saltiness benefits from the cooling contrast of mint. Mash feta with chopped mint, snipped chives and a grinding of black pepper, fold into little filo parcels and bake. On a sweeter note, in Ibiza a cheesecake-like pudding called *flaó* is traditionally made with sweetened fresh goat's cheese, mint, anise and honey.

Goat's Cheese & Mushroom: *See Mushroom & Goat's Cheese, page 77*
Goat's Cheese & Olive: *See Olive & Goat's Cheese, page 176*

Goat's Cheese & Pear: *Grazalema* is a goat's (or sheep's) cheese from the sunbaked province of Cádiz. It's a 'wolf in sheep's clothing', according to *The Murray's Cheese Handbook*, which finds 'sweet ripe pear and nectarine notes that remind us of chocolate-dipped fruit'. Which should be enough to sell you the cheese *and* the book. A buttery Chardonnay is the recommended wine pairing. Or you might try a manzanilla sherry.

Goat's Cheese & Raspberry: Raspberries combine well with young cheeses that still have their milky, lactic tang and a streak of citrus. Try them together in a fool. Crush 300g raspberries. Whip 200ml double cream to soft peaks. Whisk 150g soft, fresh goat's cheese with 1 tbsp icing sugar and a squeeze of lemon until soft. Fold into the cream with the raspberries. Check for sweetness, and divide between 4 bowls.

Goat's Cheese & Rosemary: Goat's cheese and lamb tend to share flavour affinities, including rosemary. Perroche, from Herefordshire, is a soft, lemony, unpasteurised goat's cheese that comes rolled in either rosemary, tarragon or dill. It's worth trying all three, but rosemary with gently citrussy cheese is a particularly winning combination. Or make this goat's cheese and rosemary tart. Line a 20cm flan tin with shortcrust pastry and blind-bake it. Cook 3 or 4 sliced leeks in olive oil until soft, season, then leave to cool a little. Spread them over the pastry. Whisk 75ml single cream with 100g soft, rindless goat's cheese. When well combined, beat in 2 eggs, 1 egg yolk and 1 tsp very finely chopped rosemary, and season. Pour over the leeks, top up with milk (about 100–150ml), and bake at 190°C/Gas Mark 5 for 25–30 minutes.

Goat's Cheese & Thyme: *See Thyme & Goat's Cheese, page 326*

Goat's Cheese & Walnut: There's a Persian place called Patogh off the Edgware Road in London that just might be my favourite restaurant anywhere. It serves *chelow* kebabs (see Lamb & Saffron, page 52) and enormous, cratered moonscapes of bread, hot from the oven and scattered with toasted sesame seeds. Walk in the door and the aroma of charring meat and baking bread will make the temptation of a starter irresistible. *Paneer* is a white tablet of feta, as smooth as a bar of Ivory soap and usually scattered with crisp walnuts. It's generally accompanied by *sabzi*, a thicket of fresh herbs, to offset its richness. There'll be plenty of mint, plus tarragon and dill, and bulbous spring onions and, nestled somewhere among the sprigs and leaves, little radishes, like baby robins in their nest. Quite apart from the heavenly contrast of freshness and salt, the chance to forage and eat with your hands makes this a fun and very easy appetiser or lunch to serve at home.

Goat's Cheese & Watercress: *See Watercress & Goat's Cheese, page 100*

Goat's Cheese & Watermelon: Beautiful combined in a salad. Beetroot is perhaps a more familiar partner to briny feta, but watermelon is a refreshing pretender to beetroot's earthier, more substantial sweetness, and has in fact been a common fixture in Greek salads since time immemorial. Bear in mind that both the salty cheese and olives, if you're using them, will draw juice out of the watermelon, so add the fruit just before serving to prevent sogginess. You might also consider how good goat's cheese would be with (or in?) the barbecued watermelon in Rosemary & Watermelon, page 320.

Washed-rind Cheese

Washing cheese in brine and other solutions dates back to the Middle Ages, when European monks discovered that the practice stimulated the growth of bacteria that gave the cheese less acidic, more pungent flavours, thus making abstention from meat a lot more bearable. In research conducted at Cranfield University, the beery washed-rind Vieux Boulogne was declared the world's smelliest cheese, outstinking even marc-washed Époisses, which is banned on public transport in France. As a rule, washed-rind cheeses are best left in the quiet company of bread or crackers, but they also go well with ingredients that share their piquant spiciness (like cumin, sharp apples or raw onion) or their soft earthiness (like potato). This chapter covers Stinking Bishop, Munster, Pont L'Évêque, Langres, Livarot, Vacherin and Celtic Promise.

Washed-rind Cheese & Anise: Washed-rind cheeses such as Munster or Stinking Bishop are simply too opinionated to be paired with many flavours, but anise (sweet, wonderful, beloved pet flavour of *The Flavour Thesaurus*) is up to the challenge. Slice or scoop your cheese on to these thin fennel-seed crackers. Sift 125g plain flour into a bowl with ½ tsp baking powder, ½ tsp salt and 2 tsp fennel seeds. Add 25ml olive oil and 125ml water in increments until the mixture is wet enough for a dough to be formed. Knead for 5 minutes, roll out to roughly 5mm thick, and press out your crackers with a biscuit cutter. You'll get about 24 crackers of 5cm diameter. Place on a greased baking sheet, brush with water and cook for 25 minutes at 160°C/Gas Mark 3. Substitute wholemeal flour if you prefer. Also try celery, cumin or caraway seeds.

Washed-rind Cheese & Apple: A crisp apple works well with gentler-flavoured washed-rind cheeses. Slice and core a tart green apple and eat it with a fruity, grassy Pont l'Évêque. Chef Pierre Gagnaire makes a chantilly of Pont l'Évêque and serves it with apple sorbet. Hard-core washed-rinds prefer their apple in the form of cider or the apple brandy, calvados – Celtic Promise, for example, is one of several cheeses washed in cider to help the development of its flavour and, other than a hunk of bread, a glass of cider is all the accompaniment it needs. I was so taken with Celtic Promise that I wanted to share it with the guests at my wedding, until I drove one back to London from Wales and it became all too apparent that two dozen of them in a hot room might have made my big day memorable in a way I'd want to forget.

Washed-rind Cheese & Bacon: Langres from the Champagne region of France is a salty little cheese with a flavour that's often compared to bacon. It looks like one of those unctuous yellow Portuguese custard tarts, and is every bit as rich. Each cheese has a hole in the top, into which you pour a little champagne or marc: quite a flavour sensation, and very handy if you've forgotten to pack glasses for your picnic. Langres isn't the only cheese that has a meaty quality. Some detect a beefiness in Italy's forceful taleggio. Émile Zola thought that Camembert smelt like venison. The French called Livarot from Normandy 'the meat of the poor'. I find some fresh goat's cheeses taste like a butcher's shop smells. And then there's the steak-fat blue cheese discussed in Blue Cheese & Beef, page 61. See also Potato & Washed-rind Cheese, page 94.

Washed-rind Cheese & Cumin: *See Cumin & Washed-rind Cheese, page 85*

Washed-rind Cheese & Garlic: Vacherin du Haut-Doubs, or Vacherin Mont d'Or, is a (very) soft cheese from Franche-Comté or the Swiss canton of Fribourg that frequently makes it on to lists of the world's top cheeses. Peel back the rumpled, tarpaulin-like rind and you'll discover an ivory-coloured, fondue-like liquid, with a milky, salty, slightly fruity flavour, and a whiff of spruce from the box in the case of the (always unpasteurised) Haut-Doubs version from the French side of the border. Some people eat it straight from the box with a spoon, but I find a finger sufficient. It heats well too: take the lid off the box, wrap the box in foil, prick the surface of the cheese, insert some slivers of garlic, pour over 100ml dry white wine, then bake it at 180°C/ Gas Mark 4 for 20 minutes. Scoop from the box with good bread.

Washed-rind Cheese & Pear: Livarot is a gamy, buttery cheese made from the fatty milk of Normandy cows. It has a rather spicy quality to its flavour, which makes it good with pears; no coincidence, given the abundance of orchards in Normandy. Combine them in a tart or simply sliced on a plate, served with a glass of creamy pear cider, otherwise known as perry, or *poiré* in France. Calvados is traditionally made with apples, but the Domfrontais variety contains at least 30 per cent pear and is a recommended companion for Livarot. Stinking Bishop cheese, incidentally, is washed with perry made from the Stinking Bishop pear.

Washed-rind Cheese & Potato: *See Potato & Washed-rind Cheese, page 94*

Washed-rind Cheese & Walnut: Walnut is an apt companion to all cheeses, and it's one of the few flavours that can rise to the challenge of a pungent washed-rind. Its bitter, tannic quality is apt to cut through the fatty headiness of the cheese, and its sweetness peeps through too. Walnut bread, walnut crackers, or wet walnuts when they're in season are all very good simply paired with Livarot.

Blue Cheese

What makes blue cheese blue is a powdered blue-green mould called *Penicillium roqueforti*. The dominant flavours in blue cheese are the fruity, spicy notes attributable to the ketone 2-heptanone, and a green, fatty, metallic note from 2-nonanone. Other than that, blue cheeses vary as widely in flavour as they do in provenance, depending on the animal's diet, whether or not its milk has been pasteurised, the kind of starter and secondary cultures used, and the length of time and conditions under which it's stored. Roquefort, famously, is aged in caves – its AOC depends on it having been stored in the natural caves of Cambalou near Roquefort-sur-Soulzon in the Aveyron. Stilton is aged in cellars, where cool air can penetrate the tiny holes made in the cheese to help the mould spores do their work. A notable exception to the *Penicillium roqueforti* rule is a rare blue cheese called Bleu de Termignon, made in tiny quantities in the French Alps with milk from pasture-grazed cattle, and allowed to blue naturally. Other blue cheeses covered in this chapter include Gorgonzola, Cabrales, Rogue River Blue, Shepherd's Purse, Beenleigh Blue and Fourme d'Ambert.

Blue Cheese & Avocado: Missing out on avocado and bacon is one of the drawbacks of vegetarianism, but a deep-flavoured, salty blue cheese is some compensation. Pair them Seventies-style, the fruit's cavity brimming with blue cheese dressing, or spread a toasted slice of brioche with avocado mashed with a little lemon juice and top with crumbled blue cheese.

Blue Cheese & Bacon: *See Bacon & Blue Cheese, page 167*

Blue Cheese & Beef: It's the tang of full-flavoured, properly aged beef that accounts for its successful pairing with blue cheese, according to writer Peter Graham. Steak au Roquefort is a classic, and in Spain a similar dish is made using *queso de Cabrales*, a boisterous blue from Asturias. Stilton will make an opinionated cheeseburger to shake up sluggish taste buds at a morning-after brunch. A handful of crumbled blue cheese is sometimes added, at the end of cooking, to a *carbonnade de boeuf*, melting into the stock and taking on its beery meatiness. Devotees of the combination should seek out Shepherd's Purse Buffalo Blue Cheese, made in North Yorkshire with locally reared buffalo's milk, which is higher in saturated fat than cow's milk. It has a luxurious flavour redolent of the fat on a really good, aged rump steak, with a similar melting texture. Kills two flavours with one stone – and it's suitable for vegetarians.

Blue Cheese & Blueberry: *See Blueberry & Blue Cheese, page 344*

Blue Cheese & Broccoli: A threat or a promise, depending where you stand on pungent flavours. Combine them in a soup, in macaroni cheese or, for more timid palates, a salad of chopped raw broccoli with a mild blue cheese dressing.

Blue Cheese & Butternut Squash: Pumpkin ravioli are often served with a Gorgonzola sauce (see Blue Cheese & Sage, page 63). The complex, salty cheese makes a striking contrast to the dumb sweetness of the squash, particularly if you use a bumptious *piccante* Gorgonzola rather than the milder variants sometimes referred to as *dolce*. Alternatively try roasting 2cm cubes of butternut squash and piling them on doorsteps of toast. Dot with Gorgonzola and blast under the grill. Serve with a glass of German Spätlese, a wine with a fair amount of residual sugar, which would work well with the caramelised squash and contrast nicely with the salty sharpness of the cheese.

Blue Cheese & Cabbage: The recipe for blue cheese dressing under Blue Cheese & Chicken, below, works a treat on coleslaw. But it's not the sort of thing to yank you out of bed in the morning. For that you need the kimchi butter and sweet Gorgonzola croissant from the Momofuku Bakery in NYC. Best to hold the coffee with that.

Blue Cheese & Celery: *See Celery & Blue Cheese, page 95*

Blue Cheese & Chicken: Paired with Buffalo chicken wings – see Celery & Blue Cheese, page 95 – but I think the richness of the combination is better diluted in a salad. Prepare a blue cheese dressing by thoroughly mixing 100ml mayonnaise, 150ml soured cream, 60g chopped blue cheese, 1 tbsp lemon juice, 2 tbsp parsley, 1 crushed garlic clove and some seasoning. Cool in the fridge while you slice 2 celery sticks into matchsticks. Tear Cos lettuce leaves as you would for a Caesar salad. Cut 4 boneless, skinless chicken breasts into slices, dip in seasoned flour and fry in a mixture of groundnut oil and butter. When the chicken is cooked, toss while still hot in a warmed mixture of 2 tbsp butter and 4 tbsp of hot sauce – Frank's RedHot if you can get it, but anything nice and fiery will do. In a large bowl, toss the leaves and celery in the cold dressing and pile the chicken on to a platter. Serve with a glass of IPA or a German wheat beer.

Blue Cheese & Fig: While brown dried figs are reminiscent of sweet Pedro Ximénez sherry, black-purple mission figs are more suggestive of port and, appropriately enough, make a really heavenly match for Stilton. Combine them in these Stilton and fig straws and serve with chilled tawny port. It'll make a change to savour this pair of flavours at the start of an evening. In a food processor, make a dough of 125g plain flour, 225g crumbled Stilton, 50g butter, a pinch of salt and 1–2 tbsp cold milk. Roll out into a rectangle roughly 30cm x 20cm. Using scissors, snip about 8 dried mission figs into thin strips and lightly press into the dough. Along its width, fold one half of the dough over the other, with the fig on the inside. You will now have a rectangle roughly 15cm by 20cm. Roll it out to about 5mm thick and cut into straws, using a palette knife to transfer them to a greased baking tray. Bake at 180°C/ Gas Mark 4 for about 15 minutes. You might alternatively try blue cheese and fig in a salad with sturdy leaves and a port dressing. Boil 200ml port until reduced by about half, add 1 tsp honey and leave to cool. Whisk in 3 tbsp extra virgin olive oil, 2 tbsp balsamic vinegar and season.

Blue Cheese & Grape: *See Grape & Blue Cheese, page 252*

Blue Cheese & Grapefruit: Modern in an obsolete way, like the Skylon or flying cars. Combine them in a salad with red onion, beetroot and some crisp, bitter lettuce. If you can get it, grapefruit marmalade makes a terrific sandwich combined with blue cheese.

Blue Cheese & Mushroom: *See Mushroom & Blue Cheese, page 76*

Blue Cheese & Peach: Peach is a great match for Gorgonzola. Both have a fruity, creamy quality. They're often paired in salads and on bruschetta, but all they really need is a plate and a knife. The nineteenth-century explorer, F. W. Burbidge, described the flavour of the Asian fruit durian as 'a combination of cornflour, rotten cheese, nectarines, crushed filberts, a dash of pineapple, a spoonful of old dry sherry, thick cream, apricot pulp and a soupçon of garlic all reduced to a consistency of a rich custard'. To this day in Singapore they're banned from many hotel rooms – no drugs, no firearms, no durian.

Blue Cheese & Pear: The gentler flavours of pear can be lost with some blue cheeses, but Fourme d'Ambert is at the milder end of the scale. It's sweet and milky, with a mild mustiness that comes from its ageing in caves, and is injected with a sweet wine just detectable to the palate. You might otherwise find blue cheese and pear combined in a salad (see Pear & Walnut, page 275), or in a blue cheese fondue served with slices of pear, figs and walnut bread.

Blue Cheese & Pineapple: Martin Lersch has a blog called Khymos that runs a regular TGRWT (They Go Really Well Together) recipe challenge; blue cheese and pineapple was the subject of TGRWT #10. Interestingly, Lersch notes that he was unable to find an overlap in the reported flavour odorants in these ingredients, but that this is the case with many common pairings. Other TGRWTs have investigated apple with rose, chanterelle mushrooms with apricot, Parmesan with cocoa, and banana with parsley.

Blue Cheese & Sage: Salty-sweet blue cheese craves bitterness and sage can provide it. Melt 25g butter, add 3 large sage leaves and stir for 30 seconds.

Over a low to medium heat, add 75g crumbled Gorgonzola and 150ml double cream, stirring while it melts and melds. Remove the sage, adjust the seasoning and serve on pasta or gnocchi.

Blue Cheese & Truffle: Blue cheese and truffle are commonly paired in a creamy sauce to serve with *filet mignon*. The food writer Jenifer Harvey Lang gives a recipe for choux pastries stuffed with a mixture of blue cheese, cream cheese and cream, which she tops with shavings of black truffle. I once had my head turned by the combination of truffled honey and Stilton, but even without the addition of cream, there's something about the pair that feels like wearing a low-cut top and a short skirt.

Blue Cheese & Walnut: Toasted walnuts can develop something of a blue cheese flavour. Take it as a hint. Milky, sweet, bitter-skinned walnut works wonders with all types of blue cheese. It's a classic partnership, especially crumbled Roquefort and walnuts in a salad with chicory. Good dressed with extra virgin olive oil, cider vinegar and cream, 5:3:2, shaken up with seasoning. Try walnuts on a cheeseboard with Beenleigh Blue, made in Devon from ewe's milk, which when mature has an almost fudgy texture and intensely peppery veins. Or with *queso de Cabrales* from Asturias in Spain, which has legendary strength: this cheese could fight bulls.

Blue Cheese & Watercress: *See Watercress & Blue Cheese, page 99*

Hard Cheese

This covers a wide range of cheeses, including Cheddar, Parmigiano-Reggiano, Manchego, Comté, Gruyère, pecorino, Berkswell, Mahón and Lincolnshire Poacher. Flavours vary according to milk type, milk quality, the cheesemaker's recipe, microflora and the cheese's age. A good cheesemonger will be able to furnish you with a tasting flight of the same cheese at different stages of maturation, so that you can experience at first hand the effect ageing has on flavour. Many hard cheeses are sweet, sour and salty, and gain crystals of umami as they age. It's this array of tastes, in combination with its high fat content, that makes hard cheese both a satisfying eat in itself and a complement to other ingredients, enhancing their flavours with its rich roundness. Red wine, raw onion, watercress and walnuts often work well with hard cheese, as they add a balancing touch of bitterness. And sweet partners like dried fruit, cooked tomato and cooked onion can bring out the cheese's savoury side. When tasting hard cheese, look out for creamy, buttery, coconut, caramel, fruity (especially pineapple), sulphurous (chopped boiled egg), cooked, roasted and nutty flavours.

Hard Cheese & Almond: Both Keen's and Montgomery Cheddar contain almond notes, and although walnuts are the more common nut pairing, there's no reason why almonds shouldn't work as well with a good, nutty Cheddar as they do with a Manchego. Authentic Manchego is made with sheep's milk in La Mancha, central Spain. It's as widespread in its popularity as in the redolence of its flavours. Young Manchegos have a fresh, grassy quality evocative of the cool pastures of Galicia in the north. Older specimens exhibit the hot, dry saltiness of the Andalusian coast. Both would be good cut into thin slices and served with a bowl of toasted, salted almonds. If you're lucky, they'll be heart-shaped Spanish Marcona almonds, prized for their luscious, milky flavour.

Hard Cheese & Anchovy: *See Anchovy & Hard Cheese, page 162*

Hard Cheese & Anise: Mahón, a hard cheese from Menorca, is made with pasteurised cow's milk and has a salty, lemony flavour. It's traditionally eaten in thin slices with fresh tarragon leaves, olive oil and black pepper. Leonie Glass writes about Salers, a semi-hard cheese from the mountainous Cantal *département* in south-central France, where the cows have a richly aromatic diet of liquorice, arnica, gentian and anemone, all of whose flavours are discernible in the milk. Serve with the fennel crackers described in Washed-rind Cheese & Anise, page 59.

Hard Cheese & Apple: *See Apple & Hard Cheese, page 270*
Hard Cheese & Apricot: *See Apricot & Hard Cheese, page 282*

Hard Cheese & Asparagus: People get superstitious about asparagus. Otherwise sane cooks will insist on cooking it in special pans, or turning the spears three times anti-clockwise but never under the light of a full moon. Cast aside cabbalistic practices by simply roasting asparagus in the oven, then serving with grated Parmesan, which has a harmoniously sulphurous character. Make sure to scatter lots of cheese on the tips, where it will catch deliciously between the bracts.

Hard Cheese & Bacon: *See Bacon & Hard Cheese, page 169*

Hard Cheese & Banana: Comté is made in the Alps with raw cow's milk and is the most popular cheese in France. When young, it has flavours of fresh hazelnut, dried apricot, soft caramel and boiled milk; when fully mature, according to the Comté cheese assocation, it has 'rich, persistent walnut, hazelnut, chestnut, grilled almond, melted butter and spice flavours softened by hints of matured cream or citrus fruits'. Notes of leather, white chocolate and prune may also be apparent. Try the Comté representative's recommendation of white bread topped with sliced banana, sliced Comté and a pinch of Espelette pepper (more about that in Oily Fish & Chilli, page 156), grilled for a few minutes until the cheese has melted. The banana, they say, helps bring out the cheese's multitude of flavours, whereas the chilli adds 'a final hot, persistent touch'.

Hard Cheese & Basil: If there's such a thing as a cult restaurant, La Merenda is it. The Michelin-decorated chef Dominique Le Stanc used to cook at the Hotel Negresco on the promenade in Nice. Like a disillusioned sheriff, he handed back his star and headed into the Old Town to cook in the less rarefied confines of his tiny, bead-curtained, ten-table joint scarcely bigger than a kebab shop. There's no fancy stemware, no flower arrangements, no flattering lighting, no wine list, no backs to the chairs and, advance planners should note, no telephone. The menu, chalked on a blackboard you prop on the table or your knee, is invariably Niçoise in provenance, and usually includes a *tagliatelle au pistou. Pistou* is essentially a variation on pesto, trickled around the coast from its home in Liguria, discarding a vowel on the way and picking up some new ones like souvenirs. It primarily differs from pesto in lacking pine nuts, and is sometimes made with Emmental in place of Parmesan. Le Stanc serves his *pistou* with fresh spinach pasta.

Hard Cheese & Beef: Trained tasting panels might use the term 'brothy' to describe the flavour of hard cheese, meaning it has similar properties to a beef stock cube. As any cheeseburger fan can testify, many hard cheeses make a harmonious match for beef. When I tire of reading about wonderful organic produce markets, or clod-booted laments for the good old days of subsistence farming, I like to pick up *The $100 Hamburger* by John F. Purner. It's a guide to cafés and restaurants near airfields, rating both the quality of the ribs or cheeseburgers and the runways that'll take you to them; like a gastronomic *Earth From Above*, where the aerial vantage is given on places like the Kanab Muni airfield in Utah, for example, where great burgers are available at the nearby Houston Trails End Café, or the grass airstrip at Gaston's in Arkansas, where you can stay in a cabin and eat fresh trout from the lake. Now flying, burgers and eating fish are no longer allowed, reading the book is like looking at footage of glamorous smokers in bars: nostalgia we weren't expecting to come so soon.

Hard Cheese & Broccoli: Broccoli begs for a hard, under-the-counter-strength cheese. Parmesan is ready to eat, having matured for a relatively lengthy 18 months. If you're buying it cut fresh from a deli, look for the date stamped on the wheel. Older Parmesans, matured for three or four years, are sometimes called *stavecchio* (or at their oldest, *stravecchio*), and are saltier, spicier and generally more intense. They're what you really want on your extra-bitter broccoli raab. Combine them in a pasta or risotto.

Hard Cheese & Cauliflower: *See Cauliflower & Hard Cheese, page 123*
Hard Cheese & Chicken: *See Chicken & Hard Cheese, page 28*

Hard Cheese & Chilli: Italian pecorino can be pretty spicy to begin with, but if you want it properly hot you'll need to buy it *con peperoncino* – flecked with little pieces of chopped-up, medium-hot, dried red pepper. In the US, jalapeño Jack works on the same principle, and can be used to make a fondue-style dip for tortilla chips: deconstructed nachos. The flavour of corn is particularly harmonious with hard cheese and chilli; try tossing freshly popped kernels with chilli powder, paprika, melted butter, grated Parmesan and salt. See also Butternut Squash & Chilli, page 230.

Hard Cheese & Clove: Friese Nagelkaas is a Gouda-style cheese from Friesland in Holland. *Nagel* means 'nail', referring to the nail-shaped cloves that are shattered and added to the cheese with a little cumin. If you've ever tasted Green & Black's Maya Gold chocolate, this is the cheese equivalent. The cloves and cumin contribute a heady spiciness whose hints of orange and lemon peel lend the cheese a Christmassy flavour.

Hard Cheese & Fig: The *consorzio*, or safeguarding consortium, responsible for Parmigiano-Reggiano recommends dried fig, hazelnuts, walnuts and prunes as pairings for their 24–28-month-old Parmesans. These will have lost some of the milkiness of their youth and started to develop notes of fruit and nut, alongside a melted-butter flavour – hence the pairings. As the cheese continues to age, the nut flavours get more pronounced, and spicy notes (nutmeg in particular) become detectable.

Hard Cheese & Globe Artichoke: In Italy, raw baby artichokes are sliced paper-thin and tossed with olive oil, lemon juice and wisps of Parmesan to make a salad that's bitter, sharp and salty, and an excellent appetiser. Strip your artichokes of all their dark external leaves. Lop 2–3cm off the top of each, cut most of the stem off and peel what's left of the stem with a potato peeler. Rub with lemon juice, then cut in half lengthways, checking there's no choke – if there is, remove it with a teaspoon. Slice each half into very fine strips, cutting from the top of the leaf to the stem. As you go, put the strips into water acidulated with lemon juice to prevent them browning. Once you've chopped all your stems, strain off the lemon water, pat dry and toss in olive oil. Season, and garnish with thin parings of Parmesan.

Hard Cheese & Grape: Grapes have a generic fruitiness that makes them a safe bet on the cheeseboard. Whether it was for want of fresh grapes that someone first paired tangy, slightly lemony Wensleydale cheese with a slice of fruitcake I don't know, but they make a very cosy couple. Of course, the affinity of cheese with grape is clear in countless cheese-and-wine pairings. 'Buy with crackers, sell with cheese,' they say in the wine trade: crackers cleanse the canny buyer's palate, whereas cheese coats the taste buds with fats and proteins that can attenuate a wine's harsher, tannic qualities.

Hard Cheese & Juniper: *See Juniper & Hard Cheese, page 324*
Hard Cheese & Mushroom: *See Mushroom & Hard Cheese, page 78*
Hard Cheese & Nutmeg: *See Nutmeg & Hard Cheese, page 222*

Hard Cheese & Onion: Cheese and onion was the first flavoured crisp introduced in England and Ireland. But there are countless variations on the theme. Stinky German Limburger is paired with raw onion, rye bread and mustard and served with strong dark beer. In Wales, leeks and salty, white, acidic Caerphilly are shaped into vegetarian Glamorgan sausages and coated with breadcrumbs and herbs. Classic French onion soup is *gratiné* with Gruyère, giving a lovely fruity twang to the rich onion flavour and making it nearly impossible to eat without infinitely extendable arms. A red onion tart will often include an atoll of goat's cheese, while Berkswell, a hard sheep's cheese made in the West Midlands, kills two birds by having strong hints of caramelised onion itself.

Hard Cheese & Orange: *See Orange & Hard Cheese, page 295*

Hard Cheese & Parsnip: Parsnip has a serious appetite for salty foods that emphasise its sweetness. Parmesan is a popular pairing – typically, parboiled parsnips are tossed in flour and grated Parmesan before being roasted. Or make a Parmesan cream garnish for parsnip soup by folding 1 tbsp grated Parmesan and 2 tbsp snipped chives into 4 tbsp whipped double cream. Mark Bittman gives a recipe for parsnip gnocchi, which he recommends serving with Parmesan, butter and sage.

Hard Cheese & Pea: *See Pea & Hard Cheese, page 203*
Hard Cheese & Pear: *See Pear & Hard Cheese, page 274*

Hard Cheese & Pineapple: Outsnoot snobs sneering at your sticks of cheese and pineapple. The flavours can be naturally harmonious: the pineapple note of ethyl caproate is present in some of the world's finest cheeses, including Comté, Lincolnshire Poacher and Parmesan. Ethyl caproate also occurs naturally in clove, figs and wines.

Hard Cheese & Potato: Once upon a time there was a coarse-skinned baked potato that had a lovely smell of malt but a messy thatch of Cheddar on the top, so it had to be eaten in the scullery. Everybody saw its goodness and beauty but it was never invited to the ball. One evening, when the potato was all alone, a fairy godmother appeared and asked the poor, calloused, muddy vegetable its wish. And the potato said it would like nothing better than to be rid of its rough raiments and be made smooth and silky and acceptable to people who dined in the best restaurants of France. The fairy godmother waved her wand. The potato fell into a swoon and, in the winking of one of its many eyes, awoke in a restaurant called L'Ambassade d'Auvergne, right in the very heart of Paris, as part of the richest, silkiest mashed potato all the customers of the restaurant had ever seen. It was called *aligot*, and, beside potato, was made with rich Laguiole cheese, garlic, cream and butter, all stirred up together until the *aligot* was so elastic it could be whipped out of the pan to a height of three or even four feet without breaking. The following night the fairy godmother appeared again and asked the potato what its next wish was. The potato was feeling a bit queasy from the night before and fancied something cosy but sophisticated. The fairy waved her wand and the potato found itself lying sliced in warm, creamy layers with Gruyère cheese and his old friends, cream and garlic, in a potato dauphinoise. The potato loved to be free of its tatty jacket but wasn't so sure about the roguish garlic and cream. The next evening, when the fairy godmother appeared and asked the potato what its third wish was, it has to be said that the potato came across as a little jaded. How about bathing in a sticky, fruity *raclette*, the fairy godmother suggested – perhaps with a gaggle of cornichons? Or turning into smooth, pebble-like gnocchi smothered in fontina sauce? 'Actually,' said the potato, 'what I'd like most is to stay at home with a bottle of beer. And some Cheddar. As long as it's Keen's, mind you, or Westcombe's, because if I've learnt anything it's that I'm too good for that greasy, one-dimensional pap I used to get saddled with.' 'Get you,' said the fairy godmother, and vanished in a puff of smoke.

Hard Cheese & Sage: Derby is a pressed cow's milk cheese, softer and more delicately flavoured than Cheddar. Sage Derby is the flavoured variant. Avoid the lurid green blocks found on some deli counters and go for the sort of quality cheese made by Fowlers Forest Dairy, which scatters chopped sage leaves through the centre of its Derbys. Slice it thin and pair with prosciutto in a sandwich, or use for cheese on toast topped with a fried egg. And if good sage cheese isn't available, you can always pair a strong hard cheese with sage in scones, and eat them warm with butter.

Hard Cheese & Shellfish: *See Shellfish & Hard Cheese, page 142*

Hard Cheese & Tomato: That tomatoes and cheese can transform a thin bread crust or plate of pasta into something transcendent is testament to the umami-rich splendours of the combination – although, as any Italian will tell you, the ingredients need to be good for the magic to happen. Given a high-quality English cheese, by contrast, many people will advise against cooking with it, thinking it should be preserved for the cheeseboard. The makers of Lincolnshire Poacher (a Cheddar-like cheese with a bold, nutty flavour) beg to differ, on the parallel principle that you should apply the same standards to the wine you cook with as you do to the stuff you drink: 'cooking' wine, like 'cooking' cheese, will be as inferior in your dish as it is in the glass/on the board. I use a decent Côtes du Rhône for this hearty dish, which I call Lincolnshire Poacher's Pot. Imagine that ratatouille went to a cheese and wine party, got drunk and lost aubergine and courgette along the way. Soften a chopped large onion in oil over a medium heat for 5 minutes, then add a finely chopped garlic clove and a chunkily chopped green or red pepper (green brings a pleasing freshness). Cook slowly for another 5 minutes. Add a tin of good-quality plum tomatoes and break them up with a spoon. Then add a scant tsp dried mixed herbs, 100ml good red wine, 2 tbsp water, a pinch of sugar and some seasoning. Bring to the boil and simmer for 20–30 minutes. Taste and adjust the seasoning as necessary. Before serving, cut 150–200g Lincolnshire Poacher into 1cm cubes, add to the pan, still on the heat, then stir, giving them a minute or two to warm through. Decant into 2 earthenware bowls. Eat it before the cheese melts entirely. Crusty bread is essential.

Hard Cheese & Walnut: *See Walnut & Hard Cheese, page 237*
Hard Cheese & White Fish: *See White Fish & Hard Cheese, page 147*

Soft Cheese

Many of the soft cheeses covered in this chapter are eaten young, and retain fresh dairy flavours – the clean milkiness of mozzarella and cottage cheese, for example, or the slightly richer creaminess of Brillat-Savarin and Corsican brocciu. Bloomy cheeses like Brie and Camembert have a buttery taste when young but become more pungent, earthy and vegetal as they age, recalling the farmyard more than the dairy. While fresher, younger soft cheeses work well with salty and fruity (particularly berry) flavours, the more aged types are particularly harmonious with other earthy ingredients like mushrooms and truffles.

Soft Cheese & Anchovy: Nigella Lawson decribes a sandwich-bar lunch of cottage cheese on white bread, no butter, 'but with anchovies; the saltiness, the aggressive and indelicate invasiveness of those cheap and unsoaked tin-corroded fish made me feel, after it was finished, that something actually had been eaten'. In Naples, *mozzarella in carrozza* consists of mozzarella and anchovy sandwiched between two slices of white bread, dipped in flour and egg, then fried. A few high-quality, pink anchovy fillets can be served with a ball of mozzarella for a simple lunch. If you prepare this for a solitary meal, I think you should be allowed the entire ball. Not for gluttony's sake, but simply for the pleasure of taking the whole thing in your hand and biting into it like a juicy apple. I love the initial resistance, followed by the absolute give. Chase with a sliver of anchovy.

Soft Cheese & Apple: Eat young Brie or Camembert cut into thin pieces with corresponding slivers of apple – it's like eating apples with cream or slices of butter. Or buy a whole cheese in a box, remove the wax paper, then put the cheese back in the box, prick the top and pour over some apple brandy. Bake for 20 minutes at 200°C/Gas Mark 6. Serve with wedges of apple. The sweet-toothed might prefer to drizzle a whole baked Brie with caramel, sprinkle it with walnuts and serve with wedges of sharp apple. I also like to serve apple with older Camembert. The cheese takes on something of a cooked-cabbage flavour as it ages, and this works very well with the fruit.

Soft Cheese & Aubergine: *See Aubergine & Soft Cheese, page 82*
Soft Cheese & Avocado: *See Avocado & Soft Cheese, page 200*
Soft Cheese & Basil: *See Basil & Soft Cheese, page 215*

Soft Cheese & Bell Pepper: In Corsica it's difficult to eat a meal without the local cheese, brocciu, a ricotta-like sheep's cheese, sometimes with a bit of goat's milk mixed in. Brocciu is served with fruit and jam for breakfast, with charcuterie for lunch and in cannelloni for dinner. You'll see the sheep and goats it comes from hanging around on the hairpin bends of Corsica's heart-stopping coastal-road system (they'll quite possibly be the last things you see). We stopped in Calvi to buy a beach picnic for a walk along the coast path. We had stocked up on charcuterie, bread and tomatoes when the shop owner insisted that we also try some miniature red bell peppers stuffed with brocciu. A couple of hours later we were clambering over rocks in search of a lunch spot. As we unpacked the picnic, we were joined by first one wasp, then another, then nine more, until our *al fresco* paradise began to look like the set of a B-movie. As I lifted a stuffed pepper to my lips, a wasp heli-skied into the cheese, and in my flustered hand movement shooing it away I launched a piece of prosciutto on to a rock. One wasp chased after it, and then another, quickly followed by the others, and, ingenious by accident, we got on with our picnic in peace. Which begs the question: do wasps particularly like prosciutto or are they sick to the mandibles of brocciu? I'd come round to it myself, its sweet milkiness at once complemented and offset by the sweet smokiness of the peppers.

Soft Cheese & Blackcurrant: Sharp, bitter blackcurrants offset the cloying creaminess of cheesecake. If you don't have time to make your own, or don't want a huge one lurking in the fridge, spread a digestive biscuit with cream cheese and top it with blackcurrant jam: cheatscake. Don't be too measly with the cream cheese – you need to feel your teeth sink into it.

Soft Cheese & Caper: *See Caper & Soft Cheese, page 103*
Soft Cheese & Caviar: *See Caviar & Soft Cheese, page 154*

Soft Cheese & Celery: Celery might not be as prized as it was in the nineteenth century, when it was presented at table in special glass or silver vases, but it does have a refreshing, bitter quality, with a hint of anise, that should earn it a place on the cheeseboard. Unlikely as it may seem, celery has flavour traits in common with walnut, also a classic pairing for cheese – see Walnut & Celery, page 235. In his book *Eggs*, the chef Michel Roux gives a recipe for Camembert ice cream, which he serves with tender celery leaves, little radishes and biscuits for cheese.

Soft Cheese & Cinnamon: *See Cinnamon & Soft Cheese, page 218*

Soft Cheese & Fig: In Syria, where figs are plentiful, they're eaten fresh for breakfast with dazzling-white soft cheese. They might also be turned into a rough jam, which you can make by adding 500g roughly chopped fresh figs to 200g sugar dissolved in 750ml hot water. Bring to the boil and simmer gently until good and thick, making sure it doesn't catch on the bottom. Cool and keep in a lidded pot in the fridge – it will last a week. Use the same mixture, but perhaps with some vanilla, or orange zest and Cointreau added, for a compote to serve with *coeurs à la crème*. Blend 300g cottage cheese, 225g cream cheese and 250ml double cream until smooth, then divide the mixture between 4 heart-shaped moulds and leave to drain overnight. If you don't have heart-shaped moulds, use muslin-lined flowerpots (the kind with drainage holes in the bottom). You can add a few tablespoons of icing sugar if you prefer your *coeurs* sweeter, but a little tartness is a welcome contrast to the super-sweet fig. See also Fig & Anise, page 340.

Soft Cheese & Garlic: There are worse things you can do, when your options are limited, than reach for a garlic and herb Boursin, a French stick and a bottle of Beaujolais, as in the ad: *du pain, du vin, du Boursin*. The inspiration for the product, launched in the late 1950s by François Boursin, was the long-standing custom of serving soft cheese with a mix-your-own selection of fresh herbs. At the time of writing, it's still made with Normandy cow's milk and cream, using the original production process. Presented with a smear on a slice of baguette, my husband gave a deep, Gallic shrug. 'Tastes like garlic bread.' And so it does. Which is no bad thing.

Soft Cheese & Grape: Grapes and young, buttery Brie are paid one of the highest culinary compliments in British cuisine: they're paired in a sandwich. Stronger than Brie, Arômes au Gène de Marc is steeped in grape brandy for a month with the pips, skins and stalks that are left over from grape pressing. Sold still freckled with this debris, the cheeses look as if they've been rolled along an autumn footpath on the way to market.

Soft Cheese & Mushroom: Tasting a ripe Camembert at room temperature is like sitting on a bale of fresh straw next to a basket of just-picked mushrooms while eating a truffled fried egg. The *Penicillium camembertii* that gives it its white kid-skin rind is also responsible for the characteristic mushroom note. Capitalise on this flavour harmony by taking the rind 'lid' off a

Camembert or Brie, scattering just-cooked wild mushrooms over it and placing it in the oven so the cheese melts a little before serving.

Soft Cheese & Smoked Fish: In North America the terms smoked salmon and lox have become interchangeable, though strictly speaking lox isn't smoked but cured in brine, which helped it survive its long journey to market. When Russian and Eastern European immigrants arrived in America at the end of the nineteenth century, they found that salmon, a luxury back home, was in plentiful and affordable supply, and started to eat much more of it. Cream cheese, which began to be sold on a mass scale at around the same time, had a similar taste to the dairy products familiar from the old countries, and as it softened the extreme saltiness of the lox the combination soon became a staple of Jewish-American cuisine. Some delis will gouge a trench in the bottom half of the bagel to accommodate a more satisfying depth of cheese. See also Onion & Smoked Fish, page 111.

Soft Cheese & Strawberry: *See Strawberry & Soft Cheese, page 264*

Soft Cheese & Tomato: Mozzarella is classically paired with tomato in a salad or on a pizza. Your best ripe tomatoes will be well served by real buffalo mozzarella or, even better, burrata. Imagine a mozzarella shaped like a drawstring money-bag, filled with a mixture of thick cream and off-cuts of mozzarella. Cut into it and its centre oozes like a slow groan of pleasure. The lactic freshness mingles with the sweet-sour tomato juice to make an unforgettable dressing. Enhance it with extra virgin olive oil, fresh basil and seasoning. Burrata is originally from Apulia, the stiletto heel of Italy, but cheesemakers in the US have caught on to its appeal.

Soft Cheese & Truffle: The fragrance of truffles is often compared to garlic and cheese; conversely, cheeses like Brie de Meaux and Saint Marcellin are frequently said to have a truffly quality about them. Take a good Brie and slice it in half, so you have two rounds. Cover the bottom half with thin slices of truffle, replace the top half, wrap in cling film and leave in the fridge for 24 hours before serving at room temperature. Brie can be bought already truffled, as can the soft triple-cream Brillat-Savarin.

Soft Cheese & Walnut: New-season walnuts are at their very best in autumn, which makes it as good a time as any to prepare labna, a soft yogurt cheese whose lovely lactic tang makes walnuts seem very sweet. Line a colander or large sieve with clean, damp muslin and place over a pan or bowl high enough for some of the liquid to drain off under the colander. Mix 1 tsp salt into 1 litre natural yogurt and transfer to the lined colander. Leave to drain at room temperature for about 8 hours. Serve with walnut oil, chopped walnuts, maybe some runny honey, and warm brown bread. In Syria and the Lebanon, labna is eaten for breakfast with walnuts and a few dried figs.

EARTHY

Mushroom
Aubergine
Cumin
Beetroot
Potato
Celery

Mushroom

This section covers, among others, button mushrooms, morels, porcini and chanterelles, but not truffles, which have their own section (see page 115). All of them contain a flavour-identifying (or 'character-impact') compound called 1-octen-3-one. Mushrooms vary greatly in texture and this has more bearing on how they're cooked than on their individual flavours. There are mushrooms that taste of almonds, shellfish, meat, anise, garlic, carrots and rotting flesh, but generally speaking they all prefer the same flavour partners, primarily those that enhance their own flavour – garlic, bacon, Parmesan.

Mushroom & Anise: Tarragon brings a welcome fresh, grassy note of anise to all types of mushroom and shares their love of cream. Soured cream works particularly well with tarragon and mushroom in a stroganoff-style dish. In a large frying pan, fry some garlic in a combination of butter and oil over a medium heat, adding mushrooms (chopped if necessary) when the garlic begins to colour. Season, and before all the mushroom juices have evaporated, add a dash of brandy. When that's all but gone too, remove the pan from the heat and stir in chopped tarragon and just enough soured cream to make a sauce. Heat through gently and serve on white rice. *Pleurotus euosmus* – the tarragon oyster mushroom – is a close relative of the plain oyster mushroom, but identifiable by its strong tarragon aroma. An anise note is also found in the aroma of the fleshy white horse mushroom, *Agaricus arvensis*, and in its flavour when young and unopened.

Mushroom & Apricot: Mushroom and apricot are paired in stuffings for venison, hare and quail and added to beef or lamb in the sort of towering pie that makes table legs buckle at banquets. The combination will remind mushroom foragers of the legendary apricot aroma of chanterelles (also called girolles), which the more experienced among them can apparently nose on the air. Chanterelles are very popular with chefs for their peppery, fruity flavour, which they nonetheless have only when fresh: chanterelles don't really survive drying.

Mushroom & Asparagus: *See Asparagus & Mushroom, page 130*

Mushroom & Bacon: Dried morels have a smoky, meaty flavour subtly redolent of bacon. Their complexity of flavour (and their expense) lends weight to the argument that they should be the sole focus of a meal; nonetheless, like all fungi, they take well to the flavour enhancement offered by bacon, whose salty fattiness infiltrates their many wrinkles and crevices. Morel caps look like homemade beanies, knitted with big needles after one too many parsnip wines. In the nineteenth century a dish *à la forestière* signified a garnish of morels and diced bacon; today it is more likely to mean button mushrooms. Not that button mushrooms and bacon aren't good in an omelette or crêpe, or even outstanding in a double-crust pie, when the mushroomy roux has turned to jellified umami. An old recipe worth reviving is the *croûte baron*: a savoury of grilled mushrooms and bacon on toast, covered with beef bone marrow and breadcrumbs, given another flash under the grill, then garnished with parsley. You might use a little olive oil or clarified butter if bone marrow isn't available.

Mushroom & Beef: *See Beef & Mushroom, page 46*
Mushroom & Blueberry: *See Blueberry & Mushroom, page 344*

Mushroom & Blue Cheese: Blue cheeses are made blue by fungi, so it comes as no surprise that many of them have hints, or in the case of Gorgonzola, clear enunciations, of mushroom, with which they share important flavour compounds. Polenta with Gorgonzola and porcini is a popular dish in the Trentino region of Italy; blue cheese can be stirred into wild mushroom risotto before serving; and mushrooms and blue cheese make a delicious soup with leeks.

Mushroom & Butternut Squash: Toadstools and pumpkins. A fairytale combination. Pumpkin and squash may be sweet but they have an earthy side that makes them highly compatible with the bosky mushroom. Chanterelles, in which you may detect a slightly fruity, pumpkin-like quality, are an ideal match. Philip Howard, chef at The Square in London, serves pumpkin purée, chanterelles, leeks and black truffle with scallops (he also makes a dish of langoustine with pumpkin purée, rings of trompette mushrooms, a field mushroom purée, Parmesan gnocchi and a potato and truffle emulsion). At Kitchen W8, the bistro Howard part-owns, a simpler combination of butternut squash and chanterelles is offered in a red wine risotto, topped with a soft poached egg.

Mushroom & Chestnut: Chestnut mushrooms are merely the brown form of the common mushrooms you find in plastic punnets on supermarket shelves. Japanese shiitake mushrooms take their name from *shii*, a species of chestnut tree, and *take*, meaning mushroom. The chestnut association is strong in mushrooms because of their symbiosis in the wild: mushrooms grow under chestnut trees. In northern Italy a tagliatelle is made with chestnut flour to serve with earthy-sweet dried porcini. Mushrooms and chestnuts are cooked together bourguignon-style, with shallots, bacon and red wine, and served in a pastry or suet crust. And food writer Richard Mabey combines porcini and chestnuts in a soup. It can be made with fresh, but he pronounces vacuum-packed pre-cooked chestnuts excellent. Simmer 250g vacuum-packed chestnuts in just enough water to cover for 40 minutes. Meanwhile, rehydrate 30g dried porcini mushrooms in just enough hot water to cover them for 30 minutes. Cook 1 diced onion and 4 chopped bacon rashers in a bit more butter than you ought and add to the cooked chestnuts with the mushrooms and their soaking water. Simmer for 15 minutes, then purée in batches. Reheat and season to taste, adding a squeeze of lemon and a schooner of fino sherry before serving. Apply some rouge to your cheeks and a little dab of cocoa under the fingernails, and you can claim to have foraged for the ingredients beyond the back of the cupboard.

Mushroom & Chicken: *See Chicken & Mushroom, page 29*

Mushroom & Dill: In Russia they call the porcini the tsar of mushrooms. Pair it with pine-scented dill and you'll have a dish to make you yearn for the forests of Siberia. Chopped mushrooms are stewed with dill, salt and pepper, mixed with butter and soured cream and stuffed into Eastern European dumplings called *pirozhki* or *pierogi*. Or they're cooked in the style described in Mushroom & Anise, page 75, and served with rice or boiled potatoes and a glass of chilled vodka. According to David Thompson, dill is paired with mushrooms in curries from northeastern Thailand, near the border with the dill-loving Laotians.

Mushroom & Egg: The giant puffball, *Calvatia gigantea*, has a particularly mushroomy flavour. If you like mushroom fritters, try dipping piano-key slices of giant puffball in egg and breadcrumbs before frying them. Alternatively, treat them like French toast, dipping them in egg, then frying them in butter for breakfast. The Chinese dish *mu shu* is a little more elaborate: inspired by the forest floor, its pancake base is strewn with stir-fried lily buds and delicately flavoured wood ear mushrooms and dotted with little 'flowers' of scrambled egg. Strips of pork are (sometimes) added too. See also Asparagus & Mushroom, page 130.

Mushroom & Garlic: Even the blandest mushrooms take on some of their wild cousins' intensity of flavour under the influence of garlic, but garlic and shiitake mushrooms enjoy an extra-special relationship. Shiitake contain a compound called lenthionine, chemically similar to the sulphides found in alliums such as garlic and onion, and, like them, they are prized for their flavour-enhancing properties. Lenthionine content is maximised by drying and rehydration. You won't get the same results with fresh shiitake, but you can tuck slivers of garlic into their gills and give them a drizzle of olive oil and a sprinkle of salt before grilling or frying them.

Mushroom & Goat's Cheese: A young *Agaricus bisporus* is the squeaky white button mushroom. Older, browner specimens are sold as chestnut, crimini or baby bella mushrooms, and have more flavour than their white siblings. Six or seven days later, when they open fully to display their inky gills, they become portabellas. Until the 1980s they were considered unsaleable, and mushroom farm workers took them home as perks. Then it dawned on someone that their pronounced flavour might, after all, be marketable, especially if they had a fancy Italian name. So they made one up. The portabella owes its success partly to its size and shape: it's at once an instant veggie burger and a mushroom life isn't too short to stuff. Its rusticity is particularly well paired with goat's cheese, which adds a welcome tanginess. Place 6 portabellas, cap down, on an oiled baking tray. The black gills look like lined-up 45s seen through the window of a jukebox. Scrape them out, but leave the stalks. Mash 250g goat's cheese with 1 tbsp olive oil, a handful of chopped parsley and plenty of salt and pepper. Stuff the mixture into the mushroom caps, taking care not to overfill them, as they will shrink a little in the oven. Bake at 200°C/Gas Mark 6 for 15 minutes, then serve sprinkled with more chopped parsley.

Mushroom & Hard Cheese: The species of mushroom that we commonly eat contain no salt, which is why you must either add some or pair mushrooms with salty ingredients to realise their flavour fully. Parmesan provides some saltiness in a mushroom risotto, pasta or bruschetta, while Gruyère is delicious with mushrooms on toast. And grated pecorino romano with finely chopped mushrooms is the beginning of a pesto-like sauce. Put some cooked mushrooms in a food processor with grated pecorino, toasted walnuts, garlic, parsley (or basil, or both) and olive oil – all particularly good partners for mushroom – and pulse until you've achieved your desired texture. Balance the flavours to taste. Great on pasta, clearly, but also spread on a baguette for a steak or sausage sandwich.

Mushroom & Mint: In Tuscany, porcini mushrooms are often sold alongside, and served with, the herb nepitella, or *Calamintha nepetha*. Nepitella has a woody flavour comparable to mint, which can be substituted for it. It might be worth checking your garden to see if you have some – it's a popular decorative shrub. Try it chopped and scattered over thinly sliced fresh porcini, with thin parings of pecorino cheese and your best olive oil.

Mushroom & Oily Fish: The forest-floor mustiness of mushroom particularly suits the earthy flavours of freshwater oily fish. A finely chopped crumb of shiitake brings out the best in a salmon fillet. Salmon is also paired with chopped mushrooms (and rice) in coulibiac, a French puff pastry dish descended from *kulebjaka*, a Russian pie made with yeast pastry (although not always containing fish or mushrooms). Antonio Carluccio considers chanterelles particularly good with red mullet. He marinates the fish fillets in olive oil, lime juice and seasoning before frying them, skin-side first. If you're trying this at home, serve the mushrooms on the side, cooking them as per the recipe in Mushroom & Anise, page 75, but using shallots and parsley instead of garlic and tarragon. I'd serve mackerel fillets the same way, except I'd leave out the cream and give both fish and mushrooms a quick squeeze of lemon.

Mushroom & Onion: Warm, soft and as inviting as a pair of sheepskin slippers. *Duxelles* is not, as it sounds, a kind of mushroom but a combination of finely chopped mushroom and shallot (or onion) that has been slowly sautéed in butter. Try a ratio of about 7:1 (in weight). In the largest frying pan you can lay your hands on, soften the shallots over a low heat, without browning them, then add the mushrooms, continuing to cook until all their juices have evaporated and the mixture is dark and soft. *Duxelles* can be used as a sauce – for example, with fish or chicken – as a stuffing (some include it in beef Wellington), in scrambled eggs and omelettes or simply on toast. Alternatively, make a mushroom and shallot dressing by cooking the mixture for a shorter time – i.e. until the mushroom juices have reduced to almost nothing – adding a little red wine vinegar to deglaze, then transferring to a dish to cool before whisking in olive oil. Wonderful with globe artichokes.

Mushroom & Oyster: *See Oyster & Mushroom, page 152*

Mushroom & Parsley: Parsley lends a lovely, grassy note to rich, earthy, autumnal mushrooms fried in olive oil or butter, maybe with a little garlic. Inhale that damp, turfy aroma and you could almost believe you were up at the crack of dawn, strolling through the dewy grass with a basket hooked over your forearm.

Mushroom & Pork: *Boletus edulis* are better known by the Italian term, porcini, which means 'little pigs' – perhaps after the coarse appearance of the mushroom stalks, which look (but don't feel) like bristly pigskin. Porcini also share pork's reputation for needing to be cooked thoroughly: eaten raw, they can cause stomach upsets. But their flavour is magnificent, and not only survives drying but is thought by many to be improved by it. It's the mushroom for the late-rising city dweller, who need only make a slipper-shod shuffle to the fridge for a wax-paper bag of pork and porcini sausages. You can also buy the mushroom in powdered and stock-cube form, handy for pork and porcini pasta sauces or aromatic noodle broths.

Mushroom & Potato: *See Potato & Mushroom, page 91*
Mushroom & Rosemary: *See Rosemary & Mushroom, page 318*

Mushroom & Shellfish: The soft sweetness of scallops is a great contrast to the deep, earthy intensity of cooked mushrooms – posh porcini and roasted crimini alike. In Thailand, prawns are matched with similarly nutty straw mushrooms in the coconut milk and lemongrass soup *tom yang gung*. Japanese shiitake and prawn *gyoza* dumplings give a delicious double hit of umami. In France, mussels, mushrooms and sometimes oysters are combined in *sauce normande*, which is served with fish, especially sole. In the autumn, foragers can feast on clams and chanterelles, brought together by their mutual love of garlic, wine and parsley. Shellfish is yet another of the flavours identified in mushrooms: *Russula xerampelina*, the shrimp mushroom, or crab brittlegill, is found in the coniferous forests of northern Europe and America, and some say it imparts a shellfish- or crab-like flavour to dishes.

Mushroom & Soft Cheese: *See Soft Cheese & Mushroom, page 72*

Mushroom & Thyme: Although mushrooms feel at home with grassy herbs such as tarragon and parsley, the woody herbs are their true kindred spirits. The piney, smoky nature of thyme makes a harmonious match with the thick, earthy flavour of mushrooms, especially dried ones. Combine them in a risotto or a rich white bean stew, or simply on toast.

Mushroom & Tomato: Tomatoes and mushrooms garnish a steakhouse steak and, alongside sausages, bacon and eggs, are part of a full English breakfast. They sit on the plate as separate as boys and girls at their first dance. Never an entirely easy partnership, but can work together in sauces for pasta or fish. Moti Mahal, an Indian restaurant in London, serves a mushroom *shorba* (soup) with tandoori bread and tomato chutney.

Mushroom & Truffle: Kissing cousins. Truffles are not mushrooms but they are fungi. Truffle oil, paste or butter is often used to enhance the flavour of mushroom dishes; like a culinary push-up bra, the aim is to give the more ordinary fungi the full, in-your-face sexiness of truffle. It works, but it's a little obvious. Classier to use them together but keep them distinct, as at Carlos' restaurant in Illinois, where they serve a mushroom soup topped with truffle foam and sprinkled with porcini powder, cappuccino-style.

Mushroom & Walnut: Both ligneous. Mushrooms tend to the sort of heavy, damp woodiness you greedily inhale on a forest walk in autumn; walnuts to the warmly sweet, dry fragrance of timber in a DIY store. Mushrooms cooked in walnut oil are characteristic of southwestern French cuisine, while in many parts of Europe and North America mushrooms and walnuts are frequently paired in sauces, soups and salads. Raw button or crimini mushrooms have a subtle flavour and make for a great texture contrast with crisp toasted nuts. Toss them with a walnut oil and sherry vinegar dressing, and consider adding some goat's or blue cheese. *Mousserons* you may know better as fairy ring mushrooms, although lawn owners might as well call them turf herpes: they're virtually impossible to eradicate. On the plus side, they're delicious cooked, with faint flavours of anise and almond. Dried, they take on a sweeter, nutty character that some people compare to walnut, to the extent that they recommend trying them in cookies.

Mushroom & White Fish: Italian chef Giorgio Locatelli combines turbot (or brill) with porcini, although he says his grandfather would 'turn in his grave' at the idea. In his experience, parsley acts as a bridge between the two ingredients. Mushroom expert John Wright singles out the rich, buttery horn of plenty mushroom as a 'happy companion' to fish, particularly white fish. Beech mushrooms are also frequently paired with fish: they have a nutty, some say shellfish-like, flavour, and retain their crunchy texture when cooked. Two reasons to dust off your recipe for sole *bonne femme* – sole in a white wine, butter and mushroom sauce.

Aubergine

When raw, a good aubergine tastes like a bland, sweet apple; cooked, it's transformed into something very savoury. Frying aubergines lends them a wonderful creaminess that's particularly lovely sprinkled with sweet, warming spices. Stewed or roasted, they take on a musky, mushroomy quality that works well with salty ingredients. Short of taking a surreptitious nibble, the best way to check if an aubergine has the requisite flavour and texture is to test it for tautness. Ideally an aubergine should be as tight and shiny as dolphin skin. Similarly, they squeak when you pinch them.

Aubergine & Bell Pepper: Of all Turkey's many aubergine dishes, *patlican biber* is one of the most popular, so much so that in early evening the smell of aubergines and green peppers frying in olive oil fills the air the length and breadth of the country. Once they've cooled, they are served with two simple sauces, one of cooked tomatoes and garlic and another of thick yogurt mixed with salt and more garlic. See also Garlic & Thyme, page 114.

Aubergine & Chilli: There's a Sichuan delicacy called fish-fragrant aubergines, which is an awful lot nicer than it sounds. 'Fish-fragrant' refers not to fish itself, which isn't used in the recipe, but to the seasoning, which is more often applied to fish in Sichuan cuisine. Not all versions include pork, but this one does. Take 700g small, slim aubergines and cut them lengthways into quarters. Heat 450ml oil in a wok and deep-fry the aubergine pieces a few at a time until golden and tender, then drain on kitchen paper. Discard all but a few tablespoons of the oil, get the wok nice and hot again, then add 1–2 tbsp Sichuan chilli bean paste, muddling it into the oil. Add 2 tbsp each finely chopped fresh ginger and garlic, 450g minced pork and 3 tbsp sliced spring onions. Stir-fry for 30 seconds, then add 3 tbsp rice wine (or sherry), 3 tbsp black rice vinegar (or cheap balsamic), 2 tbsp sugar, 1 tbsp roasted and crushed Sichuan peppercorns, and 2 tsp ground red chilli. Cook over a high heat for 2 minutes, add 125ml chicken stock and simmer for a further 3 minutes. Finally add the aubergines and simmer for 3 minutes. If you can't bear to deep-fry your aubergines, shallow-fry them instead. You don't get the same texture, but the sauce is so good I'm tempted to say it hardly matters.

Aubergine & Garlic: We're all either radiators or drains. Radiators are outgoing, effusive, participatory: drains suck the energy out of the room. Couples often comprise one of each. Your eagerness to see x, the radiator, is tempered by your dread of being stuck next to y, the drain. In this partnership, garlic is the radiator. It's a beguiling extrovert. Aubergine is the drain: unpredictable, often bitter, and needing a lot of attention (or an unhealthy amount of lubrication) to cajole it into a companionable mood. Together they make *baba ghanoush* – mix the flesh of roasted or grilled aubergines with raw garlic, tahini, olive oil, lemon juice and parsley.

Aubergine & Ginger: Japanese aubergines are milder than ordinary ones, if that's imaginable, thinner-skinned, and particularly worth seeking out. If you can't find them, there's no reason not to give an ordinary aubergine the Japanese treatment. They love to soak up the flavour of miso, or this ginger and soy broth. Cut a couple of aubergines into bite-sized pieces, sprinkle with salt and leave for 20–30 minutes. Rinse, squeeze gently and pat dry. Fry in groundnut oil until just golden, then add 1 tbsp grated fresh ginger, 2 tbsp soy sauce, 1 tbsp sugar and just enough water to cover. Simmer for 20–30 minutes with a foil or greaseproof paper lid on top of the mixture (not on top of the pan). Garnish with the green part of spring onions, thinly sliced, and/or a scattering of sesame seeds. Serve with boiled rice.

Aubergine & Lamb: *See Lamb & Aubergine, page 50*

Aubergine & Nutmeg: Freshly grated nutmeg puts the *ohh* into aubergines. There should be a global chain selling paper cones of nutmeggy fried aubergine slices. (Oh-bergine™. I'm rich!) Evelyn Rose writes that if you deep-fry aubergines they absorb less fat than when they're shallow-fried because the surface becomes 'sealed'. Alternatively you can salt the aubergine slices first to draw out their moisture, thus making them less fat-absorbent, before shallow-frying. Either way, don't be tempted to use ready-ground nutmeg – it has to be freshly grated to order.

Aubergine & Prosciutto: *See Prosciutto & Aubergine, page 171*

Aubergine & Soft Cheese: According to Elizabeth David, aubergines and cheese are a less than ideal combination. If you've ever wrapped a soft stole of chargrilled aubergine around the quivering white shoulders of delicate mozzarella, you may beg to differ. See also Tomato & Aubergine, page 257.

Aubergine & Tomato: *See Tomato & Aubergine, page 257*
Aubergine & Walnut: *See Walnut & Aubergine, page 234*

Cumin

Cumin seeds are too harsh and unfriendly to nibble straight out of the pot, as you might anise or coriander seeds. They're dry, woody and musty – inhale from the jar and you may recall the note in bought curry powder that smells like the inside of a second-hand wardrobe. Fortunately, they are transformed by cooking. Roasted and crushed, they release nutty, lemon notes; fried in oil, they lend dishes like dhal a lively, piquant bite.

Cumin & Apricot: There's so much going on in a tagine that, even if it's cumin-scented and full of plump apricots, you're not likely to notice how the sun-baked, floral, woody notes of apricot withstand the earthy, dusty pungency of cumin. Their reciprocity is clearer in this Armenian apricot soup recipe from David Ansel. Apricots originated in Armenia, where fruit (especially cherry) soups are popular. Dice an onion and a couple of carrots, sauté in olive oil for 10 minutes, then add 2 tsp ground cumin. Lower the heat, cover and sweat for 10 minutes. Add 250g red lentils and as much of 1.2 litres water as you need to cover them. Bring to a simmer and cook for 20 minutes, adding more of the water if necessary as the lentils expand. Remove from the heat and stir in 150g chopped dried apricots, some salt and the rest of the water. Purée, in batches if necessary. Cumin is also excellent in an apricot conserve to eat with Camembert.

Cumin & Beetroot: Aside from their shared earthiness, beetroot and cumin couldn't be more different. The sweetness of beetroot is enlivened by cumin's smoky, citric edge. They make a complex soup, with a sharp swirl of crème fraîche or soured cream. Or combine them with chickpeas for a dip.

Cumin & Carrot: See Carrot & Cumin, page 228

Cumin & Cauliflower: Roasted together, cumin and cauliflower take on a nutty sweetness without losing their essential characters. Cut a cauliflower into small florets and toss in oil before shaking over 1 tbsp ground cumin. Roast at 180°C/Gas Mark 4 for about 30 minutes, until soft, stirring once or twice. Sprinkle with salt and serve warm. Some people blanch or steam the florets first but it's not necessary. They're even more irresistible when slightly charred around the edge. I first came across this combination rolled into a falafel in Amsterdam, which was so intriguing I had to unravel it to investigate the identity of the mystery ingredient.

Cumin & Coriander Leaf: See Coriander Leaf & Cumin, page 195

Cumin & Coriander Seed: More likely to be found together than apart in Indian, Middle Eastern and North African cooking. In India they're even sold together, ground or whole. In Morocco they might be added to a hot harissa, to give it an extra aromatic edge, or shaken over deep-fried chick-peas, sold in cones by street vendors. In Egypt, cumin and coriander seed are mixed with sesame seeds, chopped hazelnuts, salt and pepper to make the famous *dukkah*, eaten with olive oil and bread. Food writer Glynn Christian believes the underlying orange flavour of coriander seed and the lick of lemon in cumin explains their powerful affinity. I think they're (beneficially) opposed in some ways, too: coriander is bright and perfumed, whereas cumin is rather murky and gruff.

Cumin & Cucumber: In *Taste*, Sybil Kapoor writes that cumin is very good combined with other bitter ingredients such as cucumber, aubergine and cauliflower – paradoxically highlighting the second ingredient's natural sweetness by deepening its bitterness. The obvious way to pair these two is by using cumin to spice up a yogurt-based cucumber soup or raita. But for something a little different, see Peanut & Cucumber, page 24.

Cumin & Egg: *See Egg & Cumin, page 134*
Cumin & Lamb: *See Lamb & Cumin, page 51*

Cumin & Lemon: Citral, a key compound in lemon flavour, is often used in cleaning fluids and furniture polish. The flavour of cumin is frequently compared to dirty socks. But don't let that put you off. To make a lovely marinade for a couple of fish fillets or some lamb chops, mix the zest of a lemon with ½ tsp ground cumin and 2 tbsp olive oil. Or make this glorious dhal. Soak 250g chana dhal in water for 2 hours, then drain and tip it into a pan with 500ml cold water. Bring to a simmer, skim off the scum and add 1 tbsp chopped fresh ginger, ¼ tsp turmeric and chilli to taste. Simmer for about 45 minutes, partly covered, stirring now and then. Add a little boiling water if it dries out. When the dhal is almost cooked, heat some groundnut oil in a pan and fry a sliced large onion until golden, adding 2 tsp cumin seeds and 1 tsp garam masala towards the end. Stir this mixture into the dhal with the zest of ½ lemon and 1–2 tbsp lemon juice.

Cumin & Lime: *See Lime & Cumin, page 302*
Cumin & Mango: *See Mango & Cumin, page 290*

Cumin & Mint: Inhale cumin and dried mint and you could be in Cairo. Use them together to season lamb kebabs or burgers. They're also delicious with broad beans and with soft, tangy cheeses. In India, a lassi might be flavoured with a few pinches of each and some salt.

Cumin & Oily Fish: Cumin is a great pairing for tuna because it's potent enough to stand up to the rich, oily fish without swamping it. Rub tuna fillets with olive oil, give them a hearty shake of ground cumin and seasoning, then fry them quickly (about 1 minute each side for a 1cm-thick steak). Let them rest for a few minutes, then cut them into strips. Pile them into warm corn tortillas or tacos with plenty of lime-tossed shredded lettuce or cabbage and some tangy mango or tomato salsa. Garnish with a little coriander.

Cumin & Pork: *See Pork & Cumin, page 35*

Cumin & Potato: Cumin has something of a musty flavour and shares an earthy quality with potato. Combine them and you might expect something reminiscent of a trudge round a ruined castle on a damp Sunday afternoon – yet they taste anything but gloomy in the Indian potato dish, *jeera aloo*. When cooked, potatoes and cumin take on a new sweetness, and the latter becomes a deal more aromatic. Boil unpeeled new potatoes until just tender, then drain, dry and cut into halves or quarters. Fry in oil with cumin and salt until browned. Garnish with chopped fresh coriander leaves.

Cumin & Shellfish: *See Shellfish & Cumin, page 141*

Cumin & Washed-rind Cheese: Cumin seeds are the classic partnership for Munster cheese. So classic, in fact, that you can buy Munster already encrusted or riddled with the seeds, and there are bakeries in France that make cumin bread specifically to go with it. In its homeland of Alsace, Munster is served with boiled potatoes and a pile of roasted cumin seeds, a very macho trio, redeemed by the company of a delicately feminine (and local) Gewürztraminer white wine. Try other washed-rind cheeses with cumin, too. At Galvin at Windows in London, they serve Stinking Bishop with a Jersey Royal potato salad and a cumin tuile. Or follow the recipe for crackers in Washed-rind Cheese & Anise, page 59, using the same amount of cumin seeds in place of fennel.

Beetroot

An unlikely sort of vegetable: dense, bluntly sweet, needing two hours' boiling, with more than a hint of the garden shed in its flavour and a habit of bleeding over everything. And yet neither golden beetroot nor the pretty pink and white tie-dyed Chioggia varieties have posed much threat to the prevalence of traditional beetroot, crimson as a Russian doll's cheeks. The secret of beetroot's success is its strange combination of sweetness and earthiness, which sets off ingredients that are predominantly sour, salty, or both, like goat's cheese. The flavour of beetroot is also found in its leaves, which can be used in salads or cooked like spinach.

Beetroot & Anchovy: Sweet beetroot is more than happy to take on salty ingredients like goat's cheese, capers and piquant anchovy. In the South of France, beetroots are diced and mixed with lots of anchovies, garlic and olive oil. *Uhlemann's Chef's Companion* notes that salad of beetroot, anchovies, small crayfish and lettuce is famous amongst epicures, and is named after the writer Alexandre Dumas.

Beetroot & Apple: *See Apple & Beetroot, page 269*
Beetroot & Beef: *See Beef & Beetroot, page 43*
Beetroot & Caper: *See Caper & Beetroot, page 102*

Beetroot & Chocolate: There's a popular, or at least widespread, cake recipe that pairs chocolate and beetroot. Its champions can hardly *believe* the lusciousness and chocolatiness of the combination. I couldn't either, and having tried it I still don't. Carrot works in cakes because it is sweet, floral and spicy, and the grated pieces create a lovely rickety-rough texture. In chocolate beetroot cake, the cocoa almost entirely overwhelms the beetroot flavour, leaving nothing but a hint of its earthiness, which makes the cake taste like a cheap chocolate cake that's been dropped in a flowerbed. And the raw cake mixture was so unpleasant that no one wanted to scrape the bowl clean. Case closed, at least in my kitchen.

Beetroot & Coconut: *See Coconut & Beetroot, page 286*
Beetroot & Cumin: *See Cumin & Beetroot, page 83*

Beetroot & Dill: The Italian gastronome Pellegrino Artusi, writing in the nineteenth century, noted that although the Florentines used lots of herbs in their cooking they were missing a trick with dill, especially dill mixed with beetroot. He had tried the combination in Romagna, where beetroot and dill were sold bundled together in the market. The ingredients have traditionally been more a feature of northern and eastern European cooking. Dill is often used to flavour borscht, and is essential for the cold beetroot soup from Lithuania called *saltibarsciai*. Whisk a little water into a sour dairy base (kefir cheese, buttermilk or soured cream) to thin it a little, then add plenty of grated cucumber, grated cooked beetroot, chopped boiled eggs, dill and chives. Chill, then serve with cold boiled potatoes and more dill.

Beetroot & Egg: *See Egg & Beetroot, page 133*

Beetroot & Goat's Cheese: A lively, stinging goat's cheese is the perfect foil to beetroot's sweetness. Just as well, as this has surely been the signature partnership of the last ten years, in the same way roasted peppers were inseparable from tomatoes in the 1990s. Goat's cheese soufflé with beetroot ice cream. Horseradish and beetroot tart with a goat's cheese meringue. Goat's cheese panna cotta with beetroot caviar. Primp them as you will, to me they're at their best muddled with warm green beans and a few crushed walnuts. And this risotto is good too, if rather pink. Soften a finely chopped small onion in olive oil, then add 150g risotto rice, stirring until the grains are coated in oil. Add a sherry glass of white wine and cook until evaporated. Mix in 250g finely diced or grated cooked beetroot, then add 750ml hot vegetable stock, one ladle at a time, stirring constantly, until the rice is cooked to your liking. Add a few tablespoons of finely grated Parmesan and some seasoning. Divide between 2 plates and serve, topped with a scattering of goat's cheese cut into 1cm cubes. Garnish with parsley leaves, if you have them.

Beetroot & Horseradish: *See Horseradish & Beetroot, page 105*
Beetroot & Liver: *See Liver & Beetroot, page 41*

Beetroot & Oily Fish: In Scandinavian and Baltic countries beetroot is commonly paired with salty fish, especially herring. The fish and beetroot are mixed with onion, potato and apple and dressed with vinegar or maybe a mustardy mayonnaise. The dish is called *sillsallad* in Sweden and *rosolje* in Estonia. On the Danish island of Bornholm, they eat salt-fried herring on dark rye bread with beetroot and hot mustard. The London-based smokers H. Forman & Son sell a beetroot-cured salmon.

Beetroot & Onion: *See Onion & Beetroot, page 107*
Beetroot & Orange: *See Orange & Beetroot, page 294*

Beetroot & Pork: From a recipe for *barszcz* (i.e. borscht) in Louis Eustache Audot's *French Domestic Cookery*, published in 1846: 'Put into a stockpot eight pounds of beef, two pounds of smoked ribs of pork, half a pound of ham, thirty morels, onions, and leeks, and some beetroot juice. Make the whole into bouillon; strain it, and add to it a hare, a roasted fowl and a duck; then, again, a quantity of beetroot liquor. Let it boil a quarter of an hour, strain the bouillon afresh, add a few whites of eggs beaten up with a little water; boil it up and strain it again; cut up the boiled viands, and serve them with the bouillon garnished with morels, onions, slices of beef intermixed with celery and sprigs of parsley, the whole stewed beforehand; together with fennel, broiled sausages, and balls of *godiveau* [a veal stuffing].' I suggest you make this while singing 'Old Louis Audot made some borscht' to the tune of 'Old Macdonald'. Incidentally, Audot goes on to give a recipe for beetroot juice, which is often cooked separately from the meat in borscht in order to keep it a vibrant crimson. It's not until right at the end that he adds, 'This soup can be made with much less meat than directed in the last receipt, and will be *barszcz* if it merely contain the juice of beetroot,' which only goes to show that you should always read the recipe through before starting to cook. See also Onion & Beetroot, page 107.

Beetroot & Potato: *See Potato & Beetroot, page 89*

Beetroot & Walnut: *See Walnut & Beetroot, page 235*

Beetroot & Watercress: Earth and iron. Like a Zola novel with a happy ending. The love of rustic, rosy-cheeked beetroot for outspoken watercress *is* requited. Combine lots of finely chopped watercress with soured cream and use to dress cooked beetroot. Serve with oily fish, liver or a rare steak.

Potato

Potatoes are sweet and slightly bitter (if the bitterness is pronounced, and the skin green, they're fit only for the compost bin). Good potatoes are characterised by combinations of buttery, creamy, nutty and earthy flavours. When baked, the skin of old potatoes can have a malty, dusty cocoa character. Cooks tend initially to divide potatoes by texture rather than flavour, as the waxiness, flouriness or firm bite dictates the ideal cooking method. Waxy potatoes usually have a more concentrated flavour, while floury are often described as bland or light tasting. A trained testing panel coordinated by the Scottish Crop Research Institute recently found a direct correlation between levels of umami-forming compounds in potato varieties and their intensity of flavour. The best-performing cultivars were derived from the 'phureja' strain – look out for Mayan Gold, whose flesh is butter-yellow, rich in flavour and makes chips so tasty you'll be tempted to skip the ketchup. The potato's sweetness is particularly heavenly when contrasted with salty foods such as fish, hard cheese and caviar.

Potato & Anchovy: *See Anchovy & Potato, page 163*
Potato & Asparagus: *See Asparagus & Potato, page 131*

Potato & Bacon: Driving past the Farmer's Market Café on the A12 in Suffolk, I saw a sign outside that read, in huge letters, Ham Hock Hash. Nothing else. No other food, no opening times, nothing. Just three little words that launched a thousand U-turns.

Potato & Beef: Harold McGee writes that the flavour of maincrop (i.e. old) potatoes intensifies when they're stored in the dark at a temperature between 7 and 10°C, and slow enzyme action creates floral, fruity and fatty notes. At too low a temperature, the starch turns to sugar, so that when the potatoes are cooked they begin to caramelise, resulting in a dark-brown chip with an unpleasantly bittersweet flavour. Which won't do. The partnership of potato and beef is too important, whether in *steak frites* or burger and chips, the fanciest rib of beef with roast potatoes or the everyday cottage pie.

Potato & Beetroot: Potato and beetroot make a very pink mash that is both sweet and earthy. Beetroot's potting-shed flavour is attributable to a compound called geosmin, which can also be detected in the smell of just-caught, bottom-feeding freshwater fish such as carp, and in 'petrichor', a term coined by two Australian researchers for the distinctive aroma released by rain on earth following a dry spell. Potato's earthy flavour comes from a different compound. If you like earthy aromas and flavours, they're also to be found in mushrooms, truffles, cooked onion and garlic, some cheeses, and aged Bordeaux and Burgundy. See also Beef & Beetroot, page 43.

Potato & Black Pudding: *See Black Pudding & Potato, page 40*

Potato & Cabbage: In Ireland, mashed potato + kale or cabbage = colcannon. The Portuguese make a similarly unadorned dish, a soup called *caldo verde*. This is a rustic blend of potatoes and onions with cabbage, often made even less decorative by the addition of a ragged hunk of chorizo. Originally from the Minho region in the north, *caldo verde* is now something of a national dish and is equally popular in Brazil. Try it and you'll see why: high-quality potatoes are used, and the Galician cabbage, with its wide, seakale-like leaves, gives the soup a dark, serious depth. Try making it anywhere else and you'd be advised to use floury, rather than waxy potatoes – they need to fall apart and thicken the broth. Galician cabbage can be hard to come by outside Portugal, and collard greens, spring greens or *kai-lan* can be used instead. Peel 1kg floury potatoes, cut into chunks and bring to the boil in 1.5 litres salted water. Simmer until tender, then roughly mash them into the water and bring back to the boil. Add 200g finely chopped greens and cook for about 10 minutes. If you like the idea of the sausage, put it in with the potatoes, remove it at the mashing stage and cut it into chunks, then return it to the soup with the greens. See also the introduction to Broccoli, page 125, and Cabbage & Onion, page 119.

Potato & Caper: *See Caper & Potato, page 103*
Potato & Cauliflower: *See Cauliflower & Potato, page 123*

Potato & Caviar: Simon Hopkinson and Lindsey Bareham write that caviar and truffles are probably better paired with potatoes than with anything else. Potato and truffle share a warm earthiness that makes for a harmonious combination, whereas caviar and potato are a contrasting pair; the sweet, bland softness of potato is pitched against the salty complexity of the taut fish eggs. They're popularly paired in a canapé of warm roasted baby potatoes topped with cold soured cream and caviar, the temperature differential creating an additional pleasing contrast. See also Potato & Truffle, page 94.

Potato & Celery: *See Celery & Potato, page 97*
Potato & Chicken: *See Chicken & Potato, page 30*

Potato & Chilli: There's a sharpness to the flavour of paprika that, along with its smoky quality, makes a successful partnership with potato. Paprika potato crisps are by far the most popular flavour in Germany. And potato and paprika make great chilli fries too. Mix 4 tbsp olive oil and 4 tsp paprika together in a freezer bag. Using a mandoline or food processor disc, cut 4 large potatoes into strips roughly 1cm square in cross section. Pat them dry, then toss them in the bag until well covered in spicy oil. Transfer them from the bag to a baking tray and roast in the oven at 220°C/Gas Mark 7 for 20–25 minutes, tossing once or twice. A pinch or two of cayenne in the oil mix will give them a bit more kick. See also Chilli & Tomato, page 211.

Potato & Coriander Leaf: *See Coriander Leaf & Potato, page 197*
Potato & Cumin: *See Cumin & Potato, page 85*
Potato & Dill: *See Dill & Potato, page 191*

Potato & Egg: The simplest, cheapest proof that you needn't be an oligarch to eat like a king. A fleshy, fluffy chip dipped deep in runny yolk. Or a fried egg on a pillow of potato purée. Add a little onion and you've got all you need for a Spanish tortilla: sweet, cakey omelette, soft, earthy potato, bittersweet caramelised onion. Eat one fresh from the pan, yellow as a Euro on a mid-afternoon pavement, or the next day, by which time it will have taken on a deeper, more savoury flavour, plus a greyish tinge that won't matter in the slightest if you slip it into a crusty white roll for an eggier take on the classic chip butty. A bit rustic, perhaps, but nothing on the *huevos con patates* we ate late one evening in Spain. We ordered it thinking it would be a tortilla, or a Brit-pandering plate of egg and chips. What arrived was a dainty saucer piled with plain potato crisps that had been knocked about the pan with a couple of eggs, not quite scrambled, not quite fried. A self-respecting two-year-old would have binned it and started again. But it was gone midnight and nowhere else was open. Once the chewy slices of potato, bound into clusters by buttery, lacy egg, had proved definitively resistant to division by fork, we rolled back our sleeves and ate with our fingers. It was quite delicious. We finished it down to the very last scrap, etching our wine glasses with greasy fingerprints. See also Ginger & Egg, page 310.

Potato & Garlic: *Skordalia* is a Greek dish made by beating pounded raw garlic into mashed potatoes with olive oil and a little white wine vinegar or lemon juice until the required consistency is achieved. An egg yolk is added sometimes too. Ground almonds, bread or mashed beans may be used instead of potato or to supplement it. You get the picture. It's white, it's garlicky and it's good with fish. Or simply scoop it up on strips of warm pitta bread.

Potato & Globe Artichoke: *See Globe Artichoke & Potato, page 129*
Potato & Hard Cheese: *See Hard Cheese & Potato, page 68*
Potato & Horseradish: *See Horseradish & Potato, page 105*

Potato & Lamb: Should get a room. They're all over each other. Stoic beef keeps its distance, even squeezed up close to potato in a cottage pie. The fattiness of lamb, on the other hand, seeps into potato in shepherd's pie, thick, spicy Indian *gosht aloo*, or Lancashire's famous hotpot. John Thornton, the mill owner in Elizabeth Gaskell's *North and South*, is surely in contention for one of the earliest bourgeois enthusiasts of peasant food. Of the hotpot he eats with his workers, he says, 'I have never made a better dinner in my life.' Years later, conceivably in homage to Mrs Gaskell, factory boss Mike Baldwin raved over Betty's hotpot in *Coronation Street*. The real secret of a great hotpot is not the use of tasty neck-end of lamb (or mutton), or browning the meat in dripping, or lots of layers of meat, onion and potato, or even adding a few kidneys under the final roof of sliced potatoes. It is time, the one thing the bustling industrialist lacks.

Potato & Lemon: *See Lemon & Potato, page 307*
Potato & Mint: *See Mint & Potato, page 332*

Potato & Mushroom: Just as a good fish soup should have a slightly disturbing oceanic depth, so a proper wild mushroom soup should live up to its name: a wolf in soup's clothing. The trick is to use a mixture of different fungi to layer the flavours, as you might use a variety of fish in a bouillabaisse. I like the Italian chef Gennaro Contaldo's recipe, not just for its mixture of fresh and dried mushrooms but for the addition of potato, which thickens the soup while contributing its own earthy flavour. Soften a chopped onion in 4 tbsp olive oil, then add 500g chopped wild mushrooms and sauté for 5 minutes. Add 1 litre vegetable stock, 25g reconstituted dried porcini (with their soaking water) and a peeled and finely chopped potato. Bring to the boil, turn down the heat and simmer for 20 minutes. Cool slightly and blend until smooth. Reheat, season to taste and serve with crusty bread and the door firmly bolted.

Potato & Nutmeg: Nutmeg is used to obscure some of potato's ruder, earthier flavours. It's often given the same purpose with pumpkin or spinach. A little grating should do the job. But then nutmeg is so lovely with all these ingredients, why restrain yourself?

Potato & Oily Fish: *See Oily Fish & Potato, page 159*
Potato & Olive: *See Olive & Potato, page 176*

Potato & Onion: Such dependable ingredients that you forget what magic they can work together. When I was a kid, there was always a sack of potatoes and a sack of onions in the garage: they had the same status as logs. Living in a poky flat in the middle of the city, as I do now, the car is parked in the street and has become a garage itself – internalising what would have housed it. Because it's dark and usually larder-cool, I keep my potatoes and onions in the boot. And yet within half an hour, these utilitarian vegetables, nestled amid the outdoor gear and plastic bottles of brake fluid, might be baked in milk, or sautéed together, or combined to make a creamy onion mash, or grated and fried in a rösti, or chopped in a simultaneously comforting and zestful potato salad, or layered with cheese for a golden-brown pan haggerty or, most transcendently of all, combined with a few eggs in a tortilla, so much more than the sum of its parts.

Potato & Parsley: *See Parsley & Potato, page 193*
Potato & Parsnip: *See Parsnip & Potato, page 225*

Potato & Pea: The presiding culinary spirits of uncontrollable children, acne, acrimonious divorce and mass unemployment. Nothing wrong with chips and peas *per se*, of course, but in too many pubs, canteens and cafés, depressing slabs of undercooked frozen potato blunder on to the plate, backed up by an entourage of hard, polyhedral peas. Best to close your eyes and think of a verdant pea and potato soup, or Indian *aloo matar*, in which the pea and potato are submerged in a sauce of fresh ginger, garlic and ground spices.

Potato & Peanut: Peanut has a meatiness that inevitably sees it paired with potato. In the city of Popayán in Colombia, they make small pasties stuffed with fried potato and peanuts called *empanada de pipián*, which are served with a peanut sauce. Boiled potatoes are usually part of an Indonesian *gado gado* salad – see Peanut & Coconut, page 24. Even in Thailand, the potato gets a rare culinary outing in the peanut-laced *mussaman* curry. Lastly, there's one of my husband's signature dishes, the Dalston Dinner, akin to a fish supper but with the added advantage that you don't need to leave the pub to eat it. Simply empty a packet of salted peanuts into a bag of salt and vinegar crisps, clench the bag shut and shake. Mysteriously more delicious than it should be. Good with lager.

Potato & Pork: *See Pork & Potato, page 37*

Potato & Rosemary: Rosemary's affinity for potato makes it irresistible on a spookily bloodless Roman *pizza bianca*, topped with potato, garlic and not even so much as a rumour of tomato. A sturdily flavoured, waxy new potato such as Yukon Gold is usually specified for this recipe, or you might try Duke of York or La Ratte. Parboil, then slice them very thinly and arrange, just overlapping, on an oiled (uncooked) pizza base sprinkled with a clove or two of finely chopped garlic. Drizzle with more oil, season well and scatter with finely snipped rosemary. You can pep up the flavour, if not the colour, with cheese (Parmesan, mozzarella, Asiago) or onion.

Potato & Saffron: *See Saffron & Potato, page 180*

Potato & Shellfish: Whole cultures have been founded on this combination: chowder in New England, *moules frites* in Belgium, potato gnocchi with spider crab sauce in Venice. At Romerijo in El Puerto de Santa María, between Jerez and Cádiz, you can tuck into net-fresh *mariscos* or *pescados fritos* with crisp, golden chips. Romerijo takes up more than its fair share of space in this lively seaside town – two branches face each other across a perpetually crowded narrow street, one specialising in fried seafood, the other in boiled. Vast glass counters house every variety of shellfish you've ever heard of, and plenty you haven't; from minuscule *camarones*, hardly bigger than the commas on the menu, to lobsters meaty enough to have rowed themselves ashore and smacked a longshoreman in the chops for his trouble. Sea-salty fried potatoes are served in paper cones printed with the restaurant's blue and white logo. Customers sit outside at Formica tables, shouting over the din as they decapitate their *langostinos*, or peel off their delicate orange armour and toss it in plastic buckets already brimming with crab claws and winkle shells as dark and shiny as ceremonial helmets. It's like a scene by Brueghel's more optimistic brother: Brueghel the Happier. Round the corner on Calle Misericordia, you'll find plenty of places for an *aperitivo*, and the trick is to drink enough oaky white Rioja to order without fear from the range of bivalved and tentacular monstrosities twitching on the ice, but not so much that you arrive at Romerijo when all that's left is a mound of *percebes* – a crustacean whose appearance can be compared only to the armour-plated trotter of a miniature aquatic pig. In English-speaking countries, *percebes* are known as goose barnacles, and were once believed to metamorphose into barnacle geese – an altogether more appropriate fate, in my book, than going anywhere near anyone's mouth. Just have the chips.

Potato & Smoked Fish: *See Smoked Fish & Potato, page 166*

Potato & Swede: A combination of mashed potato and swede is called clapshot. Mix 1:1 and add plenty of butter, plus either chives or some crisp fried onion. Conjoined but not combined, neeps and tatties are the essential side dish for haggis. The tatties, or potatoes, are mashed with butter, and cosy up to the haggis's mellow sheepishness, while the neeps, or swede, are bolstered in their natural spiciness by nutmeg, answering the spicing of the meat.

Potato & Tomato: Let's not beat around the bush – fries and ketchup. Arguably the most popular partnership in the Western world. The exact origins of *frites* are obscure but the term 'French-fried potatoes' began to appear in the mid-nineteenth century, shortly before the introduction of Heinz tomato ketchup in 1876. The singular thing about ketchup is its strength in all five basic taste categories: it is sweet, sour, bitter, salty and rich in umami. Tomato naturally contains umami, as does potato; that's deliciousness squared. Elizabeth David gives a Greek recipe for mashed potato mixed with skinned, finely chopped tomato, sliced spring onion, parsley, melted butter and flour, shaped into patties, then fried or baked. She also mentions a French recipe for a cream of tomato and potato soup: in brief, you soften the chopped whites of 2 leeks in butter, then add 225g roughly chopped tomatoes and cook them until they ooze their juice. Next add 350g diced peeled potatoes, some salt, a little sugar and 700ml water. Bring to the boil and simmer for 25 minutes. Liquidise and sieve, then return to a clean pan and add 150ml cream. Warm through and serve with parsley or chervil. On Pantelleria, an island off Sicily, *insalata pantesca* combines cooked new potatoes with chunks of raw tomato, olives, red onion and capers in olive oil and vinegar. And, of course, potato and tomato provide the background to a New York clam chowder. See also Chilli & Tomato, page 211.

Potato & Truffle: Friends of the earth. Encountering potatoes for the first time in Colombia, sixteenth-century Spanish explorers attributed truffle-like qualities to them, even naming them 'earth truffles'. Infuse a standard potato dish with truffle and their harmoniousness is clear; for example, in truffled mashed potatoes, potato gratin, or a mayonnaise made with truffle oil for potato salad. Giorgio Locatelli serves black truffles on potato gnocchi, because he believes they have a great affinity, although for pasta dishes and risotto he prefers white truffles.

Potato & Washed-rind Cheese: Let warm, fruity Vacherin Mont d'Or (see Washed-rind Cheese & Garlic, page 60) ooze slowly into the accommodating flesh of a jacket potato. In tartiflette, a dish from the Savoie region of France, nutty-flavoured, whey-washed Reblochon cheese is melted over potatoes, bacon and onion. See also Hard Cheese & Potato, page 68, and Cumin & Washed-rind Cheese, page 85.

Potato & Watercress: *See Watercress & Potato, page 100*
Potato & White Fish: *See White Fish & Potato, page 148*

Celery

This section covers celery stalks, celeriac (the swollen base of a celery relative) and celery seeds, which are harvested from smallage, or wild celery, and crushed to make celery salt. All share with the herb lovage a pair of compounds that give them their characteristic celery flavour. This is most potent in celery seeds, which are warm and bitter with a complex herbal, citrus quality; some are more lemony than others. Celery seeds can be useful when you don't have any stalks, or when they prove unwieldy. The stalks have a rather more salty, anise character, whereas celeriac is mild and adds root-vegetable sweetness and earthiness to the celery flavour. The seeds, stems and leaves of lovage are all used, and an alcoholic cordial is made of it to drink with brandy. Celery flavour is particularly savoury, recalling stocks and broths; accordingly it's used in soups and stews, where it emphasises the sweetness of meat and seafood.

Celery & Apple: In *American Psycho*, Patrick Bateman's girlfriend, Evelyn, breaks down when her Waldorf salad turns out to be gross. No need to make the same mistake. Chop 3 unpeeled, cored apples along with a stalk or two of celery and bind them to half a cup of walnuts with a tablespoon or so of mayonnaise – but don't drown it. Serve at Christmas with a thick slice of gammon and a glass of tawny port.

Celery & Beef: Cooked slowly, celery takes on a sweeter, brothier character, and the stalks (and sometimes the seeds) are used to add depth to braises and stews. The same use is made of the celery-flavoured herb, lovage, which in Germany is sometimes called *Maggikraut*, in reference to its meaty, yeasty similarity to Maggi stock cubes. Besides dropping them in a pot, you can cross-hatch celery stalks and use them as an edible rack for your beef joint, giving a deliciously deep, savoury basis for gravy. And if you're in New York, make sure you try a Dr Brown's Cel-Ray soda – probably the only celery-flavoured pop in the world – with your salt beef or pastrami sandwich.

Celery & Blue Cheese: A staple at the Christmas table. Or in a Boxing Day soup as pale and fatty as I feel after three days mainlining After Eights. Also paired in a garnish for spicy Buffalo wings – chicken wings deep-fried, then tossed in margarine and hot sauce and served on a platter with a blue cheese dip and batons of celery. I love the idea of all those strong flavours and the contrasting textures and temperatures, but the wings part leaves me cold. Eating chicken wings, I feel like a hamster nibbling on a pencil. Or like one of those crab-eating sea otters that die of starvation because the calories expended getting at the meat outnumber the calories gained when they do. For a more satisfying take on the trio, see Blue Cheese & Chicken, page 62.

Celery & Carrot: *See Carrot & Celery, page 227*
Celery & Chestnut: *See Chestnut & Celery, page 232*

Celery & Chicken: Celery makes an excellent companion to chicken, even if it's not as popular as it once was. Throughout the nineteenth century, British and American cookery writers stipulated celery sauce as the natural accompaniment to boiled fowl – indeed, celery sauce was traditionally served with an oyster-stuffed turkey at the English Christmas dinner. Hannah Glasse gives several recipes for it. One involves cutting celery stalks into pieces and simmering them in a little water. When the celery is soft, add mace, nutmeg and seasoning, then thicken the cooking liquid with butter and flour. Other versions are made with veal stock, cream or both. In recent years, scientific studies have shown that celery contains volatile compounds that, although not individually distinguishable to the human palate, significantly enhance sweet and umami notes in chicken stock.

Celery & Egg: *See Egg & Celery, page 133*

Celery & Horseradish: Early recipes for the Bloody Mary omit both celery and horseradish. As did Jacques Petiot, the cocktail's self-proclaimed inventor, in the recipe he gave in *The New Yorker* in 1964 – vodka, tomato, cayenne, lemon, black pepper, salt, Worcestershire sauce. But haven't they made themselves indispensable since? Like a couple at an okay party, who turn up late and spice things up; the horseradish makes your sinuses fizz, the celery leaves tickle your cheeks, and the stalk, with the runnels of tomato juice in its furrows, makes an ideal instrument of emphasis in drunken conversations. And of course, they make the drink a meal in itself, so your needs are pretty much taken care of.

Celery & Lamb: In Persian cooking, celery and lamb are combined in a *khoresh* much like the one given in Rhubarb & Lamb, page 255, except that the celery is fried with the herbs before being added to the meat. In Turkey and Greece, celery and lamb are stewed in a lemon sauce. At his restaurant in Langen, Germany, chef Juan Amador makes a dish of Aragon lamb cooked with celeriac, coffee and walnuts.

Celery & Nutmeg: *See Nutmeg & Celery, page 222*
Celery & Onion: *See Onion & Celery, page 108*
Celery & Oyster: *See Oyster & Celery, page 151*

Celery & Peanut: 'Ants on a log' is an American snack in which the concave groove of a celery stalk is filled with peanut butter and lined with marching raisins. Actually the combination is rather good, beyond the kitschy look of the thing – the crisp, slightly bitter bite of celery balances the salty fattiness of peanut and the sweet grapey-ness of raisin. You might take the elements and recast them in a more grown-up, Thai-influenced salad. Cut 4 tender celery stalks into matchsticks, mix with half a handful of raisins and toss with the dressing in Lime & Anchovy, page 300. Roughly crush half a handful of roasted peanuts, stir half into the celery and scatter the rest over the top.

Celery & Pork: *See Pork & Celery, page 34*

Celery & Potato: Crushed, freshly roasted celery seed stirred into your potato salad is a great way to add a little savoury spike to it. Potato and celeriac mash is good too; to avoid excessive wetness, it's best to cook the vegetables separately. Be sure to drain both vegetables well, and dry them out over a low heat before adding the butter. See also Truffle & Celery, page 116.

Celery & Prosciutto: *See Prosciutto & Celery, page 171*

Celery & Shellfish: The New England lobster roll is one of those legendary sandwiches that sound simple enough but are the cause of multiple disputes over the exact manner of their construction. Everyone agrees on the basics – that it should consist of a generous pile of lobster meat in a soft white hotdog bun – but there are different schools of thought on the presence of lettuce and/or celery and whether to robe the meat in melted butter or mayo. Waking from a coma in season six of *The Sopranos*, the first thing Tony asks for is a lobster roll from the Pearl Oyster Bar in the West Village. If you've ever wondered why mobsters are fat, you might like to note that these contain melted butter *and* mayonnaise. Mix lobster meat, a little finely chopped celery, Hellmann's mayonnaise, a squeeze of lemon and seasoning, and leave in the fridge while you open out hotdog buns like books and brown the insides in a pan of melted butter. Stuff the lobster mix into the bun. Eat lying back on a sun lounger, thinking of New England.

Celery & Soft Cheese: *See Soft Cheese & Celery, page 71*
Celery & Truffle: *See Truffle & Celery, page 116*
Celery & Walnut: *See Walnut & Celery, page 235*
Celery & White Fish: *See White Fish & Celery, page 146*

MUSTARDY

Watercress

Caper

Horseradish

Watercress

With its bittersweet, peppery, mineral freshness, watercress used to be a popular garnish for roast meats. All very well but it deserves a starrier role than culinary spear carrier. It is great paired with a salty and a sweet ingredient – blitzed into a salty stock with sweet milk or cream for a sublime soup, or pressed between slices of sweet bread and salty butter in a sandwich. Liquidised with soured cream and a pinch of salt, watercress makes a sauce that is as refreshing as dandling your feet in the river on a hot afternoon.

Watercress & Anchovy: *See Anchovy & Watercress, page 164*

Watercress & Beef: *Tagliata* is a Tuscan dish of beef steak that's seared, then thinly sliced and laid on uncooked rocket, which is dressed by the meat's cooking juices. It's a lovely means of showcasing good steak – with only the mouthwateringly peppery herb for company, you can really taste the meat. Why not anglicise the dish by substituting watercress for the rocket? A change from the more familiar practice of cramming the leaves in a thick sandwich with roast beef. Don't be tempted to serve it with potatoes, which would add a floury heaviness when the delight in *tagliata* is its lightness, in substance if not in flavour. Restrict any accompaniments to a dollop of Dijon mustard.

Watercress & Beetroot: *See Beetroot & Watercress, page 88*

Watercress & Blue Cheese: The sweet-saltiness of Stilton contrasts nicely with the bitter pepper flavour of watercress. You might also detect a faint metallic tang in them both, as if you'd let the tines of your fork linger in your mouth a moment too long. By all means combine them in a salad with pear and walnut, or in a soup, soufflé or tart. But there's nothing quite like spreading bread with buttery Stilton, deep enough to leave a pleasing impression of your teeth when you bite into it, and scattering it with watercress leaves. See also Parsnip & Watercress, page 225.

Watercress & Chicken: I think of roast chicken and watercress as a warm-weather counterpart to roast beef and horseradish. The sweetness of the meat is emphasised by the hot, peppery kick of watercress, but the leaf's refreshing greenness simultaneously lightens the combination. In France, watercress is the classic garnish for roast chicken, and works particularly well when the sweetness of the flesh and the bitterness of the leaves are balanced by crisp, salty skin – although a few olives, or a Thai dressing made with fish sauce and lime juice, do the same trick if you like to eat only the lean white meat. A warm watercress sauce for chicken can be made very quickly. Soften a couple of shallots in butter, then add 75ml white wine and simmer until reduced to about 1 tbsp. Add 400ml hot chicken or vegetable stock, simmer for 5 minutes and add 150ml cream. When heated through, add 150–200g chopped watercress, cook for 1–2 minutes, check the seasoning and blend.

Watercress & Egg: Garden cress (sometimes called peppergrass) has a rather shyer bite of mustard oil than its close relative, watercress, but both work in pleasingly prickly contrast to the cosy comforts of egg. There's no finer contrast for a sandwich to eat with your little finger in the air. The Ritz Hotel in London serves egg mayonnaise and cress bridge rolls (like miniature hotdog buns) as part of its afternoon tea. Watercress also makes a good omelette, or a salad with a soft poached egg and pieces of chorizo.

Watercress & Goat's Cheese: As an intensely blue sky sharpens the objects against it, so the bitterness of watercress gives vibrant goat's cheese a cleaner, more defined edge. And both tend to a similarly ringing minerality. Cooked watercress loses its kick but is still well matched with the cheese, particularly in a watercress soup with a goat's cheese garnish. Or pair them raw in a salad, dressed with walnut oil and sherry vinegar, as long as you're prepared, as a goat would be, to give the leaves a long, ruminative chew.

Watercress & Grapefruit: *See Grapefruit & Watercress, page 299*

Watercress & Oily Fish: Trout and cress; not so much a pairing as a reunification. Trout feed on the more tender leaves of watercress but they're really after the sowbugs, tiny crustaceans that live in its thickets. As with other natural pairings, trout and watercress are sufficiently harmonious to need a minimum of preparation. To serve two, fry a trout each in clarified butter for about 5 minutes on each side, and make a watercress sauce by blending a bunch with 150ml soured cream, a squeeze of lemon and a pinch of salt and sugar. The Japanese, who didn't come to watercress until the late nineteenth century, make a cooked salad called *o-hitashi* with it. Blanch a bunch, plunge it into iced water, drain, chop into edible lengths, dress with dashi (dried tuna stock), a little mirin and soy, leave to marinate for a while, then eat cold.

Watercress & Orange: *See Orange & Watercress, page 297*
Watercress & Parsnip: *See Parsnip & Watercress, page 225*

Watercress & Pork: In southern parts of China, watercress is slowly simmered with pork ribs to make a simple soup. It might be flavoured with fresh ginger or with jujubes, a fruit that looks and tastes like date.

Watercress & Potato: The Chinese like their watercress soup in (often pork-based) broth form. In France and Britain, the taste is for the thicker potage style, achieved with the use of cream, potatoes or both. I like all watercress but the stuff sold in posies seems to have a cleaner, mineral fragrance, as opposed to the bagged watercress that gets all pondy if you don't use it straight away. If you use a lot of watercress, you might consider growing land cress, which has a similar flavour and grows easily through the winter under a cloche. Some say land cress is stronger flavoured, and that you should use less of it in a soup than you would watercress. I say use more stock and potato and make more soup.

Watercress & Shellfish: The pepperiness of watercress tempers the overblown richness of shellfish. Nobu serves a salad of watercress with lobster and black sesame seeds, Alain Ducasse a watercress and scallop soup that's the bottomless green of a Chesterfield sofa in a gentleman's club.

Watercress & Smoked Fish: Rich, salty smoked fish and the hot pepperiness of watercress make a fine match but need some sweet relief: eggs and cream in a watercress and smoked trout tart, for instance, beetroot in a hot smoked salmon and watercress salad, or potatoes in fishcakes with a watercress sauce. See also Watercress & Chicken, page 99.

Watercress & Walnut: Watercress sandwiches are unlikely to be met with much enthusiasm, however neatly you cut the crusts off. If the leaves are trapped between slices of homemade walnut bread, it's another story. You might add a little smoked salmon, or thin slices of Brie, but don't underestimate the ability of watercress to draw out the flavour of the bread. In fact it makes rather good bread itself: in Mark Miller and Andrew McLauchlan's *Flavored Breads*, a recipe is given for a rocket and watercress flatbread, plus a variation using watercress, coriander leaf and mint. Dip in warm walnut oil.

Caper

Capers, the buds of the caper bush, can revitalise a bland meat dish or an old-fashioned seafood cocktail like a new accessory perks up an old dress. They add a fresh nip, a quirky flavour and a splash of briny liquid that's particularly pleasing with fish. Salted capers retain more of their interesting flavour than brined; soak them for 15 minutes before using and the herbal-mustard character will be more apparent. Some chefs marinate the rinsed capers in white wine and herbs before using them in salads or sauces. Caperberries, which are the fruit rather than the buds of the bush, are also covered in this chapter.

Caper & Anchovy: Just a little caper and anchovy can transform bland or oily dishes. We should carry them around in a little envelope, like a sewing kit, for culinary emergencies. Lemon mellows them somewhat; they're a good trio for a flavoured butter to use on grilled salmon, tuna steaks or lamb chops. Pound 4 anchovy fillets with 1 tsp lemon juice and ½ tsp lemon zest. Mix into

125g soft butter with 3–4 tsp small capers and season. Transfer to a square of cling film and shape into a cylinder. Chill, then slice into discs to use.

Caper & Beef: *See Beef & Caper, page 43*

Caper & Beetroot: Sugary beetroot and mustardy capers make for a kind of honey-mustard combination. They're mixed into minced beef, cooked potato and onion and fried in patties in the popular Swedish dish, *biff à la Lindström* (not unlike the *labskaus* or red flannel hash discussed in Beef & Beetroot, page 43). Add rinsed capers to an olive oil and red wine vinegar dressing for beetroot and goat's cheese salad.

Caper & Cauliflower: *See Cauliflower & Caper, page 122*

Caper & Cucumber: Cornichons, small cultivars of the cucumber family, are usually picked at 3–4cm long. Their thin, knobbly skin and crunchy flesh make them ideal for pickling. Capers and pickled cornichons are combined in tartare sauce, with herbs and hard-boiled egg in *sauce gribiche*, and in Liptauer, a soft, spicy cheese from central Europe, flavoured with paprika, mustard and chives.

Caper & Goat's Cheese: *See Goat's Cheese & Caper, page 55*

Caper & Lamb: Capers' salty bitterness smartly chaperones the sweetness of lamb. The best capers contain notes of thyme and onion, both of which go well with lamb too. This classic recipe is from Keith Floyd. He says it serves 6, so you might want to make more sauce if your leg is feeding more than that. Submerge a leg of mutton, or *gigot*, in an oval-shaped pot full of water and bring very slowly to the boil. Skim the fat from the surface and add 6 leeks, 2 swedes, 6 carrots and 4 turnips, all chopped into hearty chunks. Simmer for about 2 hours. Just before the cooking time is up, melt 25g butter in a saucepan, add 25g plain flour and stir into a creamy paste. Pour in 150ml warm milk and whisk until smooth. Then add 150ml stock from the mutton pan and simmer gently for about 20 minutes, until you have a velvety, luxurious sauce. Stir in 3–4 tbsp rinsed, drained capers, check the seasoning and pour into a jug. Remove the mutton from the stock, place on a serving plate surrounded by the vegetables and pour over the sauce. See also Goat's Cheese & Caper, page 55.

Caper & Lemon: Could wake the dead. Stir them into mayonnaise or combine them in a dressing for smoked salmon or fried fish. Or make more of a fuss of their salty acidity by cooking lemon and caper spaghetti. Follow the recipe in Lemon & Basil, page 304, substituting 1 tbsp rinsed capers for the basil. See also Caper & Anchovy, page 101.

Caper & Oily Fish: A significant flavour compound in capers, methyl isothiocyanate, has a strong mustard character, and is also found in horse-radish – a famous partner for oily fish. Capers cut through the fattiness of fish in much the way horseradish does. Oily fish and capers are especially good paired on pizza. Spread a base with tomato sauce (see Garlic & Basil, page 112, for a good one), then scatter over thin slices of red onion, flaked tinned tuna, anchovies, olives and capers. Bake for 10 minutes at 230°C/Gas Mark 8.

Caper & Olive: *See Olive & Caper, page 175*
Caper & Parsley: *See Parsley & Caper, page 192*

Caper & Potato: Capers like to razz up mild flavours and cut through fat. They're good in a Mediterranean potato salad (see Potato & Tomato, page 93), can be added to *skordalia* (see Potato & Garlic, page 90) or served with hot (especially sautéed) potatoes. It's worth remembering to add the buds to the cold oil and bring them up to heat. Tossed into hot fat, they're in danger of becoming tiny, briny incendiary devices. Note that long cooking intensifies the flavour of capers. In Greece, the leaves of the caper bush are eaten with potatoes and with fish. They have a more mustardy-thyme flavour than the buds. See also Saffron & Potato, page 180.

Caper & Shellfish: Capers work well with all seafood. The pickled variety, whose flavour, unlike salted capers, is somewhat masked by vinegar, are typi-cally used in pickled shrimp, a dish popular in the American South. It's like a ceviche – cold, piquant, with lots of citrus juice – but the shellfish is cooked. See also Caper & White Fish, page 104.

Caper & Smoked Fish: Capers make a classic garnish for smoked salmon, cutting through the fish's fattiness and, in their extreme saltiness, making it seem sweeter. Caperberries can be put to the same use, and are excellent with cured meats too. They're the size of a small olive and come with a stalk that pulls off with a satisfying *tock*. In contrast to the baggy texture of capers, caper-berries are firm and full of seeds that flood your mouth when you bite into them, like a briny, coarse mustard. The flavour is similar to capers but a little milder. Serve with smoked salmon pâté on wholewheat toast.

Caper & Soft Cheese: Famously paired with smoked salmon, but they're quite delicious together without the fish. Mix drained whole capers into a thick, rich, ivory-coloured cream cheese. Use French nonpareil capers, if you can. They're the really small ones that look like green peppercorns, and are highly regarded for their finer, radishy, oniony flavour. Spread the mix on crackers or rye bread and brace yourself for the little shocks of caper in each bite. The culinary equivalent of walking barefoot along a stony beach. See also Caper & Cucumber, page 102.

Caper & Tomato: *See Tomato & Caper, page 259*

Caper & White Fish: Skate with capers in black butter is a deservedly classic dish but, as a critically endangered species, skate is off the menu. Try the sauce on scallops instead. When skate was cheap and plentiful, crafty fishmongers used to press 'scallops' out of skate wings; some believe the sweet, delicate flavours are similar. Taking care not to let it burn, heat 75g butter in a pan until deeply golden. Add 1 tsp white wine vinegar and 1–2 tbsp drained rinsed capers. Stir, then pour over cooked scallops, any white fish, or the sauce's other classic partner, ox brains. Capers are, of course, also an essential element of tartare sauce.

Horseradish

Horseradish is a bruiser with a gentle side. Cut or grate it and its natural defence mechanism releases hot, bitter compounds to make your eyes run and your nose burn. For that reason, it's usually paired with the sort of pugnacious flavours that can stand up to it – smoked foods, roast beef, piquant cheeses and spicy, boozy tomato juice. Treated gently, however, in small doses, it can tease out the delicate flavours of raw seafood. In common with other hot ingredients such as chilli and mustard, horseradish is a showcaser, drawing attention to what's in your mouth. It has a slight freshening quality, too, knocking a little fishiness off uncooked seafood, or the earthiness from potato and beetroot. This chapter also covers wasabi.

Horseradish & Apple: *See Apple & Horseradish, page 271*

Horseradish & Bacon: Bacon and tomato find each other irresistible. Salty, sweet, sour: how could they not? Which is why so many swear by tomato sauce on their bacon butties. I understand the force of habit in these cases, but everyone should try horseradish sauce at least once, especially when smoked bacon is at stake. If it's good smoked bacon, I'd go so far as to say that horseradish is just plain better, complementing the bacon's charry brininess where ketchup puts up a fight. Mix 1 tbsp prepared horseradish with 4 tbsp mayo. Spread more than you should on toasted brown bread, lay the bacon on top, then some sickle-shapes of sliced avocado and a few leaves of crisp Cos lettuce. Sink your teeth in and feel your eyeballs begin to turn upwards. Note how the horseradish gets behind the bacon and gives it a nip on the backside.

Horseradish & Beef: *See Beef & Horseradish, page 45*

Horseradish & Beetroot: Mellow beetroot talks down headstrong horse-radish. Pair in a salad, or in a relish such as the Ukrainian *tsvikili*, a 6:1 mixture of grated cooked beetroot and grated fresh horseradish, seasoned with salt, pepper, sugar and vinegar to taste. The sweetened Jewish sauce, red chrain, works on similar principles and is served with gefilte fish. Alternatively, pay homage to the couple's Russian roots with a crimson borscht, lifted by a swirl of horseradish mixed with soured cream.

Horseradish & Celery: *See Celery & Horseradish, page 96*

Horseradish & Oily Fish: Horseradish is served as a sauce with simply cooked oily fish; chef Richard Corrigan cures herring with a horseradish mixture; and, in the form of wasabi, it provides a hot contrast to raw tuna or salmon sushi and sashimi.

Horseradish & Oyster: In New Orleans, oysters are simply dressed with horseradish, or a mixture of tomato ketchup and horseradish. The thrill of cold oyster and nose-tingling horseradish enacts a sequence of shocks, like the lime wedge after your tequila shot. New York chef David Burke pairs cooked oysters and horseradish in a risotto.

Horseradish & Pea: *See Pea & Horseradish, page 203*

Horseradish & Potato: Season mash to taste with frisky, fibrous horse-radish for a fresher thatch on your cottage pie. Or use horseradish mayonnaise (see Horseradish & Bacon, page 104) in a potato salad to accompany smoked salmon, mackerel or trout.

Horseradish & Smoked Fish: *See Smoked Fish & Horseradish, page 165*
Horseradish & Tomato: *See Tomato & Horseradish, page 260*

Horseradish & White Fish: Purists may disapprove, but I love wasabi with my sushi, pushed into the rice like a lump of green explosive. Wasabi and horseradish are close relatives. Both have a pungent, metallic flavour that comes from volatile sulphur compounds liberated as a defensive measure when the plant is damaged – i.e. grated. Horseradish has the more radishy, watercress-like flavour. Most wasabi served in Western restaurants isn't wasabi at all but horseradish dyed green; the same goes for many shop-bought varieties. Mind you, any more than a lentil's worth and you'll be weeping hot tears through your nose, so in the quantities it's appropriate to use you'd be hard pushed to notice the difference in flavour. If you do overdo it, the secret, according to Harold McGee, is to breathe out through the mouth, so the wasabi-fumes don't irritate your nasal passages, and in through the nose, to bypass the residue in your mouth. Or you could just weep and wait like the rest of us.

SULPHUROUS

Onion

Garlic

Truffle

Cabbage

Swede

Cauliflower

Broccoli

Globe Artichoke

Asparagus

Egg

Onion

The hardest workers in the food business. Across the species that comprise the *Allium* genus, onion contributes a range of distinct flavours, from the light, herbal freshness of chive to the delicate, perfumed flavour of shallots, the tear-jerking boisterousness of the bulb onion, and the more vegetal, green-tinged earthiness of leeks and spring onions. Raw, onions lend a sharp, crisp edge to dips and salads; roasted or braised, they become sweet and succulent; fried until black-edged, they add a bittersweet dimension to a hotdog.

Onion & Anchovy: On a rainy day in Venice with friends, we went hunting for lunch in the backstreets of Dorsoduro. We chose a café with a short menu and no English spoken. Dorsoduro is a little less touristy than San Marco, the other side of the Grand Canal, and the proprietor and his wife seemed delighted to entertain some *inglesi* in their restaurant, as if the very idea of foreign visitors to Venice was a novelty. We wanted to try the local dish of bigoli pasta with anchovies and onions. A platter so enormous a gondolier might have punted it on to our table arrived, along with several pitchers of Soave. Bigoli is like wholewheat spaghetti but thicker, with a nutty, rugged character. It makes an ideal carrier for the sweet and salty mixture of onions and anchovies. You can make this with wholewheat spaghetti if you can't get the real thing. For two people, soften 3 thinly sliced large onions in 2–3 tbsp olive oil over a medium heat for about 20 minutes, without letting them colour. Once they've had about 10 minutes, add 4 or 5 chopped anchovies. Mix them in, break them up a bit and season, bearing in mind how salty the anchovy is to begin with. Cook the pasta until it is *al dente*. Drain it, reserving about a tablespoon of water, and return both to the pan. Place back on the heat and stir in the sauce. For an extra touch of sweetness, add a tablespoon of currants to the onion mix. You could try some of anchovy's other matches in this too: a little rosemary, perhaps, some blanched chopped broccoli or a sprinkling of capers.

Onion & Bacon: *See Bacon & Onion, page 169*
Onion & Beef: *See Beef & Onion, page 46*

Onion & Beetroot: Beetroot's sweetness is offset to great effect by raw onion. When cooked, onion takes on a sweetness of its own, which can be balanced out by vinegar in this beetroot and onion chutney to serve with homemade sausage rolls or in cheese sandwiches. Simmer 700g diced onions with 450g peeled, cored and diced eating apples in 300ml red wine vinegar until tender – this takes about 20 minutes. Add 700g diced cooked beetroot, another 250ml vinegar, 400g sugar, 1 tsp salt and 2 tsp ground ginger. Boil for a further 30 minutes. Spoon into sterilised jam jars while still hot and seal. Makes about 5 standard (450g) jars' worth.

Onion & Bell Pepper: Stray into a residential area in Spain or Portugal in the early evening and the air will be sweet with onions and peppers being softened for supper. If the combination always smells better than it does at home, I put this down to better ingredients, the cheering late-day sunshine, and the simple fact of being on holiday. But when I came to learn more about Spanish cooking I discovered that, above all, patience is the secret ingredient. An onion and pepper mixture cooked for 20 minutes is, it turns out, actually four times better than one cooked for 5. So much so, in fact, that you can pile it straight from the pan on to coarse white bread and eat it for supper. Whether cooking them for 40 minutes would be twice as good as 20 remains to be seen. I've got *some* patience, but I'm no Job.

Onion & Black Pudding: *See Black Pudding & Onion, page 39*
Onion & Cabbage: *See Cabbage & Onion, page 119*
Onion & Carrot: *See Carrot & Onion, page 228*

Onion & Celery: Dice carrot, celery and onion and you have the aromatic base for many stocks, soups and stews known by chefs as mirepoix. Add some salty bacon or cured fat for a *mirepoix au gras* and it's a bit like being dealt three of the same-numbered cards in a hand of poker. You'd be unlucky not to end up with something winning. If you're cooking something that needs less sweetness or a fresher, more herbaceous base, skip the carrot. If you're making, say, a pale broth, and don't want carrot colour seeping into it, use a parsnip instead. The mirepoix-like combination of onion, celery and green pepper is called the holy trinity in Cajun cooking. A standard mirepoix calls for two parts onion to two parts carrot to one part celery by volume, whereas the Holy Trinity is 1:1:1.

Onion & Chicken: *See Chicken & Onion, page 29*

Onion & Clove: Pity the clove-studded onion. In bread sauce it sticks with the project all the way through, only to be discarded at the end. Bread swans in at the last minute and takes all the credit. But it's the tang of the onion, softened by the aromatic, fireside warmth of the clove, that gives the sauce its special, irresistible depth. It's the Ugg boot of sauces. You might also try the combination in a clove-infused chicken and onion sandwich. For two baguette sandwiches of about 15cm each, thinly slice a Spanish onion, then cook it nice and slowly in 1 tbsp groundnut oil, a dab of butter and ½ tsp ground cloves. Warm the bread, slice some hot, cooked chicken. When the onion is meltingly soft, you could add a few tablespoons of cream, then warm the mixture through. Spread it on to the bread before laying on the chicken slices. Great with a glass of Pinot Noir.

Onion & Cucumber: According to the Chinese, watery, cooling cucumber is very yin, warming, bright, strong, dry onion yang. Their yinniness and yanginess is never more apparent than in pancakes filled with thick, sweet hoisin sauce, crunchy-soft shreds of crispy aromatic duck, and julienned cucumber and spring onion.

Onion & Egg: *See Egg & Onion, page 135*
Onion & Garlic: *See Garlic & Onion, page 114*

Onion & Ginger: Forget Fred; spring onion's the perfect partner for ginger. A staple combination in Chinese cooking, and so versatile and delicious it can even turn tofu into a savoury feast. Fuchsia Dunlop (who learnt no fewer than nine ways to cut a spring onion at chef school in Sichuan) explains how they're used to temper unsavoury flavours in meat and seafood and, more tantalisingly, as a seasoning, shredded and scattered over steamed fish, then drizzled with hot oil to awaken their flavour before a dash of dark soy is added. For me, ginger and spring onion is never better than when stir-fried with fresh crab, a dish that can take up to an hour to dismantle with your fingers but is fortunately still delicious when cold.

Onion & Hard Cheese: *See Hard Cheese & Onion, page 68*

Onion & Lamb: Onion sauce is a classic partner for roast lamb or mutton. Food writer Charles Campion recalls this pairing was the 'banker' recipe his mother always fell back on. Largely, he recalls, because of the outstanding sauce she made with lots of onions softly fried in butter, then simmered in milk with nutmeg and black pepper and thickened with potato flour and cream. The movies are less kind to messy eating habits than books, and James Bond's fondness for lamb and onion kebabs is a notable omission from the film version of *From Russia With Love*: while his Turkish contact, Darko, tucks into what sounds like *kibbeh* (minced raw lamb, finely ground with chives and peppers), Bond plumps for particularly young, charcoal-grilled lamb with savoury rice and lots of onions. No wonder he doesn't get any action that night.

Onion & Liver: *See Liver & Onion, page 42*

Onion & Mint: As parsley is to garlic breath, mint is to onion. Remember the 1980s ad for Wrigley's Doublemint, set in a restaurant, in which Girl A, speculating about where the boys might be taking them tonight, asks Girl B whether her hair looks okay? Girl B responds that if she were Girl A she'd be less worried about her hair than her onion breath. Why didn't Girl A gently put down her fork and punch Girl B on the nose? And why was Girl B so worried about Girl A's breath, when Girl A was having the skimpiest side salad, of which the onions formed part, for her main course? Was this why they were eating *before they met the boys*? Because Girl A and Girl B were locked in a toxic cycle of narcissistic and mutually destructive sexual competitiveness? Far from encouraging me to buy gum, it instilled in me a determination to date boys in front of whom I could eat the most lingeringly pungent foods. If he still fancied me after an onion-bhaji-scented kiss, with a trailing after-note of minty raita, I would have found my match. See also Chilli & Mint, page 209.

Onion & Mushroom: *See Mushroom & Onion, page 79*

Onion & Nutmeg: Often thought of as primarily a sweet spice, nutmeg also has a bitter streak, which provides a useful counterpoint to onion's sweetness. It's good in a sauce made with cooked, puréed onions, added to a béchamel made with milk. Or cook onions very slowly in butter until soft, purée and sprinkle liberally with nutmeg. Loosen with a little chicken stock or cream if necessary. Both these sauces can be served with roast pork, lamb or duck.

Onion & Oily Fish: *See Oily Fish & Onion, page 158*

Onion & Orange: Thin sliced rounds of both can make a lovely, crisp salad. Look out for sweet onion varieties such as Viladia and Supasweet. The higher sugar levels in sweeter onions come at the expense of pyruvic acid, the defensive chemical responsible for stronger onions' pungency, aftertaste and the teardrops on your cutting board. If you can't get naturally sweet onions, you could try giving your cut onions a rinse in cold water, which arrests some of the stronger sulphur compounds released when you damage their flesh. Blood orange and red onion make a pretty pair on the plate, and red onion is often (though not always) on the sweeter, milder side.

Onion & Oyster: *See Oyster & Onion, page 152*
Onion & Pea: *See Pea & Onion, page 203*

Onion & Pork: Unpretentious pork gets along with all the onion family – garlic with roast pork, chives with Chinese pork dumplings, a tangle of onion gravy on sausages, or, best of all, pork and leek sausages. Leeks offer a creamy combination of onion and cabbage flavours – and cabbage is really pork's very best partner of all.

Onion & Potato: *See Potato & Onion, page 91*
Onion & Rosemary: *See Rosemary & Onion, page 319*

Onion & Sage: Sage and onion is the classic stuffing for a reason: sweet, herbal deep and mulchy under a crunchy crust. Perhaps mainly for associative reasons, the combination is redolent of meat, and is a knockout with cannellini beans in this bruschetta – a sort of Tuscan beans on toast. Soften a finely chopped onion in olive oil, then add a drained 400g tin of cannellini beans and a couple of finely chopped sage leaves. Cook over a low heat for 5–10 minutes, then semi-mash, season and serve on rounds of toasted French bread. See also Chicken & Sage, page 31.

Onion & Smoked Fish: Thin rings of raw red onion cut through the fattiness of smoked salmon yet match its boisterous flavour – perfect on a warm bagel spread with cream cheese. Instead of smoked salmon, you might choose lox – not the same stuff, even if the terms are often used interchangeably. Lox is salmon cured in brine, sometimes with onion and spices, but never smoked. The proper stuff is as salty as a fisherman's moustache. Russ and Daughters in New York cures its own lox and serves it with a wine or cream sauce with pickled onion. See also Soft Cheese & Smoked Fish, page 73.

Onion & Thyme: *See Thyme & Onion, page 327*
Onion & Tomato: *See Tomato & Onion, page 260*

Garlic

Adding a small amount of garlic to meat, seafood, green vegetables and even truffles is like drawing a keyline around their flavour – everything gains a sharper definition. Garlic also adds something of a succulent quality. For a mild garlic flavour, infuse warm cooking oil with a whole, unchopped clove; for something more potent, use it raw and crushed to a paste. There are two types of garlic – softneck and hardneck. Softneck is the type you're most likely to find in the supermarket or plaited into a braid, as it's easier to grow, but hardnecks tend to have the better flavour. Try a side-by-side garlic tasting by making garlic bread or aioli with a range of different bulbs, looking out for their different hot, sweet, earthy, metallic, fruity, nutty, rubbery and floral (lily) characters. Elephant garlic is milder and considered part of the leek rather than the true garlic family. Garlic can be bought in powdered, flaked, paste and salt forms, or ready chopped in jars, although I find these prepared products often have a piercing quality and miss the earthy, volatile perfume of fresh cloves. Garlic's main use is in heightening the flavour of savoury dishes but it makes a fantastic primary flavour on a sweet, bland background like bread or pasta, or, in the case of a roasted garlic risotto, rice.

Garlic & Almond: This version of the classic Spanish cold soup, *ajo blanco*, involves blending almonds with raw garlic in a food processor – a surefire way of experiencing garlic flavour at its most potent. Garlic contains a sulfoxide called alliin, which is converted into allicin when the garlic is sliced or crushed. Allicin, in turn, is converted into the sulphide compounds responsible for crushed garlic's characteristic aroma. The more brutally you rupture your garlic, the more allicin is converted. The almond in *ajo blanco* takes the edge off the pungency, as does serving it cold, so you shouldn't be tempted to underplay the garlic. Soak a handful of crustless stale white bread in water or milk. In a food processor place 200g ground blanched almonds, the bread squeezed dry and 2 peeled, crushed garlic cloves. Pulse until you have a paste. With the motor running, add 3 tbsp olive oil slowly through the feed tube followed by 750ml iced water. Season and stir in sherry vinegar (1–3 tbsp) to taste. Chill mercilessly and serve with a garnish of grapes, deseeded if necessary. See also Almond & Melon, page 244.

Garlic & Anchovy: *See Anchovy & Garlic, page 162*
Garlic & Aubergine: *See Aubergine & Garlic, page 82*

Garlic & Basil: The effect that a few garlic cloves and some basil leaves have on tinned tomatoes is nothing short of miraculous. Essentially they pull the flavours of the tomato in opposite directions, stretching it out to its fullest potential. At one end of the spectrum, garlic picks up on the strong dimethyl sulphide flavour of tinned tomato, taking it further in a savoury vegetal direction; at the other, basil replaces the green, slightly grassy flavours that tomatoes lose in the canning process, lightening and freshening the sauce. Roughly chop 4 or 5 garlic cloves and soften them in olive oil. When they've taken on a little colour, add 4 tins of whole plum tomatoes and a generous handful of roughly torn basil leaves. Break up the tomatoes, season and bring to the boil. Remove from the heat and pass through a sieve, working the mixture with a wooden spoon. Discard the garlicky, basilly tomato pulp and pour the sauce back in the pan. Bring to a simmer and let it reduce until it starts plopping like a hot swamp – it should be roughly the consistency of ketchup. Use for pasta or pizza. Gets really heavenly if you keep any excess in the fridge overnight with a couple of fresh basil leaves in it.

Garlic & Beef: *See Beef & Garlic, page 45*
Garlic & Broccoli: *See Broccoli & Garlic, page 126*
Garlic & Cabbage: *See Cabbage & Garlic, page 119*
Garlic & Cauliflower: *See Cauliflower & Garlic, page 123*

Garlic & Chicken: A drawback of chicken Kiev is having to dodge the geyser of molten garlic butter as it arcs over your shoulder. Safer to stick to the old Provençal recipe for chicken with 40 cloves of garlic. As the name suggests, you simply roast your chicken with 40 garlic cloves, unpeeled and with their pointy noses lopped off in order that the hot, sweet garlic paste can be squeezed from the skin directly on to toasted rounds of French bread. The garlic goes through a complete personality change, losing its aggressive pungency and turning caramel-sweet, with a chestnutty flavour. But for all its apparent mellowness, roasted garlic lingers no less obstinately on the breath. Last time I made the recipe, I took a cab the next morning and the driver kept giving me dirty looks in the rear-view.

Garlic & Chilli: *See Chilli & Garlic, page 209*

Garlic & Coriander Leaf: *See Coriander Leaf & Garlic, page 195*
Garlic & Coriander Seed: *See Coriander Seed & Garlic, page 346*

Garlic & Cucumber: Ken Hom writes about a pickled cucumber salad he enjoyed in Shanghai. The original was made with pungent raw garlic, but he tamps things down by using fried in his version. In tsatsiki, perhaps garlic and cucumber's most famous collaboration, yogurt moderates matters even further but the hot ardency of garlic still persists. Deseed, then coarsely grate or dice half a cucumber, squeeze as much water out of it as you can, and mix with 250g yogurt, a garlic clove crushed with salt, and a tablespoon or two of chopped mint (you might try using yogurt made with sheep's or goat's milk, the flavours of which go particularly well with cucumber). Serve with fatty lamb chops and crusty bread. Or thin with light stock to make a refreshing cold soup, remembering that cucumber will yield more of its water as the flavours meld in the fridge.

Garlic & Ginger: Good cop/bad cop. Ginger's the good cop: fresh, with a light touch, and a knack for teasing out the sweetness in meat, seafood and greens. Garlic, on the other hand, is rude, coarse, and leaves a firm, sulphurous impression. Indian chefs make a ginger–garlic paste to use as a marinade for meat or as part of a sauce. Process equal quantities by weight of peeled garlic and ginger into a paste, adding about 1 tbsp water per 100g. Will keep for a couple of weeks in the fridge or longer in the freezer.

Garlic & Goat's Cheese: *See Goat's Cheese & Garlic, page 57*
Garlic & Hazelnut: *See Hazelnut & Garlic, page 240*

Garlic & Lamb: In Barcelona there's an old coaching inn with an interior like a working forge. A grill the size of a pool table roars and spits beneath immense cuts of lamb on the bone and bundles of artichokes and leek-like *calçots*. A waiter brings you a kit of thick slabs of rough white bread, whole tomatoes and garlic cloves, with which you make your own *pa amb tomàquet*. I followed this with a stack of glistening, salty lamb chops served with a bowl of *aioli*, whose fierceness was perfectly pitched to the sweet fattiness of the meat. When the sting of garlic subsided, each mouthful of lamb tasted sweeter. When the main course had been cleared, a man at the next table leaned over and insisted we order the tangerine sorbet. We were glad he did. It tasted as if the very essence of tangeriniess, every perfumed nuance, had been cryogenically preserved.

Garlic & Liver: *See Liver & Garlic, page 41*
Garlic & Mint: *See Mint & Garlic, page 330*
Garlic & Mushroom: *See Mushroom & Garlic, page 77*
Garlic & Oily Fish: *See Oily Fish & Garlic, page 157*
Garlic & Olive: *See Olive & Garlic, page 176*

Garlic & Onion: The air our kitchens breathe. Chinese Buddhist monks, however, abstain, classing onions, garlic, shallots, chives and leeks as *wu hun*, or the 'foetid' or 'forbidden five', on the basis that they excite the senses. A similar injunction against onion and garlic exists in Hindu Brahmin culture. The Jains, for their part, avoid onion and garlic as well as root vegetables, for fear that they might contain living things. As a substitute, both Brahmins and Jains might use the resinous gum called asafoetida, which has a pungent, alliaceous flavour. That it's also known as both 'devil's dung' and 'food of the gods' might recall the equivocal gorgeous/gruesome qualities ascribed to truffles. Raw asafoetida resin smells sickeningly sulphurous (the powdered form much less so), but cooked it imbues food with an earthy, savoury tang. Although most commonly associated with Indian cuisine, it's native to Iran, where it's sometimes rubbed on to serving plates for meat. Asafoetida was so treasured in Roman times that it forms part of half the recipes in Apicius. If you're quite into having your senses excited, you might try five-onion soup, made with garlic, onion, spring onion, leek and chives.

Garlic & Parsley: *See Parsley & Garlic, page 192*
Garlic & Pork: *See Pork & Garlic, page 35*
Garlic & Potato: *See Potato & Garlic, page 90*

Garlic & Rosemary: The gutsy flavours of garlic and rosemary are an ideal combination for outdoor food. Use them on your barbecued lamb, pork or rabbit, to enrich roasted new potatoes and for an aromatic garlic bread. Or relive the summer on a cold evening by using them in a simple pasta in the 'olio, aglio' style – see Chilli & Garlic, page 209. Warm some sliced garlic in olive oil with finely snipped rosemary (½ tsp per serving) and mix into cooked spaghetti with plenty of grated Parmesan.

Garlic & Shellfish: *See Shellfish & Garlic, page 141*
Garlic & Soft Cheese: *See Soft Cheese & Garlic, page 72*

Garlic & Thyme: Kinder than garlic and rosemary, garlic and thyme work wonders on just about anything savoury: vegetables, lamb, chicken, olives. Richard Olney thinks that plenty of thyme and garlic is vital to a good rata-touille. The following (foolproof) method follows his advice and will mean that you'll never again have to consign an insipid attempt to the bin. Chop an aubergine, a red onion, a red bell pepper and 3 small courgettes into small chunks (not dice; think about half a wine cork) and put in a solid ovenproof dish with a tin of peeled plum tomatoes. Break up the tomatoes with a spoon and mix in 8 thinly sliced garlic cloves, 8 sprigs of thyme, a few generous glugs of olive oil and some seasoning. Roast at 190°C/Gas Mark 5 for an hour, stirring once or twice. Some add a tablespoon of red wine vinegar to perk it up before serving. Really good with Gruyère in buckwheat pancakes.

Garlic & Tomato: *See Tomato & Garlic, page 259*
Garlic & Truffle: *See Truffle & Garlic, page 116*
Garlic & Walnut: *See Walnut & Garlic, page 236*
Garlic & Washed-rind Cheese: *See Washed-rind Cheese & Garlic, page 60*

Garlic & White Fish: Aioli turns ordinary white fish into a bit of a feast, especially in the case of *bourride*, an aioli-thickened fish stew from Provence. *Skordalia* is a Greek dip of garlicky mashed potato that's delicious served with grilled or poached fish fillets – see Potato & Garlic, page 90.

Truffle

The price of fresh truffles usually means that they're used sparingly, and allowed to dominate without other ingredients getting in the way of their musky, pungent complexity. 'Truffle flavour' has, of course, become increasingly ubiquitous. The flavour of white truffles has been successfully synthesised in the form of a compound known as bis(methylthio)methane, which is used to make the truffle oil that is drizzled, not always advisedly, over thousands of restaurant dishes, and sometimes injected into inferior, flavourless truffles for shaving tableside. Fungal fraud aside, there's nothing wrong with synthetic truffle oil, which can work wonders pepping up mashed potato, cabbage, cauliflower or macaroni cheese, and will certainly give you an idea of what truffle tastes like if you've never had the real thing. In the same way that reading the pass notes for *Anna Karenina*, rather than the actual novel, will give you an idea of the book.

Truffle & Asparagus: *See Asparagus & Truffle, page 131*

Truffle & Bacon: Everything tastes better with bacon, so the saying goes: even truffles. From an 1833 recipe for 'Truffles with Champagne' by Richard Dolby: 'Take ten or twelve well-cleaned truffles; put them into a stewpan on rashers of bacon, add a bay leaf, a seasoned bouquet, a little grated bacon, some stock, a slice or two of ham, and a bottle of champagne; cover them with a piece of buttered paper, put on the lid, and set the stewpan on hot ashes; put fire on the top and let them stew for an hour. When done, drain them on a clean cloth, and serve on a folded napkin.'

Truffle & Beef: *See Beef & Truffle, page 48*
Truffle & Blue Cheese: *See Blue Cheese & Truffle, page 64*

Truffle & Cabbage: The characteristic aroma of truffle is attributable to a number of chemical compounds, but it's primarily dimethyl sulphide (DMS) that truffle-hunting pigs and dogs are trained to detect. Truffle grower Gareth Renowden writes that at high concentrations DMS smells like cooked cabbage – a similarity you might note in some oils made with truffle flavouring as opposed to the real thing. Marco Pierre White exploits the harmony of the two ingredients in his truffled cabbage soup, and at Nobu they're paired with beef in truffled cabbage steak.

Truffle & Cauliflower: *See Cauliflower & Truffle, page 124*

Truffle & Celery: Cookery writer Elisabeth Luard recommends mixing celeriac purée with an equal amount of mashed potato, lots of cream and some grated truffle – although not before noting that truffles are an acquired taste, redolent of 'old socks, the locker-room after a rugby match, unwashed underpants, methylated spirits, gas-pump on a wet Saturday'.

Truffle & Chicken: In the early twentieth century, Lyons was unusual in that its restaurants were dominated by female chefs, or *cuisinières*, the greatest of whom was the legendary Mère Fillioux. At her tiny restaurant on the rue Duquesne, customers would be served an unchanging menu of charcuterie, quenelles of pike, globe artichokes with foie gras, and *poularde en demi-deuil* – chicken in half-mourning – in which the golden skin of a plump bird was darkened with slices of black truffle slipped underneath. The Ivy in London pairs chicken and truffle in roast *poulet des Landes*. A. A. Gill, who wrote the restaurant's cookbook, claims to have done so in order to learn the recipe. It's a deal more fiddly than the *demi-deuil*, as it involves stuffing the chicken's partially boned legs with a mixture of shallots, mushrooms, breadcrumbs, parsley and foie gras, before they are poached and then roasted with the rest of the chicken. The leg is then served with the breast meat, *gratin dauphinoise* and a thick gravy made of a mixture of chicken and dark meat stocks, black truffle and Madeira.

Truffle & Egg: It is a truth universally acknowledged that anyone in possession of a fresh truffle must put it in a lidded container with some eggs. When the truffle has had a day or two to infuse the fatty egg yolk, make a simple omelette, scrambled egg or fried egg dish. You won't be sorry. Fat is essential for releasing and carrying the flavour of truffle; butter and goose fat give particularly good results. Some cooks use garlic to intensify the flavour of truffle served with eggs, by rubbing a cut clove either on a slice of toast or on the inside of the receptacle that the eggs are beaten in before scrambling.

Truffle & Garlic: Garlic is often invoked as a flavour descriptor for truffle. Brillat-Savarin reports that he and some 'men of unimpeachable integrity' agreed that white truffles from Piedmont had a 'taste of garlic, which mars their perfection not at all'. Black truffles are less garlicky than white and a little sweeter and mustier, with a more obvious note of mushroom in the spectrum of forest flavours. Both white and black truffles combine easily with garlic and could probably turn polystyrene into a rich, sticky feast.

Truffle & Globe Artichoke: *See Globe Artichoke & Truffle, page 129*

Truffle & Liver: Foie gras studded with pieces of black truffle is about as understated a combination as a gold-plated Ferrari. Maguelonne Toussaint-Samat writes that integral pieces of truffle detract from the singular quality of foie gras; better, in her opinion, to wrap a bacon-larded whole black truffle in paper, cook it in a low oven and serve in thin wisps over sliced foie gras. The two are often paired in dishes *à la Rossini*, most famously Tournedos Rossini, in which the fillet of beef creates an effective bridge between the ingredients, as it does in the burger stuffed with foie gras and truffle and served on a Parmesan bun at Daniel Boulud's Bistro Moderne in New York.

Truffle & Mushroom: *See Mushroom & Truffle, page 80*

Truffle & Pork: Rescued from marauding pirates, all but one of the Swiss Family Robinson decide to stay on the island, having recently discovered a wild boar and some truffles. I could sympathise, as long as there was a nice barrel of Barolo washed up somewhere. As Father says, the truffles are 'very different from the tough leathery things I remember from Europe', reasoning that he'd only ever tasted truffles robbed of their freshness during long transportation. Truffles start to oxidise as soon as they're unearthed, at first becoming quite pungent, then fading to a bland bitterness. At a charity auction in 2004, a consortium forked out £28,000 for the second-largest white truffle ever found, which was then locked up in a refrigerated safe at the London restaurant, Zafferano. Then the restaurant manager went away for four days with the key in his pocket. By the time he returned, the truffle was ruined. There's simply no effective way to keep truffles fresh – a problem the Swiss Family might have solved by making truffled wild boar salami, mortadella or pancetta – or their home country's truffled *cervelas* sausage.

Truffle & Potato: *See Potato & Truffle, page 94*

Truffle & Shellfish: Truffle and lobster enjoy an especially harmonious relationship. A key flavour compound of white truffle, bis(methylthio)-methane, which has a sulphurous, garlicky, spicy, mushroom quality, also naturally occurs in lobster (and in shiitake mushrooms and some pungent cheeses such as Camembert). Other crustaceans and scallops are also often paired with truffle, and cabbage forms a common trio.

Truffle & Soft Cheese: *See Soft Cheese & Truffle, page 73*

Cabbage

This section includes various types of cabbage, including preserved cabbage and Brussels sprouts, and a wide range of flavours, from the fresh spiciness of raw cabbage to the corridor-filling sulphurousness of well-cooked common cabbage. Somewhere between. these two extremes lie pickled sauerkraut and *kimchi*. Cooked cabbage pairs brilliantly with other pungent ingredients such as garlic, onion, truffle and mustard. Salty bacon or anchovy knocks back some of the bitter flavours – think how bacon tames sprouts. Savoy and Chinese (or Napa) cabbages are revered for their fine flavours, and their crinkly leaves are ideal for absorbing sauces in stir-fries. Intriguingly, cabbages have a clear affinity for apple, and sprouts are delectable with both dried cranberries and redcurrant jelly.

Cabbage & Apple: *See Apple & Cabbage, page 270*

Cabbage & Bacon: A big, brazen, unrefined pairing that resists gentrification. Mrs Beeton noted that a good stomach was needed to digest it. This warm autumn dish, inspired by panzanella, is so rustic it should come in a John Deere salad bowl. Tear half a slightly stale ciabatta loaf into chunks and grill them. Roast 500g halved small Brussels sprouts in olive oil at 180°C/Gas Mark 4 for 15 minutes. Meanwhile, slowly fry a chopped garlic clove, 5 spring onions cut into 1cm pieces and 200g lardons in 2 tbsp olive oil until the lardons have browned and a good deal of their fat has rendered into the pan. Remove with a slotted spoon and add to the sprouts with the toasted bread. Toss the mixture, put it back in the oven and turn off the heat. Deglaze the bacon and onion pan with 2 tbsp red wine vinegar, add 1–2 tbsp water or chicken stock and cook for 1 minute. Remove the sprout mixture from the oven and drizzle it with the contents of the pan. Season, add 2 tbsp dried cranberries and toss. Serve while still warm.

Cabbage & Beef: Irish-Americans may claim corned beef and cabbage as their own but it's not a traditional dish in Ireland, where cabbage was more likely to accompany a thick wedge of boiled gammon. During the great wave of Irish immigration in the mid-nineteenth century, beef was far more plentiful, and cheaper, in America than it was in Ireland, and the newly arrived took to curing and cooking it as they would a gammon joint, serving it with the same accompaniments of cabbage and potatoes. (In Jewish neighbourhoods a similar practice was to brine joints of brisket with spices, then smoke them to make pastrami.)

Cabbage & Blue Cheese: *See Blue Cheese & Cabbage, page 62*
Cabbage & Carrot: *See Carrot & Cabbage, page 227*
Cabbage & Chestnut: *See Chestnut & Cabbage, page 232*

Cabbage & Chicken: Some might see the presence of the Brussels sprout on the Christmas table as a Scrooge-like corrective to all the fun, but its role is essential. The bitterness of sprouts, which they owe to their high levels of glucosilonates, offsets the hefty turkey, stuffing, bread sauce, roast potatoes, parsnips, chipolatas and chestnuts. If you find their bitterness unpleasant, you might try growing Thompson & Morgan's Trafalgar F1 sprouts from seed. They're bred to be sweeter, and the company claims they'll have children coming 'back for seconds', even offering a money-back guarantee if you don't think they're the best you've ever tasted.

Cabbage & Chilli: *See Chilli & Cabbage, page 208*
Cabbage & Egg: *See Egg & Cabbage, page 133*

Cabbage & Garlic: If, as Mark Twain has it in *Pudd'nhead Wilson*, 'cauliflower is nothing but a cabbage with a college education', cavolo nero is a cabbage with a holiday home in Tuscany. It's not, however, too refined to submit to simple home cooking, as in this lovely bruschetta. Trim off the stalks from the cavolo nero and blanch the leaves for a few minutes. Drain, cool and squeeze them dry, then chop and fry in garlicky olive oil. Season and serve on toasted, robust white bread. I add a pinch of chilli flakes and maybe a short, sharp grating of Parmesan. Kale will do fine if you can't get the fancy stuff.

Cabbage & Ginger: *See Ginger & Cabbage, page 309*
Cabbage & Juniper: *See Juniper & Cabbage, page 323*
Cabbage & Lamb: *See Lamb & Cabbage, page 50*
Cabbage & Nutmeg: *See Nutmeg & Cabbage, page 221*

Cabbage & Onion: Cabbage (or sprouts) and onion add flavour to cooked potatoes in bubble and squeak, the UK's favourite leftover dish. In the nineteenth century, bubble and squeak was a fried combination of leftover beef and cabbage, but the dish is now invariably meatless. I love it so much that I often cook more potatoes than we can possibly eat with the roast chicken on Sunday. Whether premeditated surplus actually counts as leftovers is, however, a taxing philosophical problem. Processed-food companies now sell ready-prepared bubble and squeak, i.e. leftovers with no main meal from which they've been left over, which raises a number of dizzying questions. Can, for example, leftovers left over from nothing actually be said to exist? And what do you call it if you have any left over?

Cabbage & Pork: Cabbage puts pork's fattiness to good use – for example in *choucroute garnie* from Alsace, the traditional English side dish of buttered cabbage with roast pork, and the crisp, shredded raw cabbage that's served on the side of the Japanese fried pork cutlet, *tonkatsu*. My favourite use for this super-compatible pair, however, is a French *chou farci*, or stuffed cabbage.

You can stuff individual leaves, arranging them in rows like a parade of toads, or layer leaves lasagne-fashion with the stuffing mixture. But for my money the best kind of *chou farci* is the size and weight of a bowling ball, served cut into Edam-like wedges that showcase the stuffing. For the forcemeat, cook 2 finely chopped shallots and 3 finely chopped garlic cloves in oil until softened. Soak 30g crustless bread in a little milk. Mince 300g pork shoulder, 300g beef steak and 150g pork belly. Add the shallot mix and disintegrated bread to the raw meat with 1 egg, 1 tbsp each chopped parsley and chives, ½ tsp dried thyme, some seasoning and, most importantly, ½ tsp of the world's most beautiful spice mixture – and the very making of this dish – *quatre-épices*. *Quatre-épices* is a hot, sweet, potent blend of white pepper, nutmeg, clove and ginger. Parboil a whole Savoy cabbage for 10 minutes, allow it to cool, then fold back the leaves, taking care not to snap them off. When you're left with a cabbage centre about the size of a small tangerine, slice it out and replace with an equal volume of stuffing. Replace the leaves layer by layer, cramming a measure of stuffing between each, until your cabbage is fully reassembled. Tie with string to secure. Finally, melt a few tablespoons of butter in a lidded pot big enough to take the cabbage, add a chopped small onion and carrot and cook until soft. Throw in a bouquet garni and some seasoning, add 250ml chicken or vegetable stock and lower in your cabbage. Cover and simmer for 1½ hours. When it's done, take the cabbage out and keep it warm while you strain the cooking liquid into a jug to serve as a sauce. See also Clove & Ginger, page 220.

Cabbage & Potato: *See Potato & Cabbage, page 89*

Cabbage & Shellfish: Dimethyl sulphide (DMS) is an important component in the flavour of cabbage, with an odour variously described as cabbage-like and slightly oceanic – fittingly enough, as it's largely responsible for the odour of green (and some brown) seaweeds. It's also present in seafood: the primary flavour of scallops comes from a precursor that releases DMS (a precursor is a compound involved in a chemical reaction that releases another compound). DMS has been used, not always successfully, to recreate more authentic seafood flavours. More importantly from the home cook's perspective, it proves the deep affinity cabbage has with shellfish – if you needed proof having taken a single bite of a minced prawn and Chinese cabbage dumpling. See also Truffle & Cabbage, page 115.

Cabbage & Smoked Fish: *See Smoked Fish & Cabbage, page 164*
Cabbage & Truffle: *See Truffle & Cabbage, page 115*

Swede

The hot, peppery sweetness and dense flesh of swede can be sensational when you play up to its natural spiciness, as in Scotland where it's often seasoned with nutmeg. Sweet, spicy star anise is another obvious partner, and so are sweet, earthy flavours such as root vegetables and roasted garlic. Unlike parsnip and potato, swede has a rather good flavour when raw – it's hot and sweet like a radish.

Swede & Anise: Combine swede with star anise in dark, Asian braised dishes or, as Hugh Fearnley-Whittingstall does, with leftover goose in pasties. The intense sweetness of the anise accentuates swede's savouriness, while its deeply aromatic character draws attention away from the vegetable's somewhat vulgar edge.

Swede & Beef: *See Beef & Swede, page 47*

Swede & Carrot: Served as a duo of fat, waterlogged sticks at school. We would invariably eat the carrots and leave the swede on the side of the plate. Scientists now believe that the aversion to bitter vegetables, indeed all bitter flavours, is genetically determined, and boils down to sensitivity to the compound 6-n-propylthiouracil, known in flavour-scientist circles as 'prop'. If you can strongly detect the taste of prop in broccoli, for instance, you may well be one of the 25 per cent of the population known as 'super-tasters', which is more of a hindrance than it sounds. Super-tasters, who are more likely to be female, find brassicas, grapefruit and black coffee unbearably intense. Another quarter of the population can't detect prop at all. I might have put my childhood dislike of swede down to being a super-taster if it hadn't vanished overnight in my late teens, like acne or the desire to wear purple eye shadow. Carrot sweetens swede, and they're excellent mashed together with lots of butter and white pepper.

Swede & Lamb: *See Lamb & Swede, page 53*

Swede & Nutmeg: Swede is thought to be a hybrid of cabbage and turnip, and has inherited its parents' weakness for nutmeg. In Scotland, nutmeg is often used to season buttery mashed swede, known as neeps. Further north, the Finnish do something similar in a dish called *lanttulaatikko*, except the mash is creamier and it's served with ham or pork. Neither version is better than the other, unless you're playing Scrabble. See also Potato & Swede, page 93, and Lamb & Swede, page 53.

Swede & Pork: *See Pork & Swede, page 37*
Swede & Potato: *See Potato & Swede, page 93*

Cauliflower

The palest member of the brassica family in colour, but not necessarily in flavour. Cut into large florets and quickly steamed, cauliflower can be the essence of *cucina bianca*: gently tending to bland. Roasted, fried or puréed, however, it reaches its full musky, earthy potential, and makes a great match for other bold, spicy flavours. Strong cheeses, chilli, cumin and garlic all work well, and serve to emphasise cauliflower's sweetness.

Cauliflower & Almond: Anthony Flinn, who has worked at El Bulli and now cooks at his own restaurant, Anthony's, in Leeds, created a cauliflower trifle – a purée of cauliflower and cream with grape jelly and brioche. He's also conceived a cauliflower and almond crème caramel. This consists of a layer of salted caramel under a crème caramel made with cauliflower purée, topped with warm almond cream.

Cauliflower & Anchovy: *See Anchovy & Cauliflower, page 162*
Cauliflower & Broccoli: *See Broccoli & Cauliflower, page 125*

Cauliflower & Caper: Cauliflower is broccoli that can't be bothered. Where its dark-green cruciferous cousin is frisky, iron-deep and complex, cauliflower is keener on the quiet life, snug under its blanket of cheese. It needs to be livened up a bit, which is where capers come in. You don't so much add capers to cauliflower – you set them on it. Cook a chopped onion in olive oil until soft, add some chilli flakes and chopped garlic and stir for a few seconds. Add some blanched cauliflower florets, breadcrumbs and raisins and cook until the breadcrumbs are browned. Finally add capers and parsley, warm them through, then serve the mixture tossed with rigatoni.

Cauliflower & Caviar: *See Caviar & Cauliflower, page 153*

Cauliflower & Chilli: Deep-frying transforms cauliflower. It takes on a sweet, almost musky taste and a creamy texture. I like to give it the salt-and-pepper-squid treatment and serve it with a chilli sauce. Cut a cauliflower into florets the size of button mushrooms and dredge with a mixture of cornflour, salt and black pepper. Deep-fry the florets in groundnut or sunflower oil and serve with a sweet chilli dipping sauce.

Cauliflower & Chocolate: When Heston Blumenthal wanted to show cauliflower how much he loved it, he came bearing chocolate. The result was a cauliflower risotto with a carpaccio of cauliflower and chocolate jelly. The idea was that each component would release its flavour in sequence, culminating in a burst of bitterness from the specially encapsulated chocolate that Blumenthal compared to an espresso at the end of a meal. To prepare the dish, he made a cauliflower stock, a cauliflower cream, cauliflower discs, dried cauliflower, a cauliflower velouté, chocolate jelly cubes and chocolate jelly discs – and *then* he made the risotto.

Cauliflower & Cumin: *See Cumin & Cauliflower, page 83*

Cauliflower & Garlic: If you've ever tasted cauliflower and garlic soup or purée, you'll know that the cooking and pulverising processes bring out their flavours in the strongest possible way. It puts me in mind of cauliflower cheese made with a particularly ripe Camembert. Roast the cauliflower with whole garlic cloves and you'll still enjoy a rich result, with sweet nutty flavours but without the farmyard air.

Cauliflower & Hard Cheese: In New York I saw a stall in the Greenmarket on Union Square decorated with an arrangement of differently coloured cauliflowers: ivory, purple, lime green and a pale-orange variety called the cheddar cauliflower that I'd never seen before. If I was being pedantic, in colour terms it might have more accurately been called the Double Gloucester, but I kept this to myself and simply asked the stallholder what it tasted like. 'Cauliflower,' he said, as if I was dumb to ask, but I bought one anyway, as by that point cauliflower cheese was a foregone conclusion for that evening's supper. I might equally, in fact, have made it with Double Gloucester, as its rich butteriness and hints of citrus and onion make a delicious cheese sauce. But there was none to be had, so I used a heady Gruyère, whose combination of potency and nuttiness is a match for the cauliflower's.

Cauliflower & Nutmeg: It was Louis XIV who popularised cauliflower in France. He liked it boiled in stock, seasoned with nutmeg and served with melted butter.

Cauliflower & Potato: Like all cruciferous vegetables, the more you cut cauliflower, the more sulphurous it tastes. Puréed in a soup, it can go from meek to funky quicker than a Sunday-school teacher on the hooch. But its ruder notes can be tamped down with cream or potato. Choose the latter to make a sweet base for this *aloo gobi* soup. *Aloo gobi* is a popular Indian dish of spiced cauliflower and potato, served wet or dry. Spicy vegetable soups are too often let down by a curried muddiness, whereas this one captures the vivid, fresh spiciness of the dish that inspired it. Cook a finely chopped onion in groundnut oil until soft, then stir in 1 tsp very finely chopped fresh ginger, 1 chopped deseeded green chilli, ¼ tsp ground turmeric, ½ tsp ground coriander and 1 tsp ground cumin. Add 150g diced peeled potato and ½ cauliflower, chopped into florets. Stir until they are coated in the spices, then add 750ml cold water and bring to the boil. Simmer for 15–20 minutes, until the vegetables are soft. Cool a little, then blend until smooth. Serve garnished with chopped, fresh coriander leaves.

Cauliflower & Saffron: *See Saffron & Cauliflower, page 179*

Cauliflower & Shellfish: Cauliflower purée is often served with seared scallops. Its bitter flavour contrasts with the sweetness of the shellfish and chimes with the slight bitterness on its caramelised crust. On a different note, the Japanese food writer Machiko Chiba makes a salad of blanched cauliflower and broccoli mixed with fresh crabmeat and dressed with soy, mirin, sesame oil, rice wine and sugar. She recommends a Halbtrocken Riesling as the ideal wine match.

Cauliflower & Truffle: Truffle and cooked cauliflower have a flavour overlap. David Rosengarten suggests enhancing the subtle truffle notes already present in a cauliflower risotto by shaving over white truffle before serving. He describes the flavour of truffle as a combination of cheese, garlic, cauliflower and sex. Like sleeping with the greengrocer, in other words.

Cauliflower & Walnut: I used to go to a little café for lunch where they made the most delicious raw cauliflower, walnut and date salad. I only wish I'd asked for the recipe, as reconstructing the dressing has proved difficult. I'm there, pretty much, but there's still something missing (if you think you know what it is, please let me know). The white cabbage flavour of raw cauliflower combined with the dried fruit might put you in mind of a coleslaw with raisins, but the chunkier texture, the extreme sweetness of the dates, and the soured cream make it discernibly different. Cut a cauliflower into small florets about 2cm long, 1cm across. For each 100g cauliflower florets, chop up 1 Medjool date and break 5 or 6 walnut halves in half again. Mix in a bowl and (for around 200–300g cauliflower) dress with a combination of 150ml soured cream, 2 tsp lemon juice, 2 tsp caster sugar, ¼ tsp salt and a grind of black pepper. Mix thoroughly and it's ready to eat.

Broccoli

Different varieties of broccoli balance varying proportions of bitterness and sweetness. Calabrese, the familiar bushy variety, is towards the sweeter end of the scale, while purple sprouting has a more pungent depth of flavour and a bitterness taken to extremes by broccoli raab. *Kai-lan*, or Chinese broccoli, is closely related to calabrese and is similarly sweet, but has lots of stalk and leaf and not much head, which makes it juicier. Joy Larkcom remarks on its deliciousness and how easy it is to grow; she also notes its botanical similarity to the rightly celebrated Portuguese Tronchuda cabbage. All varieties have a great predilection for salty ingredients – hence their frequent pairing with anchovies and Parmesan in Italian cooking, blue cheese in Britain, or soy sauce and black beans in China.

Broccoli & Anchovy: *See Anchovy & Broccoli, page 161*

Broccoli & Bacon: Broccoli and pancetta make a delicious bittersweet, salty combination. Add sun-dried tomatoes, Parmesan, pine nuts and chilli for an Italian combination that's almost Asian in its extremes of sweet, sour, salty, hot and umami. Toast 75g pine nuts and set them aside. In a large frying pan, over a medium heat, flavour 3 tbsp olive oil with 10 dried chillies and 6 sliced garlic cloves, removing the garlic when golden along with the chillies. Put 400g linguine on to cook, meanwhile adding 200g cubed pancetta to the garlicky oil. Fry until crisp, then toss in 400g broccoli cut into small florets, making sure they are well coated in the oil. Cook for 4 minutes, add 100g sliced sun-dried tomatoes and cook for a minute longer. Add 3–5 tbsp of the pasta cooking water to loosen the mixture. Drain the pasta and add it to the frying pan with half of the pine nuts. Turn the heat off, season, and mix thoroughly. Divide between 4 plates and scatter generously with the remaining pine nuts and some grated Parmesan.

Broccoli & Beef: A partnership forged on their shared ferrous tang as much as the bittersweet contrast. Paired in a popular Chinese-American stir-fry with salty oyster sauce, ginger and garlic. If, however, you're feeling wan and actively craving the bitter iron flavour of rare meat, a quick-seared steak should hit the spot, served with broccoli cooked with garlic and anchovies.

Broccoli & Blue Cheese: *See Blue Cheese & Broccoli, page 62*

Broccoli & Cauliflower: Bushy calabrese broccoli and cauliflower both belong to the *Brassica oleracea* family. They have many flavour compounds in common, which is evident when you nibble them raw. Cooking clarifies their differences – broccoli's bitter depths of iron versus cauliflower's thick sulphurousness. A hybrid called broccoflower looks, as you might expect it to, like a queasy cauliflower and tastes like weak broccoli. In my experience people tend to love or hate broccoli, and the point of a vegetable that's just like it, except less so, is lost on me. The other variety of green cauliflower is perhaps better known as Romanesco, in equal parts famous and frightening for its custard-green colouring and fractal swirls that give it the appearance of an ancient Thai pagoda. Or a prog-rock album cover. It has a milder, less sulphurous flavour than cauliflower or broccoli.

Broccoli & Chilli: Like cauliflower, broccoli takes on a richer, sweeter flavour when roasted. Red chilli (dried and smoky or fresh and sweet) makes an ideal companion. See also Anchovy & Broccoli, page 161.

Broccoli & Garlic: The most fun you can have eating healthily. Stir-fry them with ginger in oyster sauce or cook them, with or without anchovies, in the classic style outlined in Anchovy & Broccoli on page 161 and serve with pasta. Or try this Thai-inspired noodle dish. This makes one serving. Rehydrate a sheet of fine egg noodles as per the instructions on the packet, drain them and pat dry. Heat 1 tbsp groundnut oil in a wok and fry 3 garlic cloves, cut into quarters. When golden, remove with a slotted spoon and set aside. Add the noodles and 100g small broccoli florets to the oil and fry for 3 minutes, stirring constantly. Scramble a lightly beaten egg into the pan, mixing it thoroughly with the noodles, then add a sauce made with 2 tsp light soy, 1 tsp dark soy, 1 tsp oyster sauce, 1 tsp sugar and 1 tbsp water. Mix well, heat through for a minute, sprinkle lightly with white pepper and serve garnished with the garlic pieces.

Broccoli & Hard Cheese: *See Hard Cheese & Broccoli, page 66*

Broccoli & Lemon: For all broccoli's good points, it does lose its heat very quickly after cooking. The Italian restaurant Orso in London has the answer: serve it warm, not hot, with a squeeze of lemon. If it just turned up like that at the table without any explanation, you might be disappointed, but with a cunning bit of neuro-linguistic programming they forewarn you that it comes warm, which makes it as miraculously delicious as the slow-roast pork with crackling it would be foolish not to order it with.

Broccoli & Peanut: *See Peanut & Broccoli, page 23*
Broccoli & Pork: *See Pork & Broccoli, page 33*
Broccoli & Walnut: *See Walnut & Broccoli, page 235*

Globe Artichoke

The humdrum origins of the artichoke – it's the flower of a thistle – belie its wondrous and complex flavour. See Globe Artichoke & Lamb on page 128 for a full description. Globe artichokes contain a phenolic compound called cynarin, which has the peculiar effect of making anything you eat directly afterwards taste sweet. It temporarily inhibits the sweet receptors in your taste buds, so that when you follow a bite of artichoke with, say, a sip of water, flushing the compound off your tongue, the receptors start working again and the abrupt contrast fools the brain into thinking you've just swallowed a mouthful of sugar solution. This makes for a diverting, if swiftly tedious, party game – sweet radicchio! – but it's bad news for wine. And the enemy of wine is my enemy. The problem can be minimised by using ingredients that create a bridge between the wine and the artichoke (or simply taking a bite of something else before you take a sip of wine). Or you could ditch the wine altogether and drink Cynar, an artichoke-flavoured liqueur from Italy.

Globe Artichoke & Bacon: In Lazio, a boyfriend and I were speeding through a landscape of fairytale castles, well on our way to not living happily ever after. We had been arguing with such uninterrupted intensity that it was only a promising road sign that reminded us that it was well past lunchtime and we were hungry. Our motherly Italian hostess, perhaps picking up on the friction between us, took pity and led us to a table under an olive tree. Mercifully soon, she brought a label-less bottle of cold, dry white wine, an enormous spoon and a terracotta dish of something covered in breadcrumbs and cheese, molten bubbles popping on the surface like the meniscus of a volcano. My boyfriend, or ex-boyfriend, or whatever he was at that moment, took the spoon and, breaking through the crust, emerged with a steaming heap of rigatoni, pancetta and artichokes, in a rich béchamel savoury-sweet with Parmesan. They say hunger is the best sauce, but if that lunch under the olive tree is anything to go by, the point in a relationship where *it doesn't matter any more* runs it a close second. We smiled at each other. I topped up our glasses. He piled the pasta on our plates. The bitter, nutty greenness of the artichoke cut through the richness of pancetta and cheese. It was by far the best last date I've ever had. If *your* relationship is on the rocks, get 200g rigatoni on to cook. Soften a finely chopped onion and 2 garlic cloves in olive oil with 75g sliced pancetta. Add 4–6 cooked artichoke bottoms (good jar ones will do), sliced into sixths. In a bowl, mix 125ml milk with 150ml double cream and 50g grated Parmesan. The pasta should be *al dente* by now. Drain it, empty back into the pan and add the milky, creamy, cheesy mixture and the onion and artichokes. Stir and check for seasoning, then transfer to a baking dish. Cut a ball of mozzarella into slices and lay them on top. Cover with a mixture of 50g breadcrumbs and 25g grated Parmesan and bake for

30 minutes at 200°C/Gas Mark 6, covering it with foil if it looks in danger of burning. Serve with a bottle of cold, cheap Italian white.

Globe Artichoke & Hard Cheese: *See Hard Cheese & Globe Artichoke, page 67*

Globe Artichoke & Lamb: Describing the flavour of globe artichokes could be a parlour game. Some say it's a little like asparagus but I'd say asparagus has a greener flavour, and artichoke bottoms taste more like calabrese broccoli stalks, cooked in a mushroomy vegetable stock until soft, then smothered in butter, with a hint of pewter. The flavour is wonderful, but the magic really resides in the texture – dense, yielding and velvety, it's the foie gras of vegetables. Artichokes are a spring vegetable in Italy and Spain, and make a seasonal pairing with lamb, especially in stews. Lamb seems to mellow the vegetable's bitterness in a way that beef and pork don't. The only drawback to lamb and artichoke stew is having to peel and chop globe artichokes. You end up looking as if you've been playing pat-a-cake with Edward Scissorhands. You *could* use tinned or frozen artichokes, but don't. They're no substitute in either flavour or textural terms. Like beauty, flavour is pain.

Globe Artichoke & Lemon: Fly to Rome at Easter time, and buy yourself a paper bag of *carciofi alla guida* – deep-fried whole artichokes. Find some lemon wedges and a wodge of napkins and eat them under a tree while they're still hot. Boiled or steamed artichokes can be a tough match for wine, but fried they'd go nicely with a fresh, acidic, dry Prosecco, if you can handle the social stigma of being slumped under a tree with a bottle of booze and a brown paper bag.

Globe Artichoke & Mint: The seriousness of globe artichoke is lightened by mint. The two ingredients famously come together in *carciofi alla romana*, in which the artichokes are trimmed, have chopped mint and garlic stuffed between their leaves, and are then simmered, stem-end up, in a combination of water, lemon juice, oil and more mint. Lamb and artichoke stews are also garnished with a generous scattering of mint.

Globe Artichoke & Oyster: In an early-seventeenth-century manuscript called *The Fruit, Herbs and Vegetables of Italy*, Giacomo Castelvetro cites the pairing of small cooking artichokes with oysters and beef marrow in little pies. These days the pairing of artichoke and oyster is most popular in a soup or bisque in oyster-mad Louisiana.

Globe Artichoke & Pea: *See Pea & Globe Artichoke, page 202*

Globe Artichoke & Pork: In France and Italy, globe artichokes are stuffed with minced pork or sausage meat, pushed between their trimmed bracts. It's a little fussy for both cook and diner, but the flavour combination is terrific and, allowed to infiltrate its leaves, pork lends artichoke a moreish saltiness. I combine them in a pie. Drain and rinse a tin of artichoke hearts, cut them each in half and pat dry. Line a 20cm pie tin with shortcrust pastry and spread 250g sausage meat over it. Arrange the artichokes on top, then cover with another 250g sausage meat. Cover with a pastry lid, seal the edges and make a little hole in the centre. Bake for an hour at 180°C/Gas Mark 4. Best eaten cold with plenty of salad and pickles.

Globe Artichoke & Potato: The Jerusalem artichoke is not related to the globe artichoke but was named after it because of its flavour, which many would say was a cross between globe artichokes and top-quality potatoes. Jerusalem artichokes would arguably be more popular if they weren't so famously difficult to digest. A combination of globe artichoke and potato is kinder on the stomach. In Provence, they're thinly sliced and baked together in olive oil and garlic (Escoffier ritzed the dish up by substituting truffle for garlic and butter for olive oil). Or you might pair them cold in a salad with a mayonnaise deliciously enhanced with flesh scraped from the cooked leaves. In Italy the two are combined in soup and, according to *The Silver Spoon*, in a pie.

Globe Artichoke & Prosciutto: *See Prosciutto & Globe Artichoke, page 172*

Globe Artichoke & Shellfish: Globe artichokes contain cynarin, a chemical that gives them a strange and insincere sweetness. Shellfish is a good pairing because it has a natural, more pleasing sweetness and its saltiness points up artichoke's tastier qualities. You might remove a cooked globe artichoke's tough outer leaves, purple inner leaves and hairy choke to create a 'cup' in which to serve crab, lobster or prawns in mayonnaise or vinaigrette. Or make a hot dip by mixing thin slices of cooked artichoke heart with crabmeat, mayonnaise, finely chopped shallot and grated Parmesan and baking under a herb crumb crust. Eat fresh from the oven with crackers. Hearty enough for an iron smelter's cocktail party.

Globe Artichoke & Truffle: In 1891 Anton Chekhov wrote to his brother complaining about the restaurants in Monte Carlo. 'They fleece one frightfully and feed one magnificently ... Every morsel is rigged out with lots of artichokes, truffles and nightingales' tongues of all sorts.' That artichokes have so frequently been paired with the most expensive ingredients – truffles and foie gras – is testament to the thistle's extraordinary attraction. Even today they're served together in the best restaurants. Three-star French chef Guy Savoy has a signature dish of the earthy, if not very down-to-earth, soup *d'artichaut à la truffe noire*, served with a brioche layered with mushrooms and truffle butter.

Asparagus

Salty dairy ingredients are a heavenly match for asparagus: butter, Parmesan and hollandaise sauce simultaneously contrast with and enhance its sweet, sulphurous vegetable flavour. Other sulphurous-tasting foods, such as eggs, crustaceans and garlic, also make harmonious partners. Thin spears of asparagus are called sprue, and tend to have a more piquant flavour than the full-grown variety. White asparagus is grown from the same seed as green but is covered with soil to inhibit the production of chlorophyll. It's pretty much as flavourless as it is lacking in colour, and while its apologists describe it as subtle, mild or 'dainty', I can't find a whole lot to like in a slimy, anaemic tube free of the rich nuttiness that makes proper green asparagus such a treat. For some reason, the Spanish, who have so much to recommend them gastronomically, put it in salads, where it lies hidden among the leaves like a chef's long-forgotten finger.

Asparagus & Almond: *See Almond & Asparagus, page 241*

Asparagus & Anise: Tarragon isn't quite as flimsy as its slight green leaves suggest – think how it flavours vinegars, mustards and pickles. Asparagus, none too shyly flavoured itself, is often paired with tarragon. The spears might be served with the tarragon- and shallot-flavoured Béarnaise sauce, while asparagus, tarragon and egg make a fine trio in an omelette, baked en cocotte or in a warm tart in which asparagus forms the spokes.

Asparagus & Egg: *See Egg & Asparagus, page 132*
Asparagus & Hard Cheese: *See Hard Cheese & Asparagus, page 65*
Asparagus & Lemon: *See Lemon & Asparagus, page 303*

Asparagus & Mint: American chef Daniel Boulud steams asparagus over a little water with fresh mint and lemon zest added to it, then dresses it with extra virgin olive oil, lemon juice and more mint. If you're trying this yourself, go easy on the mint. You don't want to go turning your asparagus spear into a toothbrush.

Asparagus & Mushroom: Morels are a great seasonal match for asparagus. They like to grow on charred ground, which might explain their slightly smoky character when fresh, and their love for sulphurous flavours like asparagus. Chef David Waltuck of Chanterelle serves an asparagus flan with sautéed morels in a creamy sauce made with oysters and Madeira. Egg works exceptionally well with both flavours and often forms a trio with them – the classic *oeufs Jessica* pairs baked eggs with minced morels, asparagus and a little quality meat stock.

Asparagus & Oily Fish: *See Oily Fish & Asparagus, page 155*
Asparagus & Orange: *See Orange & Asparagus, page 294*
Asparagus & Pea: *See Pea & Asparagus, page 201*

Asparagus & Peanut: This might seem as incongruous as playing darts in a ballgown but the rich, meaty flavour of asparagus is, in fact, very good with peanuts, especially when given an Asian inflection. Steam your spears and serve them with this peanut dressing: mix 3 tbsp sunflower oil, 3 tbsp lemon juice, 2 tbsp light soy sauce, a pinch of sugar and some seasoning, then stir in 100g chopped roasted unsalted peanuts.

Asparagus & Potato: Share an earthy, nutty character. Jane Grigson recommends boiling new potatoes with asparagus and serving them for lunch with a soft-boiled egg, homemade bread, butter and a Loire white wine. Sancerres from the Loire and Sauvignon Blancs from New Zealand are made from the same grape and have an asparagus quality, which makes them an ideal match for the difficult vegetable.

Asparagus & Prosciutto: *See Prosciutto & Asparagus, page 171*
Asparagus & Shellfish: *See Shellfish & Asparagus, page 139*

Asparagus & Truffle: In his book *Aphrodisiacs*, Peter Levene notes that there is a diuretic in asparagus that stimulates the kidneys and 'excites the urinary passages'. If for any reason this fails to put you in the mood for love, try shaving black truffle, or drizzling a little truffle oil, over your asparagus soup. When cooked, asparagus develops a strong sulphurous-sweet characteristic that goes particularly well with black truffle. Analysis of truffle extract reveals that it contains traces of male-pig sex pheromones, which is thought to account for the sow's happy acquiescence when dragged about the woods all day snuffling in the undergrowth. By all means, make this for your date, but if they like it, you might ask yourself what this says about them.

Asparagus & White Fish: *See White Fish & Asparagus, page 145*

Egg

Side-by-side tastings reveal that hen eggs vary noticeably in their flavour characteristics. If you're lucky, you'll find one with a buttery, naturally salty yolk that makes a mild but very satisfying dipping sauce when soft boiled. Different egg flavours are mainly attributable to their age and storage conditions, although they can also be due to variations in the bird's diet. Some claim that the rare and expensive gull's egg has a fishy flavour (as, apparently, does the penguin's), and that goose and pheasant eggs are gamier, although I can't say I've ever been able to detect either of these. Quail and duck eggs are often described as creamy, but this is mainly attributable to their higher yolk-to-white ratio.

Egg & Anchovy: If you see anchovies lying prostrate on a fried egg, there's probably a Wiener schnitzel underneath. A garnish of anchovy, egg and sometimes caper makes for Wiener schnitzel *à la Holstein*, named after the Prussian diplomat, Friedrich von Holstein, who supposedly ate them for breakfast. There are several variations on the dish, some including caviar, salmon, beetroot, pickles and lobster. Scotch woodcock is an old English recipe that sounds as if it should be a breakfast dish – scrambled eggs on toast with a garnish of anchovies – but was in fact served in genteel Victorian households as the culmination of a six-course meal. If you're going to try this, I recommend a) not eating five courses beforehand and b) soaking the anchovies in milk to soften their flavour. *Nasi lemak* is a Malaysian dish of coconut rice garnished with peanuts, cucumber, boiled eggs, fried anchovies and a spicy tomato sauce.

Egg & Anise: *See Anise & Egg, page 183*

Egg & Asparagus: Cooked asparagus spears are lovely dipped in soft-boiled eggs, especially if you follow Hugh Fearnley-Whittingstall's tip of slicing the tops off and then adding a little butter and a few drops of cider vinegar to each yolk for a hollandaise-like effect. Asparagus is also added to baked eggs (see Asparagus & Mushroom, page 130) and cooked in a frittata. I have an irrational dislike of frittata – or at least of its ubiquity. Don't throw it away: make a frittata. Can't think of anything? Make a frittata. If you've got eggs, you've always got a frittata! Frittatas are cosy, accommodating, practical and slovenly: the culinary equivalent of the tracksuit.

Egg & Bacon: *See Bacon & Egg, page 168*

Egg & Banana: In Japan, omelettes called *tamago yaki* are made with soy and sugar and served in sushi bars as a savoury dish. The sweetened omelette has classic status in French cuisine, where it might be filled with jam, fruit compote or maybe a scattering of pine nuts and served for dessert. What a great idea it is. This version is so simple you can throw it together for breakfast while you're still rubbing your eyes. Make a 3-egg folded omelette as you would ordinarily, except add 1 tbsp caster sugar and a pinch of salt as you beat the eggs. Fry in butter and then fill with a small banana, mashed or sliced as thin as pennies, before folding.

Egg & Basil: *See Basil & Egg, page 214*
Egg & Beef: *See Beef & Egg, page 44*

Egg & Beetroot: The distinguishing ingredients in a 'kiwiburger'. The McDonald's version was launched in New Zealand in 1991, and when it was later discontinued there was such widespread dismay that a campaign was launched to bring it back. At the UK's Gourmet Burger Kitchen chain, where the Kiwi chef Peter Gordon acts as consultant, the kiwiburger comes with a slice of pineapple. The beetroot and pineapple hang around in the background like a fun couple who didn't realise it wasn't a fancy-dress party. The fried egg adds richness, all right, but isn't that the chips' job?

Egg & Bell Pepper: *See Bell Pepper & Egg, page 205*
Egg & Black Pudding: *See Black Pudding & Egg, page 38*

Egg & Cabbage: *Okonomi-yaki* is often described as Japanese pizza, which is about as useful an analogy as calling salami a meaty cucumber. Roughly translated, *okonomi-yaki* means 'as you like it', and is pizza-like insofar as the base is round and flat and then customised with your choice of toppings and seasonings. But in texture and flavour it's a world away. It's made by mixing chopped cabbage, grated Japanese yam and finely chopped spring onions with egg, flour and water. The resulting batter is then poured on to a hotplate, shaped and, when cooked through, topped with pork, bacon, squid or *kimchi* (see Chilli & Cabbage, page 208), or all of them and more besides. To finish, it's decorated with a Pollockesque drip painting of mayonnaise, spicy brown sauce, *katsuobushi* (gossamer wisps of smoked tuna) and seaweed flakes.

Egg & Caviar: *See Caviar & Egg, page 153*

Egg & Celery: Celery salt and hard-boiled eggs are a classic combination. There's something in the citrussy, pine tang of celery that really lifts egg's sulphurous low notes. Quail, duck and hen's eggs are perfectly delicious served like this, although gull's eggs are the ones that make it on to the menus of fancy restaurants. Gull's eggs cost about ten times as much as hen's, not only because of the shortness of the laying season but because just a limited number of collector's licences are granted. Celery salt is, of course, widely available to buy, but you can make your own by lightly toasting celery seeds and crushing them with sea salt. Start with a 1:6 mix and adjust to taste.

Fergus Henderson, by contrast, makes celery salt by baking grated celeriac with salt, and puts a wintry spin on the combination by making a series of dents in a pile of hot, buttery mashed celeriac, placing an egg in each and baking until the white is firm and the yolk just runny.

Egg & Chicken: A stranger combination than you might suppose; you'd be hard pushed to think of a Western recipe that features them both. Chicken omelette, maybe. But do *you* fancy one? There is perhaps some deeply accul-turated discomfort at serving animal and offspring together, although this is absent from Asian culinary traditions. In China, eggs are cracked into chicken soup, chicken fried rice and a chicken congee. In Japan a rice-bowl dish called *oyakodon*, or 'mother and child', consists of chicken, egg and spring onions simmered in a mixture of soy sauce, dashi (dried tuna stock) and mirin (sweet rice wine), then served on rice. Apparently Paul Simon took the title of his song, 'Mother and Child Reunion', from the menu of a Chinese restaurant in New York.

Egg & Chilli: *See Chilli & Egg, page 209*

Egg & Coconut: *Kaya*, a sort of coconut jam (or curd), is made of coconut milk, eggs and sugar, and is spread on buttered toast for breakfast all over Southeast Asia. The same ingredients make a simple and delicious coconut custard pudding. Whisk 4 eggs with 100g sugar, then gradually mix in 250ml coconut milk. Pour into 4 ramekins and place in a baking dish. Carefully pour enough boiling water into the dish to come two-thirds of the way up the sides of the ramekins. Bake at 150°C/Gas Mark 2 for 40 minutes, until just set. See also Coconut & Cinnamon, page 287.

Egg & Cumin: Cumin is a warmer, earthier, but no less delicious seed than celery, for toasting, grinding and mixing with salt for your eggs. Try caraway too, for a trio of flavoured salts to serve with a handsome pyramid of unshelled soft-boiled quail's eggs and let your guests work through them, trying each salt as they go.

Egg & Dill: The clean, sharp flavour of dill is a contrast to egg's sulphurous homeliness. The combination is at its best when the egg's flavour has been maximised by boiling and can stand up to the insistent, citrussy greenness of dill. A simple egg and dill sandwich is hard to beat.

Egg & Ginger: *See Ginger & Egg, page 310*

Egg & Lemon: *Avgolémono* ('egg lemon') is popular in Greece in both sauce and soup form. The writer Alan Davidson noted how it demonstrates the two ingredients' affinity – as do some lemony versions of mayonnaise. To make *avgolémono* soup, bring 1 litre of chicken broth to the boil and add rice or orzo pasta. Towards the end of the rice or pasta's cooking time, whisk 2 eggs with the juice of 1 lemon. Whisk a ladleful of the hot broth into the eggs, then, off the heat, whisk the lemon mixture into the chicken stock little by little. See also Celery & Lamb, page 96.

Egg & Mushroom: *See Mushroom & Egg, page 77*

Egg & Nutmeg: Eggnog is the perfect restorative after an afternoon's Christmas shopping. Pour 3 tbsp rum, brandy or marsala into a cocktail shaker with 4 tbsp milk, 1 egg yolk and some ice. Shake well, then strain into a glass and give it a good freckling of fragrant grated nutmeg. It's like coming in from the cold. The initial warm shock of nutmeg gives way to soothing, thickened milk and the afterglow of rum. And this eggnog tart is so delicious that it's threatening to usurp Christmas pudding. Scald 150ml single cream. Whisk 3 egg yolks with 75g caster sugar, a pinch of salt and a generous grating of nutmeg. Slowly whisk the cream into the eggs. Pour into a clean pan and cook gently, stirring constantly, until the mixture is thick enough to coat the back of the spoon. Remove from the heat and set aside. Thoroughly dissolve 2 tsp gelatine granules in 4 tsp hot water and stir into the custard. Add 3 tbsp rum, 1 tbsp brandy and ½ tsp vanilla extract, stir again, then strain into a glass or ceramic bowl. Grate in a little more nutmeg and put in the fridge. Before the custard sets, whisk the 3 egg whites to soft peaks. Fold them into the custard and pour into a baked, deep sweet pastry case, 23cm in diameter. Chill until set. Serve at room temperature, with plenty more freshly grated nutmeg on top. This also works on a crushed biscuit base.

Egg & Oily Fish: *See Oily Fish & Egg, page 157*

Egg & Onion: In Jewish cookery, boiled egg and spring onion are chopped very finely, mixed with schmaltz (chicken fat), seasoned, chilled and served as an appetiser with challah or rye bread. Mollie Katzen's more piquant version adds parsley and watercress in a soured cream, horseradish and black pepper dressing. See also Potato & Egg, page 90.

Egg & Oyster: *See Oyster & Egg, page 152*
Egg & Parsley: *See Parsley & Egg, page 192*

Egg & Pea: Make it worth cooking too much rice. In China, egg fried rice is considered a meal in its own right, not just an accompaniment, and so it should be. It's quite delicious even reduced to three basic ingredients – rice, egg and peas – but add a few more and you have the mandate of heaven. Finely chop a couple of rashers of smoked bacon and a small onion and fry them in 2 tbsp groundnut oil. Add about 4 handfuls of cold, cooked white rice and give it a good stir to break up the grains. Scatter over a handful of peas and, once all is well heated, drizzle the mixture with 2 beaten eggs and a shake of soy sauce. Allow the egg to cook, giving it a turn now and then. The flavour can only improve if you invest in a carbon-steel or cast-iron wok and season it properly. To the Chinese, the wok is an ingredient in itself, and skilled chefs can impart a quality to dishes that the Cantonese describe as 'wok hay', or 'wok breath' – a combination of flavour, heat and smokiness that comes of knowing how to get the best out of your pan.

Egg & Pork: *See Pork & Egg, page 35*
Egg & Potato: *See Potato & Egg, page 90*

Egg & Prosciutto: A dish of scrambled egg yolks is the *bon vivant*'s answer to the egg white omelette. It's superbly rich, ridiculously buttery and has the simultaneously light and dense texture of clotted cream. Use 3 yolks plus 1 whole egg and a little butter. Serve with Parma ham for a luxurious take on bacon and eggs.

Egg & Sage: *See Sage & Egg, page 322*

Egg & Shellfish: Dressed crab is *the* recipe for the man who likes to spend weekends taking the car apart and putting it back together again. You have to boil and shell the crab and eggs, clean out the crab shell, finely chop the egg whites, sieve the yolks, finely chop the brown meat and mix it with mayonnaise, and mix lemon juice into the white meat. The brown meat is then layered in the bottom of the crab shell with the white meat and chopped egg arranged on top in defined bands, as in a flag. It's dressed with parsley and served with a little extra mayo on the side. You eat the white meat first, appreciating its pale delicacy before moving on to the hard stuff. The brown meat is part of the crab's digestive system and contains all the flavour that implies. If this sounds more trouble than it's worth, crab Louis is a less fussy recipe that originated on the West Coast of America in the early twentieth century. It's a white crabmeat and egg salad with lettuce and a 'Louis' dressing that's very similar to Thousand Island.

Egg & Smoked Fish: *See Smoked Fish & Egg, page 165*

Egg & Tomato: *Uova al purgatorio*, or eggs in purgatory, is a Neapolitan dish of eggs served in a thick, warm, pepper-spiked tomato sauce. Middle Eastern *shakshuka* and Latin American *huevos rancheros* operate on similar principles. Some people like to scramble their egg into the tomato sauce; others prefer to keep the eggs whole by sliding them into the sauce, putting a lid on the pan and leaving it to simmer until the eggs are cooked through. The third way is to allow the white to set, tipping and rotating the pan as necessary to ensure all the translucent liquid meets the heat, and once it has, scrambling the yolk into the sauce. If this all sounds a bit on the rustic side, you might try the very Jamesian lunch to which Strether treats Madame de Vionnet in

The Ambassadors. Over intensely white table linen at a little place he knows on the Left Bank of the Seine, they eat *omelette aux tomates* with a bottle of straw-coloured Chablis. See also Bell Pepper & Egg, page 205.

Egg & Truffle: *See Truffle & Egg, page 116*

Egg & Vanilla: Vanilla spirits away the eggy flavour that can be particularly unwelcome in pastries and desserts. Variously paired with cream, milk, sugar and flour, egg and vanilla make *oeufs à la neige* (uncooked meringues, shaped like eggs, floating in pale custard), crème caramel, crème brûlée, vanilla soufflé, vanilla ice cream and *crème anglaise*, otherwise known as custard.

Egg & Watercress: *See Watercress & Egg, page 100*

MARINE

....

Shellfish

White Fish

Oyster

Caviar

Oily Fish

Shellfish

This section covers bivalves and crustaceans, but oysters have their own chapter (see page 150). Mussels and clams have a saltier, stronger flavour than sweet prawn, lobster and scallop. Crab lies somewhere in between, depending on how much of the brown meat, which has a deeper marine flavour, you mix in with the white. The food writer Alan Davidson noted that the white claw and leg meat of crab is similar in flavour and texture to lobster. Lobster might be held in higher regard, particularly by those for whom the price is immaterial, but plenty of people consider crab to be comparable, if not superior. Hugh Fearnley-Whittingstall takes the view that while lobster costs five times as much as crab, it isn't five times more delicious.

Shellfish & Almond: The aroma of boiled prawn is often described as nutty. Roasted, it becomes more specifically almond-like. The almond note in shrimp accounts for its being paired with ground almonds in aromatic Indian curries, with almond-based sauces in Spain, and stir-fried with whole or chopped nuts in the Chinese-American dish shrimp and almond ding. The flavours work beautifully with rice, especially basmati.

Shellfish & Anise: Anise heightens and freshens the sweetness of shellfish. Tarragon butter with lobster, and mussels cooked with fennel, are justifiably classic combinations. A dash of Pernod might replace brandy in a bisque. The simple recipe for cooking chicken breast with tarragon is easily adapted for prawns – see Anise & Chicken, page 182.

Shellfish & Apple: *See Apple & Shellfish, page 272*

Shellfish & Asparagus: Like peas and sweetcorn, asparagus should be eaten as soon as possible after harvesting. Once picked, it starts to consume its own sugar – more voraciously than any other common vegetable – flattening out the flavour. At its tender best, asparagus is green heaven with prawns or sweet, fresh crab. In May or June, you could dig out your old camping stove, pack it up with some plates, cutlery, a pan and some salt and head for the Suffolk coast. Keep your eyes peeled for signs advertising pick-your-own asparagus. Harvest a couple of bundles and strike on for the sea at Southwold or Aldeburgh. While one of you cusses over the stove, the other can buy fresh crab from one of the tar-black fishermen's huts. You'll also need some good bread, salty butter, a couple of lemons and an offie-cold bottle of Sauvignon Blanc. And some early strawberries. Locate each other on the beach. Get some water on to boil and add the asparagus to it. Butter the bread. Open the wine. Quarter the lemons. When the asparagus is just cooked, dot it with butter and serve with plenty of crabmeat. Stare, shivering, towards Holland, as the tide fizzes on the pebbles and the gulls announce the onset of British summer time.

Shellfish & Avocado: *See Avocado & Shellfish, page 200*
Shellfish & Bacon: *See Bacon & Shellfish, page 170*

Shellfish & Basil: The citrus and anise notes in basil make it a gracious match for shellfish. Basil contains a compound called citral, which is partly responsible for the flavour of lemon and lemongrass. A salad of lobster and mango with basil is one of Alain Senderens' signature dishes, perhaps inspired by the classic Vietnamese combination of shrimp, papaya and lemongrass.

Shellfish & Beef: The term surf 'n' turf is thought to have originated in the US in the 1960s, although its catchiness, and the cachet conferred by the payday price ticket, are probably more responsible for its enduring popularity than any particular flavour affinity between lobster and beef. They're fine – beef's flavour tends to be intensified by marine partners such as anchovy and oyster – but I find the combination of lean, dense flesh can add up to a chewy chore. And I'm not convinced that the beef does much for the lobster in return. The basic idea has, of course, been reinterpreted by various chefs as scallops with foie gras, octopus with bone marrow and monkfish tail with oxtail. And in the late 1980s the term was applied by my hungrier male colleagues to the blow-out combination of a Big Mac and a Filet-O-Fish. Alligator meat, incidentally, is said to taste like a hybrid of shellfish and veal. See also Oyster & Beef, page 151.

Shellfish & Bell Pepper: Strips of red pepper turn up in shellfish sauces for pasta, in stir-fries and sticky, Spanish paella-style dishes, and in sweet and sour prawns. Their bittersweet vibrancy perfectly offsets the rich nuttiness of shellfish. But do we ever notice them? They're like Cyrano, selflessly eloquent in the background.

Shellfish & Black Pudding: *See Black Pudding & Shellfish, page 40*
Shellfish & Butternut Squash: *See Butternut Squash & Shellfish, page 232*
Shellfish & Cabbage: *See Cabbage & Shellfish, page 120*
Shellfish & Caper: *See Caper & Shellfish, page 103*
Shellfish & Cauliflower: *See Cauliflower & Shellfish, page 124*
Shellfish & Celery: *See Celery & Shellfish, page 97*

Shellfish & Chicken: *Mar y muntanya* ('sea and mountain') is a Catalan dish of meat and shellfish (often chicken and prawns) combined in a thick, pounded nut, tomato and garlic sauce similar to a *picada* – see Hazelnut & Garlic, page 240. Chicken is also paired with prawns or mussels in Spanish paella and Louisiana gumbo and jambalaya. The Rhône-Alpes speciality *poulet aux écrevisses* takes advantage of two local ingredients: chicken from Bresse and crayfish from the Alpine streams near the border with Switzerland. Chicken Marengo, supposedly made for Napoleon after his victory over the Austrians at the eponymous battle, consists of chicken in a tomato, garlic and wine sauce with a garnish of fried crayfish. In Brazil, chicken with a pungent mass of dried shrimp makes *xim-xim de galinha,* and in Southeast Asia, of course, untold numbers of curries and stir-fries combine chicken with shellfish both dried and fresh. Bivalves work too: clams are paired with chicken in Chinese and Korean dishes, while in Brittany chicken is sautéed with clams and samphire.

Shellfish & Chilli: Chilli crab is huge in Singapore. The crab is fried with fresh chillies, ginger and garlic, then swathed in a sticky mixture of chilli sauce, ketchup, soy, sugar and sesame oil, often with an egg stirred in at the end of cooking. It's served with rice, or a bread called *man tou,* useful for mopping up every last drop of sauce. In Malaysia and Singapore, *sambal belascan* is toasted shrimp paste and fresh chilli pounded together and loosened with lime juice; a similar concoction in Thailand is known as *nam phrik kapi.*

Shellfish & Coconut: Remind me of being on holiday. A shaggy coating of desiccated coconut turns deep-fried prawns into a trashy bar snack that demands cold bottles of beer and a sheaf of paper napkins. In Bahia, Brazil, a popular dish called *vatapá* combines shellfish and fish in a coconut milk stew thickened with bread. And in Thailand, prawns bathe in a coconut milk broth called *tom yam kha kai;* the sweetness of the two main ingredients distracts you, if only temporarily, from its fiery heat.

Shellfish & Coriander Leaf: As shellfish go, mussels are particularly rich – they have a deep, briny meatiness sometimes graced with notes of butter or caramel. This makes them especially suited to the sort of ingredients used in Thai cooking to balance out the similarly deep flavour of *nam pla,* or fish sauce. Coriander, lemongrass, lime, chilli (and combinations thereof) are all great matches. Dress mussels with finely chopped coriander leaves and a squeeze of lime after barbecuing them on the grill in a foil tray. Should take around 8 minutes, but you'll know they're done when they yawn open.

Shellfish & Cucumber: *See Cucumber & Shellfish, page 188*

Shellfish & Cumin: A cumin sauce for shellfish is given in Apicius, the oldest known cookbook in existence. The cumin is mixed with pepper, lovage, parsley, dried mint, honey, vinegar and broth. Today cumin is often paired with shellfish in India, Mexico and the American Southwest. Muddle garlic, ground cumin, ground chilli and oil to make a marinade.

Shellfish & Dill: *See Dill & Shellfish, page 191*
Shellfish & Egg: *See Egg & Shellfish, page 136*

Shellfish & Garlic: The richly sulphurous flavour of garlic has a multiplier effect on the flavour of all shellfish but hits a high with stewed clams. One evening on holiday, we stopped in Porto Ercole, on a mountainous peninsula connected to the Tuscan mainland by three dams like strands of mozzarella. After a swim in the warm sea, we drifted towards the restaurant – similarly adrift on a precariously tethered pontoon – that was playing the best music. No one else was around. The Italians would only just be digesting their lunch, but we'd driven all the way up from Rome, and the swim and the first glass of Soave had given us an appetite. We were debating how long we might be able to hold off eating when an enormous man with long, sun-ruined hair and a moustache to match sat down at our table. 'Hi,' he said, in slightly Americanised Italo-English that somehow sounded Swiss. 'What would you like to eat? I'll cook you anything.' This was a little like asking the young Hannibal if he fancied conquering any bits of the Roman Empire. I generally want *everything*. But we were by the sea, in Italy, and that can mean only one thing: *spaghetti alle vongole*. In short order, we were sitting in front of golden, tangled masses of garlicky pasta caught up with creamy, chewy clams, like Venus's hair before she'd had the chance to comb it through. Sprigs of flat-leaf parsley lifted the oily richness. I have a fairy godfather, and he's a chef the size of a grizzly bear who lives on a floating restaurant.

Shellfish & Globe Artichoke: *See Globe Artichoke & Shellfish, page 129*
Shellfish & Grapefruit: *See Grapefruit & Shellfish, page 299*

Shellfish & Hard Cheese: Controversial, but less so than fish and cheese. In lobster Thermidor, lobster meat is served in a cream sauce laced with Gruyère and mustard. Parmesan and crab meet in a boldly flavoured tart, in a soufflé, or in a mixture of spider crab, cheese and chilli sauce piled back into the shell and given a quick blast under the grill. Prawns are often paired with feta in a salad, or the feta is scattered over prawns in a tomato-rich Provençal sauce.

Shellfish & Lamb: One of the less famous meat and shellfish combinations. Nonetheless, lamb was once often cooked with cockles, and there's an early-nineteenth-century cookbook by John Farley that contains a recipe for a roast boned leg of mutton with shredded crab or lobster meat, seasoned with lemon zest and nutmeg. Marco Pierre White includes lamb with cockles and thyme on the menu at Marco, one of his London restaurants.

Shellfish & Lemon: The beach fishery at Cadgwith Cove in Cornwall is one of the last left in England. You can still see the boats huddled together on the shingle in the evening. It was a summer-holiday ritual of my childhood to help my father pick out the best live shellfish from the fishery's tank after eating crab sandwiches in a converted pilchard cellar nearby. The brown crab caught on the Cornish coast has a deep, seaweedy flavour, and in its shell looks, rather fittingly, like a pasty with legs. When it's fresh, it needs nothing but a squeeze of lemon juice backcombed through the meat to enhance its sweetness. The same goes for all shellfish, really, whether raw on a stand of *fruits de mer* or grilled on a platter of octopus and langoustines. A lemon wedge is all you need. Well, that and a suitably sharp Chablis.

Shellfish & Lime: Deep-fried conch is delicious served with a seafood-cocktail sauce laced with lime. Conch's flavour is a cross between scallop and clam. Its texture is a cross between scallop and gym mat. You can give it the ceviche treatment (see Lime & White Fish, page 303) by pounding the flesh to make it chewable, at least by humans, and mixing it with sliced onion and lots of lime juice (which will also go some way towards tenderising it). Overfishing is a problem, and farmed conch is more tender to the teeth, if less flavourful, than the wild kind.

Shellfish & Mango: *See Mango & Shellfish, page 291*
Shellfish & Mushroom: *See Mushroom & Shellfish, page 79*
Shellfish & Nutmeg: *See Nutmeg & Shellfish, page 223*
Shellfish & Oily Fish: *See Oily Fish & Shellfish, page 159*
Shellfish & Olive: *See Olive & Shellfish, page 177*

Shellfish & Parsley: Judged by the appearance of their shells on the beach, razor clams are well named, but once caught and stacked on fishmonger's ice, flopped out of the end of their shells, the edible part looks about as treacherous as a puppy's tongue on a hot day. They taste pretty much like other clams, but there's a good deal more meat on them. Serve them cooked with white wine, garlic and parsley, or do as the Italians do and slurp them direct from the shell.

Shellfish & Parsnip: *See Parsnip & Shellfish, page 225*

Shellfish & Pea: Scallops on puréed peas, or pea risotto, is something of a modern classic, but the combination of shellfish and pea is nothing new. The following recipe is from a book on medieval cookery by Hieatt, Hosington and Butler. Soak 400g split green peas (if necessary) and then simmer in 1 litre water until soft. Set aside to cool. In a food processor, blend 50g ground almonds and 15g breadcrumbs as finely as possible, then, while the machine is running, gradually add the peas with ½ tsp salt, 4 tsp white wine vinegar, ¼ tsp ground ginger, ¼ tsp ground cardamom and a pinch each of ground cinnamon and clove. Season with salt and pepper. Put the pea mixture into a pan and slowly reheat while you briefly sauté 500g shelled prawns. Arrange the prawns on top of the purée in a bowl.

Shellfish & Peanut: *See Peanut & Shellfish, page 25*

Shellfish & Pineapple: The sweet-saltiness of shellfish combined with pineapple's sweet-sourness is common to authentic Asian dishes and to their lurid, sweet-and-sour semblances in Chinese takeaways. In Indian Parsee cooking, shellfish and pineapple are paired in a sweet and sour curry with tamarind, called *kolmino patio*. And in Southeast Asia they're found in countless curries and soups. Useful to bear in mind when you're saddled with an underripe pineapple – they don't get any sweeter once they're picked.

Shellfish & Pork: In Portugal it's hard to miss *porco à alentejana*, or pork stewed with clams, peppers and onions. The magic of the dish is not just the chewy little nuggets of clam but the precious juice inside their shells, which, as is the case with oysters, contributes an essential part of the flavour. One doubtful theory on how this combination arose is that Portugal's pigs, left to wander its long coastline, had a lot of seafood in their diet, with the consequence that their meat had a fishy taste that the locals covered up by cooking it with clams. But it's just as likely to have come about because shellfish and pork were abundantly available and the combination is delicious – so much so that it's travelled to Macau, a former Portuguese colony where several variations on the dish are eaten.

Shellfish & Potato: *See Potato & Shellfish, page 93*
Shellfish & Saffron: *See Saffron & Shellfish, page 180*

Shellfish & Smoked Fish: Essential to fish pie, where the smoked fish provides a pungent flavour contrast to the white, and the prawns, besides looking cute, all pink and curled in their soft bedding of mashed potato, provide a textural contrast to them both. But you don't want too much of either: the white fish should prevail. The same principle applies to *choucroute de la mer* – see Smoked Fish & Cabbage, page 164.

Shellfish & Thyme: *See Thyme & Shellfish, page 328*
Shellfish & Tomato: *See Tomato & Shellfish, page 261*
Shellfish & Truffle: *See Truffle & Shellfish, page 117*
Shellfish & Vanilla: *See Vanilla & Shellfish, page 350*
Shellfish & Walnut: *See Walnut & Shellfish, page 237*
Shellfish & Watercress: *See Watercress & Shellfish, page 101*

Shellfish & White Fish: Scampi may refer to a type of prawn in some countries, but in the UK it's a prawn entombed in breadcrumb or batter, usually served with chips. Monkfish used to be cut into prawn shapes, coated in crumbs and passed off as scampi. Then someone realised that if it could be passed off as shellfish it might be rather good in its own right, and in the 1990s it increased in price and popularity to the extent that it is now on the endangered list. Jane Grigson notes that monkfish is often compared to lobster, which isn't, in her opinion, fair to either side, even if monkfish was her favourite fish to cook and eat after 'the four greats' – sole, turbot, eel and lobster. Lobster and monkfish certainly have a textural similarity (they're both pleasantly chewy), and taste tests reveal that the flavour of monkfish does bear comparison with shellfish, especially in the dark, gelatinous flesh nearer the skin. Monkfish aside, John Dory and turbot are classically served with shellfish sauce, and a few mussels or clams cooked with peas in butter and white wine make a beautiful brothy sauce for any white fish.

White Fish

The flavour of saltwater fish is a result of its own delicate balancing act. On average, the salinity of seawater ranges from 3 to 3.5 per cent by weight. As Harold McGee points out, animals need to keep the total level of dissolved minerals in their cells closer to 1 per cent, and so sea fish offset the saltiness of their environment by filling their cells with other compounds, namely amino acids and amines, which have their own taste and flavour implications. Glycine, an amino acid, lends sweetness, whereas the glutamic acid present in shellfish, tuna and anchovies 'is savory and mouthfilling'. Many fin fish, however, offset the salt water flowing through their bodies with the relatively flavourless amine, trimethylamine oxide, or TMAO, which is why, in contrast to strong-flavoured fish such as anchovy, most white fish are characterised by sleep-inducing flavour descriptors like 'mild', 'sweet' and 'delicate'. White fish are so often entombed in batter or slathered in sauce that it's worth trying a plate of three or four different kinds, simply fried or steamed. Once your powers of perception have acclimatised, you'll find the subtly different flavours begin to show up against the white like landmarks in a snowscape. Look out for gamy, musty, earthy and seaweedy notes. Cod can have a slightly sour, salty, cooked-potato quality, which is perhaps why it's such a hit with chips. Monkfish can be sweet and buttery, a little shellfishy, without the full butterkissed-popcorn flavour of prawns. Good sea bass is meaty, Brazil-nutty, with a faint metallic twang to match its fuse-wire grey veins. Fish covered in this chapter include cod, skate, sole, flounder, plaice, monkfish and turbot.

White Fish & Anchovy: Both Hannah Glasse in the eighteenth century and Eliza Acton in the nineteenth make mention of anchovy sauce served with boiled white fish (especially flat fish) or with fried breadcrumbed cod. You can make it by adding anchovy essence to melted butter with lemon juice.

White Fish & Anise: *See Anise & White Fish, page 185*

White Fish & Asparagus: When the Italians began cultivating asparagus in the seventeenth century, they usually served it on its own, whereas in France and England it was often used as an adjunct ingredient, especially to fowl or to fish like turbot, which has a sweet, buttery flavour that's an ideal match for sweet, butter-loving asparagus. Orange-flavoured *sauce maltaise* is the classic accompaniment – see Orange & Asparagus, page 294.

White Fish & Bacon: In *The Adventures of Tom Sawyer*, Tom and Huck cook their just-landed bass with bacon and are astonished at its deliciousness. The benefits of cooking fish with bacon fat are not to be underestimated. A pot of rendered bacon fat is worth having in the fridge. It's good with fish, cabbage and for baking cornbread. I think of it as a cross between cooking fat and stock because it has such an enriching flavour. Buy 500g very fatty bacon and chop it up into lardons or rashers (there'll be bacon meat to use up once you're finished, so cut lardons if you're tossing it with blue cheese in a salad, rashers if you're planning a breakfast or club sandwich). Cook the fat over a low heat in a frying pan with 75ml water. Be patient: it will take at least 30 minutes. When it looks as if all the water has evaporated and all the fat melted, cool a little, then strain into a ceramic or glass storage jar and keep in the fridge.

White Fish & Caper: *See Caper & White Fish, page 104*

White Fish & Celery: A rare pairing. The combination of string and bones can feel less like eating and more like some sort of therapeutic craft project. This is where celeriac – the softer face of celery – comes in. Sweeter and easier to work with, celeriac can make a great partner for all sorts of seafood. Chef Tom Aikens pairs them in dishes such as John Dory with cabbage, celeriac and horseradish, sea bass with small parsley gnocchi and caramelised celeriac, or poached turbot with poached chicken wings, crushed celeriac, truffle gnocchi and wild sorrel.

White Fish & Coconut: *See Coconut & White Fish, page 288*
White Fish & Coriander Leaf: *See Coriander Leaf & White Fish, page 197*
White Fish & Cucumber: *See Cucumber & White Fish, page 188*

White Fish & Dill: Although it is rare in other parts of Asia, dill features prominently in the cuisines of Laos and some parts of Thailand. The eponymous fish dish at Cha Ca La Vong, a restaurant in Hanoi, Vietnam, is the only thing they serve: white fish (a kind of freshwater catfish) yellowed with turmeric and stir-fried with dill fronds and spring onion. You can recreate something like it at home with any white fish that holds its shape during stir-frying, such as John Dory, sea bass or tilapia. Just don't be tempted to skimp on the dill. Cut about 500g fish fillets into large bite-sized pieces and marinate for 30 minutes in a mixture of ½ tsp turmeric, 1 tsp sugar, a 2cm thumb of galangal (or ginger), finely chopped, 2 tbsp fish sauce, 1 tsp rice wine vinegar and 1 tbsp water. Fry the fish in groundnut oil for about 4 minutes or until just cooked through, add sprigs of dill and shredded spring onion, and fry for a minute longer. Serve in bowls on cold rice vermicelli and season to taste with roasted peanuts, chilli, more dill, mint, coriander and *nuoc cham* (see Lime & Anchovy, page 300).

White Fish & Garlic: *See Garlic & White Fish, page 115*
White Fish & Ginger: *See Ginger & White Fish, page 313*

White Fish & Grape: To me, sole Véronique is the classic convalescence dish: Dover sole, lightly cooked in stock, cream, vermouth and lemon juice with halved green grapes. It fulfils the vital *cucina bianca* criterion of kindliness to the stomach, and is so pale and delicate as to make you feel robust by comparison (plus it's a way to use up all those hospital visitors' grapes). Sole is not the *sine qua non*; any firm white fish will do. To give it its due, however, Dover sole does have a unique flavour, which develops in the muscle tissue two or three days after it's caught; unlike most fish, it's not particularly tasty straight off the boat. Other flat fish such as turbot and halibut are subject to the same effect, but not as noticeably.

White Fish & Hard Cheese: A highly contentious food pairing, which is anathema to Italian restaurateurs in particular; at least one Italian restaurant in New York warns customers, 'No cheese served on seafood at any time'. The objection is essentially to the cheese overpowering the subtle flavour of fish, although it seems to have come about in relatively recent times – research has unearthed many older Italian cheese and fish combinations, dating back to a Sicilian fish recipe from around 400 BC. Fish and cheese are, of course, paired in French dishes, like skate with a Gruyère sauce, or bouillabaisse with grated Gruyère sunk into its depths. The British grate Cheddar on mashed-potato-topped fish pie to give it a flavour boost, while the Americans pair tuna with cheese in their classic toasted tuna-melt sandwich. I don't much like the *idea* of seafood and cheese, but do like it in practice, especially in an old-fashioned Mornay sauce with cod or haddock – which I suppose makes me as undecided as McDonald's, which uses only half a slice of cheese in its Filet-O-Fish.

White Fish & Hazelnut: *See Hazelnut & White Fish, page 240*
White Fish & Horseradish: *See Horseradish & White Fish, page 105*

White Fish & Lemon: White fish is so frequently accompanied by a wedge of lemon that it can look a little lonely without it. Clearly, the lemon provides a sour counterpoint to the sweetness of fish flesh, can deodorise any stronger fish flavours and cuts through the fattiness of fried fish. But the highest compliment you can pay a piece of good fresh fish is to serve it completely unadorned, like a young girl so pretty she doesn't need a scrap of makeup.

White Fish & Lime: *See Lime & White Fish, page 303*

White Fish & Mango: Briny, nutty fresh red snapper tastes great with a mango salsa. Mango is also good paired with any white fish that will hold its shape in an aromatic coconut milk curry. In Cambodia, julienned green mangoes are cooked with mudfish (although tilapia will do just as well) in a combination of fish sauce, garlic and ginger, the delicious sourness of the fruit teasing out the sweetness of the fish. Food writer Alan Davidson describes an unusual Dutch dish of haddock with a sauce made of mango chutney, sliced sharp apples, ginger and lemon juice.

White Fish & Mushroom: *See Mushroom & White Fish, page 80*

White Fish & Olive: You might think a rule applied to fish with olives – green with delicate white fish, black for richer, oily types. It doesn't. You may find, however, that the salty oiliness of olives gives subtle white fish a welcome touch of oily-fish richness. A good-quality, extra virgin olive oil, with a clean bitter streak and the flavour of expensive green vegetables, may be all the sauce a delicate piece of fish needs.

White Fish & Orange: *See Orange & White Fish, page 297*
White Fish & Parsley: *See Parsley & White Fish, page 193*

White Fish & Parsnip: 'A good cook will never send salt-fish, and but a few salt meats, to table, without parsnips,' wrote the horticulturalist, Henry Phillips, in 1822. The partnership dates back to medieval times but has recently been revived by Hugh Fearnley-Whittingstall in the form of saltfish and parsnip rösti fishcakes.

White Fish & Pea: *See Pea & White Fish, page 204*

White Fish & Potato: Some pointers for anyone seeking an authentic fish-and-chip experience:
    1. 'Fish' and 'chips' is not necessarily *fish and chips*. To qualify as the real thing – i.e. an essentially unitary quantity, *fishandchips*, wherein the chips are inseparable from the fish as opposed to just served with it – it has to come from a chippy. This is not only for sentimental reasons. To achieve the essential crispness of the chip, and to cook enough pieces of battered fish at one time to stop them losing heat or going soggy, you need the sort of hard-core double-frying equipment rarely found outside the dedicated chip shop.
    2. A chippy serves fish and chips, mushy peas, fishcakes, saveloys, battered sausages and pickles. At a stretch, Pukka meat pies.
    Avoid opportunistic 'fish bars' that offer burgers, fried chicken, kebabs or pizzas.
    3. Salt and malt vinegar are essential. Other types of vinegar are not acceptable.

4. The fish and chips must be served in proper chip-shop paper, which to the uninitiated looks, feels and most importantly smells like newsless newspaper, and is the secret ingredient in proper chip-shop fish and chips. It seasons them. If they're served in polystyrene boxes, eat elsewhere.

5. Fish and chips must be eaten in appropriate surroundings. To be truly authentic you should be eating your fish and chips by the seaside, or at the bus stop, or perched on the wall outside a petrol station, breathing steam into your hand because you couldn't wait for the chips to cool down.

White Fish & Prosciutto: *See Prosciutto & White Fish, page 174*

White Fish & Saffron: Italians turn their noses up at this combination, according to Elizabeth David in *Italian Food*, as they think the flavour of saffron overpowers the fish. She doesn't agree, and neither, surely, would anyone who's eaten a bouillabaisse. One evening in Antibes, a pharmacist slipped us the name of *the* place to get it, somewhere off the coast road between Saint Tropez and Cabasson. He didn't know the address – you just had to keep your eyes peeled. Chez Joe, it was called, or so the pharmacist's scrawl on the rumpled napkin seemed to say. We arrived at a patch of featureless headland and climbed down a rusty ladder to a narrow beach where a dozen folding tables had been pushed into the shingle. 'Joe', whose *chez* was a cave, attended to a large pot over a fire of driftwood, muttering to himself under a roof of dripping rock. Another man brought us a bottle of rosé from a coolbox and a couple of tumblers. We drank for a while, looking out to sea, before the soup was presented along with some garlic-rubbed bread. It tasted of the view: turbulent, sea-beddy, on the vaguely sinister side of complicated. When the soup was finished, the waiter brought the fish that had been cooked in it, along with more bread and more wine. A couple of diamond-shaped almond sweetmeats, called *calissons d'Aix*, in place of dessert, and a glass of eau de vie to make you forget where you'd been and preserve the secret.

White Fish & Shellfish: *See Shellfish & White Fish, page 144*

White Fish & Thyme: 'I have also removed from my cooking of fish', wrote the French chef Marie-Antoine Carême, 'those quantities of aromatics and spices that our forebears were wont to use for seasoning, for it is a strange delusion to believe that fish should taste of thyme, bay, mace, clove or pepper, whereas we have irrefutable evidence every day that fish cooked in salt water alone is excellent.' He does go on to say that a thyme-infused court-bouillon (the stock you might use for a seafood chowder) is permissible as long as the herb isn't intrusive. Fresh thyme is a safer bet than dried, which can be too strong for fish. Lemon thyme obviously makes an excellent match.

White Fish & Tomato: It's hard to beat baked bream with roasted tomatoes, or fish fingers and ketchup, but in the early 1990s researchers set out to improve on the tomato with an implanted gene from the Arctic flounder. Arctic flounders are, unsurprisingly, genetically programmed not to freeze (and rupture) in cold waters – properties the scientists thought might help tomatoes survive cultivation in hard conditions, and the bumpy trip to market. It didn't work. Splice them as nature intended by frying your flounder in butter, with a crumb coating if preferred, and serving with roast tomatoes and boiled new potatoes, or squished in a bun with ketchup.

Oyster

An oyster's flavour is more than usually expressive of the environment that supported it. The cleanliness, mineral content and temperature of the water are important factors, and account for the common practice of identifying oysters by provenance rather than species. For example, *Ostrea edulis*, the 'European flat' or 'native' oyster, is variously referred to as the English Colchester, the Irish Galway, the protected Belon and the algae-trimmed Marennes from France. They have also been successfully maricultured in California and Maine. Order a mixed platter of oysters and hold off on the lemon while you try to detect the flavour notes connoisseurs have identified: sweet, creamy, meaty, buttery, nutty, melon, melon rind, cucumber, mineral, metallic, coppery and, of course, briny or oceanic. To experience its sweeter, more complex flavours beyond the initial shock of seawater, you'll need to give your oyster a chew before it slips down. Sour flavours like lemon and vinegar dampen an oyster's saltiness and highlight its sweetness. Horseradish, or chilli-spiked tomato ketchup, makes for a hot-sweet-salt combination wherein the oyster also contributes its inherent umami. Oyster sauce is a thick, dark, salty condiment from China; brands vary in the quantity of oyster extractives, sugar, sodium and flavour enhancers they contain.

Oyster & Anise: *See Anise & Oyster, page 184*

Oyster & Bacon: Oysters individually wrapped in half a (pre-stretched) rasher of streaky bacon, impaled on a cocktail stick and grilled. I could never remember: angels on horseback? Devils on horseback? Pigs at the beach? Swine before pearls? Then someone explained: oysters are whiteish, like angels. Prunes are dark, and thus evil, especially when pitted and filled with mango chutney before they're enfolded in bacon. As ever, the devil has the best tunes: the extreme salty-sweet contrast of prune and bacon wins hands down for me.

Oyster & Beef: When Kit buys little Jacob his first dish of oysters in *The Old Curiosity Shop*, the child takes to them 'as if he had been born and bred to the business – sprinkled the pepper and the vinegar with a discretion beyond his years – and afterwards built a grotto on the table with the shells'. Before stocks collapsed, oysters were so plentiful and cheap that a servant like Kit could buy three dozen of 'the largest oysters ever seen' without fear of the debtor's prison. But it wasn't only to bulk out the more expensive ingredients that oysters were added to steak and kidney pudding. The salty oyster bolsters the flavour of beef. The same principle applies to the oyster-stuffed Australian carpetbag steak and the use of oyster sauce in stir-fried beef dishes.

Oyster & Caviar: *See Caviar & Oyster, page 154*

Oyster & Celery: Celery makes a fresh, almost citric partner for oysters: a rather genteel combination, and never more so than in this recipe for 'Oysters and Celery from Billy the Oysterman', from the charming *Esquire Handbook for Hosts*, first published in 1954. 'The man', it advises, 'who can ask his friends in after the theatre or other late functions ... is a man who is going ... to the top of his friends' hit parade.' Sauté 3 chopped celery sticks in butter until tender, add 24 shucked oysters and their liquor and simmer until the oysters curl at their edges. Splash in some sweetish white wine and season gently. Remove to a dish to keep warm, cut some toast points, tap your cigarette on its initialled silver case and bask in the adoration of your chums.

Oyster & Chicken: Fantastically luxurious to stuff a chicken with oysters before roasting it. Shuck them and stuff them in: it's as simple as that. If your cavity is bigger than your catch, you can always mix the oysters and their juices with buttery breadcrumbs. Or stuff a quail instead – they hold only about 3 oysters each.

Oyster & Chilli: My first oyster was pressed on me by a waiter in a grotty trattoria near Paddington station. It was the kind of place where you'd think twice about eating the breadsticks, let alone take your chances with the seafood. It didn't kill me, nor did it convert me. I ate my second in a bar in the French Quarter of New Orleans, a narrow, funereal room, cooled by an apathetic ceiling fan, neon signs fighting a losing battle against the gloom. A dive brasserie: exactly what I'd been hoping for. With his eyes half on the muted football game, a barman in sleeve clips shovelled oysters from an ice-filled trough in the bar and shunted them croupier-style towards the punters. The scene had the paradoxical exoticism of another culture's routine: everyone was bored except me. I raised a finger. The barman pushed an oyster my way. It was unlike any oyster I'd seen: a dark grey, shiny oval, monstrous as a whale's eye. It stared me down. I gave it a squirt of hot sauce and, trying to blank my mind, picked it up by its deep, craggy socket and swallowed it whole. I felt my scalp crackle. High on the oyster's dose of zinc, or the fiery sauce, or simply because I'd looked the beast in the eye and defeated it, I ordered a celebratory beer. And as it cooled my raging throat, the barman pushed something else my way. Bigger, greyer and shinier, and this time there were two of them.

Oyster & Egg: Make a 'Hangtown fry', invented in Hangtown in the Sierra Nevada during the Gold Rush. Some say it was made for a prospector who'd struck gold, others that it was the last meal of a convict on death row. Both myths rely on the rarity value of oysters in the desert. The likely truth is that it was devised by one of the many Chinese immigrants who found work as a cook in mid-nineteenth-century California. Hangtown fry is basically fried oysters with scrambled eggs. Some recipes include bacon but the one in M. F. K. Fisher's book, *Consider the Oyster*, doesn't: she suggests you serve it with sausages and shoestring fries.

Oyster & Globe Artichoke: *See Globe Artichoke & Oyster, page 128*
Oyster & Horseradish: *See Horseradish & Oyster, page 105*

Oyster & Lemon: Oyster purists turn their noses up at shallot vinegar or Tabasco – a raw oyster should be eaten with nothing at all, not even lemon. But I'm not a purist. For me, eating oysters is like throwing off all your clothes and jumping off the end of a jetty. Lemon juice is the mouthwatering run-up, giving way to the bracing splash of the oyster's minerality. Lemon juice also refreshes oysters deep-fried, Deep South-style, in cornmeal.

Oyster & Mushroom: Some people believe that oyster mushrooms not only resemble oysters but have a faint taste of them too, like the rubbery frills on a lady's bathing cap, fresh out of the sea. Like oysters, oyster mushrooms can be quickly fried in butter and served with a squeeze of lemon.

Oyster & Nutmeg: *See Nutmeg & Oyster, page 222*

Oyster & Onion: Finely chop shallots and mix with red wine vinegar for the classic French accompaniment to oysters, called *mignonette*.

Oyster & Parsley: Oysters Rockefeller was devised by chef Jules Alciatore, of Antoine's in New Orleans, and has been on the menu there since 1899. Oysters on the half shell are baked with a green sauce and topped with crumbs. Alciatore took the recipe to his grave, in written form at least, and his successors at Antoine's are as tight-lipped as an unshuckable oyster. Other restaurants serve imitation dishes involving spinach but, according to Antoine's, no one has ever cracked the secret of the green sauce. Research has found its primary ingredients to be parsley, capers and olive oil, but the secret ingredient no lab test can identify is secrecy itself.

Oyster & Pork: Oysters are traditionally mixed with pork and formed into sausages in the American South. They're also paired in a New England-style stuffing for poultry, and in the Louisiana stew, gumbo. But to my mind they're most electrically combined in the form of chilled, raw oysters and hot, spicy sausages. It's a perennial favourite of chefs and food writers everywhere. In Bordeaux they use *loukenkas* sausages, but mini chorizos are good too if you can find them. There's nothing like the hot, fiery snap of sausage undercut by the cool minerality of oyster. A glass of chilled white Graves and the world might fall around you like a film set.

Oyster & Watermelon: *See Watermelon & Oyster, page 250*

Caviar

Oscietra is the caviar of choice for the connoisseur: fine, nutty, complex and (some say) herbal in flavour. As with any natural product, the flavour can vary wildly, especially given the Oscietra sturgeon's omnivorous nature and its habit of evading predators by diving to the seabed, which together make its diet particularly wide. Carnivorous Beluga, whose protein-rich diet may account for the greater size of its eggs, produces a creamier, less fishy-tasting caviar. Sevruga is the commonest – or least rare – and is as black as model-village tarmac. It has a less complex, more strongly sea-salty flavour. Some estimate that stocks of Caspian Sea sturgeon may be entirely depleted by 2012. Some farmed caviars from America and Europe are nonetheless starting to receive outstanding reviews for their flavour.

Caviar & Banana: If you ever feel a bit decadent tucking into bacon and eggs at breakfast, it may help to know that in pre-revolutionary Russia the Tsar's children started the day with a dish of mashed banana and caviar.

Caviar & Cauliflower: Cruciferous vegetables are terrific paired with salty ingredients. If you like sprouts with bacon, you'll love the classic Joel Robuchon partnership of cauliflower and caviar. He makes a gelée of caviar to pair with cauliflower cream; a couscous of Oscietra caviar, cauliflower cream and asparagus gelée; and cauliflower cream with caviar and puréed potato. See also Anchovy & Cauliflower, page 162.

Caviar & Chicken: *See Chicken & Caviar, page 27*

Caviar & Egg: Frank Sinatra used to make scrambled eggs and caviar for Ava Gardner. Wolfgang Puck combines them in a buttery puff-pastry case, which must be heaven to bite into. But asking your loved one to make puff pastry first thing in the morning might be pushing your luck, even if you look like Ava Gardner. If you're all out of caviar, note that the food writer David Rosengarten believes the best caviar eggs taste of egg yolks and butter. So you could always top buttered buckwheat blini with chopped, just-cooked egg yolks and eat them with your eyes closed.

Caviar & Hazelnut: *See Hazelnut & Caviar, page 239*

Caviar & Lemon: Make an excellent sauce for scallops. Simply cook the scallops in butter, adding a little lemon juice and caviar at the end to heat through. Although lemon is often served with caviar, it's not ideal to go squeezing it on your best and most delicately flavoured eggs. I once over-heard an affronted hostess tell a guest, 'If it's taramasalata you want, darling, I'll see if I have some.'

Caviar & Oyster: If you're serving caviar and oysters, it's conceivable you're not interested in the finer points of the flavour combination. You'll have more important things on your mind, like the sable trim for your speedboat. Harold McGee reckons Oscietra caviar tastes like oysters. They certainly share a decaying-frigate palette of grey, green, rust and black, and one might put any proximity in flavour down to their similar bottom-feeding habits. One of Thomas Keller's signature dishes is oysters topped with caviar served on tapioca pearls in a vermouth sabayon. At Noma in Copenhagen, chef René Redzepi, who worked under Keller at The French Laundry, makes a caviar of gelled oyster juice and serves it on a tapioca pudding.

Caviar & Potato: *See Potato & Caviar, page 89*
Caviar & Smoked Fish: *See Smoked Fish & Caviar, page 165*

Caviar & Soft Cheese: Silver and stainless steel affect the flavour of caviar, which is why spoons made of mother-of-pearl or plastic are used instead. As to accompaniments, water biscuits or buckwheat blini are acceptable. Less fastidious fans might forgive a side dish of chopped boiled egg. White foods certainly look fantastic with caviar, drawing attention to its iridescence by bouncing light on to each taut egg, just as white fur complements high cheekbones. Try these mini caviar cheesecakes. Using a small pastry cutter, press 3cm circles from a 1cm-thick slice of dark rye bread. Leave the cutter in place while you spoon in 1cm cream cheese and a dollop of caviar. Ease off the cutter, taking care to keep the cheesecake in shape. You'll need to wash the cutter after each one.

Caviar & White Chocolate: Investigating the ability of salt to bring out the flavour of sweet foods, Heston Blumenthal paired white chocolate with ham, anchovies and cured duck before alighting on the particularly pleasing pairing of caviar. Flavour expert François Benzi noted that the two ingredients share flavour compounds that might explain their compatibility. This led Blumenthal to research the harmoniousness of pairings with compounds in common, and to conclude that while shared organo-chemical ground can often account for the compatibility of existing pairings, and, conversely, suggest unlikely pairings that turn out to work – coffee and garlic, for instance, or parsley and banana – there's no replacement for imagination and intuition. To me, the combination of caviar and white chocolate is like a heightened version of Alain Senderens' pairing of lobster and vanilla. The flavour of white chocolate is predominantly vanilla, with a slightly buttery, cream-cheesy quality that would make it all the more harmonious with the fish eggs.

Oily Fish

Oily fish are richer and more strongly flavoured than white fish. Classic flavour affinities, such as gooseberry or horseradish with mackerel, cucumber with salmon, and watercress with trout, seek to cut through the fattiness. Lemon serves this function too, as well as deodorising some of the stronger fishy aromas. Coriander leaf and/or lime juice are used to the same effect in Asian dishes. Briny capers, olives, prosciutto and shellfish bring out the sweeter side in sea-salty oily fish such as mackerel, herring, sardines and red mullet. This chapter also covers earthier-tasting freshwater fish and diadromous fish (i.e. species that live in both salt- and fresh water), like salmon, trout, grayling and eel, plus meatier-flavoured swordfish and tuna. See also the introduction to White Fish, page 145.

Oily Fish & Almond: *See Almond & Oily Fish, page 244*

Oily Fish & Anise: There are countless ways to combine fish with anise-scented herbs, spices and liqueurs, many of them quick and simple – a poached salmon steak, for instance, with a fresh, heady tarragon mayonnaise. If, however, your tastes tend more to the theatrical, you might try the recipe in Elizabeth David's *French Provincial Cooking* for fennel-stuffed grilled red mullet served on dried fennel with a measure of flaming brandy poured over it. The fennel catches and emits a puff of anise-scented smoke. Great, if you have a dine-in kitchen, where everyone can enjoy the aroma while you whip the fish off the singed twigs on to a warm serving plate. Equally sensational, if more fetishistic than rustic, is Heston Blumenthal's salmon in a tight, shiny, black liquorice gel – a recipe he developed when exploring the combination of asparagus and liquorice.

Oily Fish & Asparagus: Marsh samphire is sometimes called 'sea' or 'poor man's' asparagus. You can just imagine the resentful fenman, up to his knees in brackish marsh-water, muttering about the fancy folk inland, with their doilies and their salad forks and their 'actual' asparagus. It's certainly served the same way, with butter or hollandaise sauce, often as an accompaniment to seafood, especially salmon. As I write this, both are in season and the samphire is four times the price of the asparagus.

Oily Fish & Avocado: According to David Kamp, the California roll was first conceived in the 1960s. As the availability of raw tuna was seasonally limited in Los Angeles, Ichiro Mashita and Teruo Imaizumi, sushi chefs at Tokyo Kaikan, tried combining king crab, cucumber and ginger with avocado, on the basis that it has a buttery texture and dense fattiness somewhat reminiscent of fresh tuna. Avocados grow year-round in California, which was just as well, as it turned out Mashita and Imaizumi had invented a dish that was not only hugely popular in its own right but became a sort of training sushi; once they'd got used to the seaweed and cold, compacted rice, diners went on to try the more authentic stuff.

Oily Fish & Beef: *See Beef & Oily Fish, page 46*
Oily Fish & Beetroot: *See Beetroot & Oily Fish, page 87*
Oily Fish & Caper: *See Caper & Oily Fish, page 103*

Oily Fish & Chilli: Paired in countless sauces in India and Southeast Asia. Chilli is, of course, more sparingly used in western European cuisines, but the Michelin-starred Parisian restaurant Taillevent has been known to serve fresh tuna belly with Espelette peppers, lemon, capers and Serrano ham. At the other end of the price scale, Les Mouettes d'Arvor pairs sardines and chillies in handsome tins. Choose between the variant with Espelette chillies, a mild but tasty red pepper grown in the Basque Country, and the hotter bird's eye chilli version. The French, to their credit, still afford the tinned sardine the respect it deserves, marking the best with a *millésime*, or vintage, and a recommendation as to how long to lay them down. Chancerelle's 2001 vintage, for example, was ready to eat in 2007.

Oily Fish & Cucumber: Smelts, which are small, salmon-like fish, have a smell of cucumber when freshly caught, although some compare their aroma to violets or freshly cut grass. Elizabeth David said they are one of the nicest small fish for frying. The eighteenth-century cookery writer Hannah Glasse suggested frying them in breadcrumbs and serving with fried parsley and melted butter. Along with sweet, sour, metallic, buttery notes, salmon also has a cucumber aroma when fresh, although this recedes with cooking and is replaced with a boiled-potato character. Interesting to note that the traditional accompaniments to poached salmon, boiled new potatoes and a cucumber garnish, have a deeper affinity for the fish than you might think.

Oily Fish & Cumin: *See Cumin & Oily Fish, page 84*

Oily Fish & Dill: In Scandinavian and Baltic countries, there are many recipes for combining the strong, clean flavour of dill with oily fish. Gravadlax, probably the most famous, is salmon cured with sugar and salt, flavoured with dill and mustard, then served with more dill and mustard in the form of a sauce. The Swedish mustard used is sweeter, creamier and less pungent than Dijon or English varieties. Alan Davidson gives recipes for gravad mackerel (not as delicious as the salmon, he notes, but still pretty good), and for *makrillsopa*, a simple preparation of mackerel, dill, water, milk, peppercorns and possibly some potato. In the US, dill is used in tuna salad sandwiches, for which freeze-dried dill works just fine. My favourite dill and fish idea comes from Nigel Slater, and isn't much more work than making a sandwich. Put 2 salmon steaks in a small baking dish and cover with a mixture of 1 very, very finely chopped onion, 1 tbsp lemon juice, 1 tbsp chopped dill and 100ml soured cream or crème fraîche. Bake at 220°C/Gas Mark 7 for 15–18 minutes (just long enough to boil some new potatoes) and scatter with more chopped dill before serving.

Oily Fish & Egg: How my heart sinks when salade niçoise is served with fresh tuna. Chunks of seared tuna may share their tinned counterpart's affinity for egg, capers, green beans and potatoes but they lack the flaky, messy texture that is essential if the fish is to meld with the dressing and loose crumbs of egg yolk and infiltrate the entire salad, as opposed to sitting haughtily on top of it. If you're looking to impress, then Tre Torri's tinned Ventresca brand, which uses tuna belly, has a buttery, creamy character that makes it a world-class treat, according to the food writer David Rosengarten. Mind you, he rates it so highly as to recommend eating it by itself, using a less exalted variety for salads – understandable when you consider that Ventresca costs roughly 20 times as much as a standard supermarket brand.

Oily Fish & Garlic: This recipe from Patricia Wells is something like the fish equivalent of chicken with 40 cloves of garlic (see Garlic & Chicken, page 112). It calls for tuna, but swordfish would work well too. In fact, research has identified a 'fried chicken' character in swordfish, which suggests a compatibility with garlic. Brush two 250g fresh tuna steaks (around 2.5cm thick) with oil and season them with pepper. Grill for about 5 minutes on each side, until they turn opaque but are still pink in the middle. Meanwhile, heat 3 tbsp groundnut oil in a pan until hot but not smoking, add 20 thickly sliced large garlic cloves and sauté until golden. Add 1 tbsp red wine vinegar and stir to deglaze. Season the tuna, pour the sauce over it, and serve with *pipérade* – tomato, onion and green bell pepper stewed in olive oil. *Pipérade*, incidentally, is sometimes cooked with eggs too – see Bell Pepper & Egg, page 205.

Oily Fish & Ginger: *See Ginger & Oily Fish, page 311*
Oily Fish & Horseradish: *See Horseradish & Oily Fish, page 105*

Oily Fish & Lemon: A juicy slice of lemon is all you need for a bowl of hot, crisp, deep-fried whitebait, a dish that's popular in various forms the world over. Whitebait are served as fritters in New Zealand and tossed in chilli and turmeric in India. In the days when fish were plentiful, whitebait – a generic term for a variety of juvenile fish, or sprats, including herring – were caught in the Thames and served on summer days in pubs, moreishly salted and spritzed with lemon to help the drinks go down. See also Parsley & Potato, page 193, and Oily Fish & Dill, page 157.

Oily Fish & Lime: Lemon is excellent at cutting through the fattiness of oily fish, but lime has a spicy quality that gives it the upper hand on the richest varieties. Just a quick squeeze will tease out the sweetness of fried mackerel or barbecued sardines. For an especially intense flavour, halve your limes and place them flesh-side down on the grill to caramelise a little first. Or dress a salsa of tomatoes or mangoes with lime juice for a lively side dish. In the Arabian Gulf, fillets of oily fish are seared and served with a sauce of onions, ginger, garlic, spices and musky dried limes in a dish called *samak quwarmah*. See also Cumin & Oily Fish, page 84.

Oily Fish & Liver: *See Liver & Oily Fish, page 42*

Oily Fish & Mint: In her eighteenth-century cookbook, Hannah Glasse made a special point of stipulating finely chopped mint, parsley and fennel to stuff mackerel before grilling. In Sicilian cookery the clean, powerful flavour of mint freshens oily fish dishes such as grilled swordfish, or pasta with sardines. In Thai cuisine chopped fresh mint is used to garnish salads such as *laab pla*, a spicy, tangy mix of fish, chilli, mint, ground roasted rice and lime juice. The use of mint as a garnish is even more widespread in Vietnam, where a smooth, heart-shaped herb called fish mint is also prevalent. It has a slightly sour, fishy flavour and is often served with beef or grilled meats.

Oily Fish & Mushroom: *See Mushroom & Oily Fish, page 78*

Oily Fish & Onion: Hawaiian *poke* (pronounced pok-ay) is like sashimi going through a rebellious phase. In contrast to the strict rules and traditions applied to the preparation of its Japanese cousin, in *poke* raw tuna is cut into chickpea-sized pieces, marinated with various ingredients, then served piled on a plate. The traditional seasonings were seaweed and roasted candlenuts, a large, oily nut with a bitter taste; now lots of other flavours, especially onion or spring onion, are popular. In Japan, *toro* tuna is blanched and mixed with spring onions in a delicate dashi-based soup. The meatiness of tuna sees it minced and mixed with onions in Italian *polpette* (meatballs) and in burgers. And less exotically, if no less deliciously, tinned tuna is paired with onion on pizza, in tuna mayonnaise sandwiches and in the store-cupboard classic, tuna, cannellini bean and onion salad.

Oily Fish & Parsley: *See Parsley & Oily Fish, page 193*
Oily Fish & Pea: *See Pea & Oily Fish, page 203*
Oily Fish & Pork: *See Pork & Oily Fish, page 36*

Oily Fish & Potato: Chips go with everything in the UK, except salmon and trout – although the environmental historian Peter Coates speculates that by 2050 declining stocks will mean most of the fish fried in chippies could be salmon, a prospect I find quite unappealing. There's something about the bland saltiness of sea fish that works best with the crisp saltiness of chips, while the earthiness of freshwater fish is better served by the matching earthy quality of boiled or new potatoes. Sardines and mackerel will go with both. See also Parsley & Potato, page 193.

Oily Fish & Rhubarb: *See Rhubarb & Oily Fish, page 255*
Oily Fish & Rosemary: *See Rosemary & Oily Fish, page 319*

Oily Fish & Shellfish: Red mullet is prized for its exquisite balance of saltiness, sweetness and the meatiness you expect in oily fish, somewhere between the delicate flavour of salmon or trout and the rough sexiness of mackerel. Pliny thought red mullet tasted of oysters; comparisons with shellfish are common, and the combination is terrific. Try seared or grilled red mullet with a shellfish sauce, or served simply with langoustines and peas, which complement both ingredients perfectly.

Oily Fish & Thyme: Grayling, *Thymallus thymallus*, is an oily freshwater fish that, when just caught and pressed right up to your nose, has an aroma of thyme. As to the taste, it's like trout except not as nice. In *Good Things in England*, first published in 1932, Florence White advised that grayling is at its best grilled and sprinkled with powdered dried thyme.

Oily Fish & Watercress: *See Watercress & Oily Fish, page 100*

BRINE & SALT

Anchovy

Smoked Fish

Bacon

Prosciutto

Olive

Anchovy

Anchovies are, of course, available fresh or marinated in vinegar (as in the Spanish tapas, *boquerones*), but this chapter largely restricts itself to anchovies preserved in oil or salt and the fish sauces of Southeast Asia, made with anchovy-like fish. The richly fishy flavour of preserved anchovies can take a bit of getting used to, but when they are cooked, the slightly rancid note lifts, leaving a rich, seared, meaty savouriness that really does heighten the flavour of other fish, meats and vegetables. Anchovy-flavoured products such as anchovy essence and anchovy butter (aka Gentleman's Relish) are perhaps less popular in Britain than they used to be, but are still (fairly) widely available. Worcestershire sauce is famously made with anchovy, tamarind, vinegar, sugar and various seasonings.

Anchovy & Beef: Garum is a sauce made of sun-dried anchovies or mackerel innards and brine. It's thought to have been a Greek invention but the Romans were famously mad for garum, using it with all meats and fishes in much the same way that fish and oyster sauces are used in Asian cooking. A few salted anchovy fillets in a beef stew, or pushed into slits in a roasting joint, will perform a similar function. Don't worry if you're so-so about the flavour of anchovy: cooked like this, the fishiness disappears in favour of an intense savouriness that makes the beef taste meatier and somehow juicier. Cooks talk of anchovy adding an extra dimension, say in a spicy beef broth for a Vietnamese *pho bo*. Long cooking isn't essential; an anchovy and garlic butter will enhance the flavour of a steak. Alternatively, you could make a Thai weeping tiger salad by pouring a fish-sauce-based dressing, like the one in Lime & Anchovy, page 300, over slices of seared beef steak.

Anchovy & Beetroot: *See Beetroot & Anchovy, page 86*

Anchovy & Broccoli: Anchovy can be a model of discretion – for example, when it bolsters the flavour of a dish and then disappears like a trusted manservant. But it's indispensable to this popular Italian pasta dish. The rich saltiness of the anchovies contrasts with the bittersweet broccoli to luxurious effect – especially if you use the purple sprouting kind, which retains the sauce in its head and its frilly leaves. In a frying pan, dissolve 6 anchovy fillets in 2 tbsp warm olive oil (not hot – you don't want to fry them). Add some chopped garlic, chilli flakes and a bridesmaid's posy of cooked broccoli florets. Push the broccoli around the pan to coat it in the sauce and then serve tossed with pasta. If you top it all off with grated Parmesan, you'll have a dish fit for a peasant king.

Anchovy & Caper: *See Caper & Anchovy, page 101*

Anchovy & Cauliflower: If you like the idea of Joel Robuchon's pairing of cauliflower and caviar (see page 153) but your conscience, or wallet, baulks at Beluga or Sevruga, make do with the less handsome, but extremely delicious, pairing of cauliflower and anchovy. It's a popular combination in Italy, where cooked cauliflower is tossed with fried breadcrumbs, anchovy, garlic, chilli flakes and parsley for a pasta sauce. They also make a salad of blanched, cooled florets in an anchovy dressing made with olive oil, red wine vinegar, mustard, garlic, onion, anchovy, lemon and capers.

Anchovy & Chilli: *See Chilli & Anchovy, page 207*
Anchovy & Coconut: *See Coconut & Anchovy, page 285*
Anchovy & Egg: *See Egg & Anchovy, page 132*

Anchovy & Garlic: Two strong characters. Burton and Taylor in *Who's Afraid of Virginia Woolf?* Anchovy's saltiness and garlic's pungent sweetness combine in a slanging match where neither partner wins. Delicious nonetheless in anchoïade, a chilled dip from Provence in which garlic is pounded with anchovies and loosened with olive oil; and in *bagna cauda,* an Italian dish from Piedmont somewhere between a fondue and a dip. To make it, blend 100g butter, 175ml olive oil, 12 anchovy fillets and 6 garlic cloves until smooth. Transfer to a heavy-bottomed pan and heat slowly for 15 minutes, stirring occasionally. Place the pan over a burner on the table, or pour into a fondue dish (if you don't have one of these in the back of the kitchen cupboard, have a heart and give a good home to one of the hundreds of forlorn fondue sets languishing on eBay). Keep the mixture warm while you dip in raw morsels of cauliflower, fennel, celery, bread and anything else you think could do with a tasty 'hot bath'.

Anchovy & Hard Cheese: There's an old-fashioned English recipe for 'mock crab' in which grated hard cheese is mixed with a few anchovies, some anchovy essence, mustard, a little cold white sauce and a pinch of cayenne, then spread into sandwiches. Perfectly delicious if you banish the strangely offputting name from your mind. Anchovies were also used to flavour cheese straws, or laid on slim soldiers of bread, covered with grated Parmesan, chopped parsley and melted butter, and baked in the oven. Anchovy is a key ingredient of Worcestershire sauce, and, if you need conclusive proof that anchovy and hard cheese is a marriage made in heaven, try eating cheese on toast *without* a Friesian mottling of Worcestershire after you've tried it once. Or make a Caesar salad, a distant cousin of cheese on toast, by rubbing bread with oil and garlic, tearing it into croûtons and toasting. Toss with torn Cos leaves, anchovy fillets, grated Parmesan, olive oil, lemon juice and either a raw egg or an egg boiled for 1 minute and no more. Make sure the ingredients are well combined before serving.

Anchovy & Lamb: *See Lamb & Anchovy, page 49*

Anchovy & Lemon: Pound a couple of anchovies into a paste with a little lemon juice, then add olive oil and season to taste. This makes an excellent dressing for a salad of bitter leaves such as rocket or chicory. See also Caper & Anchovy, page 101.

Anchovy & Lime: *See Lime & Anchovy, page 300*

Anchovy & Olive: Like a couple of shady characters knocking around the port in Nice. Loud and salty, they take a sweet, simple pizza margherita and rough it up a bit. They're used to make the dotted lattice pattern on pissaladière, a simple Niçois snack sold from kiosks in the old town, where its rich, oniony fug hangs around the narrow streets on summer nights. At its best, it consists of a thick rectangle of bouncy bread, a little like focaccia, spread with a rich tomato sauce, then topped with a good depth of soft, sweet onion and a sparse noughts-and-crosses board of anchovy and olive – you don't appreciate them if they overpower every mouthful. The ideal is a detonation of brininess every few bites. See also Olive & Tomato, page 177.

Anchovy & Onion: *See Onion & Anchovy, page 107*
Anchovy & Pineapple: *See Pineapple & Anchovy, page 265*

Anchovy & Potato: Great in Jansson's temptation, a Swedish variation on potato dauphinoise. Chef Beatrice Ojakangas recommends using Swedish anchovies for this dish, as they're sweeter and less salty than the more common Spanish variety. If they're not available, she suggests smoked salmon as a possible substitute. Scatter sliced onions and anchovy fillets over the bottom of a buttered shallow baking dish and cover with fat matchsticks of potato. Pour in just enough cream to cover the potatoes, then top with breadcrumbs and dot with butter. Cover with foil and bake at 200°C/Gas Mark 6 for 25 minutes, then remove the foil and cook for another 20 minutes. I imagine Jansson as a melancholic Stockholm detective, whose sole comfort, like real ale for Morse, is a steaming plate of salty, creamy potatoes, served by a silent blonde waitress in a dark tavern by the sea.

Anchovy & Rosemary: Mix 1 tsp very, very finely chopped rosemary and a few anchovy fillets into mayonnaise for a roast beef sandwich or to serve with grilled mackerel. See also Lamb & Anchovy, page 49.

Anchovy & Sage: Italians call this combination *il tartufo di pescatore* – the fisherman's truffle. Or they should. Individually they lend a meaty character to dishes. Together they're out of this world and don't need fancy ingredients to prove it. Hannah Glasse combined them with beef suet, breadcrumbs and parsley to make a stuffing for pig's ears.

Anchovy & Soft Cheese: *See Soft Cheese & Anchovy, page 70*

Anchovy & Tomato: If you've ever wondered what umami is exactly, a mouthful of tomato and anchovy cooked together should settle the matter. They're paired in pizza, pissaladière and spaghetti puttanesca, but if you're lucky enough to have a glut of good tomatoes, cut them in half, put them flat-side up on a baking sheet, lay an inch of oily anchovy fillet on each, along with a grinding of black pepper, and cook for about 2 or 3 hours at 120°C/Gas Mark ½. Let them cool a little, then serve mixed with cannellini beans and a few shredded slices of salami. If you have any left over, blend them to make a rich tomato sauce for a simple pasta dish, or the backbone of a sturdy bolognese sauce. See also Olive & Tomato, page 177.

Anchovy & Watercress: An elegant variation on salt and pepper. Spread anchovy butter thinner than a seven-denier stocking on two slices of white bread. Load up with watercress and press down till the stalks snap. Enjoy by the river under a broad-brimmed straw hat. And *do* cut the crusts off.

Anchovy & White Fish: *See White Fish & Anchovy, page 145*

Smoked Fish

Smoked flavour is imparted by compounds including guaiacol, which has an aromatic, sweet, smoked-sausage taste, and eugenol, the main flavour component in clove. (Incidentally, both guaiacol and eugenol are found in barrel-aged wines, which is why fish pie and oaked Chardonnay are such natural companions.) You might also detect leathery, medicinal, fruity, whisky, cinnamon, caramel and vanilla notes in smoked foods. Exactly what flavour characteristics are promoted depends on how the raw ingredients were prepared. For example, ungutted fish such as bloaters will end up tasting gamier than gutted fish. The nature of the smoking process itself is another factor, including the type of wood used and the length of the smoke. Not that your herring has necessarily seen any more wood than the pencil tucked behind the delivery boy's ear. A flavouring called liquid smoke is often used in lieu of the time-consuming, expensive smoking process, not only for seafood but for meats and tofu too. In the US you can buy it off the supermarket shelf as a poke in the ribs for your barbecue beans. This chapter covers smoked salmon, trout, mackerel, haddock, eel and herring.

Smoked Fish & Cabbage: Smoked fish is to *choucroute de la mer* as smoked ham is to *choucroute garnie*: the pervasive flavour. Aside from the familiar shredded cabbage and potatoes, *choucroute de la mer* commonly includes an assortment of shellfish, white fish and some smoked fish.

Smoked Fish & Caper: *See Caper & Smoked Fish, page 103*

Smoked Fish & Caviar: Smoked salmon and caviar is a relatively common, if luxurious, pairing, but at Caviar Kaspia in Paris you can order any combination of the nine caviars on offer with smoked trout, eel or sturgeon. All good flavour pairings, but nothing looks quite as striking as the pinstriped satin flesh of salmon next to the glossy dark eggs, especially on blini with a white pillow of crème fraîche or soured cream. At his restaurant in Los Angeles, Wolfgang Puck combines smoked salmon and caviar on a signature pizza. Recreate something similar by brushing a pizza base with garlic and chilli oil, scattering it with onions and baking in the oven. Meanwhile, stir finely chopped shallots, dill and lemon juice into soured cream. When the base is crisp, remove, allow to cool, then cover with the soured cream mixture and a fairly comprehensive draping of smoked salmon. Scatter over some chives and some spoonfuls of caviar.

Smoked Fish & Cherry: *See Cherry & Smoked Fish, page 248*

Smoked Fish & Coconut: In Thailand, *pla grop* are small fish that are slowly smoked over coconut husks, tasting of smoked bacon according to the writer David Thompson, who recommends hot-smoked trout as a convenient Western approximation of the original. In *Thai Food*, he uses *pla grop* in a smoked fish and coconut soup, in a salad with Asian citron zest and in a stir-fry with holy basil and chilli.

Smoked Fish & Dill: Chopped fronds of dill are used to garnish smoked salmon and soured cream buckwheat blini and are also tossed in a creamy pasta sauce with smoked salmon. Cookery writers Julee Rosso and Sheila Lukins pair them in a quiche, while Sybil Kapoor dresses beetroot tagliatelle with a smoked trout and dill sauce. See also Oily Fish & Dill, page 157.

Smoked Fish & Egg: You could eat this combination all day. Kedgeree for breakfast – flaked smoked haddock mixed into spicy, turmeric-yellow rice with sweet peas and boiled eggs. For lunch, a two-hand sandwich of egg mayonnaise and the thinnest slivers of London-cure smoked salmon from H. Forman & Son. The salmon is lightly smoked and tastes of the fish rather than the smoker chimney. For high tea, creamy mashed potato topped with a fillet of smoked white fish, balancing a poached egg like a circus performer. Finally, head to the Savoy for a late supper of omelette Arnold Bennett, a smoked haddock dish of their own devising, doubly enriched with hollandaise and béchamel sauce. See also Egg & Cabbage, page 133.

Smoked Fish & Horseradish: Horseradish's popularity as an accompaniment to beef has meant its affinity for other flavours, especially oily fish, has become rather overlooked – at least in the UK. Not so in Eastern Europe,

Nordic countries, and wherever Jewish cuisine is eaten. Mix some horseradish into smoked mackerel pâté and spread thickly on grainy brown toast.

Smoked Fish & Lemon: Eels get a 'don't eat' rating according to the Marine Conservation Society. In *The River Cottage Fish Book*, Hugh Fearnley-Whittingstall and Nick Fisher describe them as one of the best smoked fish, on account of their rich, earthy flavour, but add, 'You must wrestle with your conscience if you want to eat smoked eel.' One way to work up an appetite for them, I suppose. But better, perhaps, to save the lemon, pepper and horseradish cream for other earthy smoked delicacies, such as trout. A wedge of lemon is the standard accompaniment to smoked salmon. The citrus juice cuts through the fattiness of the fish and freshens up the smoky flavours.

Smoked Fish & Onion: *See Onion & Smoked Fish, page 111*

Smoked Fish & Parsley: Parsley tastes of rocks, rain and lush vegetation. What could be a more fitting partner for salty Scottish smoked fish? It's the essence of the landscape in a sprig of spritely green. Chop it very finely and sprinkle over a craggy mountain of scrambled eggs with smoked salmon, Arbroath smokies or kippers.

Smoked Fish & Pea: Pea loves both fish and smoked ham, so why make it choose? Sweet garden peas are a lovely, enlivening addition to kedgeree or smoked haddock risotto.

Smoked Fish & Potato: Potato with smoked fish is a staple of northern European cooking. Potato bulks out the meal, of course, but also calms the rude flavour, which would have made it particularly welcome in pre-refrigeration days, when stronger cures were used to make the fish last longer. It's a testament to the fishcake that it's outlived these practicalities and made it on to the menus of some of the world's most fashionable restaurants, as has smoked fish chowder, or the similar Scottish soup known as cullen skink.

Smoked Fish & Shellfish: *See Shellfish & Smoked Fish, page 144*
Smoked Fish & Soft Cheese: *See Soft Cheese & Smoked Fish, page 73*
Smoked Fish & Watercress: *See Watercress & Smoked Fish, page 101*

Bacon

One of the world's best seasonings. Some people believe that there isn't a flavour that bacon doesn't enhance. Smoked bacon has a stronger, saltier, spicier flavour than unsmoked. Streaky is more fatty, and the fat is both more flavoursome and sweeter than the lean. For these reasons, just one rasher of smoked streaky bacon in a soup or stew can give a far more delicious result than a stock cube could ever hope to. Salty bacon brings out the sweetness of other ingredients and takes the edge off their bitterness. The aroma and flavour of cooked bacon is famously provocative to vegetarians, but synthetic vegetarian/kosher bacon flavour is available in the form of crisp pieces, bacon salt and a bacon-flavour mayonnaise. This chapter also covers gammon and cooked ham. For more about smoked flavours, see the introduction to Smoked Fish on page 164.

Bacon & Anise: I predict an international breakout for *lop yuk*. Otherwise known as Chinese bacon, it's cured with soy sauce, sugar, rice wine and star anise. Amongst other things, it's mixed with Chinese turnip, dried mushrooms and shrimp in a savoury cake served at Chinese New Year. It can also be sliced and cooked with broccoli, rice wine, soy and garlic in a dish that recalls the typical Italian pairing of fennel sausage with broccoli. Its strong anise accents make it a natural partner for seafood.

Bacon & Apple: Fidget, or fitchett, pie is an old English recipe in which layers of sliced apple, bacon, onions and (sometimes) potato are mixed with water, then seasoned with salt and pepper and served under a shortcrust pastry lid. As with pork, the simple combination of bacon and apple is delicious enough not to need much embellishment, although fancier versions add cider and nutmeg, and at Bubby's in Tribeca, New York, they crumble Roquefort into a combination of cooked apple, bacon, honey and thyme and bake it in a double-crust pie.

Bacon & Avocado: See Avocado & Bacon, page 198
Bacon & Banana: See Banana & Bacon, page 277
Bacon & Beef: See Beef & Bacon, page 42
Bacon & Bell Pepper: See Bell Pepper & Bacon, page 205
Bacon & Black Pudding: See Black Pudding & Bacon, page 38

Bacon & Blue Cheese: The Rogue Creamery of Central Point, Oregon, smokes its Oregon Blue cheese over hazelnut shells for 16 hours. The finished product has notes of caramel and hazelnut, while its gentle smokiness recalls the classic combination of bacon and blue cheese. Make a salad of this boldly flavoured pair by tossing them through some chilled bitter leaves – chicory or radicchio, straight out of the fridge. It's the perfect recipe for a hot day, when you feel the need for something both refreshing and salty. See also Bacon & Apple, page 167, and Washed-rind Cheese & Bacon, page 59.

Bacon & Broccoli: *See Broccoli & Bacon, page 125*
Bacon & Butternut Squash: *See Butternut Squash & Bacon, page 230*
Bacon & Cabbage: *See Cabbage & Bacon, page 118*
Bacon & Cardamom: *See Cardamom & Bacon, page 313*

Bacon & Chicken: A proper club sandwich should have one, not two, or three, or seven tiers – James Beard was very clear that two slices of toasted bread is the absolute maximum. Fill them with cooled grilled bacon, slices of chicken or turkey, sliced tomato, iceberg lettuce and mayonnaise. And don't stint on the mayonnaise. Serve with crisps – it's said that both the club sandwich and the potato chip were invented at the Saratoga Club House in upstate New York – and a glass of champagne.

Bacon & Chilli: *See Chilli & Bacon, page 207*
Bacon & Chocolate: *See Chocolate & Bacon, page 13*

Bacon & Clove: Before refrigeration became widespread, bacon and ham would have been far more strongly flavoured. To preserve meat meant smoking it intensively, lending it a rasping pungency unfamiliar to the modern palate. Degrees of smokiness are, however, still one of the main distinguishing features of bacons and hams. Eugenol, which gives cloves their characteristic flavour, is one of the compounds imparted to food by the smoking process, and I was curious to see how differently a dish (in this case, Hugh Fearnley-Whittingstall's barbecue beans) might turn out made with smoked bacon and with unsmoked bacon and cloves. I soaked 500g dried beans overnight, then slowly simmered half of them with 200g smoked bacon chopped into bite-sized pieces, 2 small onions, quartered, 1 tbsp black treacle, and 1 heaped tsp English mustard. To the other 250g beans, I added 200g unsmoked bacon, and the same quantities of the other ingredients as for smoked, with the addition of two cloves. In the unsmoked-plus-clove version, all the ingredients kept their separate identities, the clove flavour trailing just behind the others much as the toddler spaceships follow the mother ship in *Close Encounters of the Third Kind*. In the smoked version, by contrast, the smoke flavour got into everything, even under the beans' skin. It was sharper, meatier and quite the better of the two.

Bacon & Egg: The quintessentially English combination common to the full Irish breakfast, Italian spaghetti carbonara, French quiche lorraine and the classic *salade frisée aux lardons et oeuf poché* – tendrils of curly endive tangled with lardons and topped with a soft poached egg. And American bacon and egg McMuffins and eggs Benedict, a dish I felt pretty ho-hum about until I tried the version made by the chef, Denis Leary, at a narrow slice of a diner called The Canteen in San Francisco. Airy muffins, soft ham, two very fragile but perfectly poached eggs, plus a hollandaise so light it was as if the chef and his commis had simultaneously leant over and whispered 'butter' and 'lemon' as I put the first forkful in my mouth.

Bacon & Globe Artichoke: *See Globe Artichoke & Bacon, page 127*

Bacon & Hard Cheese: Cheese making and pig rearing work in pleasing symbiosis. Ham from pigs part-fed on the by-products of dairy farming has a particularly full flavour: Parma ham pigs, for instance, are fed on whey left over from the production of Parmigiano-Reggiano. The results are so harmonious they need only be paired in a sandwich to be appreciated. In fact the availability of a fine ham and cheese sandwich is usually a reliable indicator of the quality of a country's food: in Spain a crusty roll crammed with salty Manchego and chewy, spicy *jamón ibérico*; in France a baguette of cooked ham and Emmental with a *demi* of cold Kronenbourg; and in the departure lounge of Italian airports the sort of country-prosciutto and pecorino panino that's almost worth missing your flight for.

Bacon & Horseradish: *See Horseradish & Bacon, page 104*
Bacon & Liver: *See Liver & Bacon, page 41*
Bacon & Mushroom: *See Mushroom & Bacon, page 75*

Bacon & Onion: Ham and leek is a more elegantly flavoured variation on bacon and onion, and makes a steamed suet pudding or pie to rival steak and kidney. The combination is especially popular in Pennsylvania and the surrounding region, where signs for 'Ham and Leek Dinners' are posted outside community halls and fire stations in the spring. Wild leeks, or 'ramps' as they're known locally, have a pungent flavour somewhere between onion and garlic. See also Onion & Celery, page 108.

Bacon & Orange: *See Orange & Bacon, page 294*
Bacon & Oyster: *See Oyster & Bacon, page 150*
Bacon & Parsley: *See Parsley & Bacon, page 191*

Bacon & Parsnip: Pairing parsnips with salty bacon serves to emphasise their sweet, spicy, assertive flavour. Simmer them in a soup or make bacon and parsnip mash to serve with liver or scallops. Paired with pancetta rather than bacon, parsnips work well in a pasta or risotto. Like bacon, pancetta is cured, but it's not usually smoked (unless it's called *affumicata*). Cooked, its complex flavour is redolent of the floral and fruit notes in prosciutto, for which it can sometimes very effectively be substituted – say, wrapped around asparagus or seafood. Buy it sliced super-thin from a good deli and you can serve it *crudo* on your charcuterie board too.

Bacon & Pea: When I was a kid, my parents knew a couple who without variation ate a set meal for each day of the week: lamb chops on Wednesday, spaghetti bolognese on Thursday, fish and chips on Friday – always the same, every week, year in, year out. 'Even on their birthdays, Mum?' I'd ask. 'Even on their birthdays.' In Swedish schools, officers' messes, work canteens, the royal household and prisons, a thick pea and ham soup called *ärtsoppa* is served for lunch or dinner on Thursdays, followed by a dessert of pancakes, soured cream and lingonberry jam. Traditionally the soup was always eaten in the evening, to keep the tillers of the fields going through Friday's fast. To this day it often comes accompanied by a warm shot of *punsch*, a sweet liqueur bolstered by the rum-like Indonesian spirit arrack.

Bacon & Pineapple: How good is Hawaiian pizza? Better than the surfing in Naples. But only just.

Bacon & Pork: *See Pork & Bacon, page 33*
Bacon & Potato: *See Potato & Bacon, page 88*
Bacon & Sage: *See Sage & Bacon, page 321*

Bacon & Shellfish: Delicious in 'clams casino' – clams baked on the half shell with a bacon and breadcrumb topping. Fry a mixture of finely chopped onion, red bell pepper, garlic and bacon in olive oil, spoon it on to the uncooked, open clams, sprinkle with breadcrumbs and bake in the oven. If your clams are quite small, you'll need to chop the rashers finely so you can tell one chewy, salty protein from the other. Keep an eye on the quantities – you want the bacon to underpin the shellfish flavour, not overpower it. Bear the same thing in mind while making mussel and bacon soup, a lobster club sandwich or when fastening your scallops into a girdle of bacon.

Bacon & Thyme: Bacon and thyme make an agreeable savoury seasoning. Try them with Puy lentils, partridge or Brussels sprouts. Pungent thyme is used to flavour mouthwashes, toothpaste and cough medicine, and is said to have antiseptic properties. Smoked bacon also has a whiff of the first-aid box about it, as the smoking process can impart medicinal and iodine characters. Might sound unappetising on paper, but can be very delicious in practice. After all, single-malt whiskies like Laphroaig and Lagavulin are often described as having notes of iodine, seaweed, tar and sticking plasters.

Bacon & Tomato: *See Tomato & Bacon, page 258*
Bacon & Truffle: *See Truffle & Bacon, page 115*
Bacon & Washed-rind Cheese: *See Washed-rind Cheese & Bacon, page 59*
Bacon & White Fish: *See White Fish & Bacon, page 146*

Prosciutto

Although the Italian word prosciutto *can* apply to cooked ham, in this book the term is used more generically to refer to raw, cured hams primarily from Italy and Spain. Spanish Serrano ham is considered such a delicacy that some say the only thing worthy to share a plate with it is more Serrano ham. The practice of serving fruit with dry-cured ham is better suited to gentler Parma or San Daniele ham, as sweet and softly salty as a kiss from Botticelli's Venus. Serrano is more like a snog from Titian's Bacchus on the way back from getting legless in the woods. The difference is in part down to variations in the production process. During ageing, mould growth is encouraged on Serrano hams, creating mushroomy, foresty flavours, while in Parma ham mould growth is curtailed. Fat is rubbed on Parma ham to help it retain its moisture, whereas the moisture in Serrano is allowed to evaporate, concentrating the flavours. Lastly, Harold McGee notes that the nitrites used in Spanish ham production are absent in Parma and San Daniele, stimulating the development of more fruity esters than are found in Serrano.

Prosciutto & Asparagus: Wrap soft, salty prosciutto around asparagus while it's still hot and the fat in the meat will start to soften and release its flavour, providing a heavenly contrast to asparagus's sulphurous sweetness. The only trouble is it can get to be a habit. You start by twirling a little prosciutto around asparagus spears, move on to monkfish fillets and you're hooked, partly on the unique pleasure of feeling the thin slices of ham cling and mould themselves to the thing-to-be-wrapped. I have a vision of whole Christos of charcuterie, the Reichstag wrapped in juniper-smoked Westphalian ham, or the Pont Neuf in *jambon cru* from Bayonne. See also Prosciutto & White Fish, page 174.

Prosciutto & Aubergine: The American chef Judy Rodgers likes to serve a suave, slightly smoky aubergine dip with a garnish of grated bottarga (dried tuna or mullet roe) or with thin ribbons of smoked prosciutto. 'Both have a pungent feral saltiness that is perfect with the fleshy-earthy mash.'

Prosciutto & Celery: I love the Motorail train that runs from the South of France to Calais during the summer months. You drop your car off in a quiet station – rather eerily frequented only by cars – and are shuttled back to Avignon, or whichever city you're travelling from, to while away the few hours before the passenger train leaves, unburdened by suitcases, car keys, cases of wine, glass jars of duck confit or strings of flour-dusted saucissons. So unburdened, in fact, that I have without fail had to run, shoes in hand, for the train before it leaves at 11pm. I'm never so disorganised, however, that I don't buy bread, Bayonne ham, a bottle of Châteauneuf-du-Pape and a tub of creamy, crunchy, mustardy celeriac remoulade. A last-night-of-the-holiday atmosphere invariably obtains in the Motorail bar, and a late, shared snack is always welcome before you retire to your couchette at 3am to dream that you're sleeping on a train. See also Carrot & Celery, page 227.

Prosciutto & Chestnut: Parma ham pigs are often raised on chestnuts, which suggests a pleasing late-autumn combination when the usual fruit partners for ham are out of season. Nick your chestnuts at the top and roast them at 200°C/Gas Mark 6 for 8–10 minutes. Serve in a warm bowl and let everyone peel their own.

Prosciutto & Egg: *See Egg & Prosciutto, page 136*

Prosciutto & Fig: In *Italian Food*, Elizabeth David praises the brilliance of whoever had the idea of serving prosciutto with melon or, even better, fresh figs. I think the gentler, fruity-floral flavour of fig is less overpowering than melon, and the soft crunch of its seeds against the smooth ham is particularly gratifying. When neither fruit is in season, you might try the traditional practice, cited by David, of pinching thin slices of butter between folds of prosciutto. She thought it might be even better than figs.

Prosciutto & Globe Artichoke: Arriving late one night at an unpromising-looking hotel in Ancona, I entered my room to find that someone had set out a plate of prosciutto, a basket of bread, a decanter of wine and some home-marinated artichokes, green as dollar bills but of considerably more value to a half-starved, flight-stupefied business traveller. The translucent slivers of ham were like salty-sweet silk against the artichokes, chewy, sulphurous and tinged with a delicious bitterness.

Prosciutto & Juniper: During production, Tuscan prosciutto is often rubbed with a mixture of salt, rosemary, juniper, pepper and garlic to give it a more savoury flavour. Prosciutto made in this way is known as *salato*, as opposed to the better-known *dolce* varieties from Parma and San Daniele. Speck, from the culturally (and linguistically) Italo-German region of Alto Adige, is a type of prosciutto soaked in brine, juniper, sugar and garlic, then dried and wood-smoked for a few weeks before ageing.

Prosciutto & Melon: Harold McGee writes that during its ageing process, unsaturated fats in prosciutto break down and form an abundance of volatile compounds, some of which have an aroma characteristic of melon. Prosciutto and melon are, of course, a classically harmonious flavour pairing, and so simple to prepare. Orange cantaloupe is the most common choice but a less heady Galia can be as good, if not better. Whichever cultivar you use, don't overwhelm the ham with huge briquettes of melon, or use underripe melons – the lovely, buttery texture of a ripe melon is half the point of the pairing.

But then it shouldn't be so ripe that its aroma catches like hair lacquer at the back of your throat. Make sure that neither the melon nor the ham is too cold. But then they shouldn't be warm either. And don't plate too far in advance of serving. The salt in the prosciutto is liable to draw out the melon juice, leaving you with spoilt, soggy meat. Like I said, *so* simple.

Prosciutto & Olive: Tiny Arbequina olives can be hard to find but they make a very fitting flavour partner for prosciutto. What Arbequinas lack in good looks they make up for in flavour – they're nutty and buttery, with delicious background notes of tomato and melon.

Prosciutto & Pea: Pellegrino Artusi (1820–1911) wrote enthusiastically about the pea dishes served in restaurants in Rome. They were the best he'd ever eaten, which he attributed to the chefs' use of smoked prosciutto. He suggests stewing them together to serve as a side dish, or using them to make a pea risotto or a pea and ham soup. Other than oversalting, it's quite hard to mess this combination up; the most difficult thing will be sourcing good, affordable prosciutto. My local deli sells rough offcuts of Serrano ham. They're hard and chewy and great for soup – that's if I manage to get them home. It's all too easy to eat them one by one out of the bag as if they were dark, salty toffees.

Prosciutto & Peach: If you're lucky enough to come across good white nectarines, try one with some Parma ham. Zuni Café owner Judy Rodgers writes that the fruit has a little bitterness, a floral note and a length of flavour that brings out qualities in the ham obscured by sweeter fruit.

Prosciutto & Pear: *See Pear & Prosciutto, page 275*

Prosciutto & Pineapple: If the definition of an intellectual is somebody who doesn't think of the Lone Ranger when they hear the 'William Tell Overture', the definition of a foodie is someone who doesn't think *Hawaii!* when they see this combination. A foodie may smugly inform you that the Consorzio del Prosciutto di Parma recommends pineapple as a complementary flavour for Parma ham. And it's true that the caramel note in pineapple chimes particularly nicely with the nutty caramel flavours created during the process of curing prosciutto – flavours that are normally found only in cooked meat. Still, no foodie worth his or her *fleur de sel* would dream of threading pineapple chunks and S-bends of ham on a cocktail stick. But I might.

Prosciutto & Sage: *See Sage & Prosciutto, page 323*

Prosciutto & Tomato: Split a panino and drizzle a little fruity olive oil on either side. Fill with silk-thin slices of prosciutto, mozzarella and seasoned tomatoes, press flat and grill. Eat while conducting an unbelievably petty argument with your boyfriend on the back of his scooter at the same time as yelling into your mobile phone. If you don't have the energy for that, lay a little Serrano on a hunk of bread rubbed with garlic and tomato – see Tomato & Garlic, page 259.

Prosciutto & White Fish: One of the factors that saw monkfish become an endangered species so quickly was the mania for wrapping whole tails in prosciutto. Sure, it tastes good, what with the ham's donation of fat, flavour and saltiness to the lean, light flavour of white fish, but there are more plentiful fish that take to the treatment just as well, even if they don't slice into neat rounds like monkfish. A similar flavour, incidentally, can be achieved with some fish without using prosciutto. Scale and clean a skin-on fillet of sea bass or black bream, then run the back of a knife along it, like a window cleaner's squeegee, to remove the moisture. Salt and leave at room temperature for 15 minutes, then give it another scrape and pat dry. Place the fillet skin-side down in hot oil, cook for a few minutes, then flip for a quick final cook or finish in the oven. Properly crisped, the skin is as salty, flavourful and texturally pleasing as bacon and a delicious contrast to the soft, creamy flesh. Works on oily fish such as salmon and trout, too.

Olive

Black olives are ripe green olives and are thus sweeter. Green olives tend to be sour. Both are naturally bitter, which is why to be palatable they need to be cured. Proper curing is a slow process. The fruit is packed in salt, or sun-dried, before being steeped in brine for months. By contrast, the industrial process, in which the olives are preserved in lye solution, takes less than a day. Both the traditional and industrial processes draw out the olive's bitter glucosides, but in the latter too much of the flavour is lost too. Find a good olive supplier and you can appreciate the variety of cultivars available, each with their own flavour and textural characteristics: Gaeta, a small, wrinkled, dry-cured olive from Italy that has a slight dried-fruit/plum flavour; Nyons, also dry-cured, then aged in brine, with a pleasingly leathery, slightly nutty flavour; tart, crunchy Picholine, a green olive that puts up a satisfyingly crisp resistance to the teeth and will cut through fattier meats in much the same way as cornichons; and Lucques, a gently flavoured, buttery green olive from the South of France, touched with almond and avocado flavours. Olive oil encompasses a similarly broad range of flavours, from the mild and sweet to the dark, peppery and throat-catching. As a rule, pressings of early fruit produce greener, more peppery oils, the later, riper olives softer flavours. Cook with the cheaper stuff and save expensive oil for salads, or for use as a sauce over warm vegetables. Flavour notes in olive oil include floral, melon, apple, butter, pepper, artichoke, herbal, tomato leaf, green leaves, green banana, avocado and grass, which leads us neatly on to the next section, Green & Grassy (see page 178).

Olive & Almond: Aged West Country Cheddar and Balsamic Marinated Onions? Wild Mushroom with Garlic and Parsley? Buffalo Mozzarella and Basil? Have crisp manufacturers gone out of their minds? It's a source of genuine puzzlement to me that the crisp should have become the focal point for the rhetorical excesses of late-stage global capitalism. Something to discuss over green olives and almonds. If you miss the descriptive frills and furbelows, you can always call them Tree-grown Valencian Manzanilla Olives and Pan-roasted Marcona Hand-salted Almonds.

Olive & Anchovy: *See Anchovy & Olive, page 163*

Olive & Anise: A natural combination. The olive sellers Belazu say that black, wrinkly olives have a strong liquorice flavour. Deli owner and food writer Ari Weinzweig notes that green Picholine olives have an anise undertone. And *Cook's Illustrated* magazine found that the liquorice-flavoured liqueur, sambuca, made a harmonious marinade for olives. Extend the idea by making an anise martini, substituting Pernod for vermouth and garnishing with an olive.

Olive & Beef: A good handful of stoned black olives, salty and shiny as a pirate's boots, can lend a dark, briny depth to a land-lubber's beef daube. In the Camargue they call this *gardiane*, and use little black Nyons olives, which have a leathery, nutty flavour. Follow a standard beef bourguignon recipe but use a spicier wine (a Syrah/Shiraz would be ideal) and add the olives about ten minutes before serving with white rice, pasta or potatoes.

Olive & Bell Pepper: *See Bell Pepper & Olive, page 206*

Olive & Caper: The first time I tried tapenade I wasn't sure whether to swallow it or smear it on my face and declare war on the hostess. It was henceforth filed in my flavour memory as a dank paste mulched in the oily seepage of discarded farm machinery. More than two tapenade-free decades later, I stayed at a *chambre d'hôte* in Rouen, where Madame la Patronne welcomed us with a tinkling decanter of chilled Muscadet and a plate of her homemade tapenade on toast. It was heavenly. The trick is not to pulverise the ingredients, which tends to make them bitter and tarry, but to pulse them carefully and stop while the mixture is still relatively coarse. Try 1 tbsp drained capers to 100g unpitted olives (or 85g pitted), a pinch of dried thyme and roughly 1 tbsp olive oil, depending how loose you want it. Add an anchovy or two and/or some raw garlic, if you like.

Olive & Carrot: *See Carrot & Olive, page 228*
Olive & Chilli: *See Chilli & Olive, page 210*

Olive & Coriander Seed: Olives are often split or 'cracked' before steeping, so the marinade can fully penetrate the flesh. It's common practice in Greece and Cyprus, where green olives are marinated in crushed coriander seed and lemon. Rinse the brine from 250g unpitted green olives and pit them. In a glass or earthenware jar or bowl, mix them with ½ unwaxed lemon, cut into 8 and the pips removed, and 1 heaped tsp crushed coriander seeds. Cover with olive oil, squeeze over the other half of the lemon, add a grinding of pepper and stir. Cover and leave in the fridge for at least 12 hours. This typically Cypriot marinade might also include garlic and/or dried oregano.

Olive & Garlic: Pity the green olive that's had an entire garlic clove shoved into it. It looks so uncomfortable. The best are hand-stuffed, probably by the kind of women who can, through sheer force of will, get their feet into shoes the next size down when their own isn't available. And is it worth it? You can't really taste the garlic; it just lends a slightly sinister texture, like a chemically softened bone. Better to marinate the olives in garlic and oil.

Olive & Goat's Cheese: A salty, tangy feta cheese meets its match in a Greek salad with meaty, inky purple kalamata olives. Kalamata, from the Peloponnese city of the same name, are cured in red wine vinegar and brine, and have a similar strength of character to the cheese, but a juicy, vinous flavour that cuts through it too. Chop the feta, and some peeled, deseeded cucumber and tomato, into 2cm chunks. Slice red onion into thin separated rings. Keep the olives whole. Dress with grassy Greek olive oil, red wine vinegar and a shake of dried oregano. Like bacon, even average feta is pleasingly fatty and salty, and the temptation can be to make do. But – like bacon – it also keeps well, and so it's worth stocking up when you can get your hands on the good stuff. By good stuff, I mean barrel-aged feta made with sheep's milk, or a combination of sheep's and goat's milk. Feta made with cow's milk is bleached, to mask the carotene that makes butter yellow, and lacks the natural piquancy and pepperiness of cheese made from the milk of hardier, hairier animals. Barrel-aged feta develops a stronger, spicier flavour than its modern, tin-aged counterpart, and can be kept in brine for up to a year. It's worth remembering that not all good feta-style cheeses come from Greece – look out for Bulgarian and Romanian brands.

Olive & Juniper: *See Juniper & Olive, page 324*
Olive & Lemon: *See Lemon & Olive, page 306*
Olive & Orange: *See Orange & Olive, page 296*

Olive & Potato: Stew them together in olive oil with tomatoes, onions and garlic to serve with fish, or chop some olives into a new potato salad dressed with vinaigrette. Cookery writer Mary Contini uses potato and fennel sautéed in garlicky olive oil and a scattering of chopped black olives to stuff poussins. And in Heston Blumenthal's opinion, olive is the best oil for roasting potatoes, as it imparts the most flavour and reaches a higher temperature than fashionable goose fat, for example. And a higher temperature means crisper spuds.

Olive & Prosciutto: *See Prosciutto & Olive, page 173*

Olive & Rosemary: A hardy combination to put you in mind of Italy. Scattered with olive and rosemary, focaccia becomes an edible postcard of the Maremma, the irrigated flatlands that span southern Tuscany and northern Lazio. A bite of olive gives the salty tang of the sea breezes that sweep in from the west, rosemary a hint of the *maquis*, so thick in places that there are local vineyard owners who claim you can taste it in the wine.

Olive & Shellfish: Just the thought of the combination of salty-sweet shellfish and salty-bitter olives is mouthwatering. Especially as described by Elizabeth David: 'At Nénette's they bring you quantities of little prawns, freshly boiled, with just the right amount of salt, and a most stimulating smell of the sea into the bargain, heaped up in a big yellow bowl; another bowl filled with green olives; good salty bread; and a positive monolith of butter, towering up from a wooden board. These things are put upon the table, and you help yourself, shelling your prawns, biting into your olives, enjoying the first draught of your wine.'

Olive & Tomato: You're late home from work. You call for a pizza. It arrives. It's horrible. Lukewarm and flabby with cheap mozzarella. Bin it, along with the pizza-delivery flyer you keep in your letter rack. Here's a quick alternative that's sweet and mouth-filling and doesn't oblige you to wrestle an uncollapsible box into a binbag the next morning. Call it a lazy puttanesca. To serve one, put 100g pasta on to cook. Chop a garlic clove and put it in a small frying pan with 1–2 tbsp olive oil, 3 sliced sun-dried tomatoes, 6 roughly chopped, pitted black olives, 2 anchovy fillets, 1 tsp capers and some red chilli flakes. Warm through. Once the pasta is cooked, drain it and toss with the sauce. Use angel hair pasta and you can be curled on the sofa with something quite delicious in 5 minutes.

Olive & Thyme: *See Thyme & Olive, page 327*

Olive & White Chocolate: The chocolatiers Vosges make a white chocolate bar with bits of dried kalamata olive in it. Not so unusual when you consider other chocolate/salty combinations, such as Domori's Latte Sal (a milk chocolate with flecks of salt). See also Caviar & White Chocolate, page 154.

Olive & White Fish: *See White Fish & Olive, page 148*

GREEN & GRASSY

Saffron

Anise

Cucumber

Dill

Parsley

Coriander Leaf

Avocado

Pea

Bell Pepper

Chilli

Saffron

Saffron is inimitable. Turmeric, safflower and annatto are often used in its stead but can only ever hope to impart an approximation of its colour, and maybe a little saffron-ish bitterness. Saffron combines the flavours of sea air, sweet dried grass and a hint of rusting metal – it's the spice equivalent of Derek Jarman's garden on the bleak shingle beach at Dungeness, defiantly strange and beautiful. This rarefied, and accordingly expensive, spice is most often paired with sweet ingredients, especially those pale enough on the eye and palate to show off its colour and complex flavour – rice, bread, fish, potatoes, cauliflower and white beans. It also combines well with other bitter flavours, like almonds or citrus zest, and is especially harmonious with other bittersweet florals like rose.

Saffron & Almond: The sweetness of almond, boosted by sugar, offsets saffron's sometimes militant bitterness, just as cigarette manufacturers attenuate harsh tobacco with sugar, chocolate and honey. (Sweet tobacco, in fact, is the chief aroma I get opening a box of dried saffron stamens.) I like to call the following recipe my Saffron Induction Cake. Heat the oven to 180°C/ Gas Mark 4. Place 4 or 5 saffron threads in a heatproof dish and leave in the hot oven for a minute or two. Remove and crumble the threads into a tablespoon of warm milk sweetened with a pinch of sugar. Leave to infuse while you get on with the cake mixture. Cream 125g butter with 150g caster sugar. Your saffron milk should by now be the colour of a desert sunrise. Add it to the butter-sugar mixture and beat well. Beat in 3 eggs and 75g ground almonds, adding them 1 egg and 25g almonds at a time. Fold in 3 tbsp plain flour. Put the mixture in a greased and lined 18cm springform cake tin and bake at 180°C/Gas Mark 4 for 45 minutes. Leave to cool, then cut into 8 slices and eat one every day for a week, leaving one spare to induct a friend into the cult of which you will hopefully now be a devoted member.

Saffron & Anise: Cookery writer Anne Willan advises against combining saffron with strongly flavoured herbs or spices. It's best unchaperoned, although fennel, she concedes, is a good match in fish soups and stews. For an idea of just how good, put a single thread of saffron on your tongue; when the medicinal flavour passes, you should detect clear notes of liquorice. You'll also notice, next time you look in the mirror, that your teeth are the colour of a leering Dickensian villain's.

Saffron & Cardamom: *See Cardamom & Saffron, page 315*

Saffron & Cauliflower: In search of a flavour reminiscent of white truffle, the American food writer David Rosengarten added cauliflower to a risotto Milanese (traditionally flavoured with saffron) and found the end result superb.

Saffron & Chicken: Classically paired in chicken biryani and some versions of paella, where the saffron enriches the overall dish while providing a bitter contrast to the sweet chicken and rice. I also notice a distinct almond flavour emerges when saffron and chicken are cooked together, which suggests a very harmonious trio. See also Lamb & Saffron, page 52.

Saffron & Lamb: *See Lamb & Saffron, page 52*
Saffron & Lemon: *See Lemon & Saffron, page 307*

Saffron & Nutmeg: These spice the traditional Cornish saffron cake, which is really more of a bread and was traditionally eaten on Good Friday, spread with clotted cream. Saffron was once grown in Cornwall, which accounts for its prevalence in Cornish cooking long after the rest of the country had given up on this expensive, high-maintenance spice. These days, of course, it's hard to find a Cornish saffron cake that uses real imported saffron, let alone the local stuff, and most bakers just dye their wares yellow: cakes with a fake tan. Which is a pity, as the astringent background flavour of saffron provides a beautiful contrast to the sweetness of the dried fruit. In the old days, bakers would leave the saffron stamens in the dough, which according to Elizabeth David suggests that they understood the superior flavour of the whole stamen over powdered saffron, and that the stamens acted as a visual sign of quality.

Saffron & Orange: *See Orange & Saffron, page 297*

Saffron & Potato: The liquid gold leaked by saffron makes potatoes look particularly appetising. Maybe a primitive part of my brain thinks they've been mixed with reckless quantities of butter from pasture-grazed cows. A little saffron may be added to a Spanish tortilla or Italian potato gnocchi. In Peru, *causa* is a mashed-potato salad whose many variations boil down to what's spread between its layers: it might be a piquant mix of olives, capers, garlic and herbs, or of tuna, egg, avocado and onion in mayonnaise. The *causa* should be made a day in advance, to allow the flavours to develop and the salad to set into shape, ready to be turned out on to a serving dish. Some versions are striped with different colours of potato – blue, white and yellow, the last from either the natural colour of the potato or the addition of saffron.

Saffron & Rhubarb: *See Rhubarb & Saffron, page 256*
Saffron & Rose: *See Rose & Saffron, page 343*

Saffron & Shellfish: The American food writer Gary Allen points out that saffron is especially good with shellfish, as it has a slightly iodine-like, oceanic scent, redolent of just-caught seafood. Next time you order a bouillabaisse, or a saffron-scented shellfish dish, take a deep inhalation before you eat. I guarantee this will bolster your appetite just as well as a stroll by the harbour in your espadrilles.

Saffron & White Chocolate: *See White Chocolate & Saffron, page 352*
Saffron & White Fish: *See White Fish & Saffron, page 149*

Anise

This chapter covers anise seeds, liquorice, fennel, tarragon, star anise and anise-flavoured drinks like pastis. Anise seeds and fennel seeds share a primary flavour compound, anethol. They can be adequately substituted for one another, but what difference obtains between them is most noticeable when you nibble them straight from the jar – where anise seeds are sweet enough to please a liquorice eater, fennel seeds are less sweet and greener, somehow more rustic. A better substitute for anise seeds is star anise, which is also anethol-dominated, and is the closest in flavour terms. A different, if chemically similar, compound, estragol, is primarily responsible for the anise flavour of tarragon and chervil (and is, incidentally, present in basil, too). Anise is a popular flavouring for alcoholic drinks: pastis, absinthe, ouzo, raki, arrack, sambuca and Galliano all share its liquorice sweetness. It's a very combinable flavour, equally successful in sweet or savoury dishes, and gets on famously with seafood and sharp fruit.

Anise & Almond: Anise can do for almond what a half-decent heckle does for a tired comedy routine. They're found together in biscotti, those Italian biscuits that are somewhere between a sweet treat and hard labour. The following crumbly cookies, which wouldn't seem out of place in the bakeries of Sicily either, deliver the pleasures of this combination without the jaw ache. Cream 75g soft butter with 60g caster sugar. Add 1 egg yolk, 90g plain flour, 60g ground almonds, 1 tsp anise seeds and ½ tsp almond extract. Mix well, shape the dough into walnut-sized balls and bake at 160°C/Gas Mark 3 for 25 minutes. When cool, sift over some icing sugar. Good with coffee but at their best with mint tea.

Anise & Apple: In recent years star anise has been worthy of the name, eclipsing plain old anise despite the fact that their flavour-containing oils are almost identical. The compound most responsible for their flavour is anethol, which is also sometimes used to bolster the aniseed flavour of liquorice confectionery. Star anise is obtained from the fruit of *Illicium verum*, an evergreen tree native to China, where the spice is commonly used in pork and duck dishes. Its autumnal, cinnamon-like sweetness makes it very good with fruit, especially apples, and it works well in strudels, mulled apple juice, or spiced apple sauce to serve with pork.

Anise & Asparagus: *See Asparagus & Anise, page 130*

Anise & Bacon: *See Bacon & Anise, page 167*
Anise & Banana: *See Banana & Anise, page 277*
Anise & Basil: *See Basil & Anise, page 213*

Anise & Beef: Béarnaise sauce is basically hollandaise flavoured with tarragon, shallots and sometimes chervil. It's most commonly served with steak, but its grassy, subtly anise-scented flavour abets most grilled meats, fish and egg dishes. See also Cinnamon & Anise, page 216, and Tomato & Anise, page 257.

Anise & Blackcurrant: *See Blackcurrant & Anise, page 333*
Anise & Carrot: *See Carrot & Anise, page 227*

Anise & Chicken: The reason the chicken crossed the road. Roasted with tarragon, it's a classic of French cuisine. Served cold, the pair works well in a salad – see also Anise & Grape, page 183. If you can't get fresh tarragon, freeze-dried is an acceptable second-best in cooked dishes, and will turn a dull chicken breast into as luxurious a meal as you can make in 15 minutes. Cut 4 skinless, boneless chicken breasts into bite-sized pieces and brown in a mixture of butter and groundnut oil. Cover and leave over a fairly low heat until cooked through. Remove the chicken from the pan and keep hot. Soften a couple of finely chopped shallots in the pan, then deglaze it with 200ml dry white vermouth. Allow to reduce a little, then return the chicken to the pan with 1 tbsp chopped tarragon leaves (or 2 tbsp freeze-dried tarragon) and 300ml crème fraîche. Heat through and check the seasoning. Serve with white rice. If you have a little more time on your hands, massage roughly 2 tbsp soft butter into a whole oven-ready chicken, and scatter a little chopped tarragon over the surface and in the cavity before seasoning and roasting as normal. The Chinese might improve the flavour of chicken by placing a couple of star anise in the cavity before roasting it.

Anise & Chilli: *See Chilli & Anise, page 207*

Anise & Chocolate: Anise seeds were just one of the spices used by the Spanish to flavour chocolate in the sixteenth century. It's an unusual combination now, but La Maison du Chocolat makes a dark chocolate ganache infused with fennel, named Garrigue after the kind of fragrant scrubland that lacerates walkers' ankles in the South of France.

Anise & Cinnamon: *See Cinnamon & Anise, page 216*

Anise & Coconut: Like soy sauce, the syrupy Indonesian condiment *kecap manis* is made with fermented soya beans, but with the addition of coconut sugar, fennel and star anise. This gives it a sweet spiciness beyond the typical salty, umami notes it shares with soy. If you love the anise flavour of Thai basil leaves in a green curry, you might have just found your new favourite ketchup.

Anise & Cucumber: *See Cucumber & Anise, page 186*

Anise & Egg: Tarragon joins chervil, parsley and chives in the classic French mixture, *fines herbes*. Fresh, grassy and potent, they make an omelette fit for fine dining. See also Anise & Beef, page 182.

Anise & Fig: *See Fig & Anise, page 340*

Anise & Goat's Cheese: Star anise is very fashionable but the real aniserati have already moved on to fennel pollen. The New York chef Mario Batali pairs it with goat's cheese and orange zest in tortelloni. Much has been written about the beautiful flavour of fennel pollen; the general consensus is that it's like fennel, but more so, with a sweet, almost honeyed quality particularly suited to goat's cheese. However, less rarefied sources of anise flavour work equally well. Donna Hay combines goat's cheese with shaved fennel bulb, pomegranate seeds, snow pea leaves and yellow pepper in a salad dressed with pomegranate juice, balsamic vinegar and black pepper.

Anise & Grape: Fennel seeds might be used instead of rosemary to season *schiacciata*, the grape-scattered bread described in Grape & Rosemary, page 253. Some recipes call for anise-flavoured sambuca instead of water in the dough. Less rustically, Delia Smith dresses a salad of chicken, green grapes, spring onions and leaves with a combination of mayonnaise, double cream and chopped fresh tarragon.

Anise & Hard Cheese: *See Hard Cheese & Anise, page 65*
Anise & Lamb: *See Lamb & Anise, page 50*

Anise & Lemon: Trans-anethole, the principal flavour compound in anise, star anise and fennel, is 13 times sweeter weight for weight than table sugar, according to Harold McGee. No wonder anise seeds are used to partner bitter lemon in some biscotti. Pastis, meanwhile, makes an odd but successful match for lemon in a sorbet.

Anise & Melon: *See Melon & Anise, page 279*

Anise & Mint: While the British tend to marry liquorice with coconut or sugary, fruit-flavoured fondant in the form of Liquorice Allsorts, the Dutch and Scandinavians pair it with mint, or ammonium chloride, otherwise known as sal ammoniac, in sinisterly dark confections known as *zoute drop* in Holland and *lakrisal* in Sweden. See also Anise & Coconut, page 182.

Anise & Mushroom: *See Mushroom & Anise, page 75*
Anise & Oily Fish: *See Oily Fish & Anise, page 155*
Anise & Olive: *See Olive & Anise, page 175*

Anise & Orange: Chefs and diners alike rave about the partnership of thinly sliced fennel and orange. But spare a thought for the poor, neglected Harvey Wallbanger, as unfashionable in its combination of anise-flavoured Galliano, vodka and orange juice as the (similarly well flavour-matched) piña colada. Make a pitcher for a summer party, call it a Galliciano and see if your guests aren't bowled over by its loveliness. The anise seems to enhance the citrus juiciness of orange.

Anise & Oyster: A splash of anise-flavoured spirit is added to Oysters Rockefeller (see also Oyster & Parsley, page 152). But most commonly, oysters get their anise kicks from tarragon; try them raw, sprinkled with a tarragon-enriched vinaigrette, or baked with a button of tarragon butter.

Anise & Parsnip: *See Parsnip & Anise, page 224*
Anise & Pea: *See Pea & Anise, page 201*
Anise & Pear: *See Pear & Anise, page 273*

Anise & Pineapple: The Australian chef Philip Searle is famous for his chequerboard dessert of pineapple, vanilla and star anise ice creams. British chef Aiden Byrne notes that pineapple and fennel are delicious paired both in savoury dishes such as roasted foie gras with fennel and caramelised pineapple and in sweet dishes like yogurt with roasted pineapple and fennel foam. Or try a dash of Pernod in pineapple juice for a refreshing long drink.

Anise & Pork: *See Pork & Anise, page 32*

Anise & Rhubarb: Take a lead from Mark Miller, one of the great masters of Californian cuisine, and add anise seeds to the topping for a rhubarb crumble. Roast and crush the seeds first and stir them in with the sugar. Use 2–3 tsp for a topping made with 175g plain flour and 100g each sugar and butter. This works for apple and plum crumbles too.

Anise & Saffron: *See Saffron & Anise, page 179*
Anise & Shellfish: *See Shellfish & Anise, page 139*

Anise & Strawberry: Anise is beautiful with strawberries – in a sauce, jam, or simply ground with sugar and sprinkled over them. As a variation on Cherries Jubilee, cook strawberries in sambuca and serve on vanilla ice cream. If you're keen to serve strawberries and cream but are saddled with inferior ingredients, the chocolatier Jean-Pierre Wybauw gives some useful tips: a) a little anise stirred into whipped cream gives it a farm-fresh flavour, and b) bland strawberries benefit from ten minutes or so in water with a good dash of raspberry vinegar.

Anise & Swede: *See Swede & Anise, page 121*

Anise & Tomato: *See Tomato & Anise, page 257*

Anise & Vanilla: Galliano, the sweet yellow liqueur that comes in a baseball-bat-shaped bottle to make a bar designer weep, is flavoured with anise, herbs and lots of vanilla. In Spain, the Basque liqueur Patxaran is made by steeping sloes in an anise spirit (where the Brits would use gin), with the addition of aromatics such as vanilla or coffee beans, according to which brand takes your fancy. See also Anise & Orange, page 184.

Anise & Walnut: *See Walnut & Anise, page 234*
Anise & Washed-rind Cheese: *See Washed-rind Cheese & Anise, page 59*

Anise & White Fish: Anise is both fish's downfall and its redemption. Fishermen sometimes keep a bottle of anise oil in their bait box to flavour the bait, as trout in particular are attracted to the smell. And just as both pigs and pork love apples, anise is a great match for fish: see the classic recipe for fish with fennel under Oily Fish & Anise, page 155, which works just as well with white fish like sea bass. If you can't get your hands on fresh fronds of fennel, try poaching fish in a Chinese stock enriched with star anise. Put 2 litres of water, 250ml Shaoxing wine (a fermented rice wine), 200ml soy sauce, 100g brown sugar, 6 star anise, 2 cinnamon sticks, a 6cm piece of fresh ginger, thickly sliced, and 5 garlic cloves in a large pan. Bring to the boil and simmer for an hour. Strain the stock through a sieve and either use straight away or freeze. Use to poach any white fish, or reduce to make a velvety sauce.

Cucumber

Russ Parsons, the *Los Angeles Times* food editor, notes that cucumber varieties are of more interest to the gardener than the cook: they all have the same distinctive green aroma and flavour that we recognise, logically enough, as cucumber-like. Even the lemon cucumber, which is yellow and lemon-sized, is named after its visual resemblance to the fruit rather than any discernible lemon flavour. Any differences that do exist between varieties generally boil down to levels of bitterness, and crispness on the teeth. The texture and refreshing cleanness of cucumber clearly lend themselves to garnishes and salads, but try pairing it with sour ingredients to knock the bitterness back a bit – goat's cheese, yogurt and dill all make cucumber shine, as does vinegar. Pickled cucumbers, gherkins, cornichons and dill spears are indispensable with fatty pâtés, charcuterie and heavy sandwiches. Borage, which is also covered in this chapter, is a cucumber-flavoured herb that can be used in salads, to flavour alcoholic cordials or as a garnish in drinks.

Cucumber & Anise: A study in 1998 by the Smell and Taste Treatment and Research Foundation in Chicago concluded that of a range of scents, women found a combination of cucumber and a liquorice-flavoured confectionery the most arousing. Canny suitors may thus dispense with the scented candles and serve fish with a simple salad of cucumber and fennel. To find out what fragrance men liked the most, see Butternut Squash & Rosemary, page 231.

Cucumber & Avocado: *See Avocado & Cucumber, page 199*
Cucumber & Caper: *See Caper & Cucumber, page 102*

Cucumber & Carrot: These make a terrific pairing in a fast pickle for serving with a piece of chargrilled chicken and sticky rice or in a spectacular sandwich. Cut a large carrot and a quarter of a cucumber into fat matchsticks. In a sieve, sprinkle them with 1 tsp salt and leave for 5–10 minutes before rinsing, gently squeezing them dry, and mixing with 4 tbsp rice wine vinegar and 1–2 tbsp sugar. Keep in the fridge until needed. Drain before using. You have to try these in a *bánh mì*, the house speciality of Nicky's Vietnamese Sandwiches in New York and an ingenious mixture of indigenous and colonial French ingredients. You can make one at home by spreading mayonnaise and a good amount of (non-herby) pork pâté into a baguette (along with some sliced cooked pork too, if you like) and heating it through in the oven. Once it's nice and hot, stuff the sandwich with the pickle and a thicket of fresh coriander. Some people paint the inside of the bread with an oil, soy and fish sauce mixture before filling. Don't stint on the pickle: as well as giving the sandwich its deeply satisfying crunch, it freshens up the heavy meat with its sweet-and-sour liveliness. See also Cinnamon & Pork, page 218.

Cucumber & Cumin: *See Cumin & Cucumber, page 84*

Cucumber & Dill: When I first lived in America, I was surprised to find sandwiches accompanied by a stubby green pickled cucumber, shiny in its foil like a miniature zeppelin. It tasted of dill, and as I was in Minneapolis I assumed this was a Scandinavian quirk, like saying 'oh yah' and enjoying ice fishing. Soon I was mournfully searching under my coleslaw if lunch arrived without its pickle. The doubly fresh combination of dill and cucumber was like taking your appetite to the laundromat. Just when consuming the second half of the sandwich, creeping up the constraining cocktail stick like rising dough, seemed a complete impossibility, you took a negligent crunch on your pickle and were ready for more. Pickles and gargantuan American portions are not accidental bedfellows. Neither are dill and cucumber. Dill seed is known for its digestive properties; it's the main ingredient in gripe water. Cucumbers, conversely, are known for their indigestibility. And so – aside from the beautiful flavour combination – your digestion is held in perfect balance, at least until the half-kilo of turkey, bacon, avocado and Monterey Jack hits your stomach and you're gestating a belch that would reinflate the

Hindenburg. 'Sour pickles' are fermented in brine, not vinegar, and 'half sours', fermented for a shorter time, are also available.

Cucumber & Garlic: *See Garlic & Cucumber, page 113*

Cucumber & Goat's Cheese: On the rue Armand Carrel in the nineteenth arrondissement of Paris, there's an unassuming brasserie called the Napoleon III. It's the sort of place you find all over France – neither rough-and-ready nor haute cuisine but the sort of mid-range establishment that in Britain often leaves something to be desired. There I was served a starter of cucumber salad with goat's cheese. Nothing more than an arrangement of slices of cucumber, translucently thin, topped with four slices of cheese and a garnish of flat-leaf parsley, but the cucumber's floral perfume and alkaline nature set off the cheese's lactic acid tang to perfection.

Cucumber & Melon: *See Melon & Cucumber, page 279*

Cucumber & Mint: Colder than a couple of contract killers. Add yogurt, also known for its cooling properties, and you have a form of gastronomic air-conditioning found the length and breadth of the 'tsatsiki belt' that runs between India and Greece. It's called *cacik* in Turkey, *raita* in South Asia, *talatouri* in Cyprus. Each cuisine imposes its subtle variation – *cacik* often includes lime juice, *raita* onion – but the core remains the same. Dried or fresh mint may be used. The English use mint and cucumber to lend a summer-garden freshness to drinks, most famously to Pimm's and lemonade, although the combination is so good it's worth adding to other sweet, fruity concoctions on a hot day.

Cucumber & Oily Fish: *See Oily Fish & Cucumber, page 156*
Cucumber & Onion: *See Onion & Cucumber, page 108*
Cucumber & Peanut: *See Peanut & Cucumber, page 24*

Cucumber & Pork: The French delicacy *rillettes* is succour to the pâté-lover who's built up a resistance to richness. Goose, duck or pork meat is cooked very slowly in fat, then shredded and cooled with enough of the fat left on it to bind the meat into a mouth-coating, variegated brown-and-white paste. It's usually spread on toast, into whose crisp cavities the heated fat melts, and served with a ramekin of tiny pickled cornichons, whose vinegariness cuts through the fat and distracts you from the feeling that your arteries are furring like the crystal boughs of Magic Trees.

Cucumber & Rhubarb: *See Rhubarb & Cucumber, page 254*

Cucumber & Rose: Share a summery, herbal quality. This natural affinity is picked up and extended in Hendrick's Gin, hand-crafted in small batches by

William Grant & Sons in Ayrshire, Scotland. Oddly for a Scottish product, the addition of Bulgarian rose and a cucumber mash was inspired in part by the quaintly English notion of eating cucumber sandwiches in a rose garden. Neither is distilled *into* the drink, like the other botanicals, but are added during the final blending process to preserve their flavour, as you might a delicate herb in a curry or a stew. The cucumber lends Hendrick's its distinctive freshness, the rose a hint of sweetness.

Cucumber & Shellfish: The freshest shellfish has a soft saltiness that offsets the bracing minerality of cucumber. Exaggerate the contrast with these Chinese-inspired sesame-prawn toasted sandwiches, served hot and crisp with a brisk cucumber garnish. Peel a 10cm length of cucumber, cut it in half lengthways and slice into thin semi-circles. Mix with 2 tsp rice wine vinegar and a few pinches each of salt and sugar. Leave in the fridge while you make the sandwiches. Dry-fry 2 rashers of smoked bacon, leave to cool, then pulse in a food processor until quite finely chopped. Add 200g cooked peeled prawns, 1 tsp sesame oil, 1 tsp soy sauce and 1 tbsp sesame seeds. Pulse a couple of times until the mixture has the texture of white crabmeat. Brush vegetable oil on to 8 slices of white bread, crusts removed, and make up 4 sandwiches by piling the prawn mixture on the *unoiled* sides. Sprinkle extra sesame seeds over the oiled top of each sandwich and toast in a sandwich toaster until golden on the outside. Serve while hot, with a little of the cold cucumber on the side.

Cucumber & Strawberry: *See Strawberry & Cucumber, page 263*
Cucumber & Tomato: *See Tomato & Cucumber, page 259*
Cucumber & Watermelon: *See Watermelon & Cucumber, page 250*

Cucumber & White Fish: In defence of Dr Johnson, when he said that cucumber should be 'well sliced, and dressed with vinegar and pepper, and then thrown out as good for nothing', he was only voicing the commonly held medical opinion of the day. Nonetheless, he should have tried cucumber with fish. Pickled, and in salsas, cucumber makes a crisp, cool counterpoint to fried, spicy or fatty dishes like goujons, smoked salmon pâté, fishcakes and fish kebabs. Chopped gherkin, along with caper, provides the bite in tartare sauce. Some note that cooking cucumber intensifies its flavour while retaining a little of its soft crispness, and recommend cutting it into strips and stir-frying it with firm white fish.

Dill

Dill takes its name from the Norse word *dilla*, meaning to lull, as the seeds are said to have a relaxing effect on the muscles. They're anything but relaxing to the palate, however: dill seeds have a considerably stronger, sharper flavour than dill weed (i.e. the fresh herb). Dill weed (which is what these entries mean by 'dill', unless otherwise specified) strikes me as having a nervy flavour in keeping with its frayed fronds. It initially seems sweet, before a sour, clean taste takes over, to the benefit of rich fish, meat and creamy dishes. It also rubs along very well with other sour ingredients like lemon and vinegar. Not a flavour, in other words, for a Sunday afternoon slumped in front of a box set. Dill is complex, demanding and opinionated. Think Velma in *Scooby-Doo* (basil is Daphne).

Dill & Avocado: Both grassy, but in different ways. The flavour of dill is a neat, blue-green lawn tended with an assiduousness verging on mania. Avocado is the rich greensward whose springiness speeds you downhill on a moorland walk. Mix the buttery flesh of a Hass avocado (the one that looks as if it's been covered in woodchip and spray-painted purple-green) with dill clippings and a little vinaigrette and spread generously into a crayfish, tuna or chicken sandwich.

Dill & Beef: The essence of a Big Mac. Odd that Big Macs are so popular, particularly amongst British teenagers, who aren't known for their love of dill or dill pickles. (Admittedly, judging by the pavement outside my local branch, a lot of them jettison the pickles, but there's still a heavy hit of dill flavour in the mysterious orange sauce.) My husband calls this Big Mac pie. Try it on your friends and see if they make the connection. Corned beef may strike you as an odd choice, but I've tried this using freshly ground beef and it doesn't work anything like as well. Line a 21cm tart tin with shortcrust pastry. Slice and deseed 2 tomatoes and lay the slices on the bottom. Mash a 340g tin of corned beef with 4 tbsp dill relish, 1 tbsp dried dill and 1 tbsp American mustard. Spread the mixture over the tomatoes, cover with a pastry lid, brush with milk or beaten egg, then scatter with sesame seeds. Bake for 35–40 minutes at 190°C/Gas Mark 5. Serve hot or cold.

Dill & Beetroot: *See Beetroot & Dill, page 86*

Dill & Coconut: A common pairing in Indian and especially Laotian fish and vegetable curries. In Laos dill is treated more like a vegetable, and the entire plant, stalk and all, is often thrown in the pot with the fish and other vegetables. Dill and coconut also crop up, rather more unexpectedly, as flavour notes in some red wines aged in American oak barrels. The coconut flavour comes from lactones in the wood, and dill is one of the herbaceous notes naturally present in oak. Worth trying to detect them in a Ridge Lytton Springs, safe in the knowledge that if all you can taste is wine it'll still be a terrific bottle of Californian Zinfandel. For more about oak flavours in wine, see Vanilla & Clove, page 348.

Dill & Cucumber: *See Cucumber & Dill, page 186*
Dill & Egg: *See Egg & Dill, page 134*

Dill & Lamb: Finnish *tilliliha* ('dill meat') is a simple stew of slow-simmered lamb or beef, to which vinegar, sugar, cream and dill are added towards the end of cooking. In Greece, the offal of just-slaughtered lamb is mixed with dill in a soup called *mageiritsa*, eaten at Easter to break the Lenten fast. And in Iran, heavily dilled rice is alternately layered with skinned broad beans and cooked lamb (shank or chop meat), possibly with the addition of turmeric or saffron or both, in a dish called *baghali polo*.

Dill & Lemon: *See Lemon & Dill, page 305*

Dill & Mint: Spearmint and dill seed contain different forms of the same naturally occurring flavour compound, carvone. In either case the carvone molecule is the same shape but the mirror image of the other, and thus perceived differently by the flavour receptors in our noses and mouths. There are hundreds of these, each evolved to receive different molecules according to their shapes, a bit like a vastly complex version of a toddler's shape-sorting puzzle. Spearmint contains the left-oriented form of the molecule (l-carvone), dill the right (d-carvone). Aromatically they are quite distinct, and thus unlikely to be effective substitutes for each other, unless, of course, you're prepared to cook the entire recipe backwards.

Dill & Mushroom: *See Mushroom & Dill, page 77*
Dill & Oily Fish: *See Oily Fish & Dill, page 157*

Dill & Pea: Used to hook up with diced potatoes and carrots in a Russian salad, now as rare a summer sighting as socks with sandals, found only in hotel restaurants and old-fashioned tapas bars. But dill's brightening quality is ample reason to revive this dish. Peel and cube 500g new potatoes, then simmer until just tender. Do the same for 250g carrots. Cook 100g frozen peas. Let them all cool, then mix with a dill mayonnaise. You could add a drained, diced dill pickle for an extra bit of bite. Serve with cold cuts and crisp lettuce.

Dill & Pork: Cabbage, leek and chives are often mixed with pork in Chinese dumplings, as a freshening counterpoint to its meatiness. So is dill, though far less frequently, except in dishes originating in north-eastern China. Here dill weed, along with beetroot and parsley, was cultivated by the indigenous population for the large number of Russian immigrants who had arrived to work on the construction of the Chinese Eastern Railway. You can make Chinese dumplings in minutes if you can get your hands on the dumpling wrappers. Chinese supermarkets sell them in the chiller cabinet and they freeze very well. To make about 15, mix together 250g finely minced pork, 1 tbsp chopped dill, a crushed garlic clove, 1 tbsp soy sauce, 1 tbsp Shaoxing wine, a shake of sesame oil and a little salt. Place about 1 tbsp of this on each wrapper, brush the edges with water, then fold the wrapper pasty-style over the filling and press the edges together to seal. Cook in boiling water (or a tasty stock) for 5–8 minutes. Serve with soy sauce.

Dill & Potato: In Poland, a potato salad without dill is like a union leader without a bushy moustache. In India, potatoes are cubed and fried with garlic, turmeric and chilli, then tossed with plentiful quantities of dill. Dill (called *sowa* or *shepu*) is indigenous to India, but the variety has a lighter flavour than its European relative.

Dill & Shellfish: In August in Sweden, dill and crayfish are paired in the grand outdoor feast known as a *kräftskiva*, or crayfish party. The crayfish are boiled in water (and sometimes beer) flavoured with crown dill, which is straightforward dill harvested after the plant has flowered, supposedly giving it a stronger flavour. The crayfish are slurped from their shells with simple accompaniments of bread, beer, aquavit and a strong hard cheese riddled with tiny holes called *Västerbotten*.

Dill & Smoked Fish: *See Smoked Fish & Dill, page 165*
Dill & White Fish: *See White Fish & Dill, page 146*

Parsley

Parsley's fresh, green, woody notes are described as 'generic' by Harold McGee, which is, according to him, why the herb complements so many foods. It is at its best with briny ingredients, especially gammon and all types of fish, to which it brings a welcome coolness, and a bitterness that offsets the salt-sweetness in meat. Its generic herbal flavour also makes it great for mixing with other herbs. The flat-leaf variety usually has a stronger flavour and leaves that are more tender than those of curly parsley.

Parsley & Bacon: Thickly sliced gammon is traditionally served hot with a roux-based parsley sauce. Some recipes call for ham stock and a little cream, but milk alone makes for a purer parsley flavour and a gentler counterpoint. In France they make a jellied terrine of ham and (lots of) parsley called *jambon persillé*; the one from Burgundy has the best reputation. Parsley's fresh, green flavour makes a cool, clean contrast to the saltiness of the meat.

Parsley & Beef: *See Beef & Parsley, page 47*

Parsley & Caper: A pair of green avengers, battling the palate-numbing tedium of fried foods. Pitch them, possibly in the form of a *salsa verde*, against fried aubergine slices, battered fish and crumbed escalopes. Great too with more strongly flavoured fatty foods – roughly chop and stuff into sardines before a skin-blistering turn on the barbecue.

Parsley & Carrot: *See Carrot & Parsley, page 229*
Parsley & Coriander Leaf: *See Coriander Leaf & Parsley, page 196*

Parsley & Egg: American cookery writer Fannie Farmer specifically recommends a garnish of parsley for poached eggs if they're cooked for an invalid. I'd recommend them if you're cooking for a geologist. Parsley has a lean, metallic crispness and there's an echo of that minerality in parsley's scientific name, *Petroselinum*, or 'rock celery'. To my mind, cooked egg white has the mineral edge of Perrier in cans, and so caution should be exercised when combining it with parsley – especially an egg white omelette – unless you get your kicks from licking rocks.

Parsley & Garlic: By reputation, parsley is the Hail Mary to the sin of garlic breath. Hold a little back when you chop it finely with garlic for a *persillade*, mixed with breadcrumbs for lamb. Or stir the two into sautéed potatoes just before the end of cooking, when you'll retain some of parsley's bright minerality while taking the pungent edge off the garlic. The juice and zest of a lemon added to parsley and garlic will create a *gremolata*, used as a last-minute seasoning, most famously in *osso buco*. Or hold the lemon and add olive oil for the simple *chimichurri* sauce served with roasted meats in Argentina (see Beef & Parsley, page 47, for more about that). Seek out the Spanish *rojo* variety of garlic, which has an excellent reputation for flavour, even in its raw state.

Parsley & Lemon: *See Lemon & Parsley, page 306*

Parsley & Mint: I love tabbouleh. There's a great little place called Istanbul Meze on Cleveland Street in London that serves it as it should be – overcome with parsley. You need about five parts parsley to one part mint, and much less cracked wheat than you get in supermarket versions (it should come as a pleasant surprise – oh, there's a bit – rather than the dominant force). As to the parsley, chop so much that you can hardly bear to chop more. Then chop more. Be as restrained with the tomato as you were with the wheat. Dress with plenty of lemon juice, a little oil and a touch of crushed garlic. If the result is as juicily green as a mouthful of meadow, you've got it the right way round. The herb-light, wheat-heavy stuff they sell in shops gets it back to front: it should be called *heluobbat*.

Parsley & Mushroom: *See Mushroom & Parsley, page 79*

Parsley & Oily Fish: For a cold parsley sauce to serve with fried mackerel or herring, fold 75g finely chopped parsley into 300ml whipped double cream with 1 tsp Tabasco and some seasoning.

Parsley & Oyster: *See Oyster & Parsley, page 152*

Parsley & Potato: Lest old potatoes be forgot: didn't you just love those fist-size floury spuds, peeled, quartered and simmered till soft and pale yellow, with a halo of buttery fuzz? In Britain they've all but disappeared. In Lisbon they're everywhere: in stews and chunky soups, beside garlicky pork chops and robust sausages. Any attempt to disguise their country frumpiness, other than an offhand strewing of chopped parsley, is mercifully resisted. Seek them out at Patio 13, one of those small, family-run restaurants that materialise as casually as a cat or a line of bright washing as you explore the labyrinthine backstreets of Alfama, the oldest district of the city. Traditionally Alfama was renowned for *fado*, a genre of folk music characterised by *saudade*, which is one of those untranslatable Iberian concepts roughly corresponding to our notions of nostalgia and loss. Sit on a parched terrace drinking tart, spritzy *vinho verde* and watch the host turn sardines on a grill the size of a church organ. A stainless-steel tray of boiled potatoes patterned with parsley provides a perfect foil for the charred, meaty fish. You can't help feeling something like *saudade* for the simple boiled potato, in its prime here but unsung elsewhere, pushed out by mash and the ubiquitous chip.

Parsley & Shellfish: *See Shellfish & Parsley, page 143*
Parsley & Smoked Fish: *See Smoked Fish & Parsley, page 166*
Parsley & Walnut: *See Walnut & Parsley, page 237*

Parsley & White Fish: There was a time when a piece of passed-out parsley was to be expected on almost any savoury plate. It was gastronomic junk mail: something you were wearily accustomed to throwing away. But as a partner for white fish it's indispensable. The saltiness of the fish is offset by the herb's leafy freshness. For a parsley sauce to serve with firm white fish such as cod or haddock, add a generous amount of chopped parsley to a béchamel sauce and season with lemon zest and a little lemon juice. Or, for a lighter, faster variation, dip your fish fillets in seasoned flour, cook in olive oil and add a little white wine and fish stock (or water). Allow to reduce a little and, when the fish is cooked through, scatter with chopped parsley. See also Lemon & Parsley, page 306.

Coriander Leaf

In common with its lookalike, flat-leaf parsley, coriander leaf is characterised by fresh, green and woody notes. But in place of parsley's cold-rain flavour, coriander is more redolent of the monsoon, with hints of warm earthiness and fruity citrus peel. It has a bittersweet taste, and is often used as a garnish, partly because its flavour isn't heat-stable and therefore needs to be added at the end of cooking, and partly because it has so many useful tempering qualities. Coriander leaf calms saltiness, deodorises fishiness, cuts fattiness and lends a cooling note to hot, spicy food.

Coriander Leaf & Avocado: A popular pairing in salsas and guacamole. They have harmonious, grassy flavours in common, but the freshness of coriander leaf cuts through avocado's fattiness, especially in the spin taken on the pairing by Ferran Adrià at El Bulli, where the avocado is deep-fried in tempura batter. Cooked avocado is not to everyone's taste – it's thought that tannins in the flesh become increasingly bitter when cooked – but I've not been able to detect anything unpleasant in gratinéed avocado, which used to be popular in trattorias, or in my own experiments with tempura. Whether or not you can handle the double fat-whammy of deep-fried avocado, even with the mediation of coriander leaf, is another matter.

Coriander Leaf & Chicken: *See Chicken & Coriander Leaf, page 28*
Coriander Leaf & Chilli: *See Chilli & Coriander Leaf, page 208*

Coriander Leaf & Coconut: Coriander may well have sailed into our hearts on a sea of coconut milk but that shouldn't limit the way these two are used together. Sweet, juicy coconut is a natural partner for fresh, zesty coriander in this flatbread. Put 225g self-raising flour in a food processor with ½ tsp baking powder, ½ tsp salt, 1 tsp sugar and 25g soft butter and pulse until the mixture resembles breadcrumbs. With the motor running, drizzle 125ml lukewarm milk or water through the tube and your mixture will become a dough. Remove and knead for 5 minutes. Cover with a damp cloth and leave to rest for 20 minutes. Divide the dough into 4 and roll each piece into a rectangle roughly 20cm x 15cm. Mentally dividing each in half lengthwise, scatter the right-hand side with some coriander leaves and desiccated coconut, then fold the left side over and gently roll out until it's as thin as it will go. Set the grill to high and line the grill pan with greased foil. Grill your flatbreads just below the heat source for 90 seconds, then turn and grill on the other side for about 60 seconds, by which time they should have developed some golden patches. Brush with butter and serve.

Coriander Leaf & Coriander Seed: *See Coriander Seed & Coriander Leaf, page 345*

Coriander Leaf & Cumin: Toast cumin and you bring out a bitter note in its warm earthiness. Coriander leaf shares these qualities, although where cumin's earthy bitterness is downbeat, smoky and autumnal, coriander's is zingily fresh. Together with chilli, these two are found in Indian curries, dhals and chutneys, and sometimes in Mexican bean and meat stews. Add toasted ground cumin and chopped coriander to a guacamole, especially if the avocados are a little lacklustre. Also try adding toasted cumin to scrambled eggs with chopped coriander. So simple you'll have time to make your own flatbread to scoop it up with – see Coriander Leaf & Coconut, above.

Coriander Leaf & Garlic: In Spain, *sofrito* is a mixture of slowly fried onions, garlic, tomato and sometimes bell pepper. In other Hispanic cuisines the term might denote a similar mixture that's added to dishes in its raw state. In Puerto Rico they add coriander and *culantro* – the leaf of a related plant, *Eryngium foetidum*, which is like coriander but more coriandery. Not to be confused with the American term for coriander leaf, cilantro, *culantro* has long, saw-toothed foliage and looks more like a salad leaf than a herb. Keep an eye out for it in Caribbean food shops. Puerto Ricans make *sofrito* in huge batches and use it in soups, stews, rice dishes, and anything that will benefit from its perfumed zinginess. Roughly chop 2 large Spanish onions, 1 green pepper, the peeled cloves of half a garlic bulb and a fistful of coriander (or half each of coriander and culantro). Finely chop some fresh chilli in whatever amounts you can tolerate – although the authentic choice is the mild *aji dulce*, which has a smoky, fruity character rather than intense heat. Add a few tablespoons of olive oil, and maybe 1 tomato, skinned and chopped, and whiz in a food processor until finely minced. Keep it a little loose by adding water a tablespoon at a time. The mixture can be stored in the fridge for a few days, or you could freeze it in ice-cube trays.

Coriander Leaf & Goat's Cheese: *See Goat's Cheese & Coriander Leaf, page 56*

Coriander Leaf & Lamb: The Lebanese dish, *yaknit zahra*, translates as 'cauliflower stew', although lamb and the large amount of coriander leaf used dominate its flavour. The Indian flatbread *keema naan* is often stuffed with lamb and coriander leaf, but coriander addicts may prefer the following version of the lamb and spinach dish, *saag gosht*. Coriander has a tendency to lose its flavour when cooked but the sheer amount used in this recipe, plus the inclusion of the stalks, ensures its leafy freshness survives, mingling with the spinach, the lamb juices and yogurt to make a curry that's very luscious in the mouth but not in the least bit rich or cloying. In an ovenproof pot, fry a chopped large onion in a little butter and oil until soft. Add a crushed garlic clove, 1 tsp salt, a thumb of fresh ginger, finely chopped, 1 tbsp ground coriander, ½ tsp turmeric and chopped fresh chilli to taste. Stir, and cook for a few minutes, then add 1kg diced lamb. Brown the meat and stir in

250g (defrosted) frozen whole-leaf spinach and most of a good bunch of coriander – leaves roughly chopped, stems quite finely chopped. Gradually add 300g yogurt. Cover, transfer to the oven and cook at 160°C/Gas Mark 3 for 2 hours. Before serving, stir in the coriander leaves you've held back, to restore some of the top notes lost in the cooking. Serve with rice.

Coriander Leaf & Lemon: *See Lemon & Coriander Leaf, page 305*

Coriander Leaf & Lime: The first time I ordered Vietnamese beef and coriander noodle soup, a wedge of lime turned up in it, I put it to one side and left it there, grinning at me as it leaked tangy beef stock into my paper napkin. Lime, I thought, is sweet. Bear in mind I was brought up on Rose's lime cordial and its matching alien-plasma marmalade: sweet and then some. The more I ate Vietnamese and Thai food, however, the more lime began to turn up in savoury dishes, most often in partnership with coriander. It wasn't long before I was ordering dishes simply because they came with lime and coriander, which is a bit like buying a song because you like the backing vocals, and no worse a habit for that. Coriander and lime are the *wooh woohs* in 'Sympathy for the Devil' – completely and utterly indispensable.

Coriander Leaf & Mango: *See Mango & Coriander Leaf, page 290*
Coriander Leaf & Mint: *See Mint & Coriander Leaf, page 330*

Coriander Leaf & Orange: When people say coriander leaf adds 'zest' to food, they're closer to the literal truth than they may realise. Harold McGee writes that the main component of coriander's aroma is a fatty aldehyde called decenal, which is also responsible for the waxy note in orange peel. Decenal is highly unstable, so coriander leaf quickly loses its characteristic aroma when heated, and is mostly used uncooked, as a garnish. Try a salad of orange slices, sweet onion and radish, strewn with torn coriander leaves. Some Thai spice pastes include coriander root, which contains no decenal, instead contributing woody, green notes not dissimilar to parsley. Coriander leaf is often used to pep up orange, mandarin and other citrus notes in manufactured flavourings. Coriander's oranginess is markedly more apparent in its fruit – see Orange & Coriander Seed, page 295.

Coriander Leaf & Parsley: Poor parsley. Coriander was once the herb of choice in South America, Asia and the Caribbean, while parsley held sway in Europe and North America. Slowly and surely coriander is doing for parsley what the grey squirrel did for the red. It's the most consumed herb in the world. But, if it can't beat coriander, parsley can join it. It shares a green grassiness with coriander and so can be used to dilute it in a dish without skimping on the quantities of herb. And you needn't feel too sorry for parsley in any case. It'll always have ham.

Coriander Leaf & Peanut: Substitute coriander and peanut for basil and pine nuts and you have a delicious Vietnamese-style take on pesto. Roughly chop about a handful of coriander leaves and half a handful of roasted peanuts. Holding some of each back for garnish, mix them with a sheet of cooked (and still warm) egg noodles with 1 tsp groundnut oil and a dash of fish sauce, maybe with a shake of dried chilli flakes and a squeeze of lime. Garnish and serve immediately.

Coriander Leaf & Pineapple: *See Pineapple & Coriander Leaf, page 266*
Coriander Leaf & Pork: *See Pork & Coriander Leaf, page 34*

Coriander Leaf & Potato: Fans and foes of coriander often cite its earthy flavour, which I think makes it a winning partner to potato, sustaining some of the earthiness lost in boiling or mashing. *Caldo de papa* is a potato soup eaten in many Latin countries, especially Colombia. Made with generous amounts of coriander and with either beef or beef stock, it's renowned as a hangover cure. I don't know about that, but it would be easy enough to rustle up *with* one. Homemade beef or veal stock would be heaven, but I've made it with bought concentrate and, as the potato starts to disintegrate, the soup thickens, and deepens in flavour. So: cook a chopped large Spanish onion in oil, then add 500g floury potatoes, peeled and cut into small-roast-potato-sized chunks. Cover with 500ml beef stock and simmer until the potatoes are on the point of falling apart. Stir in 2 generous handfuls of chopped coriander leaves and some slices of fresh green chilli.

Coriander Leaf & Shellfish: *See Shellfish & Coriander Leaf, page 141*

Coriander Leaf & Tomato: Dancing partners in a salsa. So popular that sales of prepared salsa have overtaken ketchup in North America – and that's not counting the huge amounts made from scratch. Basil needs to watch its back... Somewhere in the warehouse district in Minneapolis, a short gust of freezing wind from the Mississippi, stands the Monte Carlo, a supper club dating from 1906, when the lumber trade was at its height. The place isn't retro: you're just late. It has a tin ceiling and a copper bar and serves the kind of martinis to make you see the Prohibitionists' point. Once your eyes have uncrossed, you'll find yourself with the appetite of a timber baron, easily satisfied with one of the Monte Carlo's trademark flatbread pizzas, topped with tomato, havarti cheese and coriander pesto. Every time I ate one I thought, they should make more pizzas with coriander. And that, basil, is the way the world ends. Not with a bang, but a pizza.

Coriander Leaf & Watermelon: *See Watermelon & Coriander Leaf, page 250*

Coriander Leaf & White Fish: Coriander leaf's citric quality makes it a good match for fish. Like lemon, it complements the delicate flavour while countering its 'fishiness'. In Southeast Asian cuisine, with its heavy use of fish sauce, shrimp paste and dried fish, coriander leaf is an essential balancing element. See also Lemon & Coriander Leaf, page 305.

Avocado

No wonder it's hard to stop grazing on avocados: they taste like grass and have the texture of butter. Delicate avocado goes well with other subtly flavoured ingredients, such as mozzarella and crustaceans; the latter love the light anise note in avocado flesh. Often buried under stronger flavours, like lime and garlic, the flavour of avocado arguably runs second to its lovely, unctuous texture, and the cooling, fatty quality it brings to sandwiches, salads and salsas. Avocado oil is even more delicately flavoured than the flesh, and lacks the grassy note, for which you'd be advised to seek out an olive oil instead.

Avocado & Bacon: As rich as Jonathan and Jennifer Hart and just as gorgeous. When these two meet it's not exactly murder, but you might want to have your cardiologist on speed dial. The green flavour of avocado makes a fresh counterpoint to bacon's heavy, salty meatiness, but it's at least as fatty. Get the max out of these in a salad made with baby spinach or in a hefty wholemeal sandwich with mayonnaise.

Avocado & Blue Cheese: *See Blue Cheese & Avocado, page 61*
Avocado & Chicken: *See Chicken & Avocado, page 27*

Avocado & Chilli: The Gwen avocado is a variety derived from the Hass cultivar in 1982 and is worth seeking out for the hint of smokiness that *Saveur* magazine notes is redolent of chipotle chillies. If Gwens aren't available, you can always make an avocado and chipotle chilli soup with any variety of ripe avocado you can get your hands on. For two servings, blend the flesh of 2 avocados with the juice of 1 lime, 100ml yogurt or soured cream, 150ml water, 1 tsp chipotle chilli paste and some salt. Check for taste and texture (add a little more water if it needs thinning) and chill for a short while before serving garnished with a minimal pinch of cayenne pepper.

Avocado & Chocolate: Adherents of the raw-food movement make a silky chocolate mousse from these two, using cocoa powder for the chocolate flavour, sometimes supplemented by banana or date. Avocado takes care of the texture. The aim of the rawist is to eat as much of their food uncooked as possible. If this sounds quite hardcore, rawism's a cakewalk compared to being an instincto. Instinctos eat only one, raw ingredient per sitting, selected according to what smells right. This might be fruit, vegetable, egg, fish, badger or grub, as long as it's uncooked, unseasoned and neither juiced nor ground. The method is straightforward: the instincto sniffs at a range of foods until they find one that smells instinctively right (instinctos are easy to spot at the Pizza Hut salad bar). In time they reach a state of such instinctive receptiveness that they only have to pass, say, a freshly road-killed rabbit to stop and with lizard-like relish snatch it from its final resting place in the hedge. Then they feast on it until they can eat no more – or 'reach their stop' (in this regard they're less easy to spot at the Pizza Hut salad bar). A typical instincto meal might thus consist of 52 egg yolks at a single sitting, or 210 passion fruit in a day.

Avocado & Coffee: An unlikely mix to Western tastes, maybe, but the avocado is a fruit, and is treated as such in Vietnam, Indonesia and the Philippines. It's puréed into a shake with milk and sugar (or condensed milk) and sometimes flavoured with a coffee or chocolate syrup. In Mexico, avocados are sprinkled with sugar or rum to make a simple dessert.

Avocado & Coriander Leaf: *See Coriander Leaf & Avocado, page 194*

Avocado & Cucumber: I make a cold soup with these two. Blend the flesh of an avocado with a peeled, deseeded cucumber and a squeeze of lemon juice, then season to taste. Avocado dominates, but the fresh, green notes of cucumber aren't far behind. Thick, silky, but refreshing. Like a guacamole with its kit off.

Avocado & Dill: *See Dill & Avocado, page 189*
Avocado & Grape: *See Grape & Avocado, page 252*
Avocado & Grapefruit: *See Grapefruit & Avocado, page 298*

Avocado & Hazelnut: According to the Mexican food expert Diana Kennedy, avocados can contain notes of hazelnut and anise. The Guatemalan-Mexican hybrid Fuerte – 'the strong one' – is particularly prized for its hazelnut flavour. Avocado leaves are dried and used for seasoning stews, soups and bean dishes in Mexico. They too have an anise-like flavour, and food writer Rick Bayless recommends a combination of bay leaf and anise seeds as a substitute.

Avocado & Lime: Lee Hazlewood and Nancy Sinatra singing 'Some Velvet Morning', Lee the velvety baritone note of avocado, Nancy the high-pitched lime that cuts through the smoothness just when you're getting too comfortable. At once beautiful together and distinctly separate. The association may largely be down to my having played the song over and over again, driving down Highway 1 in California on honeymoon. While others toast their future together over lightly grilled fish and flutes of champagne, served on a lapping pontoon in the Indian Ocean, we stopped at striplit *taquerías* and ate burritos the size of shotputters' forearms. Tender strips of grilled steak come rolled in a floury, slightly crisp tortilla packed with rice, beans, soured cream, mouth-watering, lime-laced guacamole and salsa so fiery you have to grip the sides of the little plastic serving basket till your eyes stop streaming tears. On the subject of guacamole, some say that leaving the avocado stone in will prevent discoloration. My view is that if the guacamole's around long enough to find out, you're not making it right.

Avocado & Mango: Delicious together but you have to be accurate with your timing. Avocados don't ripen on the tree – their leaves supply a hormone to the fruit that inhibits the production of ethylene, the ripening chemical. That's why you have to buy them unripe and pinch them on the nose every day until there's give. Although mangoes *do* ripen on the tree, most of the mangoes for sale in supermarkets have about as much give as the stone inside them, which means leaving them at room temperature until they soften and release their complex, spicy perfume. If you haven't managed to synchronise your avocado to your mango, put the ripe one in the fridge, where the cold will arrest the ripening process, and nip out for some fresh crab to serve with them as a reward for your patience. Mix the crab with mayonnaise and press into a ramekin, followed by a layer of chopped mango and another of avocado, mashed or chopped and mixed with lime juice. Turn out, like a sandcastle, on to a plate with some tender watercress leaves. Or simply make an avocado and mango salsa and serve with freshly fried crab cakes.

Avocado & Mint: For a salad dressing, blend an avocado, 4 tbsp yogurt, 1 tbsp olive oil, a handful of mint leaves and a pinch of salt.

Avocado & Nutmeg: *See Nutmeg & Avocado, page 221*
Avocado & Oily Fish: *See Oily Fish & Avocado, page 156*
Avocado & Pineapple: *See Pineapple & Avocado, page 265*

Avocado & Shellfish: If God hadn't meant us to fill avocado cavities with seafood in Marie Rose sauce, he wouldn't have made the stone so big, would he? Simon Hopkinson and Lindsey Bareham suggest mixing homemade mayonnaise with shop-bought ketchup and hot sauce. For about 200g peeled prawns, stir 4–5 tbsp mayo with a few drops of Tabasco, 1 tbsp tomato ketchup, a little lemon juice and 1 tsp cognac.

Avocado & Soft Cheese: Mozzarella is the classic cheese pairing for avocado. If the cheese is made without gums and fillers, the two should share a mild, milky sourness that combines with the soft springiness of mozzarella and the velvet depth of avocado to create comfort food suitable for the summertime. Add slices of tomato for an Italian *tricolore*.

Avocado & Strawberry: *See Strawberry & Avocado, page 262*

Avocado & Tomato: Out of mozzarella? Make do with a *bicolore*. Or pair them in a sandwich with a jalapeño mayonnaise. See also Walnut & Chilli, page 236, and Avocado & Soft Cheese, page 200.

Pea

A tiny pouch of sweet and savoury: under its simple grassy sweetness the garden pea is a rich source of umami. Peas make harmonious matches with salty seafood, bacon and Parmesan, and the herbal flavours of mint and tarragon. The field pea, most commonly eaten dried in the form of split green peas, is the garden pea's country cousin. It's less fresh tasting, in part because of the farinaceous texture of its flesh, which swells and bursts from the skin when cooked. Marrowfat peas are also a type of field pea. Peas and green bell peppers share dominant green flavour compounds.

Pea & Anise: The sweet anise flavour of tarragon has a slightly bitter edge that suits pea, which is sweet enough itself, very well. Try these light pea fritters with a sharp tarragon cream sauce. Defrost 500g frozen peas and pat them dry, then roughly process them with 1 egg, 1 tbsp olive oil, 4 tbsp plain flour and some seasoning. Using a pair of dessertspoons, shape the pea mixture into 12–15 quenelles. Shallow-fry them in vegetable oil for a few minutes, turning them twice so they cook on all 3 sides. Serve 3 to a plate with a dollop of sauce made from finely chopped fresh tarragon leaves stirred into seasoned crème fraîche. See also Pea & Chicken, page 202, and Pea & Hard Cheese, page 203.

Pea & Asparagus: Raw asparagus tastes like freshly podded peas, but when cooked it takes on a nuttier, more savoury flavour. Cooked peas, by contrast, retain their sweetness, as well as their own strong savoury character. The combination of asparagus and pea might sound light but it's remarkably flavourful, and very good in risottos or egg-based dishes. The 'asparagus pea', incidentally, is claimed by some to recreate the delicious subtleties of asparagus. Sadly, it doesn't.

Pea & Bacon: *See Bacon & Pea, page 170*

Pea & Beef: From *The Horticulturist and Journal of Rural Art and Rural Taste* (1851): 'Everybody knows how to cook peas, or at least everybody thinks so – and everybody boils them. That is excellent, but by no means the only way to taste this vegetable in perfection; an Old Digger may not be supposed to know much about cooking, but in fact no place lies so close to the kitchen as the kitchen-garden, and it must be a dull digger who does not know something of what the cook does with his "truck". So I will tell you that the neatest little dishes that any cook ever sends to the table are very small joints of lamb or veal, or perhaps a pair of spring chickens, stewed in a close pot or stew pan very gently, over a slow fire, for two or three hours, till quite done, with peas – butter, pepper, and salt being added, of course. The juices of the meat penetrate the peas, and the flavor of the peas is given to the whole dish, so that I doubt that there was more savory dishes among the flesh-pots of Egypt, than one of these stews.'

Pea & Chicken: Liking pea and chicken is about as interesting as liking warm sunshine. But the combination needn't be as boring as it sounds. *Poulet à la clamart* is a dish to please adventurous and conservative palates alike. Clamart, a suburb about five miles to the southwest of central Paris, has long been famous for the quality of its peas, and lends its name to any dish that makes extensive use of them. In *poulet à la clamart*, pea and chicken's stale marriage comes under the refreshing influence of light, anise-scented tarragon. Brown 8 chicken pieces in a mixture of butter and olive oil. Add 50g smoked streaky bacon, cut into matchsticks, a dozen trimmed and chopped spring onions, 2 tbsp chopped tarragon leaves and half a glass of white wine, then shake the pan. Season, cover with a lid and cook in the oven at 160°C/Gas Mark 3 for 30 minutes. Add 450g peas and 2 tsp sugar, then return to the oven for another 30 minutes. Transfer the casserole to a hob and the chicken to a warmed plate. Add 1 shredded Cos lettuce to the sauce, give it a good stir and cook, covered, over a low heat for 10 minutes. Finally, stir in about 300ml double cream and heat gently. Taste, adjust the seasoning and serve with a garnish of parsley.

Pea & Dill: *See Dill & Pea, page 190*
Pea & Egg: *See Egg & Pea, page 135*

Pea & Globe Artichoke: In his 1891 cookbook, Pellegrino Artusi admits his recipe for artichoke and pea pie is strange, but will nonetheless appeal to many. Me included. Parboil 12 fresh globe artichoke bottoms and 150g peas, drain them, then cut the artichokes into eighths. Slowly stew both vegetables with 50g butter and some seasoning until cooked. In a separate pan make a sauce with 1 tbsp butter, 1 tbsp plain flour and 125ml meat stock and stir into the vegetables. Place this mixture in a heatproof dish in layers, sprinkling grated cheese (Parmesan or pecorino) between them, and cover with a short-crust pastry lid. Brush with a beaten egg yolk and bake at 220°C/Gas Mark 7 for 10 minutes, then 180°C/Gas Mark 4 for 20 minutes or until the crust has browned. If you fancy something lighter than pie, another classic Italian recipe is to stew chopped artichoke hearts with broad beans, sliced onion and pancetta for about 15 minutes, then add peas and cook for an additional 10–15 minutes, keeping the mixture moist with a few tablespoons of white wine and/or water as necessary.

Pea & Hard Cheese: On St Mark's Day, 25 April, the Doge of Venice would be presented with a dish of *risi e bisi*, made with the pick of the new vegetables arriving at the Rialto market. Edward Lear would have appreciated it, too: it's essentially a soup that you eat with a fork. The classic version adds a stock made of the pea pods to peas and onions cooked with a (very) short grain rice called *vialone nano* and finished with plenty of grated Parmesan. Venetian cuisine is full of sweet-sour combinations, furnished in this case by the contrast of sugary pea and sharp, sour cheese. Bacon, parsley and (less frequently) fennel are common additions to the dish.

Pea & Horseradish: Is there a deeper cultural chasm anywhere than the uses to which the English and Japanese put the marrowfat pea? The English boil them to a green sludge and ladle them into a polystyrene cup, fragments of pea skin protruding like the eyelids of crocodiles; the Japanese turn them into neat, brittle, deep-fried spheres in pale wasabi crash helmets, vacuum-packed in foil bags that look like pretentious design magazines costing £20.

Pea & Lamb: *See Lamb & Pea, page 52*
Pea & Mint: *See Mint & Pea, page 331*

Pea & Oily Fish: According to New England tradition, gardeners make sure to plant their peas by Patriot's Day (19 April), in the hope that they'll be ready for the traditional Independence Day feast of poached salmon, fresh green peas and new potatoes. Strawberry shortcake is served for dessert.

Pea & Onion: Petits pois are a small breed of pea with a super-sweet flavour. Canned petits pois are sometimes just small peas untimely ripp'd from the pod, and will have neither the sweetness nor the tenderness of the variety they're passing themselves off as. For *petits pois à la française* you should really seek out the real thing, fresh or frozen, to give the lettuce in the dish its due as a bitter counterpoint to the sweetness. The small onions often stipulated in French recipe books are hard to find outside France but the white socks of spring onions, shorn of their tendrilly toes, will do just as well, as will the sliced white bits of leek. Slice a bunch of spring onions (or the white parts of 3 leeks), soften them in 30g butter, then add a few handfuls of shredded butter lettuce (or a couple of Little Gems, cut into wedges), 100ml stock or water, salt and ½ tsp sugar. When the lettuce has wilted, add 450g frozen petits pois and simmer for about 10 minutes, stirring infrequently so as not to damage the peas. Taste for seasoning and add a little more butter before serving.

Pea & Parsnip: *See Parsnip & Pea, page 224*

Pea & Pork: As fitting a pair as legs in breeches, according to Ibsen's *Peer Gynt*. Deemed worthy of inclusion in the 1850 *Oxford English Dictionary*, the most famous pork and pea dish in Britain (particularly in Wales and the

Black Country) is faggots and peas. Faggots are essentially pig's offal mixed with pork belly, onion, sage and mace, then rolled into balls, either wrapped in a caul or breadcrumbed, and baked. Opinion is divided over whether dried or fresh peas make the best accompaniment, even if tradition would have favoured dried, as pigs were slaughtered long after the pea harvest was over. *Crépinettes* are the French equivalent and, wrapped as they are in caul, look similar to faggots but are usually made with a more standard sausage meat mixture of lean and fatty pork, seasoned with sweet spice and sage, thyme or parsley. Additions of chestnut, truffle or pistachio are common.

Pea & Potato: *See Potato & Pea, page 92*
Pea & Prosciutto: *See Prosciutto & Pea, page 173*

Pea & Rosemary: The field pea, which is dried and split and used primarily these days for soup, is thought to be a close relation of the far more culti-vated, vibrant garden pea. Where the garden pea is sweet, with a grassy-fresh flavour attributable to the compound that gives green peppers their charac-teristic aroma, field peas are more akin to another member of the legume family, the lentil. They have a meatier flavour, and are most commonly cooked with ham or bacon, but rosemary's woody eucalyptus notes suit them too. The following is a recipe for soup, but can be cooked with less water to make a side dish for lamb or pork. Soften a chopped onion in olive oil, then add 250g dried green split peas, a sprig of rosemary and 1.5 litres of stock. Bring to the boil, turn down the heat and simmer for 1–1½ hours, until the peas are soft, seasoning towards the end of the cooking if necessary. Add boiling water if the pan is running dry. You can reduce the cooking time by pre-soaking the peas for a few hours. You might alternatively use yellow split peas, but note that they tend to be milder and sweeter than the green ones and have a less earthy taste.

Pea & Shellfish: *See Shellfish & Pea, page 143*
Pea & Smoked Fish: *See Smoked Fish & Pea, page 166*

Pea & White Fish: Surf 'n' turf is all very well but fish goes best with ingre-dients that truly taste of turf, not just graze on it – and there's nothing much more grassy than the garden pea. (Other grassy flavours like parsley, fennel and tarragon also make classic pairings.) The natural sweetness of pea emphasises the savouriness of the fish, whether in a humble polystyrene cup of mushy peas with fish and chips or the turbot served with scallops, pork belly and pea purée at Michael Caines' Michelin-starred Gidleigh Park. And as pea loves salty ingredients, it pairs exceptionally well with *bacalao*, or salt cod.

Bell Pepper

Green peppers are immature red peppers. Green and red differ substantially in flavour but for the purposes of concision share one chapter here. Yellow and orange have more in common with the flavour of red than with green. As you might imagine from an unripe fruit, green peppers are more bitter and have a fresher, grassier flavour than the heat-ripened red, which is sweeter and fruitier. They can sometimes, but not always, be substituted for one another, although you wouldn't stuff a bitter olive with green pepper, and red peppers don't have quite the freshening quality that makes green so good in a stir-fry.

Bell Pepper & Aubergine: *See Aubergine & Bell Pepper, page 81*

Bell Pepper & Bacon: The combination of salty bacon and oily red pepper lends dishes a sort of smoky, sweet charriness without the hassle of setting up the barbecue. It might remind you of chorizo too. A little goes a long way: even a couple of rashers and a wrinkled, punctured old pepper will season a hearty rice or chickpea dish.

Bell Pepper & Beef: Face it, you don't go to a barbecue to eat well. Even good cooks produce dog chews of cindered meat and trays of chicken *à la* salmonella. In my experience, only one outdoor-cooked meal ever came within a smoke wisp of the campfire meatfeasts that made my stomach rumble during cowboy films, and it was in the middle of the New Forest in the 1970s. It was August, baking hot; I must have been eight or nine. We were with my parents' best friends – a chef, originally from Italy, and his wife. Having found a shady spot by a stream, Piero built a fire while my father made a rope swing. I busied myself making star-shapes on the swing until a whiff of searing meat lured me off the rope, over to where the grown-ups were holding sticks – real sticks from the forest floor! – threaded with beef and green peppers over the fire. It tasted like nothing I've ever eaten since. Maybe because the beef was aged rump steak, cut into chunks large enough to stay tender and juicy on the inside while crisp, salty and charred on the outside. Maybe because the peppers were quartered like cups so they caught and held the juices of the meat. And maybe because real and highly illegal wood fires will always lend more flavour to food than barbecue briquettes.

Bell Pepper & Chicken: *See Chicken & Bell Pepper, page 27*
Bell Pepper & Chilli: *See Chilli & Bell Pepper, page 207*

Bell Pepper & Egg: I refer anyone bemused as to why there should be an album of music featured in *The Sopranos* called *Peppers and Eggs*, when said album doesn't contain a song of that name, to a paper published by

Dr Maria-Grazia Inventato, Chair of Cultural Studies at the University of Eau Claire, Wisconsin: 'Peppers and Eggs: Red-Blooded Males and Mother-Worship in Italian-American Crime Culture'. As she says, 'For many mafiosi, the capsicum, with its erect stalk, blood-red juice, and consanguinity with the violent fieriness of the chilli pepper, stands as a potent symbol of Latin masculinity, at once contradicted and confirmed by the strong maternal attachment represented by the egg. However, it should be noted that the recipe requires both the *softening* of the pepper, and the *scrambling* of the mother-symbol, a double-trauma whose significance will not be lost on anyone familiar with mother-son dynamics even in second- or third-generation immigrant communities.' Fry a couple of sliced red (or green) peppers until soft and juicy, scramble in 4 large eggs, then season and pile into 4 crusty ciabatta or white rolls. The recipe was traditionally served during Lent, when meat was forbidden, but it tastes more feast than fast to me. The Basque dish of *pipérade* similarly combines chopped peppers, onion and tomato with scrambled eggs. See also Chilli & Egg, page 209.

Bell Pepper & Olive: A green olive stuffed with a sliver of red pepper is the classic gin martini garnish, although anchovy and Gorgonzola make tasty, if less attractive, alternatives. Some experts say the meatier quality of an unpitted olive is a better match for gin's juniper-dominated flavour. They might have a point – think how well juniper goes with game – but the stuffed olive definitely pips it when it comes to sparing drinkers the inconvenience of hacking up seeds like a parrot, while sitting at the bar trying to radiate seductiveness or discourse on American foreign policy. And besides, the red bull's eye, pierced through the middle with the cocktail stick, serves as a handy visual metaphor for the effect a properly made martini has on the brain.

Bell Pepper & Onion: *See Onion & Bell Pepper, page 108*
Bell Pepper & Shellfish: *See Shellfish & Bell Pepper, page 140*
Bell Pepper & Soft Cheese: *See Soft Cheese & Bell Pepper, page 71*
Bell Pepper & Tomato: *See Tomato & Bell Pepper, page 258*

Chilli

The heat of chilli can make it difficult to appreciate its various flavour characteristics. As with their close relatives, bell peppers, green chillies are unripe and have a fresh green-bean/pea flavour. Red chillies are sweeter and less easy to characterise. Dried chillies are sweeter still, and tend to the same rich, fruity, sometimes smoky, leathery flavours as sun-dried tomatoes and olives. Chilli fans might like to familiarise themselves with the flavours and heat-intensities of a range of cultivars, and with chilli products such as oils, sauces, vodkas and pastes.

Chilli & Almond: Spicy, nutty romesco sauce comes from Tarragona, 70 miles southwest along the coast from Barcelona. It's made with pulverised almonds (and/or hazelnuts), tomato, garlic and a dried sweet chilli pepper from which the sauce takes its name, otherwise known as the nora. Noras are always dried, are red-brown in colour and have a smoky flavour. They're one of the dried red peppers that are ground to make Spain's ubiquitous pimentón, or Spanish paprika. If you can't find noras, try anchos. Romesco sauce is classically served with chargrilled *calçots*, a leek-like vegetable, and seafood. But why deprive lamb chops or barbecued chicken of its company?

Chilli & Anchovy: *Phrík náam pla* is a simple mixture of sliced fresh chillies and fish sauce that you'll find on most tables in Thailand. It's a less unfamiliar idea than it might seem at first, operating on the same principles as salt and pepper but turned up a few notches. Sea salt is rarely used as a seasoning in Thailand – it's considered a rather crude ingredient. Peppercorns, although still used in Thai sauces and pastes, lost ground to chilli peppers as the major contributor of heat when the latter arrived from the New World in the sixteenth century.

Chilli & Anise: When spicy Italian sausages are called for but you can't get any, try a few pinches of fennel seeds and crushed dried chilli with a good-quality, herb-free pork sausage. See also Pork & Broccoli, page 33.

Chilli & Aubergine: *See Aubergine & Chilli, page 81*
Chilli & Avocado: *See Avocado & Chilli, page 198*

Chilli & Bacon: Sweet, crumbly cornbread tends to be cakey until you lend it the savouriness of bacon. This recipe is quick and easy enough to rustle up warm for breakfast. Whisk 2 eggs in a large bowl, then add 450g plain yogurt and 50g melted butter and whisk again. Sift together 65g plain flour, 2 tsp salt and 1 tsp bicarbonate of soda, gradually stirring it all into the egg mixture. Then add 275g fine cornmeal and fold in 4 crumbled, well-cooked bacon rashers and 1 tsp dried chilli flakes. These will lend some welcome smokiness, as well as a flicker of heat, but you could also use an equivalent amount of finely chopped fresh green jalapeños. Grease a muffin tray (use the fat from frying the bacon), fill to about halfway with the mixture and bake at 200°C/ Gas Mark 6 for about 20 minutes, until golden and risen. Alternatively, pour the whole lot into a 23cm square tin and cook for 25–30 minutes before cutting into squares. Whatever the shape, it's excellent spread with cold cream cheese and a piquant chilli jelly.

Chilli & Beef: *See Beef & Chilli, page 43*

Chilli & Bell Pepper: Although they're both members of the capsicum family, bell peppers lack the capsaicin that gives chilli peppers their fire.

Chilli heat is measured on the Scoville scale, with habanero and Scotch bonnet chillies scoring 80,000–150,000 and jalapeños 2,500–8,000. Bell peppers score a big fat zero. But remove the seeds and ribs from a green jalapeño and, with its heat reduced, a nibble will reveal a very similar flavour to its mild-mannered relative. They share a dominant flavour compound, 2-methoxy-3-isobutylpyrazine, which is also present in Cabernet Sauvignon and Sauvignon Blanc wines. Similarly, red chillies taste like red peppers, although unlike green they lack a shared single character-impact compound (i.e., a compound that can summon up an ingredient in one sniff). Nonetheless, green or red, big or small, all are highly combinable. Try an Indian chilli-laced potato mixture stuffed into green peppers: mix roughly mashed potato with onion fried with an Indian spice blend and chilli, stuff into halved, deseeded peppers, put a little knob of butter on each and bake until the peppers are cooked through – about 30–40 minutes at 180°C/Gas Mark 4. You can speed up the process by blanching the peppers first.

Chilli & Broccoli: *See Broccoli & Chilli, page 126*
Chilli & Butternut Squash: *See Butternut Squash & Chilli, page 230*

Chilli & Cabbage: *Kimchi* is a Korean side dish of pickled vegetables, often made by fermenting cabbage and chillies in brine. Before the arrival of chillies from the New World, ginger and garlic provided the kick; now very hot, sweet red peppers called *koch'u* have taken their place, in both fresh and coarsely ground form. The cabbage is usually the sweet Chinese variety, kept whole in the very best *kimchi*, but often shredded to keep the jar size manageable. Plenty of other vegetables, including cucumber and aubergine, are given the *kimchi* treatment; several different types of *kimchi* might be offered at the same meal. Buy some from an Asian grocery if you feel the need to try it before making your own and burying it in the garden to mature.

Chilli & Cauliflower: *See Cauliflower & Chilli, page 122*
Chilli & Chicken: *See Chicken & Chilli, page 28*
Chilli & Chocolate: *See Chocolate & Chilli, page 15*

Chilli & Coconut: Coconut milk enfolds Thai ingredients in a sweet, forgiving embrace. It knocks the sharp edges off lime, shushes foul-mouthed fish sauce and soothes the heat of chilli, whose active component, capsaicin, is soluble in fat but not in water. The medium-hot *phrik chii faa*, or 'sky-pointing chilli' (known as the Japanese chilli elsewhere), is often used in Thai curries, most often in dried form but sometimes fresh.

Chilli & Coriander Leaf: Frequently used together. Green chillies have a particularly pleasing affinity for coriander, lending a sharper freshness to its lush, just-after-the-rain grassiness. Blend them with a little lemon juice and sugar to serve as a condiment.

Chilli & Egg: Experience and innocence; as uncomfortable an incongruity as a baby with its ears pierced. Until the plate of *pad thai* arrives, that is, sweetly fragrant of scrambled egg and garnished with rounds of fresh red chilli. Or *huevos Mexicanos* – the patriotic breakfast that scrambles egg with the colours of the country's flag; green chilli, red tomato and white onion. Literalists, or committed carnivores, might want to add some chopped eagle and serpent.

Chilli & Garlic: Finding out that *not all food in Italy is good* was as big a disappointment as discovering that Santa was a fraud. Within the first few days of our holiday in the Italian lakes, my sister and I had exhausted our restaurant options. On day four we hatched Plan B: eat nothing but *aglio, olio e peperoncino*. Spaghetti with garlic, oil and chilli. It's not always on the menu, but rest assured that the kitchen will have the ingredients, and be sufficiently aroused by the mark-up not to turn down the request. *Aglio olio* is the sort of dish Italians knock up late at night for friends, and if you try it yourself you'll see why – it's mysteriously more delicious, and satisfying, than the sum of its parts. Certainly good enough to eat four nights in a row. While your spaghetti is boiling, warm enough olive oil in a pan to coat the pasta without drenching it. Finely slice some garlic (a clove per serving, as a rough guide), slide it into the oil and fry until it just turns golden. Don't burn it. You might alternatively fry the garlic whole or crushed, depending on how garlicky you want it – sliced is the *via media*. Remove the garlic, or don't (depending, again, on levels of garlic tolerance), shake in a teaspoon of dried chilli flakes and toss your perfectly cooked spaghetti in the flavoured oil. Serve with chopped parsley and grated Parmesan.

Chilli & Ginger: *See Ginger & Chilli, page 309*
Chilli & Goat's Cheese: *See Goat's Cheese & Chilli, page 56*
Chilli & Hard Cheese: *See Hard Cheese & Chilli, page 67*

Chilli & Lemon: The heat of a chilli can disguise its fruity qualities. The habanero, for example, is so fiery you'll almost certainly have missed its lovely citrus notes, which pair so nicely with lemon in both savoury and sweet sauces. As the name suggests, Aji Lemon Drop is another variety of citrussy chilli pepper, but it also scores highly on the Scoville scale of chilli heat. In the US, Toad Sweat, a range of chillified dessert sauces, includes a lemon-vanilla sauce with a hint of habanero, good with ice cream and fruit salads.

Chilli & Lime: *See Lime & Chilli, page 301*
Chilli & Liver: *See Liver & Chilli, page 41*
Chilli & Mango: *See Mango & Chilli, page 290*

Chilli & Mint: *Vada pav*, a popular fast-food snack indigenous to Mumbai, is essentially a patty of mashed potato combined with onion and spices, deep-fried in chickpea batter and spread with a vibrant chutney made of mint leaves ground with fresh green chillies, lemon juice and salt. It comes in a soft white roll. Chilli-mint jelly is delicious, and easy to make at home: simply add a couple of finely chopped jalapeños to a standard mint jelly recipe.

Chilli & Oily Fish: *See Oily Fish & Chilli, page 156*

Chilli & Olive: The pleasing counterpoint of sweet flecks of chilli in olives is lent scientific weight by research conducted at the University of California, Davis. Capsaicin, the compound responsible for chilli heat, also suppresses our ability to detect bitterness, thus moderating the harshness of the olives.

Chilli & Orange: *See Orange & Chilli, page 294*
Chilli & Oyster: *See Oyster & Chilli, page 151*

Chilli & Peanut: Is it the peanut's mission to neutralise chilli? Capsaicin, the sinisterly flavourless, odourless, heat-giving compound in chilli, is fat- but not water-soluble, and thus foiled (some say) by oily peanut. Peanut also comes armed with tryptophan, which induces sleep, and undermines the endorphins produced by the body to counter the pain of chilli heat (and which, it's argued, constitute the otherwise counterintuitive pleasure of removing the top of your scalp with a prawn vindaloo). Or are they working together? Chilli and peanut combine to make a complex garnish for soups and noodle dishes, are ground into a paste for satays, and in Mexico take centre stage in *mole de cacahuate*, a smoky sauce made with lots of dried chillies and peanuts.

Chilli & Pineapple: *See Pineapple & Chilli, page 266*

Chilli & Pork: Sweet dried red chilli meets pork in chorizo sausages, which were exotic a decade ago, then suddenly hit the big time and have been painting the world's menus red ever since. According to the strength of pimentón used to flavour it, chorizo comes *dulce* (sweet/mild) and *picante*, although the spice is also available in *agridulce*, or bittersweet, form. Pimentón is made from a variety of chillies, including nora and choricero, and also varies regionally and according to production technique. In La Vera valley in Extremadura, the ripe peppers are hung in smokeries in the fields and left for up to two weeks to develop the characteristic deep, rich quality that's substantially different from the flavour of chillies left to dry in the sun. There's a lot to be said for trying out the full range of pimentón varieties to understand quite how different one is from the other, and (note to self) not just because they come in such pretty tins. Paprika from Hungary is similarly prepared with dried red chillies and is available in a similar range of styles, but is said to be fruitier than pimentón. It's used in roughly the same way pimentón is used in Spain – i.e. with everything.

Chilli & Potato: *See Potato & Chilli, page 90*
Chilli & Shellfish: *See Shellfish & Chilli, page 141*

Chilli & Tomato: In the early 1990s, a tapas bar opened near where I worked in London. A pokey little place, with room for maybe 20 or 30 customers, but the food was great. Well, I say the food, but what I really mean is the *patatas bravas*. 'Fierce potatoes', as any tapas lover will know, are fried potato wedges or cubes, draped in a tomato sauce spiked with fiery pimentón. Here they came with *aioli* too, Barcelona-style. Sure, we tried the manzanilla clams, the spicy *albondigas*, the tortilla and the *gambas al pil-pil*. But after a few visits all we ever ordered was the *bravas. Bravas, bravas, bravas.* In time, people would make the pilgrimage to Soho, as they do to the famous Las Bravas in Madrid. Or they might have done had the place not abruptly shut down. I wonder in hindsight if the owners, dreaming of converting numb British palates to the glories of Spanish cuisine, had grown tired of running a glorified chip shop, packed with increasingly ample women glugging over-oaked Rioja and stubbing out Marlboro Lights in smears of garlic mayonnaise.

Chilli & Walnut: *See Walnut & Chilli, page 236*
Chilli & Watermelon: *See Watermelon & Chilli, page 249*

SPICY

....

Basil

Cinnamon

Clove

Nutmeg

Parsnip

Basil

Sweet basil is the warmest, most fragrant, beautiful, fresh and irritatingly likeable of herbs. It has strong notes of spice – clove, cinnamon, anise and tarragon – combined with a minty grassiness that's particularly noticeable when it is pulverised in quantity to make pesto. Basil comes in many 'flavour variants', such as lemon, lime, cinnamon and the liquorice-flavoured Thai basil, all of which share a rich spiciness and an enlivening freshness. Dried basil is no substitute for fresh, but it's not to be sniffed at. Sure, with drying, the beautiful, perfumed top note disappears, but carefully dried basil develops a spicy, liquoricy, mint character that works well in fish stews or baked lamb dishes.

Basil & Anise: If you love basil and star anise, you'll walk over hot coals for Thai basil. Identifiable by its purple stem, Thai basil has a liquorice flavour with a hint of cinnamon. Unless you live near a Thai or Chinese supermarket, it's probably easier to grow your own than find it to buy, and well worth it if you cook a lot of Thai curries or stir-fries.

Basil & Chicken: A sort of wish-fulfilment combination: less charming together than you'd hope they'd be. Basil mayonnaise is good in a chicken baguette, and sweet basil leaves are an adequate substitute for Thai basil in a Thai-style stir-fry, but please: spare us the chicken with pesto on pasta.

Basil & Clove: Some of sweet basil's spiciness comes from eugenol, which gives cloves their distinctive flavour. I've heard of Italian housewives putting a pinch of ground cloves in their pesto if the basil isn't pulling its weight. The flavour of holy basil, used in Thai cooking, is dominated by eugenol and, when fresh, shares some of clove's anaesthetic effect on the mouth. Which is maybe why the herb is often paired with chilli in stir-fries such as *bai kaprow*: the basil takes the edge off the chilli's heat. Pound 3 cloves of garlic, fresh red chilli to taste and a little salt into a paste. Heat 2 tbsp groundnut oil over a high heat and cook the paste for 30 seconds. Add 2 minced or thinly sliced chicken breasts and stir-fry until cooked through. Pour in a sauce mix of 3 tbsp water, 2 tbsp soy sauce, 1 tsp sugar, ¼ tsp white pepper and a handful of holy basil leaves. Serve with plain rice. Season to taste with the sauce in Lime & Anchovy, page 300.

Basil & Coconut: Freshly torn basil leaves make an ideal counterpoint to rich, fatty coconut. Strewing standard sweet basil over a creamy Thai curry works wonders, not just on the flavour but also by giving it the floating-market prettiness that makes Thai soups so appetising to the eye. Even better, if you can get it, Thai basil has a similar flavour to its sweet relative, but with stronger aniseed notes.

Basil & Egg: When in the mood to make eggs green
(To clarify just what I mean,
Not 'eco' green, like Prius cars
But *coloured* green, like men from Mars),
In your mental pan you should
Consider only what tastes good.
Rule out at once the croquet lawn,
The waistcoat of a leprechaun.
Green ink will only make you ill,
As would a mashed-up dollar bill.
Avocado'd be a waste:
In scrambled eggs it's hard to taste.
Green tea – a very current fad –
Would be preposterously bad.
Leeks and lettuces lack the might:
When cooked they'll be less *green*, more *white*.
Peas and peppers taste persuasive,
But their colour's not pervasive.
Broccoli all but makes the mark,
Except its green's a trifle dark;
Celery, okra, courgettes, kale
In hue and flavour mostly fail.
Of the green things that we tested
Basil simply can't be bested.
To scrambled eggs you add pesto,
Stir it well, and then, *hey presto* –
Green eggs. Season. Serve with ham.
(Do not prepare for folk named Sam.)

Basil & Garlic: *See Garlic & Basil, page 112*

Basil & Goat's Cheese: In tomato and mozzarella salad, basil's all ring-a-ding sweetness and light, but in rougher company it can turn quite raunchy, as in pesto. Pair it with a lusty goat's cheese – preferably something piquant, well chilled, and soft enough to be spread on these pesto scones. Place 375g plain flour in a food processor with a pinch of salt and 1 tbsp baking powder and pulse to mix. Add 75g diced cold butter and resume pulsing until the mixture has the texture of breadcrumbs. Mix 4 tbsp pesto with 125ml cold milk and add through the feed tube with the machine running. Mix until you have a dough, adding a little more milk or flour respectively if it's too dry or too wet. Remove the dough, knead briefly on a floured surface until smooth, and roll out to 1.5cm thick. Cut out 12 rounds with a 6cm biscuit cutter, place on a greased baking sheet and bake at 220°C/Gas Mark 7 for 12–15 minutes.

Basil & Hard Cheese: *See Hard Cheese & Basil, page 66*

Basil & Lemon: *See Lemon & Basil, page 304*
Basil & Lime: *See Lime & Basil, page 300*

Basil & Mint: A mint character can often be detected in basil, especially when dried, although this is not always welcome. Ligurian basil is the preferred type for making pesto because of its lack of mintiness. Make the most of both herbs' abundance in summer with this courgette pasta. Cut 4 courgettes into 2cm-thick coins and place on a well-oiled baking tray. Drizzle with more oil and roast at 180°C/Gas Mark 4 for about 30 minutes. Meanwhile, cook 200g pasta (conchiglie or farfalle) so that it's *al dente* by the time the courgettes are well browned on both sides and a bit collapsed. Drain the pasta and mix it with the courgettes and the oil in the tray. Stir in a couple of handfuls of grated Parmesan and some finely chopped basil and mint. Garlic cloves, roasted with the courgettes and peeled, are a good addition.

Basil & Raspberry: *See Raspberry & Basil, page 338*
Basil & Shellfish: *See Shellfish & Basil, page 140*

Basil & Soft Cheese: Basil could be considered the herbal equivalent of the allspice berry, combining the flavours of clove, cinnamon, mint and anise. And where spices can be awkward to include in a sandwich, basil can just be smoothed on to the bread like a transfer, preferably with some sliced mozzarella, prosciutto and tomato. Aside from the beautiful flavour released by its essential oils, it will contribute a satisfying snap on the teeth – the plant world's answer to the pleasures of biting into a sausage.

Basil & Tomato: Tomato's sweet and sour flesh loves the bitter, spicy flavour of fresh basil. With both to hand, even the least experienced cook can make something delicious – consider them culinary stabilisers. Combine them in a thick sauce for pasta or pizza (see Garlic & Basil, page 112), a soup, a risotto, an omelette or a tart. If that's too much trouble on a hot summer's day, in less than ten minutes you could chop and pile them on to toasted rustic bread for bruschetta, or made a salad with mozzarella, or a panzanella salad with yesterday's bread. Or try tossing chopped tomato and torn-up basil leaves through just-cooked angel hair pasta with a little olive oil and seasoning; so rewarding for such little effort. Jars of ready-made tomato and basil sauce should blush for shame. See also Tomato & Clove, page 259.

Basil & Walnut: Walnut and basil mingle pleasingly with cooked green beans. Toss the just-drained beans in warm walnut oil and scatter with torn basil, maybe with some chopped walnuts too. If you don't like the resinous flavour of pine nuts in pesto you'll find that walnuts make a fine, and far less opinionated, substitute.

Cinnamon

Homely *and* exotic. Sweet, warm, slightly bitter cinnamon flavours apple pies, Christmassy confections, Moroccan tagines and salads, Mexican *moles* and Indian dhals. Cassia (*Cinnamomum cassia*), cinnamon's rougher cousin, comes in shards of bark in contrast to true cinnamon's neat scrolls. It's considerably cheaper and so is sometimes sold ground with the real stuff by spice merchants. Sniff it and you'll detect something of a star-anise quality – it's sometimes called Chinese cinnamon – although for me it's so redolent of cola you can almost hear it burp.

Cinnamon & Almond: *See Almond & Cinnamon, page 243*

Cinnamon & Anise: Chinese five-spice powder is a combination of ground cinnamon, star anise, fennel seed, clove and Sichuan pepper. If you're a few spices short, even a stick of cinnamon and a carpel of star anise can give bought beef stock a rich, Oriental depth. Throw in shreds of leftover roast beef, rice noodles, spring onion, mint and chilli for a phoney (but delicious) Vietnamese *pho*.

Cinnamon & Apple: *See Apple & Cinnamon, page 270*

Cinnamon & Apricot: The old English name for cinnamon was 'pudding stick'. It's like a wand to transform all manner of sweets. Poach apricots with a little water, a cinnamon stick and sugar to taste.

Cinnamon & Banana: *See Banana & Cinnamon, page 278*
Cinnamon & Beef: *See Beef & Cinnamon, page 44*
Cinnamon & Blueberry: *See Blueberry & Cinnamon, page 344*

Cinnamon & Butternut Squash: Sweeter than a basket of kittens sharing a lollipop. Delicious roasted together or paired in a soup. See also Ginger & Butternut Squash, page 308.

Cinnamon & Cardamom: *See Cardamom & Cinnamon, page 314*

Cinnamon & Carrot: Carrot has a woody character with hints of pine. Cinnamon is the dried inner bark of a tropical tree. Bring them together in a classic carrot cake and plant an arboretum in your flavour memory.

Cinnamon & Cherry: Whirl like folk dancers in Hungarian cherry soup. Pit 500g sour (e.g. morello) cherries. Put the stones in a freezer bag and bash with a rolling pin until some of them are cracked. Empty into a pan with 500ml wine (Riesling, Bordeaux and fruity rosés are all commonly used in this type of soup), a 6cm cinnamon stick, 50g sugar, a strip of lemon zest, the juice of ½ lemon and a pinch of salt. Bring these to a simmer, cover and cook for 15 minutes. Strain the mixture into a clean pan over a medium heat. Hold back a few tablespoons and mix them with 1 tsp cornflour to make a paste. Add this to the warming, boozy cherry juice and stir until it thickens a little. Add the cherries and simmer for about 10 minutes, until soft. Leave to cool a little, then stir in 150ml soured cream and liquidise in a blender. Serve chilled as an appetiser or a dessert, perhaps using more sugar in the latter case. If you can only find sweet cherries, use just 25g sugar to begin with, add a little more lemon juice, then adjust to taste accordingly.

Cinnamon & Chocolate: A popular combination in Mexico, where they go nuts for it in both drinking chocolate and chocolate bars. It's also found in their famous *mole* sauce for meat – see Chocolate & Chilli, page 15. Elsewhere in the world, vanilla has replaced cinnamon as the aromatic of choice for flavouring chocolate – although Nestlé in Canada recently launched a limited-edition cinnamon Kit Kat.

Cinnamon & Clove: Kicks the holly and the ivy into touch. A simmering pan of mulled wine. Plum pudding. Mince pies. Such a gorgeous combination shouldn't be limited to Christmas or sweet stuff. Drop a 6cm cinnamon stick and 3 cloves into a pan of basmati rice while it's cooking to make a non-specifically festive accompaniment to curry. Add ½ tsp turmeric if you like it yellow.

Cinnamon & Coconut: *See Coconut & Cinnamon, page 287*
Cinnamon & Coffee: *See Coffee & Cinnamon, page 20*

Cinnamon & Fig: There's a kind of sherry called Pedro Ximénez that's as syrupy and dark as old-fashioned cough mixture and as sweet as figgy pudding. Simmer 15 chopped dried figs in 100ml warm water, 100ml Pedro Ximénez and ½ tsp ground cinnamon until the liquid is thick and sticky. Cool slightly, and serve with vanilla ice cream.

Cinnamon & Ginger: *See Ginger & Cinnamon, page 310*

Cinnamon & Grapefruit: A half grapefruit sprinkled with cinnamon is a fine partnership. So how about this grapefruit cheesecake with a biscuit base enriched with cinnamon and honey? Melt 75g butter and stir in 10 crushed digestive biscuits, 2 tsp ground cinnamon and 2 tbsp honey. Press into a 20cm loose-bottomed flan tin. Stir 3 tbsp icing sugar into 500g mascarpone cheese, then carefully fold in the juice and grated zest of 2 grapefruit plus the finely chopped flesh of another. Spoon on to the biscuit base and refrigerate for a few hours before serving. You could alternatively set the topping with gelatine but I like the loose, unctuous creaminess the simpler recipe gives.

Cinnamon & Lamb: As night falls on the Djmaa el Fna in Marrakech, the air fills with the aroma of spiced meat cooking on charcoal grills, drawing in locals and tourists, weaving like charmed snakes between neat stacks of sheep's heads, to sit at smoky stalls lit by gas lanterns. Harassed parents wishing their kids were as keen to arrive at the dinner table might try the same trick – simply grill lamb chops with a sprinkle of cinnamon. It's great in a slow-cooked lamb tagine, too, or in minced lamb kebabs made with finely chopped onion. Try roughly 1 tsp cinnamon per 500g meat.

Cinnamon & Lime: *See Lime & Cinnamon, page 301*

Cinnamon & Mint: A hot yet herbaceous mix that works well with red meat. Or add a few cinnamon sticks to the mint syrup in Mint & Watermelon on page 332 to make a cinna-mint variant. Dilute with sparkling water for a long, refreshing drink.

Cinnamon & Orange: After a few seconds in the mouth, a piece of cinnamon should take on a complex character as its essential oils rehydrate, according to spice expert Tony Hill. Essences of orange and cedar come first, followed by a heat reminiscent of clove or mild pepper. Cinnamon not only combines beautifully with orange but its sweetness offsets the fruit's sharpness. Orange slices sprinkled with a few pinches of ground cinnamon and a drop or two of orange-flower water are a classic combination. Or try cinnamon added to the cake in Orange & Almond, page 293.

Cinnamon & Peanut: *See Peanut & Cinnamon, page 24*
Cinnamon & Pear: *See Pear & Cinnamon, page 274*
Cinnamon & Pineapple: *See Pineapple & Cinnamon, page 266*

Cinnamon & Pork: In Vietnam this pairing is found in a popular kind of charcuterie called *cha que*. Blitz 500g lean pork leg in a food processor with 3 tbsp fish sauce, 3 tbsp water, 2 tbsp groundnut oil, 1 tbsp cornflour, 1 tsp ground cinnamon, 1 tsp baking powder, ½ tsp salt and a little white pepper. Place on a baking sheet covered with foil and fashion into a rough cylinder 6cm thick. Wet the palm of your hand and smooth the surface of the cylinder before pricking it all over with a cocktail stick, pushing the stick all the way through to the foil underneath. Bake at 190°C/Gas Mark 5 for 25–30 minutes, until the cylinder is light brown on top and a skewer comes out clean. When cool, cut into 5mm-thick slices. This makes an authentic addition (or alternative) to pâté in *bánh mì* sandwiches – see Cucumber & Carrot, page 186.

Cinnamon & Soft Cheese: Chalk might seem a better match for cheese but these two are a common pairing in America. Mind you, everything goes with cinnamon in America. Sure, Europeans like cinnamon in cakes and pastries, but not necessarily in chewing gum, confectionery, breakfast cereal, cola, coffee, tea and booze. In every airport and mall in the US, the Cinnabon baker slides a fresh tray of rolls out of the oven every 30 minutes and gives them a rich cream-cheese frosting. Cinnabon rolls are basically butch Danish pastries. They're deeper, stickier and deliver a far stronger cinnamon hit – maybe because in the US (in common with China, Vietnam and Indonesia) cinnamon flavour comes from the cinnamon-like cassia plant, *Cinnamomum aromaticum*. Cassia grows in China and Indonesia and is harder and darker than the true cinnamon from Sri Lanka that we get in the UK. It's also stronger, hotter, simpler and generally more intense in the mouth compared to true cinnamon's sweeter, more complex flavour. Basically cassia's the hard stuff, which may explain why America is addicted.

Cinnamon & Strawberry: *See Strawberry & Cinnamon, page 262*

Cinnamon & Thyme: The recipe for Colonel Sanders' unique blend of 11 herbs and spices is kept in a vault in KFC's headquarters in Louisville, Kentucky. I, on the other hand, make no secret of this finger-lickin' crumb crust for Fitzrovia baked chicken. Thoroughly mix 4 tbsp seasoned flour with 1 tsp cinnamon and 1 tsp dried thyme. Sprinkle it over 6 skinless chicken thighs, dip the thighs in beaten egg and coat in breadcrumbs. Bake on a rack at 200°C/Gas Mark 6 for 30 minutes, turning halfway through. Add a pinch or two of cayenne to the flour if you fancy some heat. Serve in a bucket, although a washing-up bowl works just as nicely.

Cinnamon & Tomato: Cinnamon adds a warm bass note to shrill tomato. Try a pinch instead of sugar to sweeten tinned tomatoes. A subtly spiced tomato sauce does wonders for meatballs, lamb shanks, prawns and aubergines. See also Beef & Cinnamon, page 44.

Cinnamon & Walnut: *See Walnut & Cinnamon, page 236*
Cinnamon & Watermelon: *See Watermelon & Cinnamon, page 249*

Clove

The word clove is derived from *clavus*, Latin for nail, which, aside from the visual likeness, suits the spice's hard, direct, hot-headed flavour. The nail association becomes literal in the case of *clouté*, wherein a clove is used to fasten a bay leaf to half an onion in order to season soups, stews and sauces. The singular flavour of clove often sees it paired with other flavours to modify or round it out, although British clove-flavoured boiled sweets are one exception; another is the cordial made with pink cloves from Zanzibar, once popular in the south of England, and still made today. In Indonesia, the majority of cigarettes are flavoured with clove and, when fresh, Thai holy basil has a similar flavour and numbing effect on the lips.

Clove & Apple: *See Apple & Clove, page 270*
Clove & Bacon: *See Bacon & Clove, page 168*
Clove & Basil: *See Basil & Clove, page 213*

Clove & Beef: Use a clove or two in beef stew (as most French recipes do for beef *pot au feu* or stock) or a pinch of ground cloves in gravy. The flavour of clove will be scarcely distinguishable but its bittersweet warmth enhances the beef in a way that makes it seem darker and more concentrated. Just don't forget to remove whole cloves before serving.

Clove & Cinnamon: *See Cinnamon & Clove, page 217*

Clove & Coffee: Like cardamom and coriander seeds, clove is sometimes ground with coffee, specifically in Ethiopia. Quite a double-hit of bitterness, this one, so if you prefer a softer, more latte-style beverage, heat up a mugful of milk with a couple of cloves in it, then discard them and add to the coffee. See also Cardamom & Cinnamon, page 314.

Clove & Ginger: Clove needs company. It's rare to find it in anything other than an ensemble recipe, perhaps because most of its flavour comes from just one compound (eugenol), and needs complementary flavours to round it out and make it subtle. The spice blend *quatre-épices* combines clove, ginger (or cinnamon), nutmeg and white pepper, and has a hot, sweet, fruity character that gives depth to meat dishes, especially pork. See also Cabbage & Pork, page 119. Five-spice, incidentally, isn't just *quatre-épices* plus one – see Cinnamon & Anise, page 216.

Clove & Hard Cheese: *See Hard Cheese & Clove, page 67*
Clove & Onion: *See Onion & Clove, page 108*
Clove & Orange: *See Orange & Clove, page 295*

Clove & Peach: A fair few fruits contain clove's identifying flavour compound, eugenol, and peach is one of them. Perhaps that's what made pickled peaches such a popular recipe in the American South. You peel the peaches before you stick the cloves in. Although who would have the heart to pierce that delicate, downy skin?

Clove & Pork: Clove pairs very well with pork, not just on the grounds of flavour but because it acts as a natural preservative. The eugenol and gallic acid in clove have a strong anti-oxygenic effect at fairly low concentrations, so as food companies respond to growing consumer unease at synthetic additives, we may see a lot more of this partnership. Which would be no bad thing.

Clove & Tomato: *See Tomato & Clove, page 259*
Clove & Vanilla: *See Vanilla & Clove, page 348*

Nutmeg

The botanical name for nutmeg, *Myristica fragrens*, makes it sound like a Bond girl – appropriately enough for such an exotic, beautiful double-agent of a spice, apt equally to make sweet, creamy dishes less cloying and cruciferous vegetables less bitter. Mace, nutmeg's outer coating, is composed of the same flavour compounds but in different proportions, and contains slighter greater quantities of essential oil. They can be used interchangeably, but always opt for fresh rather than the pre-ground form of either. Nutmeg is easier to grate than lacy pieces of mace, and is a little cheaper to buy.

Nutmeg & Apple: I love using nutmeg, partly because of the dinky grater. Also because it's simultaneously rich and fresh, and wonderful for perking up warm apple purée. Grate a light dusting over it and serve with vanilla ice cream. Like falling in love in the autumn.

Nutmeg & Aubergine: *See Aubergine & Nutmeg, page 82*

Nutmeg & Avocado: Avocado mixed with nutmeg is said to have an aphrodisiac effect on men. Avocado contains vitamin B6, which supposedly stimulates the production of testosterone. Nutmeg turns *everyone* on. Together they transform the mildest-mannered mummy's boy into Javier Bardem. Grind a little nutmeg over cold avocado soup or avocado stuffed with shellfish, then stand back.

Nutmeg & Butternut Squash: Butternut squash, lovely as it is, can send the palate to sleep. That's where nutmeg comes in – to keep things interesting. Italians use nutmeg in a pumpkin and ricotta filling for pasta. In America, it forms part of the spice mix in pumpkin pies and baked pumpkin custards. But it doesn't need heavy dairy to come to life: try some freshly grated on butternut squash that's been roasted with a mixture of 2 parts olive oil to 1 part balsamic vinegar.

Nutmeg & Cabbage: Nutmeg can have an enlivening effect on dreary greens. Dot cooked cabbage or sprouts with butter and speckle them, like bare winter trees decked in fairy lights, with freshly grated nutmeg.

Nutmeg & Cauliflower: *See Cauliflower & Nutmeg, page 123*

Nutmeg & Celery: Many nineteenth-century recipes for celery sauce are seasoned with nutmeg, or its conjoined twin, mace. In *The American Sportsman* (1855), Elisha Jarrett Lewis demurs. Either she found it the height of vulgarity to flavour one's celery or she was suffering from an attack of indecision: 'If fond of spices, put in a little mace and a clove or two; we don't, however, recommend it. A shallot or so, a bay leaf, lemon juice, or a little parsley, might also be advocated by some of our friends.' See also Celery & Chicken, page 96.

Nutmeg & Chocolate: *See Chocolate & Nutmeg, page 16*
Nutmeg & Egg: *See Egg & Nutmeg, page 135*

Nutmeg & Hard Cheese: Nutmeg has a crispness that lends itself to fatty foods. Macaroni cheese is a case in point. The flavour of nutmeg is a complex mixture of pine, flower, citrus and warm peppery notes from a compound called myristicin, which is said to give nutmeg its hallucinogenic qualities. When nutmeg is added to bland foods, like cheesy pasta, custards and potato, the complexity is especially notable – even more so if you add enough to begin hallucinating about it.

Nutmeg & Lamb: Long before I learned to cook, I ate 'spaghetti bolognese' in a taverna in Corfu. It was delicious, but unfamiliar for a reason that dawned on me only recently, cooking a Greek meal in which the minced lamb was flavoured with sweet, peppery nutmeg: they were using their moussaka sauce on the pasta. To make *spaghetti corfiote*, chop ½ small onion and soften it in 3 tbsp butter or lard. Add 450g minced lamb and cook until well browned. Stir in 250ml tomato passata, 250ml white wine, 250ml water, 2 tbsp chopped parsley, ¼ nutmeg, freshly grated, and a good pinch of sugar. Season, bring to the boil, and cook gently for about 1 hour, stirring intermittently, until most of the liquid has been absorbed. Add an extra grating of nutmeg, check the seasoning and serve on pasta. The taverna served this on bucatini, a long, thin pasta similar to spaghetti but hollow, like a tiny water main. Note that some moussaka recipes substitute cinnamon for nutmeg, in a similar vein to the Greek dish *pastitsio* – see Beef & Cinnamon, page 44.

Nutmeg & Onion: *See Onion & Nutmeg, page 110*

Nutmeg & Oyster: Nutmeg is a classic companion for oysters in cooked dishes, especially with cream. It's the seasoning that's used for oyster loaves, which are said to have originated in Massachusetts in the late eighteenth century. Cut lids from the tops of some crusty bread rolls, scoop out their soft, bready centre and paint the cavity with melted butter. Put the hollowed rolls and lids in a 200°C/Gas Mark 6 oven for no more than 10 minutes while you cook the filling. Take enough oysters to fill the rolls and stew them along with their liquor, and the torn-up excavated bread, in some butter for 5 minutes.

Add a little cream and a grating of nutmeg and cook for another minute. Fill the hot rolls with the oyster mixture, replace their lids and serve.

Nutmeg & Parsnip: Some chefs have noted that the flavour of parsnips is partly reminiscent of nutmeg. That's because parsnip contains myristicin, a key component of nutmeg's flavour, which is particularly noticeable when the vegetable is roasted. I'd steer clear of baking pears with nutmeg for pudding: the combination is too parsnip-like for comfort.

Nutmeg & Potato: *See Potato & Nutmeg, page 91*
Nutmeg & Saffron: *See Saffron & Nutmeg, page 180*

Nutmeg & Shellfish: Nutmeg, or a combination of nutmeg and mace, is traditionally used to season potted shrimps. Mace is the lacy outer shell of the nutmeg fruit. Both have a clear, citrussy, fresh-pepper quality that makes them equally natural partners for creamy or buttery prawn and lobster dishes.

Nutmeg & Swede: *See Swede & Nutmeg, page 121*

Nutmeg & Tomato: In Bologna they use nutmeg to tamp down the harsh acidity tomato can bring to a ragù. For an even silkier sauce, try adding milk to the meat once it's browned, in place of some of the stock or tomato you might otherwise have used, and your bolognese will be as round and smooth as a Brancusi. See also Nutmeg & Lamb, page 222.

Nutmeg & Vanilla: *See Vanilla & Nutmeg, page 349*

Nutmeg & Walnut: A few pinches of grated nutmeg can enhance the flavour of walnut cakes and biscuits in the same way that sweetmeats made with hazelnut are heightened by a teaspoon of cocoa powder.

Parsnip

Cooked parsnip has the sweet, slightly earthy flavour typically associated with root vegetables but with its own strong hints of nutmeg and parsley. Raw, its flavour is rather dispiriting, especially in combination with its fibrous, woody texture, for which you might as well substitute a macramé plant holder. Roasted, mashed or chipped, in plenty of fat and salt, parsnip takes on a gorgeous sweet spiciness that can recall coconut or banana.

Parsnip & Anise: There's a trace of herbal, anise flavour in parsnips. Nibble one raw and you should get it. It's subtle – don't expect pastis on the *pétanque* pitch at St Paul de Vence – but it's there. A welcome change from the usual curry treatment, then, is to pair parsnip with tarragon in a soup.

Parsnip & Bacon: See Bacon & Parsnip, page 169

Parsnip & Banana: When bananas weren't available in Britain during the Second World War, mock bananas were made from parsnips. Aside from their ivory flesh, parsnip and banana share a sweet spiciness. Try a piece of roasted parsnip, close your eyes and think of banana – more convincing than carrots posing as apricots, another wartime substitution. Add a little ground cloves and rum to them and it's even more of a match. Now that bananas are no longer threatened by U-boats, a mock parsnip made of banana might lend a Caribbean lilt to your Sunday roast, but better to pair them in a moist cake – parsnips were once as popular a cake ingredient as carrots are now.

Parsnip & Beef: Carrot and parsnip are similarly sweet but parsnip's greater complexity of flavour makes it a more interesting partner for beef. Serve roast beef with parsnips roasted in the dripping, a basic beef stew with parsnips cut into chunks, or oxtail cooked in red wine with a parsnip and potato mash. On a less homely note, Charlie Trotter makes a terrine of beef cheek, salsify and endive with a parsnip purée. And as parsnip has a passion for salty flavours, I pair slices of the Italian air-dried salted beef, bresaola, with slices of parsnip and Parmesan bread made to Delia Smith's recipe.

Parsnip & Chicken: See Chicken & Parsnip, page 29
Parsnip & Hard Cheese: See Hard Cheese & Parsnip, page 68
Parsnip & Nutmeg: See Nutmeg & Parsnip, page 223

Parsnip & Pea: It's generally thought that the compounds most responsible for parsnip's characteristic flavour are terpinolene (also found in some essential oils derived from pine trees), myristicin (present in nutmeg and, to a lesser extent, parsley and dill) and 3-sec-butyl-2-methoxypyrazine, which has a slightly musty, green-pea quality and is present at higher levels in parsnip than in any other vegetable, conceivably accounting for the unique affinity parsnips have for peas. Try them together in a winter pea soup. The parsnip acts as a thickener and also brings a lightly spicy flavour; it's like a sunny winter's day. Peel and chop 3 parsnips, then cook in olive oil with a sliced onion until softened. Add 750ml vegetable or chicken stock, bring to the boil and simmer for 10 minutes. Then add about 500g frozen peas and season. Bring back to the boil, simmer for 5 minutes, then leave to cool a little. Liquidise, reheat and serve.

Parsnip & Pork: The parsnip has recently gained 'exotic' status among French gourmands, who historically considered it fit only for feeding livestock. Parsnips are not just excellent for fattening the herd: they're known to have an enriching effect on the flavour of pig meat, and are often fed to prosciutto pigs. Reciprocally enough, in the nineteenth century the flavour of parsnips was often improved by boiling them with salt pork, then mashing and frying them in butter – which sounds great, but would probably also improve the flavour of cotton wool.

Parsnip & Potato: The introduction of the potato to Europe in the sixteenth century was responsible for the decline in parsnip's popularity, and entirely did for the skirret, which has a flavour somewhere between the two. Salsify, another pale root, is sometimes called the oyster plant, as it's said to taste like oysters, although I'd say a delicate, more savoury parsnip is probably closer. Scorzonera, sometimes known as black salsify, looks and tastes similar to regular salsify but has a dark skin, as its name suggests.

Parsnip & Shellfish: Scallops will perch on almost anything, as long as it's puréed. Parsnip is no exception. Nestle the scallops on top and enjoy the complementary sweetness and nuttiness.

Parsnip & Walnut: See *Walnut & Parsnip, page 237*

Parsnip & Watercress: Watercress and roasted parsnip make a good basis for a winter salad. Both have a bitter spiciness, offset in watercress's case by its freshwater cleanliness and in parsnip's by its sweetness. Toss cubes of warm cooked parsnip with watercress leaves, croûtons and crumbled blue cheese, then dress with a piquant French dressing. If you grow parsnips, the White Gem variety, whose leaves are edible when very young and have a recognisable parsnip flavour with a satisfyingly bitter aftertaste, would make an interesting addition to this dish.

Parsnip & White Fish: See *White Fish & Parsnip, page 148*

WOODLAND

Carrot

Butternut Squash

Chestnut

Walnut

Hazelnut

Almond

Carrot

Carrots vary both in their levels of sugariness and in the pine/parsley flavour notes that can tend to a certain woodiness. They have a strong flavour affinity for other umbellifers, and their sweetness, and hint of woodiness, make for a harmonious match with the same quality in nuts. Nantes carrots are renowned for their excellent flavour.

Carrot & Anise: Guy Savoy offers a carrot and star anise soup as an *amuse-bouche,* and uses the same flavours to complement lightly grilled lobster. The combination is perfect: star anise flatters carrot's fresh, woody quality, which is all to the good, as carrot flourishes under a surfeit of praise. Chef John Tovey makes a homely carrot and anise side dish by mashing 450g cooked carrots with 20g butter and 1 tbsp Pernod. Try with confit of duck.

Carrot & Apple: Children tend to like this sweet and sour salad. Grate both and dress with a little neutral-tasting oil and lemon juice. Strew with a potluck handful of mixed seeds, nuts and raisins for a more exciting texture.

Carrot & Beef: *See Beef & Carrot, page 43*

Carrot & Cabbage: Both crisp, clean and spicy-sweet when raw. Carrot brings a little fruitiness to the mix. A dependable basis for a coleslaw with apple, celery, walnuts, caraway or blue cheese (or all of them). I'm more than happy with just cabbage, carrot and a little onion. Unless it's to be eaten straight away, you can salt the shredded cabbage first, leave for about an hour, rinse, drain, then dry. This will draw out some of the water and prevent the coleslaw turning soupy. It also gives the dish a more complex, savoury quality in place of the sweet, innocent fruitiness.

Carrot & Cardamom: Combined in a popular Indian dessert *gajar halwa,* which is served at wedding feasts and during the autumn festival of Diwali. There are many ways of making *gajar halwa,* but essentially it's finely grated carrot, slowly simmered in milk until most of the moisture has been absorbed, then enriched with sugar, ghee (or unsalted butter/flavourless oil) and crushed cardamom seeds. Garnishes vary, but almonds, pistachios and dried fruit are typical. Eat warm or at room temperature. Some say an accompaniment of vanilla ice cream is good, but I think its sweetness calls for the contrasting sourness of crème fraîche or thick yogurt.

Carrot & Celery: When it comes to diet foods, which do you prefer, the carrot or the stick? That's right: neither. Or both, soused in dressing. In a game of word association, my response to 'France' would not be 'Paris' or 'terroir' but 'celeriac remoulade'. A pot of that, the same of *carottes râpées,* some slivers of Bayonne ham, a boxed ripe Camembert, a French stick, a bottle of Côtes du

Rhône. The perfect picnic. Inevitably I'll forget to bring cutlery and have to make do scooping up heaps of vegetable with the bread. To make *carottes râpées*, finely grate the carrot (preferably in a food processor, which makes for silkier strands) and toss with a dressing made with a light-flavoured olive oil, lemon juice, a touch of Dijon mustard and pinches of sugar, salt and pepper. For celeriac remoulade, grate your celeriac (not too fine, or it'll taste like coconut), toss with lemon juice to prevent it browning, then dress with a mayonnaise mixed with a little grain mustard and season to taste.

Carrot & Cinnamon: *See Cinnamon & Carrot, page 216*

Carrot & Coconut: A signature dish of Wylie Dufresne, chef-owner of wd~50 in New York, is Carrot-Coconut Sunny-Side-Up – a perfect replica of a fried egg. The (fully pierceable) yolk has flavours of carrot and maple, while the white tastes of coconut and cardamom. Those of us without the necessary industrial gum pastes (or know-how) to knock this up in our own kitchens might have to limit ourselves to a coconut frosting on a carrot cake.

Carrot & Cucumber: *See Cucumber & Carrot, page 186*

Carrot & Cumin: It's rare to sit down at a Moroccan feast without being offered a plate of sweet carrots in a robust, cumin-flavoured dressing. Cut into crinkly discs, like the metal from which Ingersoll keys are cut, they remind me, cumin's efforts notwithstanding, of the sorry rounds of orange matter you get in tins. Home-grown carrots, on the other hand, tugged from the ground when they're long, thin and pointed, are perfect for this combination. Toss them, washed but unpeeled, in olive oil and sprinkle with cumin before roasting. This will intensify both their earthiness and their sweetness, coaxing the sugars to the surface, where they caramelise and mingle deliciously with the spice.

Carrot & Hazelnut: *See Hazelnut & Carrot, page 239*

Carrot & Olive: I love those inexpensive restaurants – often Turkish or Greek – where they bring you a complementary dish of wrinkly black olives and sticks of raw carrot to nibble on while you read the menu. It shows a little care. And the combination of oily, salty olives with fresh, sweet carrot stimulates your taste buds while you consider your options.

Carrot & Onion: To make carrots *à la nivernaise*, first blanch peeled whole young (or chopped older) carrots for a few minutes and drain. Stew them slowly in butter and just enough stock to cover, until all that's left of the liquid is a small amount of thick syrup. At the same time, cook peeled small onions via the same method, bar the blanching. Combine the carrots and onions with seasoning and a little sugar. Just a little: remember how candied both carrots and onions can get anyway. And if you're scrumping them from Mr McGregor's garden, watch out for the cat.

Carrot & Orange: Over 80 years ago, the French polymath Paul Reboux wrote, 'I am not interested in a compote of spiders, a salmis of bats or a gratin of blindworms. All I want to do is break the traditional association of certain ingredients in cookery. My mission is to ally the unexpected with the delectable.' Having thus set out his stall, he goes on to give a recipe for a salad of lettuce leaves and sliced cooked potato in a creamy dressing, garnished with orange zest and carrots, both cut into one-inch lengths and 'as thin as pine needles'. This, claims Reboux, is guaranteed to capture the attention of the gourmand. 'Orange? Carrot? How is it that the orange tastes of carrot and the carrot of orange?' A game for the palate to play.

Carrot & Parsley: Carrot flavour can be accentuated by adding one of its umbelliferous relatives, such as parsley, parsnip, cumin, coriander or dill. A fine scattering of parsley is often used to finish both carrot soup and Vichy carrots (new carrots cooked over a low heat in a combination of butter, sugar, salt and the non-chalky water of the Vichy region of France).

Carrot & Peanut: *See Peanut & Carrot, page 23*
Carrot & Swede: *See Swede & Carrot, page 121*

Carrot & Walnut: Carrot juice has a sweet, fruity flavour and can taste a little like a thin milkshake. Walnuts, when fresh, also have a milky sweetness. The last of the summer's carrots with the first of the year's walnuts will make a lovely salad to accompany good bread and cheese. As they age, and thus become woodier, they might need a little sweetening up, say, in a carrot cake.

Butternut Squash

Butternut squash and pumpkins share a chapter as they have similar flavour affinities and are often used interchangeably. Bear in mind, though, that butternut squash is naturally sweeter and will need less sugar in sweet recipes. There's also a difference in texture: the dense flesh of butternut squash is fine-grained and silky, whereas pumpkin can be rather fibrous. The pronounced sweetness of butternut squash works well with salty ingredients; cut through with something spikily sour; or, in combination with the density of its flesh, as a background for potent herbs such as rosemary and sage.

Butternut Squash & Almond: In northern Italy they fill pillows of pasta called tortelli with amaretti biscuits and pumpkin. The bittersweet biscuit lifts the sweetness of the pumpkin. Nadia Santini, chef at Dal Pescatore in Mantua, makes legendary pumpkin and amaretti tortelli, which also contain mostarda di Cremona (fruits preserved in a thick mustard syrup), nutmeg, cinnamon, clove and Parmesan.

Butternut Squash & Apple: One autumn lunchtime at the Beacon restaurant on West 56th Street in New York, I ordered the pumpkin and apple soup. The waiter brought it in a pitcher, poured it into the bowl and put a puff of spiced candyfloss on top. It fainted instantaneously into the soup, leaving a trace of cinnamon sweetness and the gentlest lick of heat. Back in London a week later, trying to recreate the experience in my own kitchen, I left the soup chilling in the fridge as I riffled through eBay for a candyfloss machine. I came to my senses. Who needs another large device, solely in order to make a soup taste *slightly* better, when you already have to stack tea towels on top of sieves on top of an ice-cream machine? And in the meantime, as it happened, the flavour of apple had been intensifying in the fridge, to the extent that by the time I got around to eating the soup it didn't need a spicy puff of candyfloss at all.

Butternut Squash & Bacon: The sweet-saltiness of this combination reminds me of crabmeat, which was the inspiration behind this landlubber's version of crab cakes – butternut squash and bacon cakes with lime mayonnaise. Grate 200g butternut squash. Combine with 4 cooked, crumbled bacon rashers, a generous handful of breadcrumbs and a pinch of salt. Bind together with about 1 tbsp mayonnaise. Shape into cakes about 4cm in diameter and 1cm deep, then leave to firm up in the fridge for about 30 minutes before deep-frying in vegetable oil. Top each cooked cake with a little mayonnaise mixed with lime juice and zest, with an extra sprinkle of zest to finish.

Butternut Squash & Blue Cheese: *See Blue Cheese & Butternut Squash, page 62*

Butternut Squash & Chestnut: Sounds like a couple of fat Shetland ponies, but a good winter combination nonetheless. Try them paired in a wild rice pilaf. Or detect both flavours in a Potimarron, a French heirloom squash variety whose name is derived from *potiron* (pumpkin) and *marron* (chestnut). Bright orange and the shape of an outsize fig, the Potimarron has a wonderfully aromatic chestnut flavour that's made it widely popular, and fairly widely available. In Japan it's known as *hokkaido* and is often cooked in miso.

Butternut Squash & Chilli: Squashes make great fillings for pies and pasta because they're dry(ish), and their sweet, uncomplicated flavour lets other ingredients have their say. A quesadilla provides the perfect opportunity to pitch butternut squash against chilli. Take a tortilla that'll fit in your frying pan. Top with mashed butternut squash to a depth of 1–2 cm, scatter over a sour-hot mixture of pickled jalapeños and chopped fresh chillies, then a layer of grated mild Cheddar. Top with another tortilla and cook over a medium heat, on both sides, until heated through and the cheese has melted. Cut into quarters and serve.

Butternut Squash & Cinnamon: *See Cinnamon & Butternut Squash, page 216*
Butternut Squash & Ginger: *See Ginger & Butternut Squash, page 308*

Butternut Squash & Goat's Cheese: Sweet beetroot is a classic match for salty goat's cheese, but butternut squash is even better. Roast cubes of squash and the edges will caramelise and take on a honey flavour – and we all know how gruff old goat's cheese takes to a slick of golden honey. Some pair squash and goat's cheese in a gratin but I find that a little heavy; better, in my opinion, to toss them in a sharp dressing with baby spinach leaves, or in a couscous with chickpeas, toasted pine nuts, finely chopped red onion and lots of chopped parsley and mint.

Butternut Squash & Lime: *See Lime & Butternut Squash, page 300*
Butternut Squash & Mushroom: *See Mushroom & Butternut Squash, page 76*
Butternut Squash & Nutmeg: *See Nutmeg & Butternut Squash, page 221*

Butternut Squash & Pork: Take kindly to all sorts of stews. Can be given a Western slant in cider with apples, bacon and onions, or sent East in chicken stock with soy, Shaoxing rice wine, five-spice and brown sugar. To help thicken the sauce, flour the pork – shoulder, ideally, cut into 3cm cubes – before browning. Add the butternut squash pieces 20–30 minutes before the end, as they'll disintegrate if cooked for too long.

Butternut Squash & Rosemary: To roast these together is to remember how intensely sweet and fragrant they both are – so much so that they can carry a whole dish, like this rib-sticking butternut squash, cannellini bean and rosemary stew. Chop an onion and soften in olive oil, adding 3 finely chopped cloves of garlic towards the end. Add 500g peeled, deseeded butternut squash cut into 2cm cubes, 2 tins of cannellini beans, drained, 1 tin of cherry tomatoes, the very finely chopped spikes of 1 sprig of rosemary, 250ml dry white wine, 250ml water and some seasoning. Stir, bring to the boil, then cover and simmer for about 20 minutes. Remove the lid and continue cooking until the butternut squash is tender and most of the liquid has evaporated. Serve this as it is, or top with breadcrumbs mixed with a little Parmesan and grill until lightly browned. If you feel more than usually excited by the smell of this dish, you may be interested to note that butternut squash and rosemary are close relatives respectively of pumpkin and lavender. In a study of a range of scents by Dr Alan Hirsch's Smell and Taste Treatment and Research Foundation in Chicago, men found the fragrance of pumpkin pie with lavender the most arousing; for women it came second – see also Cucumber & Anise, page 186.

Butternut Squash & Sage: *See Sage & Butternut Squash, page 322*

Butternut Squash & Shellfish: You had us at the butter, say lobsters, who love butter more than anything: you could just poach them in it. Squash is a lovely match, providing a harmonious sweet nuttiness as well as an appropriately expensive texture, variously described as like velvet, satin or silk.

Chestnut

Like pine nuts and cashews, one of the sweeter nuts, but it's chestnut's low fat content that makes it unique. Nonetheless, as with its oily cousins, roasting – over an open fire, naturally – brings out its full flavour and sweetness. Its earthy quality makes it a good match for other autumnal flavours, such as game, mushrooms and apples. Chestnuts can be ground into a flour for rather rustic-flavoured bread, pasta and cakes, or stuffed to the cell walls with sugar to make purées and *marrons glacés*. A chestnut liqueur called *crème de châtaigne* is also available.

Chestnut & Butternut Squash: *See Butternut Squash & Chestnut, page 230*

Chestnut & Cabbage: Having cut crosses in your Brussels sprouts and nicks in your chestnuts, you'll have the knife skills to whittle everyone their Christmas presents. Cutting a vent in chestnuts is essential to stop them exploding in the oven. You really needn't bother with sprouts: it'll only risk overcooking them. And you'll need all your energy to peel the chestnuts, and suppress the yodel of agony when a shard of superheated shell insinuates itself behind your thumbnail. If you have gone to the trouble of gathering them yourself, don't squander it by eating them too soon – sweet chestnuts need a few days to dry out, giving the starch a chance to convert to sugar, thereby intensifying the flavour. The sprout and chestnut pairing is delicious, of course, but why not try braising chestnuts with apple and red cabbage, or, if your hands have recovered, stuff a cabbage, adapting the recipe in Cabbage & Pork on page 119, using chestnut and bacon in place of the pork and beef.

Chestnut & Celery: A *brunoise*, or fine dice, of celery is recommended as a pairing for chestnuts in soup, not only for the flavour compatibility but because celery and chestnut have similar cooking times, according to the French cookery writer Madame E. Saint-Ange.

Chestnut & Chicken: Edward A. Bunyard writes that 'the chestnut finds its best end within a bird of some sort – preferably a dead bird. Here its soft pastiness makes an admirable ground on which more pungent flavours may display themselves, a more attractive background than the (nearly) all conquering potato.' Bunyard was most likely thinking of how chestnuts pair with fattier, boldly flavoured game birds such as goose or duck, although the pairing is just as common in stuffings for chicken and turkey.

Chestnut & Chocolate: *See Chocolate & Chestnut, page 14*

Chestnut & Lamb: For those who find apricots and prunes too sweet, chestnuts make an excellent sweetish substitute in a North African lamb stew or tagine. Add vacuum-packed chestnuts to the simmering pot about 10 minutes before the end of cooking and they'll hold their shape.

Chestnut & Mushroom: *See Mushroom & Chestnut, page 76*

Chestnut & Pear: Hold back some of the chestnuts you bought for the stuffing at Christmas and serve them on Boxing Day in a salad of chopped pear, the best bits of dark turkey meat and some dark green leaves.

Chestnut & Pork: Alexandre Dumas opines that chestnuts are very good with all meats. In *Le Grand Dictionnaire de Cuisine*, he gives a recipe for a chestnut purée to serve with pork sausages. Peel roasted chestnuts, removing the thin inner skin too. Soften them in butter, white wine and a little stock, then purée. Mix the cooking juices from the sausages into the chestnut mixture before serving. Chestnuts have an unusually high carbohydrate content for a nut, which accounts for their traditional use as a potato substitute; it also allows them to be ground into flour for baking. Its farinaceous quality earned the sweet chestnut the nickname 'bread tree' in Corsica. The chestnut is also used to brew Pietra, Corsica's first native beer, which has a roasted, smoky quality.

Chestnut & Prosciutto: *See Prosciutto & Chestnut, page 172*

Chestnut & Rosemary: *Castagnaccio* is a Tuscan cake originally made with nothing but chestnut flour, olive oil, water and salt. Through more prosperous times, it has accrued a variety of rosemary, pine nuts, dried fruit, walnuts and candied peel. Chestnut flour has a curious aroma, somewhere between cocoa and silage, which makes for a rustic flavour experience. And I mean really rustic: it tastes like the floor of a shepherd's refuge. Not to everyone's tastes, then, but if you want to try it for yourself, mix 250g sifted chestnut flour and a pinch of salt to a smooth batter with 350ml water. Stir in some finely snipped rosemary leaves and pour into a buttered 23cm flan tin – it's a shallow cake. Scatter with pine nuts, brush generously with olive oil and bake at 190°C/Gas Mark 5 for 30–45 minutes, until the top is dark brown and fretted with cracks like old varnish. You'll notice the recipe contains no raising agent, and pretty much the only sweetness comes from what's naturally present in the chestnuts, so if you have guests you might want to recalibrate any expectations the word 'cake' may arouse.

Chestnut & Vanilla: Most commonly combined in *marrons glacés*, a sweet-meat so sugary it warrants a wanted poster in every dental surgery. They are made with particularly sweet, large, single-kernel nuts, infused over days with a vanilla-flavoured syrup before a final glazing with an even more concentrated syrup. In France Clément Faugier makes a *marron glacé* spread that tastes like a subtly nutty toffee, with the pleasantly powdery quality you'd expect of a chestnut. It's served simply mixed with whipped cream or spread on to thin crêpes.

Walnut

After almond, the second most popular nut in the world. Walnuts are easy to take for granted in cakes and confectionery, where their wrinkly lobes are often more interesting than their mild flavour. Toasting brings out their full character – stronger nutty notes with a hint of nicotine bitterness. Walnuts work particularly well with other 'brown' flavours, such as cinnamon, nutmeg, maple syrup, honey and pears. They can be bought pickled, steeped in syrup, as a liqueur (*nocino* or *vin de noix*) and as walnut oil, which makes a great dressing for vegetables and salads.

Walnut & Anise: I urge you to try ½ tsp crushed anise or fennel seeds in a sticky walnut or pecan pie (pecans and walnuts are nearly always interchangeable, although pecans are sweeter, less bitter and easier to slide under doors). Simply stir the spice into the mixture before decanting it into the pastry case. Brings a fresh note to what can be a rather monotonous sweetness. If sweet's not your thing, try a dressing made with walnut oil and tarragon vinegar.

Walnut & Apple: *See Apple & Walnut, page 272*

Walnut & Aubergine: Frequently paired in Russian and Turkish dishes and in Georgia, where baby aubergines are halved, fried and stuffed with a combination of ground walnuts, garlic and coriander leaf mixed with chopped onion, celery, tarragon vinegar and paprika. They're served at room temperature, scattered with pomegranate seeds. In the Lebanon, baby aubergines are almost split lengthways, stuffed with walnut and garlic and preserved in oil. Italian chef Giorgio Locatelli stuffs pasta parcels with a mixture of walnut, aubergine, ricotta, nutmeg, egg and Parmesan. He recommends buying unshelled walnuts while they're in season (December to February), for their freshness and intensity of flavour.

Walnut & Banana: Here's a novel idea for bananas. Novel because it calls for ones that aren't overripe. Peel a pristine banana and slice it into coins. Top each one with a walnut half, using a neat dollop of dulce de leche as cement. The art here is to get the dulce de leche on to the banana without it clinging to the spoon and trailing messily. It's worth the effort, though. Twice as satisfying, even, as a carpaccio of chilled Mars Bar. If the bananas *are* overripe, the traditional combination is banana bread mixed through with walnuts that show in each slice like stranded jigsaw pieces.

Walnut & Basil: *See Basil & Walnut, page 215*
Walnut & Beef: *See Beef & Walnut, page 48*

Walnut & Beetroot: As wrinkly and red-faced as a couple of weather-beaten peasant farmers. Give them a fresh start by mixing broken walnut pieces and chunks of roasted beetroot and sweet potato into cooled, cooked red quinoa (which is crunchy, and has something of a roast-walnut flavour itself). Dress with a maple syrup vinaigrette – just add maple syrup where you might ordinarily use honey.

Walnut & Blue Cheese: *See Blue Cheese & Walnut, page 64*

Walnut & Broccoli: Combine them in a pasta dish or a stir-fry: broccoli makes an incongruously healthy addition to the heart-furring dish described at Walnut & Shellfish, page 237.

Walnut & Carrot: *See Carrot & Walnut, page 229*
Walnut & Cauliflower: *See Cauliflower & Walnut, page 124*

Walnut & Celery: Celery and walnut share distinctive aroma compounds called phthalides, which you can also detect in lovage. Chew a walnut and you will clearly taste the connection. This flavour overlap ensures they combine beautifully in stuffing and in Waldorf salad. As celery also has a magical effect on chicken stock (see Celery & Chicken, page 96), try this recipe, which brings all three together in a soup. In a little butter or oil, gently fry a chopped onion, a large potato, peeled and cubed, and 4 or 5 chopped celery sticks. When the onion has softened, add 750ml chicken stock, bring to the boil, then turn down the heat and simmer until the potatoes and celery are cooked. Finely grind 50g walnuts and set aside. Liquidise the soup, return it to the pan and add the nuts. Stir until thickened. Serve with some suitably coarse brown bread.

Walnut & Cherry: *See Cherry & Walnut, page 249*
Walnut & Chicken: *See Chicken & Walnut, page 32*

Walnut & Chilli: *Chiles en nogada* are stuffed green chillies served with a ground walnut sauce and scattered with pomegranate seeds. A signature dish of Puebla in Mexico, *chiles en nogada* was devised to celebrate the country's independence, as the green chillies, white walnut sauce and red pomegranate seeds match the colours of the national flag (see also Chilli & Egg, page 209, and Avocado & Tomato, page 201). In the book *Like Water For Chocolate*, the dish is served at the climactic wedding of Tita's niece, Esperanza, to Dr Brown's son, Alex, where it makes everyone so randy that Pedro (spoiler alert) expires after a bout of post-prandial lovemaking (even Mrs Beeton knew you should always wait 20 minutes to let the meal go down).

Walnut & Chocolate: *See Chocolate & Walnut, page 18*

Walnut & Cinnamon: Walnuts have a kinship with sticky-sweet autumnal flavours like cinnamon, toffee, maple syrup and apple. There's even a walnut cultivar called Poe that's said to taste like butterscotch. The common Persian walnut is sometimes called the English walnut in the US, because it was imported from (if not necessarily grown in) the UK, and had to be distinguished from the native black walnut. The British used to call it the Madeira nut, because that's where *they* imported it from, although I like to think it might have something to do with the way the nut's rich sweetness is offset by the astringency of its skin, just as golden Madeira wines (full-flavoured with notes of caramel, nuts, dried fruit, marmalade and toffee) are balanced by their pronounced acidity.

Walnut & Coffee: *See Coffee & Walnut, page 22*
Walnut & Fig: *See Fig & Walnut, page 341*

Walnut & Garlic: In the early eighteenth century, *aillade* sauce from the Languedoc was described by a M. Duchat as 'a mess which the poorer sort make with garlic and walnuts pounded together in a mortar, and which prepares the stomach for the reception of certain meats of an undigestive and disagreeable nature. As for the *aillade* itself, it is so much admired by some persons of distinction, even in Italy, that the historian, Platina, could not forbear telling the world, that a brother of his would often put himself in a sweat by the pains he took in preparing this ragoo.' Poorer sort or not, you can make this mess in a food processor, although the flavour will be better if you pound it in a mortar. Pulse 100g walnuts and 4 garlic cloves until crushed. Season, then slowly add 150ml olive oil (or a mixture of olive and walnut oils) until you reach sauce consistency. For a Turkish variation known as *tarator*, add 3 crustless slices of white bread in chunks, 2 tbsp lemon juice, 1 tsp red wine vinegar and 100ml stock to the garlic and walnuts before pouring in the oil.

Traditionally this sauce is served with roasted meat, but works well with a spinach, red pepper and chickpea paella.

Walnut & Goat's Cheese: *See Goat's Cheese & Walnut, page 58*
Walnut & Grape: *See Grape & Walnut, page 253*

Walnut & Hard Cheese: Cheese expert Patricia Michelson writes that wet walnuts enhance strong-flavoured cheeses like Parmesan and pecorino. Wet walnuts have a fresh-milk flavour similar to the note lost in cheese during the ageing process. That's not to say that dried walnuts aren't good partners too. They're particularly well matched with aged Gouda, with its deep butter-scotch flavour and colour.

Walnut & Mushroom: *See Mushroom & Walnut, page 80*
Walnut & Nutmeg: *See Nutmeg & Walnut, page 223*
Walnut & Orange: *See Orange & Walnut, page 297*

Walnut & Parsley: Parsley adds welcome freshness to walnut's woody astringency. They're often paired in a sauce related to the more famous pesto. Heat 3 tbsp olive oil in a pan and add 2 chopped garlic cloves, 75g finely chopped walnuts and a handful of roughly chopped flat-leaf parsley. Season and allow to warm for a few minutes. You might toss this sauce with pasta, or use it over gnocchi, beetroot or a cheese soufflé.

Walnut & Parsnip: Like gnawing on Pinocchio's leg. Counter excess woodiness by removing the tough cores from older parsnips.

Walnut & Pear: *See Pear & Walnut, page 275*

Walnut & Shellfish: There's a dish they serve in American Chinese restaurants that tends to divide humanity fairly straight down the middle: deep-fried prawns tossed in a honey and lemon mayonnaise and mixed with candied walnuts. Tribe A sees the potential in chewy, salty shellfish mixed with sugar-crisp, slightly spicy nuts. Tribe B suppresses instant emesis at the thought of the calories and sheer inauthenticity. I'm with Tribe A.

Walnut & Soft Cheese: *See Soft Cheese & Walnut, page 73*

Walnut & Vanilla: Black walnut is a boisterously flavoured alternative to the common Persian variety, with a fruitier, musty quality. It lacks the paint-like notes that in Persian walnuts recall the smell that hits you on reopening an old can of gloss. Persians also tend to be woodier and more astringent. Native to northeast America, the black walnut is prized for its wood, which is used in furniture making and for the stocks of upscale shotguns. They're notoriously hard shelled, and have to be whacked with a hammer, driven over by a station wagon or taken to the local shelling depot. Once cracked, they're often paired with vanilla to make legendary cakes, ice cream and a sweetmeat called divinity candy, made with sugar, egg whites and corn syrup. The result is like a cross between a meringue and a nougat.

Walnut & Washed-rind Cheese: *See Washed-rind Cheese & Walnut, page 60*
Walnut & Watercress: *See Watercress & Walnut, page 101*

Hazelnut

Hazelnuts have a sweet, buttery flavour, with hints of cocoa that make them a sensational match for chocolate. Hazelnuts grown in the Piedmont region of Italy are particularly renowned for their quality. Less glorious specimens can taste woody, with a metallic streak, rather like pencil shavings. Like all nuts, hazelnuts become more flavourful when heated: research has shown that the key hazelnut flavour compound increases tenfold when the nuts are roasted. The bittersweet richness of hazelnuts is also good ground into a coating for delicate, buttery seafoods or as the basis for a luxurious sauce. Hazelnut oil is useful for baking and is a treat in dressings. Frangelico and *crème de noisette* are hazelnut-flavoured liqueurs. And health-food shops sell a hazelnut butter that tastes like the inside of a delicious praline truffle on a spoon.

Hazelnut & Almond: Emergency Cake. It's one of life's paradoxes that the need for cake often arises from conditions that make you incapable of either making it or going out to buy it. Ideally, the following ingredients would be kept under glass with a little hammer hung underneath, but it was desperate improvisation that initially led me to this combination. A ciabatta roll was excavated from the bottom of the freezer, defrosted in the toaster, given a drizzle of hazelnut oil, sprinkled with a few almonds and sultanas picked from my husband's muesli, squashed together and eaten while still warm. It tasted amazing, somewhere between fruitcake and pain au chocolat, without the sickliness of either. Happily the bread's air holes turned out to be perfect pockets for the fruit and nuts, deepening its similarity to fruitcake.

Hazelnut & Apple: *See Apple & Hazelnut, page 271*
Hazelnut & Avocado: *See Avocado & Hazelnut, page 199*

Hazelnut & Banana: Hazelnut butter, not to be confused with *beurre noisette* – see Hazelnut & White Fish, page 240 – is a posh version of peanut butter. It tastes like a Ferrero Rocher denuded of its chocolate shell but without the sugar, although still possessed of a mellow sweetness that brings out the fruity side of banana. Spread it on to a loaf of fine white bread *before* you slice it (to prevent the bread ripping) and make sandwiches with slivers of banana. Or thin a little out with milk and maple syrup to make a sauce for banana pancakes, scattered with roasted nuts.

Hazelnut & Carrot: Recipes for carrot cake often call for vegetable oil rather than butter or margarine, so you might add some depth of flavour by using hazelnut oil. It's not cheap, but neither does the oil last very long, so if you have a bottle nearing its use-by date this recipe will amply consecrate its memory. If you find the hazelnut flavour too strong, dilute it with sunflower oil, which has a hint of hazelnut flavour itself. Ground hazelnuts can be used to flavour your baking too – you'll need to substitute them for a third to a quarter of the flour called for in cake recipes. By all means grind them yourself in a food processor, but roast them first to activate all the flavour compounds, then remove the bitter skins – unless you're making a coarser cake, in which case leaving the skins on can be rather good.

Hazelnut & Caviar: Could hazelnut be the finest flavour in the world? It is detectable in aged white burgundies, champagne, oysters, *jabugo* ham, Sauternes, Beaufort and Comté cheese, French farmhouse butter, lamb's lettuce, toasted sesame seeds, wild rice, many of the most revered potato cultivars and Oscietra caviar.

Hazelnut & Cherry: *See Cherry & Hazelnut, page 248*

Hazelnut & Chicken: Filbertone is a key characteristic of hazelnut flavour. It has nutty, cocoa flavours with some meaty, earthy notes, which might suggest a Mexican *mole* sauce (see Chocolate & Chilli, page 15). Hazelnut flavour is intensified by roasting or dry-frying the nuts; a good pairing for chicken is the *picada* sauce given in Hazelnut & Garlic, page 240. Or use them to thicken an aromatic stew like the one in Almond & Chicken, page 242, as they do in Turkey, where so many of the world's hazelnuts are grown. Or simply combine cold roast chicken, toasted hazelnuts and rocket with fresh figs in an autumnal salad.

Hazelnut & Chocolate: *See Chocolate & Hazelnut, page 16*
Hazelnut & Coffee: *See Coffee & Hazelnut, page 21*

Hazelnut & Fig: Frangipane, the lovely, soft nut paste used to fill French fruit tarts, is usually made with almonds, but it needn't be. Hazelnut is a great alternative, particularly for a tart made with velvety, dark-skinned figs. Beat 100g skinned, toasted ground hazelnuts with 100g soft unsalted butter, 100g caster sugar, 20g plain flour, 2 eggs and ½ tsp vanilla extract. Pour this into a 22cm blind-baked sweet pastry case, place your figs on top, slightly pressing them in and bake for 25 minutes at 180°C/Gas Mark 4. Some like to position the figs so their luxuriant red interiors face up, but I prefer to see them rump-up, protruding from the golden paste like baby elephant seals softly snoring on the beach.

Hazelnut & Garlic: Spanish *picada* is, at its most basic, a sauce made with pounded nuts, garlic, bread and oil. Sometimes hazelnuts are used, sometimes almonds and sometimes a combination. There are endless variations that might include saffron, tomato, parsley or pine nuts. It's not unlike the French *aillade* and Turkish *tarator* described in Walnut & Garlic, page 236. Use it to thicken stews (see Almond & Chicken, page 242), to mix into meatballs before shaping, or to serve as a sauce with meat or seafood. Take 15 hazelnuts, 15 almonds (both roasted and skinned) and a slice of good white, crustless bread that's been fried in olive oil, and pound them together in a mortar with 2 garlic cloves. When the mixture has become a paste, add 1 tbsp olive oil and seasonings as desired.

Hazelnut & Pear: Although its flavour dissipates somewhat on cooking, hazelnut oil is very flavourful drizzled on steamed vegetables or mixed with vinegar in salad dressings. It combines particularly well with raspberry vinegar for a salad of goat's cheese, pear and lamb's lettuce – a dark green leaf (also known as mâche) with its own trace of hazelnut flavour.

Hazelnut & Raspberry: *See Raspberry & Hazelnut, page 338*

Hazelnut & Rosemary: Heston Blumenthal once gave a recipe for hazelnut and rosemary couscous in which he toasted the couscous in groundnut oil in a pan before adding the water. But not just any water. He heated it with fresh rosemary stems to infuse it with flavour, before discarding them and reheating the water. After adding it to the couscous, he raked skinned, roasted chopped hazelnuts, finely snipped rosemary, butter and plenty of seasoning through the cooked couscous to finish the dish. You could also combine hazelnut and rosemary in a sweet biscuit or ice cream, providing the nuts are roasted to boost their sweet, chocolatey character.

Hazelnut & Strawberry: *See Strawberry & Hazelnut, page 263*

Hazelnut & Vanilla: The hazelnut liqueur Frangelico, from the Piedmont region of Italy, is made with toasted wild hazelnuts, vanilla, cocoa and a number of the usual secret ingredients. It has a smooth, buttery, hazelnut flavour with a noticeable vanilla finish, and can be whisked to great effect into whipping cream – say 2 tbsp Frangelico and 2 tbsp icing sugar to 250ml cream. Serve with any number of chocolate, pear or raspberry desserts.

Hazelnut & White Fish: *Beurre noisette* is most often served with fish and vegetables but it's good on poultry too. Butter is heated in a pan and, when the milk proteins and sugar in the whey caramelise, it turns brown, taking on a nutty colour and flavour. If allowed to go darker, it becomes *beurre noir* which is traditionally served with skate, brains or eggs. Sometimes a few chopped hazelnuts are added to a *beurre noisette*, making it *beurre de noisette*.

Almond

There are two distinct kinds of almond flavour, bitter and sweet. Bitter almond is the pronounced marzipan flavour that is found in almond extract, almond essence and Amaretto. The extract is derived from bitter almond kernels and from other stone fruits, such as apricot and peach; it must be treated to remove its cyanide content before it is suitable for human consumption. The primary compound responsible for bitter almond flavour is benzaldehyde, which was first synthesised in 1870 and is the second most used flavouring in the world. Aside from bitter almonds, it is also naturally found in a number of foods, including the prince mushroom and the cinnamon relative, cassia. Bitter almond goes particularly well with fellow members of the rose family – stone fruits, berries, apples, pears and rose itself. It's used to boost the flavour of other nuts; you may detect a hint of bitter almond in some dyed green pistachio ice creams. The sweet almond is the world's most popular nut. It has hints of bitter almond flavour but is mild, milky and slightly grassy when raw, and richer when roasted, with a slight toffee-popcorn flavour. Sweet almond's soft, rounded flavour makes it highly compatible. Almond milk and almond butter are available from health-food shops.

Almond & Anise: *See Anise & Almond, page 181*
Almond & Apple: *See Apple & Almond, page 268*

Almond & Apricot: Charles Arrowby in Iris Murdoch's *The Sea, The Sea* rhapsodises on how well anything made with almonds goes with apricot, thumbing his nose at the peach along the way. At one point he prepares a meal of lentil soup, chipolatas with boiled onions and apples stewed in tea, accompanied by a light Beaujolais and followed by almond shortcake with dried apricots. Clearly he's no stranger to tins and packets, but he's right about the apricot and almond. For a plain almond biscuit to serve with poached dried apricots or an apricot fool, follow the recipe in Anise & Almond on page 181 but leave out the anise.

Almond & Asparagus: The flavour of asparagus is often described as nutty. Unsurprising, then, that it has such an affinity for almonds, particularly toasted almonds, whose buttery quality complements the sulphurous bass notes of asparagus. Cook a handful of slivered almonds in a knob of butter over a low heat for 6–7 minutes, until golden. Remove from the heat, add 1 tsp lemon juice and ½ tsp salt, and pour over your cooked spears.

Almond & Banana: *See Banana & Almond, page 277*

Almond & Blackberry: There's no such thing as a free crumble. The price you pay for the astonishing late-summer abundance of inkily delicious black-berries is to walk away with pulls in your jumper and stains on your skirt. Almond's sweetness calms some of blackberry's wild spiciness in this black-berry and almond crumble. Butter a deep 21cm dish and fill with blackberries to a depth of 3–4cm. Sprinkle with 2 tbsp sugar. In another bowl, rub 175g plain flour and 75g butter together until they have a breadcrumb-like consist-ency. Stir in 75g golden caster sugar and 50g roughly chopped, toasted flaked almonds. Sprinkle this on top of the blackberries and bake at 200°C/Gas Mark 6 for about 30 minutes.

Almond & Blackcurrant: *See Blackcurrant & Almond, page 332*

Almond & Blueberry: Fine in your muesli, but you wouldn't want to meet them at a party, would you? Almond is pale, characterless and shy unless toasted. Blueberry is usually just plain insipid. The Spartan, Ivanhoe and Chandler cultivars of blueberry are worth looking out for, but beware the faint-praise-worthy Duke, described variously as mild and moderately flavoured. Things improve considerably if you add some almond extract or, even better, Amaretto, to whipping cream and whisk until the cream holds its shape. Fold in a handful of blueberries and some toasted almond slivers, holding back a few of the almonds to sprinkle over the top.

Almond & Butternut Squash: *See Butternut Squash & Almond, page 229*
Almond & Cardamom: *See Cardamom & Almond, page 313*
Almond & Cauliflower: *See Cauliflower & Almond, page 122*
Almond & Cherry: *See Cherry & Almond, page 247*

Almond & Chicken: In Spain, the Moorish influence is easily discernible in almond-thickened recipes such as *gallina en pepitoria*, a favourite dish at fiestas. Fry 1.5kg chicken joints in olive oil until golden, then set aside. Soften a finely chopped large onion in a little oil with 2 crushed garlic cloves and a bay leaf. Put the chicken back into the pot and pour over 150ml fino sherry and just enough chicken stock or water to cover. Bring to the boil, put a lid on and leave to simmer while you make the *picada* in Hazelnut & Garlic (page 240), except use 30 almonds and no hazelnuts and add a pinch of saffron, a few pinches of ground cloves and 1 tbsp parsley. When you have a paste, add it to the chicken mixture and continue to simmer until the chicken is completely cooked (45–60 minutes from beginning to simmer). Just before serving, you may need to remove the chicken and keep it warm while you boil the sauce to reduce and thicken it. Many recipes suggest adding a couple of finely chopped boiled egg yolks at the end for the same reason. Serve with boiled rice.

Almond & Chilli: *See Chilli & Almond, page 207*
Almond & Chocolate: *See Chocolate & Almond, page 13*

Almond & Cinnamon: These work well together in cakes, pastries and biscuits. They also meet in one of the strata of Morocco's legendary *bastilla* pie. Spiced poached pigeon meat, very lightly scrambled eggs and a mixture of ground almonds, ground cinnamon and sugar are layered between super-fine leaves of *warqa* pastry. Be warned, *bastilla* is fiddly and time-consuming to make. It's faster to fly to Fez and back than attempt it at home – meaning, of course, it's utterly exquisite. As is *keneffa*, the lesser-known sweet version that's often served at weddings. This intersperses the same delicate *warqa* pastry with cinnamon and almonds. My anglicised take on this treat is to make puff pastry horns and fill them with a cinnamon- and almond-flavoured *crème pâtissière*.

Almond & Coconut: When vanilla extract is called for in coconut cakes, biscuits and puddings, try substituting almond extract for half of it. You'll get the same flavour-bolstering, rounded quality but with a nuttier, more sympathetic edge.

Almond & Coffee: *See Coffee & Almond, page 19*
Almond & Fig: *See Fig & Almond, page 339*
Almond & Garlic: *See Garlic & Almond, page 111*

Almond & Ginger: Gingerbread and marzipan on cold night air is the smell of a Christmas market. Add the warm notes of cinnamon, clove and lemon basking in simmering red wine, with chestnuts and bratwursts scorching over coals, and you can enjoy your own miniature *Weihnachtsmarkt* in the comfort of your own home. It's traditional to cut the gingerbread into the shape of buildings and people, the marzipan into animals. In 1993, Roland Mesnier, the Clintons' pastry chef, made a gingerbread White House and no fewer than 21 marzipan likenesses of Socks the cat.

Almond & Grape: *See Grape & Almond, page 251*
Almond & Hard Cheese: *See Hard Cheese & Almond, page 65*
Almond & Hazelnut: *See Hazelnut & Almond, page 238*
Almond & Lamb: *See Lamb & Almond, page 49*

Almond & Lemon: Ground almond soothes lemon's sharpness in cakes and tarts. In Kew, southwest London, deep little tarts called maids of honour are baked and sold at The Original Maids of Honour Shop. They're said to date back to the time of Henry VIII – in Hilary Mantel's novel *Wolf Hall*, Thomas Cromwell sends flat baskets of them to console Anne Boleyn's ladies-in-waiting. The recipe is a secret, but broadly speaking they're puff pastry tarts with a cheesecake-like lemon and almond filling. Further north, Lancaster lemon tart is a variation on Bakewell tart (see Raspberry & Almond, page 337) that omits jam in favour of a thick spread of lemon curd under the cooked almond and egg mixture. In Italy, *torta della nonna* is usually made with lemons and pine nuts, or occasionally almonds – perhaps when *la nonna* has squandered her pension on sweet wine. And in both Italy and Spain, ground almonds are combined with lemon in a moist cake the Spanish call *torta de almendros de Santiago*. You could try using the whole fruit (zest, juice, pith) as described in Orange & Almond on page 293, increasing the amount of sugar a little to compensate for the lemon's extra sourness, but expect quite a mouth-drying result. Better to skip the pith in lemon's case.

Almond & Melon: Grapes may be the standard garnish for the cold Spanish soup, *ajo blanco* (see Garlic & Almond, page 111) but melon is sometimes used instead. You might be able to make perfect spheres with your melon baller but they don't burst in the mouth quite as satisfyingly as an ice-cold grape.

Almond & Oily Fish: According to Elizabeth David, the French writer Jean Giono dismissed trout and almonds as packaging rather than cooking (she didn't have much time for it herself). Alice Waters was more positive. In fact, her biographer recalls that the chef once visited a restaurant in Brittany where a meal of cured ham and melon, trout with almonds, and a raspberry tart constituted her idea of good food.

Almond & Olive: *See Olive & Almond, page 175*
Almond & Orange: *See Orange & Almond, page 293*

Almond & Peach: There's a pleasing symmetry to the classic Italian dessert of baked peaches with amaretti. The biscuits, which share an almond flavour with peach stones, are crushed and stuffed in the cavities left where the stones have been removed. Like the stones, the leaves of the peach tree have a peachy-almond flavour, and can be steeped in water and sugar to make a delicious syrup used in drinks, sorbets and fruit salads.

Almond & Pear: *See Pear & Almond, page 273*
Almond & Raspberry: *See Raspberry & Almond, page 337*
Almond & Rhubarb: *See Rhubarb & Almond, page 254*

Almond & Rose: In France you'll find an almond and rose syrup called Orgeat that tastes like Amaretto getting ready for a date. It's mixed with water to make a refreshing summer cordial, with rum, lime, orange Curaçao and mint to make a Mai Tai, and with pastis to make a Moresque. In Iran, slivers of almond coated with rosewater-flavoured sugar are served on festive occasions. If you like *ajo blanco*, the soup from Andalusia (see Garlic & Almond, page 111), you might try a sweet version in which rosewater and a little honey replace the garlic. A similar principle operates in the *sharbat* of milk, almonds and rose petals offered by the bride's family to the groom's at Muslim weddings in Bangalore.

Almond & Rosemary: Almonds tossed in oil and then lightly salted have a surprising smoky-bacon flavour enhanced by a sprinkling of chopped rosemary. Serve with chilled fino sherry before dinner. Alternatively, fry the almonds in olive oil for an extra-toasty flavour – use 250g almonds to 1 tbsp very finely snipped rosemary.

Almond & Saffron: *See Saffron & Almond, page 179*
Almond & Shellfish: *See Shellfish & Almond, page 139*
Almond & Strawberry: *See Strawberry & Almond, page 262*
Almond & White Chocolate: *See White Chocolate & Almond, page 351*

FRESH FRUITY

Cherry

Watermelon

Grape

Rhubarb

Tomato

Strawberry

Pineapple

Apple

Pear

Cherry

In common with the apple, a fellow member of the *Rosaceae* family, cherries come in sweet and sour form, with something of a grey area in between. And like apples, they have a predominantly fresh, green, fruity character and an almond-scented seed, although almond flavour is far more strongly present in cherry stones than in apple pips – so much so, in fact, that the bitter-almond compound, benzaldehyde, forms the basis of synthesised cherry flavouring. In real cherries, almond flavour is most easily detectable when the fruit is cooked with the stones in. Cherries also have floral and spicy notes, plus a tannic quality that is particularly noticeable in the dried form of the fruit. Cherries are especially lovely with spices such as vanilla and cinnamon, and are paired with them to make cherry liqueurs. Kirsch and maraschino are clear, distilled spirits with a clean cherry flavour that goes very well in fruit salads or with flambéed fruit.

Cherry & Almond: Cherry stones and bitter almonds contain a volatile oil that can be used to produce a compound called benzaldehyde. Benzaldehyde is the second most popular flavour molecule in the US flavour and fragrance industry, after vanillin, and is used to synthesise both almond and cherry flavours. Sip a cherry cola and think of Amaretto and you'll taste the proximity. It's the cherry stone that tastes most like almond, not the flesh. Unless it's a maraschino cherry. Brined while unripe and green, maraschino cherries were originally steeped in a liqueur made from the juice, stones and leaves of cherry, which gave them a lovely, drunken marzipan flavour. These days most maraschinos are steeped in sugar syrup and given an almond flavouring, which doesn't taste half as nice – so if you want the best garnish for your Manhattan you'll have to steep your own, or seek out an artisan producer. Make a Manhattan by stirring 60ml good rye or bourbon, 30ml sweet vermouth and a dash of angostura bitters with ice and then straining over a maraschino cherry.

Cherry & Banana: *See Banana & Cherry, page 277*

Cherry & Chocolate: A winning combination. Even if you turn your nose up at Black Forest gâteau, or Ben and Jerry's Cherry Garcia ice cream, you can't deny that cherry, with its fruit *and* nut flavour, is a natural partner for chocolate. Sour morello cherries, grown in the orchards of the Black Forest in southwestern Germany, are the usual choice for combining with chocolate. Delia Smith makes a roulade of them, while Nigella Lawson makes chocolate muffins with morello cherry jam mixed into the batter. If you're not in the mood for baking, a good chocolate counter should furnish a half-pound of cherries slouching kirsch-drunk in their chocolate shells.

Cherry & Cinnamon: *See Cinnamon & Cherry, page 216*
Cherry & Coconut: *See Coconut & Cherry, page 286*
Cherry & Coffee: *See Coffee & Cherry, page 20*

Cherry & Goat's Cheese: Sweet cherries work well with young goat's cheese, particularly when fresh, grassy examples of both are available. Keep an eye out for them in high summer and, if you love long walks punctuated by picnics but can't bear to lug around a hamper or a coolbox, this less-is-more lunch is ideal. Wrap fresh cherries and a few rounds of goat's cheese in a paper bag with only as many slices of crumbly, nutty bread as you plan to eat, then head off to your picnic spot. I like to eat some of the cheese piled on the bread first and then relish the rest of it with the cherries, ending the meal with the remaining cherries on their own. Edward Bunyard writes that to enjoy cherries at their best you should walk through an orchard just after they've been harvested and pick the ripe remainders, so maybe you should plan your route accordingly.

Cherry & Hazelnut: Added to your muesli, a handful of hazelnuts and some dried sour cherries recall a mug of sweet, milky tea and a cigarette. Dried cherries have a tangy sweet-sourness with strong hints of tobacco and a clear tannic tea flavour, which marry well with hazelnuts' milky sweetness.

Cherry & Lamb: *See Lamb & Cherry, page 51*
Cherry & Peach: *See Peach & Cherry, page 284*

Cherry & Smoked Fish: Hugh Fearnley-Whittingstall suggests a seasonal combination of hot-smoked sea trout and a tart morello cherry compote made with fresh stoned cherries simmered with a little brown sugar. Serve both warm with a watercress salad and slices of walnut bread.

Cherry & Vanilla: The anise-like quality of pure Tahitian vanilla is particularly complementary to cherry flavour, which will no doubt put you in mind of Cherries Jubilee. Created by Escoffier for Queen Victoria's Golden Jubilee in 1887, the dish originally consisted of sweet cherries cooked in a thick, sugary sauce to which kirsch or brandy was added before being set alight. In later versions, Escoffier ladled the cherries over vanilla ice cream, which is almost certainly how you'd be served it today. Cooks who value their eyebrows might settle for cherry clafoutis, a French dessert of cherries cooked in a sweet batter, sometimes flavoured with almond, although vanilla is more common. The cherries are left unpitted, as the stones bring a balancing bitterness to the dish. Put 500g sweet cherries in a buttered 23cm round ovenproof dish. Split a vanilla pod and scrape the seeds out into a saucepan containing 250ml milk. Throw in the pod while you're at it, then scald the milk and set aside to cool. Whisk 2 eggs, 1 egg yolk and 125g caster sugar until well combined. Add 75g melted butter and whisk some more. Sift in 50g plain flour and whisk until smooth. Remove the vanilla pod and whisk the milk into the batter. Pour this over the cherries and bake for about 30 minutes at 200°C/Gas Mark 6, until set and golden on top.

Cherry & Walnut: The sort of partnership Alan Bennett might get wistful about. Poor walnut is in danger of being squeezed out by more newly fashionable nuts – macadamia, pecan, pine – and glacé cherries by overqualified, under-sweet fruits such as blueberry and cranberry. Make a cherry and walnut cake, just for old times' sake.

Watermelon

A bite of cold watermelon: like cherryade and cucumber juice with a hint of grass, chilled into a soft granita. Mark Twain called the watermelon 'chief of this world's luxuries', and if you get your hands on a ripe one you may be inclined to agree. Look for a watermelon that's as heavy as a medicine ball and sings a low B-flat when you thump it. As a rule, the seeded varieties taste better than the seedless ones. Watermelon juice is the colour of rubies and has a lovely sweet flavour with a vegetable undertone, a little like carrot juice. The compatibility of watermelon flesh with other ingredients is limited by its tendency to waterlog them, but herbal and sour flavours make fine pairings.

Watermelon & Chilli: A favourite combination in Mexican confectionery. Watermelon lollies come with a chilli sherbet for dipping, watermelon gummy sweets with a sugar and chilli coating, and watermelon hard candy with chilli powder in the centre.

Watermelon & Chocolate: The Sicilian dish *gelo di melone* is a watermelon soup thickened with cornflour, sweetened with sugar, spiced with cinnamon and flavoured with either crushed pistachio, grated chocolate or candied peel, or a combination of all three.

Watermelon & Cinnamon: The Baptiste mango of Haiti is said to have the fragrance of pine and lime, and a flavour reminiscent of sweet watermelon with a mild cinnamon aftertaste. Chances are readers outside of Port-au-Prince won't be finding one in their local greengrocer's any time soon. But you can make the watermelon sorbet from Jane Grigson's *Fruit Book*, in which the sugar syrup is enriched with Haiti-conjuring cinnamon. Try the cinnamon-flavoured sugar syrup in Lime & Cinnamon on page 301, except with unflavoured sugar. When it's cool, add to strained watermelon juice with a squeeze of lemon until it tastes right. Freeze.

Watermelon & Coriander Leaf: Sniff a slice of watermelon and it might remind you of a hot day at the beach – the watery, salty tang, with the candied wafts of a distant funfair. Combine it in a salsa with coriander leaf, a little red onion and some fresh green chilli, and it's more dripping jungle after a rainstorm. (I need to get out more.)

Watermelon & Cucumber: Watermelon is related to cucumber and shares many of its flavour characteristics. Unsurprisingly, then, watermelon goes well with cucumber's classic partners, especially feta cheese and mint. It's also worth considering it as a cucumber replacement in, say, a gazpacho, where its fruity take on cucumber's wateriness lends an essentially savoury dish a lovely melting-ice-lolly quality.

Watermelon & Goat's Cheese: *See Goat's Cheese & Watermelon, page 58*

Watermelon & Lime: Serve watermelon pieces with lime zest, juice and a sprinkle of corrective sugar if needed. Or combine them in a long, refreshing drink, like they do in Mexico. The crisp flesh of watermelon holds its chill particularly well, and the noise it makes when cut into chunks for liquidising is like the creak of boots on snow.

Watermelon & Melon: Although part of the same family as cantaloupes, ogdens, honeydews and Galias, and combinable with all of them, watermelon is not of the same genus. It lacks the fruity-smelling esters that are characteristic of its cousins. That's not to say that cantaloupes and the other sweet, petite melons don't have some of the vegetal funk that is common to the squash family. Their seedy bellies have a composty low note that often comes as an unpleasant surprise, like hearing an otherwise delicate woman speak in a booming baritone.

Watermelon & Mint: *See Mint & Watermelon, page 332*

Watermelon & Oyster: The cucumber notes in watermelon work well with oysters, which in turn bring out the juicy sweetness of the fruit. And far from being swamped by the wave of wateriness, oyster positively basks in it. At the restaurant O Ya in Boston, chef Tim Cushman combines *kumamoto* oysters with watermelon pearls and a cucumber mignonette. Along similar lines, a 2006 menu at El Bulli included a selection of seaweeds arranged like a garland around a piece of watermelon covered with an intensely sea-flavoured foam. You ate the seaweeds in order of increasing saltiness, and the watermelon provided sweet solace at the end.

Watermelon & Pork: In 2006 The Fatty Crab, Zakary Pelaccio's Malaysian street-food restaurant in New York's West Village, won *Time Out New York*'s award for Most Deliciously Unhealthy Salad with its watermelon pickle and crispy pork appetiser. Pork belly is marinated in *kecap manis* (a kind of soy-dark, Satanic ketchup), rice vinegar, fish sauce and lime juice, roasted, then cubed and deep-fried. The cubed pork is mixed with cubes of sweet water-melon dressed with seasoned sugar, lime and vinegar, and little pieces of pickled white watermelon rind. Finally it's topped with a thatch of spring onion, coriander and basil, and a shake of white sesame seeds.

Watermelon & Rosemary: *See Rosemary & Watermelon, page 320*

Watermelon & Tomato: Delicious paired in salads and salsas. Shake Shack in New York combines them in its frozen custard – a sort of posh soft-serve ice cream. It's one of their special flavours, as are coffee and doughnuts, cucumber and mint, and raspberry jalapeño.

Grape

Impossible to write about grapes without writing about wine; the sheer variety of wine grapes, and of the flavours coaxed from them by vinification, is simply astounding. Regrettably, the same can't be said for the sorts of table grape available in shops. Broadly speaking, the difference between table and wine grapes is that the former are bred to be thin-skinned and seedless, and thus easy to eat. The skin of a grape is where much of its flavour resides, and it also gives red and rosé wines their colour. The table/wine divide is not absolute, however: some varieties fulfil both functions. Muscat wine, for example, has the unusual quality of tasting like the grapes it was made from (consider how often wine tastes of apples, grapefruit, gooseberries, apricots, melon and blackcurrants, and how rarely of grapes). With their honeyed, floral quality and notes of rose and coriander seed, muscat grapes are also delicious plucked off the bunch. Other white table grapes have similar flavours, while red grapes can have hints of straw-berry or blackcurrant, at least when given time to develop on the vine. This, sadly, is rare, and all too often we're saddled with slightly unripe, seedless varieties whose flavour could at best be described as generic-ally fruity. The unobtrusive, sweet-sour fruitiness of grape works well with other fruits, or as a refreshing counterpoint to meat. You might want to savour the good ones by themselves.

Grape & Almond: Likeable, bland grape and almond must be sent to extremes to arrest your attention. Freezing the grapes concentrates the flavours, and the resulting texture is somewhere between a sorbet and a Gummi Bear. You could bring out the flavour of almonds by toasting them for almond brittle; serve the brittle and the frozen grapes with the cheese course in separate glass or silver bowls, the brittle broken into sticky fragments. Another take on this pair is almond-studded cantuccini biscuits dipped into rustic, raisiny Vin Santo, the (usually) sweet Tuscan wine that's made with dried grapes. See also Garlic & Almond, page 111.

Grape & Anise: *See Anise & Grape, page 183*

Grape & Avocado: The California Table Grape Commission helpfully suggests that grapes can in most cases be used in place of tomatoes. Remember that next time tomatoes are out of season and you need something to serve with your mozzarella and avocado. Not sure it works both ways, even in the case of the small tomato cultivar called Green Grape, which like its namesake has translucent skin and a zesty flavour.

Grape & Blue Cheese: It goes without saying that port with Stilton is one of the great cheese and wine pairings. They share a richness, but it's the contrast between the sweet wine and the salty cheese that makes it so satisfying. Sauternes with Roquefort works on the same principle. Similarly, a black grape that floods your mouth with deep, sweet, spicy juice will make a good partner for Stilton, not just on the cheeseboard but in a salad of lamb's lettuce with a few nuts.

Grape & Chicken: Grapes complement light meats such as chicken or, more famously, delicately flavoured quail. Quail with grapes, stalwart of the high-gloss coffee-table cookbook, often calls for vine leaves and wine too; in the bad old days you might have been required to blanch, peel *and* deseed your grapes before adding them. These days the practice of deseeding green grapes is next to obsolete, thanks to the market dominance of the seedless Thompson variety, developed in mid-nineteenth-century California by the English viticulturist, William Thompson. Thompsons have medium-thick skin, so you'll still need to peel them for your quail or chicken dish. As with tomatoes, blanching them beforehand will make the job that much easier if they're not quite ripe.

Grape & Hard Cheese: *See Hard Cheese & Grape, page 67*
Grape & Melon: *See Melon & Grape, page 280*
Grape & Peach: *See Peach & Grape, page 284*

Grape & Peanut: Grape is the jelly of choice for a classic American peanut butter and jelly sandwich (see also Blackcurrant & Peanut, page 333). Grape jelly is made with Concord grapes, a flavour experienced in the UK only in the form of imported juice, or occasionally in 'grape-flavoured' sweets that, until you try the fruit itself, invite you to ponder the nature of subjectivity ('Grape? Are you *kidding*?'). I finally sampled a Concord grape from a stall in New York's Union Square Market. Crikey, I thought. It tasted simultaneously cheap and very expensive, like a penny sweet heavily laced with jasmine. Back home, I get my Concord fix from Welch's grape juice, which makes a lovely perfumed sorbet. Mix 500ml unsweetened juice with 250ml sugar syrup, chill, then freeze in the usual way. Serve with a scoop each of peanut-butter and brown-bread ice cream for a peanut butter and jelly sandwich sundae.

Grape & Pineapple: On a hot summer's afternoon, seedless grapes and chunks of super-ripe pineapple in a bowl of iced water will keep everyone chilled, at least until the ice-cream van arrives.

Grape & Pork: Pellegrino Artusi suggests serving sausages with grapes, on the assumption that the sweet and sour fruit will partner pleasingly with the pork. Simply cook the sausages (Italian pork, if you can get them), and when they're nearly done, add whole grapes to the pan and cook until they collapse. See also Chilli & Anise, page 207.

Grape & Rosemary: Never mix the grape and the grain, unless you're making *schiacciata con l'uva*, a kind of bread that Tuscans cover with luscious crushed grapes at harvest time. The bread itself is not dissimilar to focaccia but is baked longer and is crisper for it. The grapes used are wine cultivars, either semi-dried or fresh from the vine, with the seeds left in. Rosemary or fennel might be sprinkled over the bread before it's baked. Eat warm from the oven while watching Éric Rohmer's *Autumn Tale*, which makes viniculture look a deal more romantic than it undoubtedly is.

Grape & Soft Cheese: *See Soft Cheese & Grape, page 72*

Grape & Strawberry: The grape known in Italy as *fragola uva*, the strawberry grape, is an American import known in its country of origin as the Isabella. Its juice has a pronounced strawberry flavour and can be mixed with Prosecco, in the style of a Bellini, to make a Tiziano (I don't know much about art, but I know what I like to drink). Isabella and a wild strain of grape native to North America were crossed to create the more commonly grown Concord (see Grape & Peanut, page 252), and they share distinct candy notes. *Fragola uva* can be grown in the UK: there's a vine on the roof garden of the Coq d'Argent restaurant in the City of London.

Grape & Walnut: Jeremy Round wrote about the excellent autumn pairing of mild, creamy, fresh walnuts and muscat-flavoured grapes. He recommended the richly sweet Italia variety, a milder muscat grape that's most often used for wine-making.

Grape & White Fish: *See White Fish & Grape, page 147*

Rhubarb

Rhubarb is a vegetable native to Siberia. The leaves are poisonous; it's the pink petioles, or stalks, that we eat. Once its intense sourness has been countered with sufficient quantities of sugar, the flavour becomes fascinating – a combination of aromatic, candied strawberry notes with a cooking-apple fruitiness, plus a strong, thick note redolent of a greenhouse full of ripening tomatoes. The fruity notes are able to withstand cooking, and retain their freshness even after sugar has been added. Rhubarb is best paired with overtly sweet ingredients, such as maple syrup, honey or anise, then smothered with even more sweetness in the form of vanilla, almonds, cream or butter. Some take advantage of its gooseberry/cooking-apple sourness to pair rhubarb with fatty meat and oily fish.

Rhubarb & Almond: The Scottish dessert cranachan originally consisted of cream, cream cheese, honey and toasted oatmeal – the sort of recipe that was invented before it was compulsory to worry about your heart. More recently it's likely to include whisky and raspberries. As the only raspberries you can buy in January are those tasteless grenades of pure sourness they flog in supermarkets, one Burns Night I devised this spin-off using rhubarb instead. Rhubarb has a similarly pleasing sharpness to raspberry, and I used Amaretto in place of the whisky – partly because almond is a natural partner for rhubarb, partly because its sweetness and lower alcohol content make it less of a hot shock than Scotch. Toast 50g oatmeal until golden brown and set aside to cool. Cut 6 sticks of rhubarb into 2cm pieces, place in a buttered ovenproof dish, sprinkle over 150g sugar, cover with foil and bake at 180°C/ Gas Mark 4 for about 30 minutes. Remove and cool. Whip 200ml cream until it holds its shape, then fold in four-fifths of the toasted oatmeal, the cooked rhubarb, 2 tbsp Amaretto and 2 tbsp runny honey. Divide between 4 dishes and top each with the remaining oatmeal and a Highland fling of toasted almond slices.

Rhubarb & Anise: *See Anise & Rhubarb, page 184*
Rhubarb & Black Pudding: *See Black Pudding & Rhubarb, page 40*

Rhubarb & Cucumber: I used to love dipping raw rhubarb sticks in sugar and biting off sections that always threatened to be face-tighteningly sour. The secret was to overdo the sugar, which is surely what rhubarb's celery-like, natural scoop-shape encourages you to do. The effect was like a marginally healthier version of the sour fish and fizzy laces you find in sweet shops – the mouthwatering citric shock at once tempered and intensified by the intense, crunchy sweetness. Until I read Paula Wolfert, I'd never thought of dipping rhubarb in salt, which a friend of hers reported people doing in Turkey. Further investigations yielded an Iranian recipe for thinly sliced cucumber and rhubarb tossed and left to stand for a while in salt, then mixed with rocket, lemon juice and a little mint, which Wolfert suggests as an accompaniment to poached salmon.

Rhubarb & Ginger: *See Ginger & Rhubarb, page 312*

Rhubarb & Juniper: At Alinea, in Chicago, Grant Achatz offers a dish of rhubarb cooked in seven ways – pairing it with goat's milk jelly, for example, with green tea foam and with gin. Rather than mask it with sugar, Achatz likes to highlight the inherent sourness of rhuburb, which he plays off against bold flavours such as lavender and bay leaf. I pair it with juniper in a gin and rhubarb sorbet; like vodka, the gin lends the sorbet a satisfying smoothness.

Rhubarb & Lamb: You can see how rhubarb might work in the sweetly spiced, fatty tagines of North Africa, or in this Iranian *khoresh*. Soften a large onion in a mixture of groundnut oil and butter, then add 500g cubed lamb and brown. Stir in a pinch of saffron and 1 tsp pomegranate syrup, then pour in enough water to cover the meat. Simmer, covered, for 1½ hours. Half an hour into the cooking, fry a finely chopped large bunch of both parsley and mint in butter and add to the *khoresh*. About 5–10 minutes before the stew is ready, add 3 sticks of rhubarb, cut into 3cm pieces, stir once, cover and leave until the rhubarb is cooked but still holding its shape. Fried herbs are often added to *khoresh*; although fresh herbs generally lose their flavour when cooked, in this instance they're present in sufficient quantities for some flavour to survive, and their bulk serves the secondary purpose of thickening the sauce. Serve with basmati rice.

Rhubarb & Mango: Chef Richard Corrigan rhapsodises over the combination of rhubarb and Alphonso mango, whose seasons, he notes, overlap. He poaches the rhubarb in a rosemary-flavoured sugar syrup with a splash of grenadine, leaves it to cool, then serves it in a bowl with slices of Alphonso mango, nutmeg-freckled vanilla ice cream and stem ginger shortbread.

Rhubarb & Oily Fish: Sour gooseberry might be the better-known companion for mackerel but rhubarb can be equally ruthless in tackling the fish's oiliness, and the combination is just as delicious. Soften 2–3 finely chopped shallots in vegetable oil, add 3 chopped rhubarb stalks and cook, covered, over a medium heat until the rhubarb is well broken down. Stir in 2–3 tsp red wine vinegar and 2 tsp brown sugar, and cook for a few minutes until most of the vinegar has evaporated. Taste, season, and serve with crackling-hot mackerel.

Rhubarb & Orange: *See Orange & Rhubarb, page 296*
Rhubarb & Pork: *See Pork & Rhubarb, page 37*
Rhubarb & Rosemary: *See Rosemary & Rhubarb, page 320*

Rhubarb & Saffron: Rhubarb invites experimentation. *New York Times* food writer Mark Bittman described his trials with a number of flavour pairings. He rejected tarragon, mint, cumin and coriander before settling on saffron, in which he detected an almost smoky 'elusive depth of flavour' that works perfectly with the rhubarb. He recommends serving them with simply cooked fish. See also Rhubarb & Juniper, page 255.

Rhubarb & Strawberry: A standard pairing in the US, where it's hard to find a rhubarb pie or tart that doesn't include strawberry. Ripe rhubarb contains a juicy, floral strawberry flavour, and the two share pronounced fresh, green notes. A tip from Edmund and Ellen Dixon, writing in 1868, is to add a couple of tablespoons of strawberry jam to your rhubarb tart, which, they claim, will result in a pineapple flavour.

Rhubarb & Vanilla: Rhubarb is easy to grow, and by the late nineteenth century most people in England had a crown or two in their garden. In *Plenty and Want*, John Burnett cites a week's worth of menus for a typical English family in 1901. Rhubarb makes it into no fewer than six meals. Such ubiquity and ease of cultivation was a blessing during the wars but by the second half of the twentieth century the nation had grown heartily sick of rhubarb, boiled to a pulp and burbling in lumpy custard, especially as so many new foods became available. Rhubarb might have disappeared altogether had it not been for the diplomatic skill of vanilla. Which is just as well, as rhubarb is one of vanilla's best friends: the contrast of luxurious, floral creaminess with rhubarb's mouthwatering sour-fruity flavour – somewhat akin to passion fruit but without the heavy muskiness – is completely heavenly. And so rhubarb clung on, skirting obsolescence on the back of rhubarb crumble with vanilla ice cream and rhubarb tart with proper custard (which is out of this world, by the way, if you cook the rhubarb and custard together in the tart). And those shocking pink and yellow boiled sweets. Now, of course, rhubarb is popular again, thanks to renewed interest in seasonal food and growing your own. And how does it repay vanilla for sticking by it through the hard times? By looking for newer, more exotic partners, of course. See Rhubarb & Saffron, above, and Rhubarb & Mango, page 255.

Tomato

Buying decent tinned tomatoes is a good deal easier than buying tasty fresh ones. Look for Italian tinned plum tomatoes – if it says San Marzano D.O.P. on the label, they'll be good. The original San Marzano cultivar was more or less wiped out in the 1970s by the cucumber mosaic virus, but the kind available today is an approved replacement, with a fleshy texture that's hard to beat for cooking. There are also some excellent organic brands from California. Tinned tomatoes have been cooked a little (common for canned products) and will have developed a more sulphurous, jammy, spicy flavour than their raw counterpart. Raw tomatoes taste sour, sweet and salty, and have leafy, fruity and floral flavours. They're at their best when they've been left to ripen properly on the vine, developing their optimal bold sweetness and acidity. If you can't grow your own, shop-bought cherry tomatoes are often the best bet for flavour. Or you could invest the money you might otherwise have wasted on premium-priced, but stingily flavoured, varieties in a bottle of high quality balsamic vinegar, which will furnish the sweetness and acidity the tomatoes lack. (Incidentally, the flavour of strawberry is also intensified by balsamic vinegar; see Tomato & Strawberry, page 261, for their alleged interchangeability.) Tomato has an umami taste too. Heston Blumenthal, acting on a hunch that tomato seeds contain more flavour than the flesh, worked with scientists from Reading University to confirm that they are in fact richer in glutamic acids, which not only makes them particularly tasty but also boosts the flavour of other ingredients.

Tomato & Anchovy: *See Anchovy & Tomato, page 164*

Tomato & Anise: Add a few tablespoons of tomato purée to tarragony Béarnaise sauce and it becomes the rosy-pink *sauce Choron*, named after Alexandre Étienne Choron, the great French chef. When the Prussian siege of Paris in 1870 cut off supplies to his restaurant, he turned to the zoo in the Bois de Boulogne and devised a menu that included elephant consommé, bear shanks in a roasted pepper sauce and cat with rat. Assuming supply lines are open as you read this, you might serve *sauce Choron* with salmon, fishcakes or red meat. As to the purée, you want the good stuff. Giorgio Locatelli writes that a quality tomato purée should taste good straight out of the tube, with a flavour reminiscent of tomatoes dried naturally in the sun.

Tomato & Aubergine: Both members of the nightshade family and, used incautiously, can be deadly for the cook. You have to manage tomato's acidity and the bitterness of aubergine, while not undercooking the aubergine or using so much oil that it oozes from its pores. No wonder so many *imam bayildi* can be as delicious as a plate of boiled plimsolls. Handled sensitively, however, this Turkish dish of aubergines stuffed with garlic and tomatoes, amongst other things, can be sublime, as can *melanzane parmigiana* (baked aubergines in a cheese-enriched tomato sauce), *pasta alla norma* (the classic Sicilian pasta dish with aubergines, tomato, basil and ricotta) and caponata (a cold, sweet and sour aubergine and tomato salad, also from Sicily).

Tomato & Avocado: *See Avocado & Tomato, page 201*

Tomato & Bacon: What a contrast! Salty bacon and sweet-sour tomato, Famously good with crisp, bittersweet lettuce in a BLT. Not so good in the first dinner I cooked my then husband-to-be: pasta all'amatriciana. A safe bet, you'd think. I fried a dozen chopped rashers of pancetta in olive oil until crisp, removed them from the pan and set them aside. Having softened a sliced onion in the bacon fat, I emptied in a tin of whole plum tomatoes, broke them up with my wooden spoon and added 1 tsp each of chilli flakes and sugar before seasoning. While that slowly simmered, I slipped into the bedroom and crammed all the discarded shoes, recipe books, home-gym equipment and sweet wrappers into the wardrobe before nonchalantly returning to the kitchen to give my sauce a stir. A little more sugar, I thought, to balance the sharpness of the tomato – a sharpness that lingered on my palate, worryingly, as I withdrew to the bathroom. So much so that once I'd applied my eyeliner I had to pop back to the kitchen and add an extra teaspoon. And so on, teaspoon after teaspoon, until the sauce had taken on a candied glaze and might as well have been called pasta alla diabetica. I added the bacon to the sauce and reheated it. Cooked the pasta and drained it. Mixed it with the sauce and served it with pecorino romano. He ate it, but I'm sure I saw him wince. Nervous hosts should note that stress and anxiety can dull the ability to taste. Research carried out on people with seasonal affective disorder has shown a marked difference in the sufferer's taste thresholds during the winter months.

Tomato & Basil: *See Basil & Tomato, page 215*
Tomato & Beef: *See Beef & Tomato, page 48*

Tomato & Bell Pepper: Not long after the second summer of love came the first summer of Delia. The ungainly chilli con carne pots of our youth were cleared away in favour of the roasted vegetable couscous salad with harissa-style dressing, oven-roasted ratatouille and chicken basque in *Delia Smith's Summer Collection*. And, of course, the Piedmont roasted peppers, which Smith had eaten at Bibendum, whose chef, Simon Hopkinson, had in turn eaten them at Franco Taruschio's Walnut Tree Inn. If 1993 had a flavour, it was halved red peppers stuffed with half a skinned tomato, an anchovy fillet, a little garlic and some olive oil, roasted and then garnished with a scattering of torn basil. See also Bell Pepper & Egg, page 205.

Tomato & Caper: The volcanic soil on the Greek island of Santorini is said to give the capers grown there a unique intensity of flavour. A quantity of them are sun-dried until pale and very hard, then cooked in a tomato sauce to accompany the island's prized yellow split peas. See also Potato & Tomato, page 93, and Olive & Tomato, page 177.

Tomato & Chicken: *See Chicken & Tomato, page 31*
Tomato & Chilli: *See Chilli & Tomato, page 211*
Tomato & Chocolate: *See Chocolate & Tomato, page 18*
Tomato & Cinnamon: *See Cinnamon & Tomato, page 219*

Tomato & Clove: Eugenol is the predominant flavour compound in dark, spicy cloves. It's responsible for some of basil's flavour too, and occurs naturally in tomatoes. Clove is often added, along with other spices, as a flavour enhancer in cooked tomato dishes and sauces, such as ketchup. See also Basil & Clove, page 213.

Tomato & Coriander Leaf: *See Coriander Leaf & Tomato, page 197*

Tomato & Cucumber: Although tomato and cucumber may seem to be the lifeblood of gazpacho, the dish pre-dates their arrival from the New World. Gazpacho was originally made with bread, garlic, olive oil, vinegar and water – a less fancy version of *ajo blanco*. The first gazpacho I made – or had a hand in making – was in Portugal, on a day I'd cheated death twice (landslide, drowning). It took 12 of us to prepare it, variously assigned to the peeling, grating, chopping, blending, sieving and so on: a kitchen orchestra conducted by a brusquely efficient hostess. Even with a dozen of us, it took an hour. But it was the best gazpacho I've ever tasted, tangy and seemingly containing every fresh salad flavour under the Cascais sun.

Tomato & Egg: *See Egg & Tomato, page 136*

Tomato & Garlic: *Pa amb tomàquet*: the only way to start the day in Catalonia. Not a bad way to finish it either. Served with most meals, it's a simple dish of bread, toasted, or a day old so it's hard enough not to tear when you rub on the garlic, then the tomato, pieces of whose flesh, along with the juice and the seeds, get caught in the air pockets and enrich the flavour. To finish, it's drizzled with olive oil and sprinkled with salt. It's usually eaten on its own, though sometimes accompanied by anchovies or *jamón jabugo*. In his *Teoria i pràctica del pa amb tomàquet*, which runs to more than 200 pages, Leopold Pomés tells of a famous musician who liked to take alternate bites of tomato bread and chocolate. See also Chocolate & Tomato, page 18.

Tomato & Ginger: *See Ginger & Tomato, page 312*
Tomato & Hard Cheese: *See Hard Cheese & Tomato, page 69*

Tomato & Horseradish: Mix tomato ketchup with horseradish to make a simple sauce for raw oysters or cooked shrimp. A little dash of chilli sauce will pep it up if the horseradish alone is too tame. See also Celery & Horseradish, page 96.

Tomato & Lamb: Like coconut, tomato can add instant summer to a dish: it even lightens roast lamb. In Greece they cook lamb joints with tomatoes and add orzo, the rice-shaped pasta, towards the end. The pasta soaks up the lamb and tomato flavours. All it needs is a simple spinach salad on the side. Noting how long it will take to roast the meat to your taste, make slits in your lamb joint, poke slivers of garlic into them and season. Transfer the joint to a rack in a roasting tin and place on the middle shelf of an oven preheated to 190°C/Gas Mark 5. Roughly chop the contents of two 400g tins of tomatoes, then stir in some oregano, a bay leaf, ½ tsp sugar and some seasoning. When the meat has an hour left to cook, working quickly, take the roasting tin out of the oven, set the lamb aside and drain the fat from the tin. Pour the tomatoes into the tin, rest the lamb on top of them and return to the oven. When the lamb's cooking time is up, remove it and wrap loosely in foil to rest. Stir 250g orzo and 100ml boiling water into the tomatoes and return to the oven. Once the meat has rested for 15 minutes, carve it, by which time the orzo should be cooked. Double-check it is, then serve slices of lamb on the pasta. See also Lamb & Anise, page 50.

Tomato & Lemon: A light squeeze of lemon will remove the metallic taste from a tin of tomatoes. Worth knowing, especially if you've just retrieved a tin from the depths of the cupboard, as the tinned flavour develops with age.

Tomato & Lime: *See Lime & Tomato, page 302*
Tomato & Mushroom: *See Mushroom & Tomato, page 80*
Tomato & Nutmeg: *See Nutmeg & Tomato, page 223*
Tomato & Olive: *See Olive & Tomato, page 177*

Tomato & Onion: Tomatoes open up perhaps the widest gap between ideal and actual flavour. Elizabeth David writes about the tomato and onion salad she ate every day one summer in Spain, noting that both ingredients were so delicious they could only have been spoiled by the addition of cucumbers, olives or lettuce. She goes on to lament that such a pleasure was becoming increasingly rare in England. It's almost non-existent now. The only tomatoes that have ever really lived up to the ideal for me were the ones I ate at a beach restaurant in El Puerto de Santa María, between Jerez and Cádiz on the Costa de la Luz. It had garish plastic tablecloths covered by a layer of rough paper, held in place by fluorescent green table-clips. The tomatoes were fringed with green, the onions, just, well, onions. But both were exquisite: the tomato deep with chlorophyllic greenhouse flavour, the onions so sweet you could have blindfolded someone and convinced them they were slices of fruit.

Tomato & Peanut: *See Peanut & Tomato, page 25*
Tomato & Pork: *See Pork & Tomato, page 37*
Tomato & Potato: *See Potato & Tomato, page 93*
Tomato & Prosciutto: *See Prosciutto & Tomato, page 173*
Tomato & Sage: *See Sage & Tomato, page 323*

Tomato & Shellfish: *Linguine alle vongole* is served either *rosso* or *bianco* – with or without tomatoes. I'm firmly in the *bianco* camp, but if you prefer *rosso* you may be more comfortable than I was with the concept of Clamato, a sort of liquidised *vongole rosso* (minus the pasta) in much the same sense that gazpacho is liquidised salad. A mix of tomato juice, clam broth and spices inspired, in fact, by Manhattan clam chowder, Clamato is the sort of novelty item you bring back to your holiday rental, and, as I did, stick in the fridge, taking the bottle out now and then to send the air bubble on a futile mission to the bottom and back, searching for signs of lurking clam meat. Steeling myself, largely by reasoning that I liked tomato-shellfish concoctions like prawns Provençal, lobster américaine, the Catalan fish stew *zarzuela*, and the Italian-influenced San Franciscan seafood stew cioppino, I popped the lid. And fell in love. Clamato is pure liquid umami, nothing more challenging to the palate than a very savoury, salty tomato juice, perfect for Bloody Marys. In Mexico they mix it with beer to make a *michelada*.

Tomato & Soft Cheese: *See Soft Cheese & Tomato, page 73*

Tomato & Strawberry: These are interchangeable, according to some scientifically minded chefs, as the two share many flavour compounds. In the mid-1990s, Ron G. Buttery and his team discovered that tomatoes contain what's known as the strawberry furanone, also found in raspberry, pineapple, beef, roasted hazelnuts and popcorn. Later research discovered the highest concentrations were found in home-grown tomatoes in high summer. Try substituting one for the other in your favourite strawberry and tomato dishes. Strawberry, avocado and mozzarella salad is a no-brainer. How about strawberries in your burger or tomatoes on your fruit tarts? Wimbledon may never be the same again.

Tomato & Thyme: *See Thyme & Tomato, page 328*
Tomato & Vanilla: *See Vanilla & Tomato, page 350*
Tomato & Watermelon: *See Watermelon & Tomato, page 251*
Tomato & White Fish: *See White Fish & Tomato, page 150*

Strawberry

The most popular berry in the world, and one of the sweetest tasting. When ripe, fresh strawberries contain a combination of fruity, caramel, spice and green notes. Some cultivars have strong pineapple flavours. Wild strawberries have flavour notes in common with wild grapes, and can have a distinct, spicy clove character. The strawberry makes harmonious matches with warm, sweet spices and with other fruits, and its natural confectionery quality comes to life in the company of sugar or dairy (famously cream, but also yogurt, fresh cheeses and buttery pastry).

Strawberry & Almond: Blend 250g ripe strawberries with 2 tbsp icing sugar and 3 tbsp each of Amaretto and water for a sauce to go with ice cream or Madeira cake. Sweet and sharp, like the descant to your favourite hymn.

Strawberry & Anise: *See Anise & Strawberry, page 184*

Strawberry & Avocado: Prue Leith acknowledges that the combination of strawberry dressing and avocado might seem bizarre but points out that mixing oil and strawberries makes a sort of vinaigrette, with the strawberries taking the place of the usual wine vinegar. Purée 250g strawberries with 100ml olive oil and 100ml sunflower oil mixed together, adding the oils in increments until the balance seems right. Season with pinches of salt, pepper and sugar to taste. This should be enough for 3 avocados, peeled, stoned, halved and neatly sliced (i.e. 6 servings). Top with toasted almond slivers.

Strawberry & Chocolate: *See Chocolate & Strawberry, page 18*

Strawberry & Cinnamon: Strawberries have a hint of candyfloss about them. Cinnamon loves sugar and fruit. Warmed together, the pair gives off a seductively seedy fug of the fairground. For an irresistible sweet snack, dig out the sandwich toaster, butter 2 slices of white bread, spread one slice (on its unbuttered side) generously with strawberry jam, and the other with more butter and a good shake of ground cinnamon. Sandwich together, with the just-butter sides facing out, and press in the toaster till the bread is crisp, golden and, essentially having been fried rather than toasted, more like a doughnut than plain old jam on toast. Do wait until the lava-hot jam has cooled a little before biting or you won't be able to tell anyone how good this is. You could also try the combination in a sorbet, milkshake or a layered sponge cake filled with strawberry jam and fresh whipped cream, topped with a shake of cinnamon sugar.

Strawberry & Coconut: The French chef Michel Bras halves and slices fresh strawberries, then sets them into a coconut cream to make an elegant terrine. Against the pure white background, the strawberry slices look as delicate as Japanese printed fans. It's a restrained take on a partnership that might otherwise scream cupcakes, iced biscuits and experiments with jelly.

Strawberry & Cucumber: At wedding breakfasts in provincial France, newlyweds were traditionally served a soup made with strawberry, borage (a cucumber-flavoured herb), thinned soured cream and sugar. Borage is often planted next to strawberries in the garden, as they are believed to have a stimulating effect on each other's growth, which is perhaps where the pertinence to weddings comes from. Like all enduring partnerships, they improve each other's flavour too. Slice some strawberries as thin as a bride's nightie and layer them with borage leaves in delicate tea sandwiches enriched with cream cheese.

Strawberry & Grape: *See Grape & Strawberry, page 253*

Strawberry & Hazelnut: The flavour of roasted hazelnuts is deep without being overpowering. It's great with strawberries, allowing the fruit's flavour to shine in a way that chocolate rarely can. It's even better when strawberry's sweetness is further emphasised by sugar – say, in a hazelnut meringue roulade filled with strawberries and whipped cream. For the hazelnut meringue, whisk 4 large egg whites to soft peaks. Continue to whisk while gradually adding 225g caster sugar. Fold in 100g toasted ground hazelnuts, then spread the mixture on to a lined 25cm x 35cm Swiss roll tin. Bake for 20 minutes at 190°C/Gas Mark 5. Remove from the oven, cool, then turn out, peeling off the paper lining if still attached to the meringue. Cover with whipped cream and chopped strawberries. While the meringue is still pliable, roll it up with care. It's not supposed to look perfect. And if you really make a hash of it, you can always go nuts and turn it into an Eton mess. Hazelnuts share strawberry's love of toffee-nosed flavours, so a swirl of caramel sauce is an excellent addition.

Strawberry & Melon: *See Melon & Strawberry, page 281*

Strawberry & Mint: Freshly torn mint, a squeeze of lemon juice and a few pinches of sugar can really amplify strawberry's sweetness. Heston Blumenthal describes mint as a classic partner for strawberry, and one that he initially considered, along with coconut, black pepper, olive oil and wine, when developing his dish of macerated strawberries with black olive and leather purée and pistachio scrambled egg.

Strawberry & Orange: *See Orange & Strawberry, page 297*
Strawberry & Peach: *See Peach & Strawberry, page 285*
Strawberry & Pineapple: *See Pineapple & Strawberry, page 268*

Strawberry & Raspberry: Like wearing black and navy blue: they *can* work together. Raspberry is the black: classic, classy, sophisticated. Works well with other classics such as chocolate and vanilla. Strawberry is the navy blue: seems straightforward, safe even, but is really quite a tricky one to match. You need to be very sure, combining raspberry and strawberry, that you wouldn't be better off just plumping for one or the other. Note that when they are combined, it's almost always for decorative purposes – on tarts, cheesecakes or pavlovas – but that as soon as the berry is blended or juiced beyond recognition they tend to go it alone, in jams, ices, drinks and jellies, which has to tell you something about the flavour combination.

Strawberry & Rhubarb: *See Rhubarb & Strawberry, page 256*

Strawberry & Soft Cheese: Strawberries have both buttery and creamy notes, which is why they go so well with cream, clotted or otherwise. There's also a distinctive cheesy note in there, which might explain the near-mystical aptness of a strawberry topping on cheesecake. So, as a variation on grapes, why not add some to your summer cheeseboard? Ideal with a young Brie or a Brillat-Savarin – a triple-cream cheese that's glorious with strawberries.

Strawberry & Tomato: *See Tomato & Strawberry, page 261*

Strawberry & Vanilla: A fine partnership. They are paired in a millefeuille, the vanilla in the form of a pastry cream, or in the tidy glazed tarts in the windows of French pâtisseries. But – hear me out on this one – isn't strawberry better with unadulterated dairy? With whipped, pale-yellow cream in an Eton mess or a pavlova, sitting pretty on a dense cheesecake, or, best of all, with clotted cream on a scone? For me, the combination of strawberry, with its strong candy flavour, and perfumed vanilla is too much – it almost tastes synthetic. On a slightly more positive note, of the three permutations available to the consumer of 'classic' Neapolitan ice cream, strawberry and vanilla is the least bad. Isn't it time for a new take on Neapolitan? It was originally made from a combination of all sorts of flavours, including pistachio, raspberry and coffee. And then it became that dull greatest-hits compilation of chocolate, vanilla and strawberry: a threesome of convenience. Pistachio in place of the chocolate would be an improvement. Rhubarb, strawberry and vanilla, a delight.

Strawberry & White Chocolate: In fancy chocolate shops, I sometimes see slabs of white chocolate spattered with clots of freeze-dried strawberry, like stucco after a shoot-out. White chocolate makes for a better combination with strawberry than milk or dark because, like strawberry, and gangland comparisons, it's a little cheesy.

Pineapple

A cocktail all on its own. When properly ripe, pineapples combine an array of juicy fruit flavours with a spicy, boozy, confectionery quality redolent of the fruit's classic partners – vanilla, rum, coconut and caramel. As they stop ripening once picked, commercially available pineapples are often seriously underripe, having failed to reach their full flavour and ideal balance of sourness and sweetness. To check the ripeness of a pineapple, smell its base – the fruitlets there are the oldest, and therefore the sweetest and most fragrant.

Pineapple & Anchovy: *Nuoc nam* is a Vietnamese dipping sauce made of fish sauce (in Southeast Asia, usually made with fermented anchovies), lime juice, chilli and sugar. A similar but even more pungent dipping sauce for beef or fried fish is made by mixing a thicker, unstrained fish sauce, *mam nem*, with pulverised pineapple, chilli, sugar, garlic and lime juice.

Pineapple & Anise: *See Anise & Pineapple, page 184*

Pineapple & Apple: According to the *Oxford English Dictionary*, the first instance of the word pineapple in English dates back to 1398, when it was used to describe the fruit of the pine tree, i.e. the pine cone. The first recorded use of 'pineapple' as the common name for the tropical fruit *Ananas comosus* is attributed to the diarist and botanist John Evelyn in 1664; it's thought the term was coined by European explorers struck by the similarity of the fruit to what we now refer to as pine cones. 'Apple' had long been used to describe not only fruits that resembled apples themselves but all manner of fruit and vegetables; the Anglo-Saxon poet, Aelfric, uses *eorbaeppla* (earth-apples) as a synonym for *cucumeres* (cucumbers). As it happens, a fresh, sweet, green-apple character is one of the fruit flavours you can detect in pineapple; correspondingly there are apple cultivars that taste profoundly of pineapple, like the Allington Pippin, the Claygate Permain and the Pitmaston Pine Apple.

Pineapple & Avocado: In 1557 a Brazilian priest wrote that pineapple was so 'immensely blessed by God' that it 'should be cut only by the holy hands of Goddess Venus'. In the same century, the Spanish historian Fernández de Oviedo wrote that pineapple was similar to peach, quince and very fine melons, and tasted 'so appetising and sweet that in this case words fail me properly to praise the object itself'. With typically English restraint, the adventurer Edward Terry, who travelled to India in 1616, described the flavour of pineapple as a 'pleasing compound made of strawberries, claret-wine, rosewater and sugar'. In the eighteenth century, the German philosopher and poet Heinrich Heine spoke of pineapple in the same breath as fresh caviar and Burgundian truffles. With reviews like that, no wonder it's such a diva. Pineapple won't allow jelly to set, curdles cream and reduces other foods to a pulp if you're not careful. It's least problematically served *à la Garbo*, i.e. alone. Jane Grigson feels much the same way about avocado, with the exception of a handful of 'magnificent partnerships' – including, incidentally, pineapple. Dice them for a salsa or slice them thinly and layer into a fried fish sandwich.

Pineapple & Bacon: *See Bacon & Pineapple, page 170*

Pineapple & Banana: The cherimoya, or custard apple, looks like a cross between a Granny Smith and an armadillo, and tastes like a cross between pineapple, banana and strawberry.

Pineapple & Blue Cheese: *See Blue Cheese & Pineapple, page 63*

Pineapple & Chilli: Buying a ripe pineapple is a bit of a lottery. Leaves that come away on tugging as an indicator of ripeness is an old wives' tale. Sniffing its bottom isn't: the juice in this part of the fruit tends to be sweeter, and when ripe its perfume will penetrate the armoured peel. If it smells as if it's been in the pub all afternoon, avoid it. I've found that medium-sized fruits tend to be sweeter and more flavourful than the larger varieties; and you're generally safer, in the UK at least, buying them in winter and spring. If you do end up with a sour pineapple, try dipping pieces in chilli and salt, as they do with green mangoes in Southeast Asia and Mexico. Sweet pineapple is good mixed with fresh red chillies too, especially in a salsa to accompany fish, or chopped up very finely and served with a mango sorbet.

Pineapple & Chocolate: The Québécois chef and Japanese-food enthusiast David Biron serves a chocolate club sandwich with 'fries' made of pineapple. Strawberry and basil take the place of tomato and lettuce.

Pineapple & Cinnamon: Pineapple, like strawberry, combines with sugar and cinnamon to create a flavour not unlike a natural version of candyfloss. A similarly lovely caramelised effect can be achieved in a cinnamon and pineapple tarte Tatin.

Pineapple & Coconut: *See Coconut & Pineapple, page 288*

Pineapple & Coriander Leaf: Author Leanne Kitchen notes pineapple's affinity for Asian dishes and ingredients such as curries and coriander leaf. Pineapple and coriander leaf are a common pairing in Mexico, where they're both grown. See Pineapple & Pork on page 267, or try this striking black bean soup when you have some gammon stock. Soak 250g black beans in water overnight, drain and rinse, then bring them to the boil in a litre of ham stock. Cover and simmer for 45 minutes–1 hour, by which time the beans should be soft. Remove about a quarter of the contents, blend and add back to the soup to thicken it. Before serving, stir in some coriander leaves and shredded fresh pineapple (cut a peeled, cored pineapple lengthways into 8 spears and then chop along the grain for short shreds). You can add some shredded ham if you fancy that, and if you don't have good ham stock, you can always try softening an onion and some smoked bacon in the soup pot before adding the beans and a litre of water.

Pineapple & Grape: *See Grape & Pineapple, page 253*

Pineapple & Grapefruit: Take a sip of pineapple and grapefruit and like as not you'll be transported to a hammock in the tropics. Or at least Uxbridge, where Lilt is bottled by the Coca-Cola Company. But the moon? In 1969 the crew of Apollo 11 washed down their first lunar meal – bacon squares, peaches, sugar-cookie cubes – with a pineapple and grapefruit drink. Not Lilt, which wasn't launched until six years later and wouldn't have been appropriate anyway. Drinks taken on space missions had to be ones you could rehydrate, and, since carbon dioxide bubbles lack buoyancy in weightless conditions, even if an astronaut did manage to slurp down the frothy mass they wouldn't be able to burp, leaving them with a gassy back-up they'd have to wait till re-entry to relieve. Zero gravity is also believed to have an adverse effect on flavour perception, as the particles by which we detect aroma are less likely to make it to our olfactory bulbs. Chances are the big flavours of pineapple and grapefruit were very welcome. For more about the particular potency of grapefruit flavour, see Grapefruit & Shellfish, page 299.

Pineapple & Hard Cheese: *See Hard Cheese & Pineapple, page 68*
Pineapple & Mango: *See Mango & Pineapple, page 291*
Pineapple & Orange: *See Orange & Pineapple, page 296*

Pineapple & Pork: Worth travelling to Mexico just for *tacos al pastor*, a street snack containing spiced pork topped with fresh pineapple and spit-roasted. As it cooks, the pineapple juice flows over the meat, simultaneously creating a dark-brown, caramelised crust and tenderising the meat by means of a protease enzyme called bromelain, which breaks down its collagen. The pork is served sliced in warm corn tacos, garnished with sweet onion, pineapple, lime juice and lots of coriander.

Pineapple & Prosciutto: *See Prosciutto & Pineapple, page 173*
Pineapple & Raspberry: *See Raspberry & Pineapple, page 339*

Pineapple & Sage: Pineapple sage (*Salvia elegans*) is used to flavour drinks or fruit salads. Dolf de Rovira Sr writes that it tastes like pineapple or piña colada. Imagine dancing to Wham's 'Club Tropicana' in white stilettos with a bunch of pineapple sage in one hand. George would have loved it; Andrew would have thought you were weird.

Pineapple & Shellfish: *See Shellfish & Pineapple, page 143*

Pineapple & Strawberry: On the basis of its acidity, strawberry is one of the fruits that Richard Olney singles out as particularly good with pineapple, along with raspberries and orange juice. There can be an overlap between the flavours, and some believe the best strawberries have a hint of pineapple about them. If you want to grow your own pineappley strawberries, look out for Cleveland and Burr's New Pine, described in Edward James Hooper's *Western Fruit Book* (1857).

Pineapple & Vanilla: The pineapple growers Dole published the recipe for pineapple upside-down cake as part of a marketing campaign in the 1920s. It was an instant success, and rightly so – the pairing of toffeeish, slightly caramelised pineapple on creamy vanilla sponge is delicious. Other upside-down cakes have come in its wake (cranberry and peach, maple and pear, orange and cardamom), none matching the magical fragrance of the original.

Pineapple & White Chocolate: *See White Chocolate & Pineapple, page 352*

Apple

Inseparable from the refreshing, fruity, green flavour of apples is their crucial balance of sour and sweet. Imagine a continuum running from sweeter varieties such as Fuji and Gala, through middling Golden Delicious, tart Braeburn, Pink Lady and Granny Smith to the Bramley cooking apple at the sour extreme. The cultivar also dictates the presence of idiosyncratic flavour characteristics, such as floral (rose) or fruit notes like damson, pear, pineapple, strawberry and rhubarb. Apples might contain spicy notes too, such as nutmeg and anise, dairy notes like butter, cream and cheese, nutty notes – especially near the core, as the pips have an almond flavour – or hints of honey, wine and bubblegum. Apples are the most cultivated fruit in temperate climates, not only on account of their superb flavour but because they are so versatile. Apart, of course, from their consumption raw, they're excellent cooked in cakes, pies and puddings or made into jelly, piquant sauces, juice, cider and brandy.

Apple & Almond: Butterfly an almond croissant, spread thickly with cream cheese on one side and apple purée on the other, and close its wings. More delicious than strudel.

Apple & Anise: *See Anise & Apple, page 181*
Apple & Bacon: *See Bacon & Apple, page 167*

Apple & Beetroot: I adore beetroot for its warm earthiness, which reminds me of the smell of garden centres. If, however, this is not your bag, a sharp apple will temper its richness. Try one part diced Braeburn to two parts diced cooked beetroot. Oh, and keep the apple skin on for the texture contrast. In time, the beetroot stains the mix a uniform red, which is pleasingly confusing to the brain when, expecting the soft resistance of beetroot, you crunch into a sweet morsel of apple. Both flavours work well with horseradish, so maybe mix a little into some mayonnaise for a dressing. Or walnut – another great match. Apple and beetroot with a walnut oil-based dressing. Delicious with grilled oily fish.

Apple & Black Pudding: I first ate this simple combination in a brasserie called Aux Charpentiers in the St Germain district of Paris. Once through the heavy door, you have to part a thick, faded velvet curtain to enter the dining room. This made me feel like Edmund stepping through the wardrobe into Narnia, except instead of arriving in a magical land of snow and ice and being seduced by Turkish Delight, I arrived in a 1930s Parisian working men's café and was seduced by black pudding. Make this on a chilly autumn night when you yearn for something satisfying but snappy. Choose an eating apple that holds its shape, preferably a tangy one to offset the rich spiciness of black pudding. Peel and core the apple and cut into 8 wedges. Cook in a tablespoon each of butter and groundnut oil until softened and lightly browned. Heat the black pudding in the same pan when the apples are nearly done: it's already cooked, so it takes only a few minutes to heat through. Serve with nothing but a glass of cold, peachy Viognier.

Apple & Blackberry: Like Simon and Garfunkel: perfectly respectable solo careers, can sell out Central Park together. Simon is the apple, by the way, the dominant partner. Blackberry does the high notes. Blackberries have a spicy character, although not a specific spice. Pick a bagful of blackberries from a hedgerow. Mix these in a pan with 4 peeled, cored and chopped cooking apples and about 4 tbsp sugar. Cook on a low heat for about 20 minutes, until the apples are soft and the blackberries have stained the mixture a shiny crimson. Check for sweetness and add more sugar if necessary. We used to call this stewed fruit, but supermarkets now insist on calling it compote, which is more elegant on the ear but misses the sweet rustic rowdiness. Just a little cream will sweeten it further.

Apple & Blueberry: No doubt who does all the work in this partnership. A little apple will give a fruity boost to the diffident blueberry. Try them in a tart or crumble – the one that you make with the blueberries you bought to eat instead of chocolate-covered peanuts but which now sit in your fridge as baggy as your good intentions.

Apple & Butternut Squash: *See Butternut Squash & Apple, page 230*

Apple & Cabbage: You might pair pineapple or orange with spicy raw cabbage in a coleslaw but apples are the only fruit that go with sulphurous slow-cooked cabbage. That said, braised red cabbage with apple and onion (and the optional addition of bacon and/or chestnuts) is one of the best side dishes for pork you could think of. Just make sure to add something acidic to the braising liquid, such as lemon juice or red wine vinegar, to prevent the cabbage turning blue.

Apple & Carrot: *See Carrot & Apple, page 227*
Apple & Celery: *See Celery & Apple, page 95*

Apple & Cinnamon: A classic. The spice graces the sharpness of apple with a sweet, slightly woody warmth. Like the sitar on a Stones track. Similarly, shouldn't be overdone.

Apple & Clove: In Robert Carrier's opinion, no apple pie is complete without a hint of clove. In Elizabeth David's, no apple pie is edible *with* one. Not wishing to sit on the fence, but it might simply come down to the apples and the time of year. An apple that packs plenty of character and acidity, like many cooking varieties, will make a lovely contrast to soft, buttery pastry, crumble or sponge, with no need to call for any back-up on the flavour front. Some dessert apples also make the grade; Simon Hopkinson recommends Golden Delicious for apple tarts. Most dessert apples, however, don't have enough acidity for that gorgeous fresh fruitiness to survive the cooking process, and are better eaten raw. Nonetheless, if needs must, the flavour of cooked dessert apples can be improved by a squeeze of lemon juice and a sweet spice such as clove or cinnamon. If you grow your own apples, or keep fresh apples bought from a farmer's market in a cold store, you'll notice that over time both cooking and dessert apples become less acid and more sweet: even a puckersome Bramley can develop into an eater, albeit a sharp one, by March.

Apple & Coriander Seed: *See Coriander Seed & Apple, page 345*

Apple & Hard Cheese: Glorious. A friend once told me rather sniffily that the ploughman's lunch was a marketing confection. But I'm hardly going to turn my back on a centuries-old combination of cheese, apple and bread simply because somebody gave it a slightly naff name. A wedge of tangy mature Cheddar or Stilton, like a road sign warning of a steep hill ahead, with a whole apple, half a loaf of crumbly brown bread and some home-pickled onions and chutney. The sharpness of the apple cuts through the salty creaminess of the cheese, making it just the thing with good beer or cider. You could also try a sharp hard cheese with apple pie, as is the custom in Yorkshire and parts of America. Some take the cheese on the side, others bake it under the pastry crust. In Wisconsin a law was once passed banning the consumption of apple pie without cheese; Eugene Field (1850–95) wrote a poem to the pairing, and in *Taxi Driver* Travis Bickle orders apple pie with melted cheese in a coffee shop, some say in reference to a similar request made by the psychopath Ed Gein in exchange for a full confession.

Apple & Hazelnut: The combination of hazelnut and apple can make you wish for summer to be over and done with. Stuff a pork loin with them, make a hazelnut pastry for your apple pie or try my autumn cake. This has *lots* of apple in it. You might think it's not going to work, but have faith. In a large bowl, mix 100g roasted (or blanched), skinned and ground hazelnuts, 125g plain flour, 100g very soft butter, 100g sugar, 2 tsp baking powder, 1 egg, 1 tbsp hazelnut oil and 1 tsp cocoa powder. Peel, core and quarter 3 medium cooking apples, then halve each quarter and cut each piece into 4. Fold them into the mixture and transfer to a greased and lined 20cm springform cake tin. Bake at 180°C/Gas Mark 4 for about 45 minutes. You can serve this as a rustic dessert on its own, with caramel sauce or with ice cream. The hazelnut flavour will be more pronounced once the cake has cooled. Bear in mind that with so much apple it's very moist, and so is best eaten within two days.

Apple & Horseradish: Grate a tart green apple and mix it with 1½ tbsp grated fresh horseradish. Add 3 tbsp soured cream, a pinch each of salt and cayenne and ¼ tsp each of lemon juice and brandy. Serve with cold meats, especially beef and duck.

Apple & Liver: *See Liver & Apple, page 41*
Apple & Mango: *See Mango & Apple, page 289*
Apple & Nutmeg: *See Nutmeg & Apple, page 221*

Apple & Orange: Incomparable maybe, but not incompatible. Nigel Slater suggests cooking a couple of peeled dessert apples, segmented into eight, in 50g butter for 6–7 minutes. Transfer to a warm dessert dish. Add 2 tbsp brown sugar to the pan and stir for 2–3 minutes while the appley butter caramelises. Pour in the zest and juice of one big orange followed by 150ml double cream. As soon as the mixture begins to bubble and thicken, pour it over the apple and divide between two plates.

Apple & Peanut: *See Peanut & Apple, page 22*

Apple & Pear: Sara Paston-Williams makes the point that this combination must be very old, as pear and apple were the first two fruits grown in Britain. She gives a recipe for pears in nightshirts, in which whole pears are poached in cider, set on a bed of spiced apple purée, covered in meringue and baked until crisp and golden. You could replace the apple with a purée of quince, which, like apple and pear, is a pome fruit. Quince is famous for its heavy, sensual perfume, which at autumn farmers' markets hangs as thickly in the air as Dior's Poison on the platforms of London Underground stations circa

1987. Quince's aroma is a combination of apple, pear, rose and honey, with a musky, tropical depth. Jane Grigson believed that it couldn't be beaten as a flavouring for apple or pear tarts. Grate or finely chop a quince and mix it into a pie or tarte Tatin. Be sure to include the skin, where most of the flavour compounds are concentrated.

Apple & Pineapple: *See Pineapple & Apple, page 265*

Apple & Pork: Apple-fed pork was only one of many of the benefits that came from giving your pigs the run of the orchard. They also fertilised the ground and, in scoffing themselves to a healthy weight, cleared it of pest-attracting fallen fruit. The Old Spot pig from Gloucestershire is, in fact, also known as the orchard pig, and legend has it that its black spots are bruises caused by apples. On the plate, these two are made for each other. With a plate of proper roast pork, by which I mean one with a curly roof of crackling, your apple pulls back the curtains and throws open the window of your palate. Make more apple sauce than you need. Lots more. Nobody ever had too much of it – it's so versatile. Put a kilo of peeled, cored, chopped Bramleys, 75g sugar and 1–2 tbsp water in a saucepan. Bring to the boil over a medium heat, cover and cook for about 5 minutes, keeping an eye on it and stirring now and then, until you have the texture you like. Taste for sweetness and adjust. See Apple & Almond, page 268, and Nutmeg & Apple, page 221.

Apple & Rose: *See Rose & Apple, page 342*
Apple & Sage: *See Sage & Apple, page 321*

Apple & Shellfish: Grate a cold, sharp apple into soft, sweet crab mayonnaise to freshen it up.

Apple & Soft Cheese: *See Soft Cheese & Apple, page 70*
Apple & Vanilla: *See Vanilla & Apple, page 347*

Apple & Walnut: These two have lots of robust, autumn flavour matches in common. Mix them with beetroot, orange and watercress and the result is like New England in October.

Apple & Washed-rind Cheese: *See Washed-rind Cheese & Apple, page 59*

Pear

Pear is less acidic than its relative, the apple, and less hardy, but it isn't as dainty as you might think. The characteristic flavour of pear survives the canning process and, even more impressively, distillation into eau de vie. The Williams pear is the variety most commonly used in canning and eau de vie, as well as in many pear-flavoured products. The Doyenne du Comice is a highly regarded pear for eating raw. Unveiled in 1849, it has been treasured for its quality ever since. It's a butter pear, as are Bosc and Anjou, similarly prized for their rich, aromatic flavour and (as the name suggests) buttery texture. The sweet, vinous character of pear makes it a great partner for sharp cheeses or ingredients with a tannic edge, such as walnuts and red wine. The juicy crispness of the Nashi (or Asian) pear suits similar flavour combinations but has a more pear/melon character.

Pear & Almond: A natural couple: classy and restrained. Save them from an excess of tastefulness by making an unctuous pear and almond croissant pudding. Like bread and butter pudding in an Armani suit, and great if you have three almond croissants to use up – which is unlikely, admittedly, so buy three more than you need. Cut them into 2cm strips, arrange in a buttered shallow 1 litre dish with a couple of pears, peeled, cored and sliced. Scald 500ml each of milk and double cream together in a pan. Whisk 1 egg, 4 egg whites and 1 tsp almond extract with 3 tbsp sugar, and add the milk mixture to the eggs. Pour over the pears and leave to stand for 10 minutes, before baking in the oven at 180°C/Gas Mark 4 for 45 minutes.

Pear & Anise: Asian, or Nashi, pears taste like pear but have an apple's crisp bite. This makes them particularly enjoyable raw in salads – finely sliced fennel bulb is a perfect, subtly perfumed partner. Or play up their Asian origins by peeling, coring and poaching them whole in a syrup flavoured with star anise. Excellent with plum ice cream, but vanilla will do. See also Beef & Pear, page 47.

Pear & Apple: *See Apple & Pear, page 271*

Pear & Banana: Banana-flavour sweets and pear drops share a fruit ester called isoamyl acetate, which is also released by a honeybee's sting apparatus, acting as an attack pheromone to alert other bees to the presence of something, or somebody, it would be a good idea to sting a lot. The moral of which is, choose your confectionery wisely when strolling past beehives.

Pear & Beef: *See Beef & Pear, page 47*
Pear & Blue Cheese: *See Blue Cheese & Pear, page 63*

Pear & Cardamom: Can combine in an upside-down cake or a tarte Tatin, but they're particularly good when the pear flavour retains some of its crisp fruitiness as a contrast to the lovely floral character of cardamom, say in a sorbet. Just make a cardamom-flavoured sugar syrup to add to your puréed pear. A little poire eau de vie will pep it up.

Pear & Chestnut: *See Chestnut & Pear, page 233*
Pear & Chicken: *See Chicken & Pear, page 30*
Pear & Chocolate: *See Chocolate & Pear, page 17*

Pear & Cinnamon: Cook pears in an unflavoured sugar syrup and it becomes clear why they are normally poached in cinnamon and wine. Without strong flavours to bolster them, cooked pears can all too easily taste like overboiled turnips. For the same reason, cinnamon is a welcome addition to hearty hot pear puddings such as tarte Tatin, upside-down cake and clafoutis. Stuck for more traditional apricots, dates or prunes, I once used dried pear in the Moroccan cinnamon-sugared sweet couscous known as seffa. Toast a handful of flaked almonds until golden, and set aside. Snip 4 dried pears into pea-sized pieces. Empty 200g couscous into a bowl and mix in 4 tbsp brown sugar. Pour over 250ml boiling water, add 25g butter, cover and leave for 5 minutes. Rake the couscous with a fork to separate the grains. Add most of the pear and almonds, sprinkle over 2 tsp orange-flower water and ½ tsp ground cinnamon and stir well to combine. Serve piled into small bowls with a little pear and almond on the summits. In Morocco, seffa is often accompanied by a glass of milk or buttermilk. A small, chilled maple-syrup lassi in Moroccan tea glasses works well for me.

Pear & Goat's Cheese: *See Goat's Cheese & Pear, page 57*

Pear & Hard Cheese: Peter Graham quotes an old French proverb: *Oncque Dieu ne fist tel mariage / Comme de poires et de fromage.* 'Never did God make a marriage / Like that of pears and cheese.' The Italians are more aggressive: *Al contadino non far sapere quant'è buono il cacio con le pere.* 'Don't tell the peasant how good cheese is with pears.' I tried this once, striding through an Apennine valley with my nose in the air. 'Come here, my good man,' I said. 'Do you know how well a Williams pear goes with fontina?' Whereupon he chased me off his land with a stick. The principle applies wherever you are. Try a nutty Bosc pear with mature Cheddar, or a Comice with Brie. You can't go wrong, really.

Pear & Hazelnut: *See Hazelnut & Pear, page 240*

Pear & Pork: Apples are such a popular pairing with pork that it's hard for pears to get a look in. Nonetheless they marry nicely with the sweet notes in the meat. One reason apples work so well is that their acidity cuts through pork's fattiness, so pears will be better roasted with leaner cuts such as fillet. Mind you, London bakers Konditor & Cook make a pie topped with puréed pear and slices of fatty chorizo and it's magnificent.

Pear & Prosciutto: I've seen them combined on a pizza, in panini and any number of ritzed-up salads, but really they want nothing more than to be left alone together. They're perfect.

Pear & Walnut: A mellow autumnal pairing, classically enlivened by piquant blue cheese in a salad. Start by nibbling one of your pears to see if they need peeling – if it's not too tough, keep the skin on for flavour and texture. Core, quarter and slice 2 pears and drop into 500ml acidulated water (i.e. water with 1 tbsp lemon juice added). Wash, drain, and, if necessary, chop your leaves: watercress, radicchio or chicory would work well. Crumble or cut 125g blue cheese. Roughly chop a generous handful of walnuts, toasting them first for a fuller flavour, or leaving them raw, which is fine. Make a dressing with 3 tbsp walnut oil, 1 tbsp olive oil, 2 tbsp sherry vinegar and some seasoning. Dress the leaves and toss with the walnuts, half the blue cheese and the drained pears. Scatter over the rest of the cheese and serve. Pear and walnut will also make a rich cake or tart.

Pear & Washed-rind Cheese: *See Washed-rind Cheese & Pear, page 60*

CREAMY FRUITY

Banana

Melon

Apricot

Peach

Coconut

Mango

Banana

Fresh banana, when it still has a streak of green on the skin, has a noticeable astringency at the heart of its bland, slightly grassy flavour. As it ripens, this develops into the familiar fresh, fruity banana flavour with a distinct note of clove. By the time the peel is mottled with brown, the fruit's flavour is reminiscent of vanilla, honey and rum, as if anticipating its conversion into banana bread or its flambéing in a pan. Banana has a great affinity for roasted flavours such as coffee, nuts and chocolate, and for heavily spiced flavours like rum.

Banana & Almond: A banana split without a sprinkling of toasted almond flakes? Like a Bee Gee in a buttoned-up shirt.

Banana & Anise: Giorgio Locatelli pairs tiramisù with a banana and liquorice ice cream. Sounds pretty good to me. Liquorice has spicy and salty notes, both of which marry well with banana. Sceptics might try chasing a banana with a liquorice toffee.

Banana & Bacon: Wind thin streaky bacon rashers around peeled bananas, secure with a cocktail stick and grill for 8–10 minutes, turning frequently. Can't you just taste this in your mind's mouth? The bacon's powerful saltiness held back by the sweetness of the banana? Not in the least bit sophisticated, but fun.

Banana & Cardamom: *See Cardamom & Banana, page 314*
Banana & Caviar: *See Caviar & Banana, page 153*

Banana & Cherry: Kirsch, the clear spirit distilled from stone-in cherries, has a strong note of bitter almonds that betrays the flavour's family relations (almonds are the seed of a stone fruit, or 'drupe', that's closely related to plums, peaches, cherries and apricots). Splashed on fruit, kirsch triangulates the sweet-sourness with a delicious bitterness. There's an old French recipe called *bananes baronnet* that sounds far more tra-la-la than it is to make. Slice a banana per serving, then squeeze over a little lemon juice, add a sprinkling of sugar, 2 tsp kirsch and finally 1 tbsp (unwhipped) double cream. Mix thoroughly and serve.

Banana & Chicken: Banana meets chicken in chicken Maryland, which usually consists of fried breaded chicken, fried banana and cornbread (or fritters), served with a creamy gravy. The last dish you'd associate with the Riviera set, and yet in *Tender is the Night* we find Nicole Diver leafing through a recipe book in search of it. And it was served in the first-class restaurant of the *Titanic* on the night it sank. Jamie Oliver suggests a baked take on the combination, in which banana-stuffed chicken breasts are wrapped with bacon and baked on fresh sweetcorn kernels and cannellini beans in white wine, double cream and butter.

Banana & Chocolate: Slash the skin of an unpeeled banana almost end to end without damaging the fruit. Make slits in the flesh about an inch apart and then push a chunk of chocolate into each. Pinch the skin back together, wrap in foil and put on the barbecue embers for 5 minutes. Open and eat the warm chocolatey, gooey banana with a spoon.

Banana & Cinnamon: The presence of the clove-flavoured compound eugenol increases in banana as it ripens. Think how spicy mottled bananas are. Consequently they're particularly harmonious with other spices – for example, cinnamon or vanilla in banana bread, that great redeemer of the ruined banana. If you have only one banana, peel it and halve it lengthways, then sprinkle with 1 tbsp flour and ¼ tsp ground cinnamon. Fry in 2 tsp each of butter and groundnut oil and serve. It looks better on the plate with a scoop of ice cream, but it's sweet and satisfying enough by itself.

Banana & Coconut: *See Coconut & Banana, page 286*

Banana & Coffee: Before Brangelina and Bennifer there was banoffee, the sickliest and most enduring supercouple of all: banana and toffee. Banoffee pie consists of a pastry or biscuit base topped with caramel, banana slices and coffee-flavoured cream – so you could say the etymology of 'offee' splits two ways. I'd choose a digestive biscuit base over pastry, as its salty, malty flavour sets off the fresh green notes in just-ripe banana better. Coffee beans contain highly volatile aldehydes and esters that lend coffee its fragrant, floral notes and hints of sweet spices such as clove. Banana also has floral and clove components, so the two flavours combine rather pleasingly. Note how the coffee and bananas aren't just lending flavour; they contribute bitter and sour tastes that strain against the pie's desire to become a sweet, cloying headache.

Banana & Egg: *See Egg & Banana, page 132*
Banana & Hard Cheese: *See Hard Cheese & Banana, page 65*
Banana & Hazelnut: *See Hazelnut & Banana, page 238*
Banana & Parsnip: *See Parsnip & Banana, page 224*

Banana & Peanut: Fried peanut butter and banana on white was Elvis Presley's favourite sandwich. Some say there was bacon in there too, but my contact at the Elvis Presley Estate Archive confirms that this was not the case. The confusion arose, they told me, from another of Elvis's sandwiches that has passed into myth. Seized with nostalgic cravings one night in Graceland, he bundled some friends into his private jet and flew a thousand miles to Denver, Colorado, there to feast on a local speciality – an entire loaf hollowed out and filled to the brim with peanut butter, grape jelly and fried bacon.

Banana & Pear: *See Pear & Banana, page 273*
Banana & Pineapple: *See Pineapple & Banana, page 266*

Banana & Vanilla: We stopped in Benson, an old mining town 25 miles north of Tombstone, Arizona. Excusing himself with an actual tug of the Stetson, my cowboy got out and came back with a can of oil that stops horses' hooves cracking, a birthday cake that looked as if it were made out of shaving foam and a bouquet from a store where the flowers were cooled like corpses in refrigerated cabinets. Sweltering in the truck, I felt like an abandoned pet. Noting how hot and tired I was, he opened the truck door and, with all the unironic courtesy of the Old West, escorted me to Dairy Queen, where he bought me a cup of banana and vanilla ice cream. Both flavours have floral, spicy notes to them, and the almost citric sourness of banana is beautifully blunted by creamy, sweet vanilla. I relished each tiny, cool spoonful, kicking my heels on the side of the dusty road as an endless freight train clanked past along the railway, and my cowboy finished his unlikely chores.

Banana & Walnut: *See Walnut & Banana, page 235*

Melon

This covers cantaloupe, Galia, Charentais and honeydew, while watermelon, a relative of melon cultivars, has its own chapter (see page 249). When allowed to ripen, all varieties of melon become sweet and share a basic melon flavour note; other than that there's some variation, notably in depth of flavour and in the presence of fruity (pear and banana), floral and sulphurous characters. Cantaloupes develop a particularly floral and persistent flavour. Galias are known for their sweetness, and have a cucumber streak, sometimes with a hint of glue. Melons are easily mixed with other fruit, but their wateriness is one reason for their limited number of classic flavour affinities.

Melon & Almond: *See Almond & Melon, page 244*

Melon & Anise: Stuck for things to do with the melon, chefs used to cut it in half, then get it half-cut on some sort of booze: port, cassis and champagne were popular. At Petersham Nurseries, Skye Gyngell serves slices of Charentais melon with crushed toasted fennel seeds and a splash of sambuca.

Melon & Cucumber: From the same family. Melons, especially the Galia variety, share cucumber's green, grassy flavour notes. Harold McGee writes that Galias also contain sulphur compounds that give them a deeper, savoury dimension. Combine them in a salsa, a chilled soup or a mint-dressed salad.

Melon & Ginger: A marriage of convenience. Ginger was traditionally paired with melon because its warmth and stomach-soothing properties were thought to counter melon's chilliness and resistance to easy digestion. With a tasting panel, I tried ground, preserved, fresh, crystallised and liqueur ginger with five different varieties of melon, and all combinations proved considerably worse than melon with no ginger at all. Even honeydew tasted worse with ginger, which is saying something, as this melon variety has always reminded me of those brands of attractively packaged European chewing gum that lose their flavour within one grind of the teeth. The marriage is therefore annulled. In this household at least.

Melon & Grape: Melon will fare just fine in a mixed fruit salad but it enjoys a particularly happy relationship with the grape. Simply served as a twosome, grape's rather plain, crisp flavour contrasts well with melon's peculiar and slightly tropical alkaline fruitiness. The textural contrast – melon's soft granularity against the jelly pop of grape – only adds to the pleasure. Melon notes, by the way, often turn up in Chardonnay wines, including *blanc de blancs* champagne, made from 100 per cent Chardonnay grapes. If you're planning on juicing a melon to make a cocktail, make sure you taste it before adding it to the fizz: it can sometimes become a little too cucumbery when liquidised.

Melon & Mint: Forget ginger. Mint is melon's real best friend. In Syria they combine the two in a drink with milk, yogurt and a little sugar. Or you could try them in a soup, using a few different types of melon. Cut them into neat pieces (or balls) and float them in the slightly sweetened, liquidised juice of the remaining flesh, scattered with torn mint leaves.

Melon & Orange: The Melon de Cavaillon consortium suggests flambéing its Charentais melons in orange liqueur and serving them on a nest of dark chocolate tagliatelle. You might alternatively serve them with a simple drizzle of Cointreau, but then again the tutti-frutti, honeysuckle flavour of Cavaillon melons is so heavenly you may prefer to eat them as they are. So prized have they been throughout the ages that, when asked by the Mayor of Cavaillon if he would donate some of his books to the town library, Alexandre Dumas pledged his entire oeuvre in return for an annuity of 12 Cavaillon melons. To experience them at their very best, you really have to go to Provence in midsummer – although if you (or a friend) do make the trip, bear in mind that a bottle of the Cavaillon melon syrup made by the Domaine Eyguebelle will give a year-round glimpse of the deep beauty of this flavour.

Melon & Prosciutto: *See Prosciutto & Melon, page 172*

Melon & Rose: For a fruity take on the classic Indian dessert, *gulab jamun*: find the muskiest, most floral cantaloupe melon you can, cut it in half and deseed it. With a melon baller, scoop out as many spheres as possible, then drape them in a chilled, rose-flavoured syrup. Let the flavours infuse before serving. See also Rose & Cardamom, page 342.

Melon & Strawberry: According to one of my trusted reference books, melon fritters with strawberry sauce is a popular combination in France. When I tried making fritters with a Charentais melon, my kitchen smelled of the most exquisite jam doughnuts imaginable, but they disappointed in the eating. The melon flavour survived the hot oil treatment, just about, but the texture was quite unpleasant. Better, perhaps, to stick to simple, unheated pairings, like cantaloupe with wild strawberries, as suggested by Elizabeth David. Anna del Conte, by contrast, is adamant that melon and strawberry are not a match, but notes how good they are individually sprinkled with caster sugar and balsamic vinegar. Some say kiwi fruit combine the flavours of melon and strawberry: see if you can detect them yourself.

Melon & Watermelon: *See Watermelon & Melon, page 250*

Apricot

Apricots are sour-sweet, with a creamy, floral character and a mixture of fresh and tropical fruit notes. Dried, they lose some of their perfume and take on a sweeter, cheesier character. When dried with sulphur dioxide, they are particularly tangy; without it, they tend to the toffee-fruity. Apricots have a great affinity for dairy flavours as well as other fruity florals.

Apricot & Almond: *See Almond & Apricot, page 241*
Apricot & Cardamom: *See Cardamom & Apricot, page 313*

Apricot & Chocolate: Even when sweetened, the sharpness of apricots persists in bringing a fruity tang to bitter dark chocolate. That they work together is undisputed. How they should be paired is more contentious. Take the notorious chocolate- and apricot-flavoured Sachertorte. The Hotel Sacher and the Demel bakery in Vienna had a full-scale bunfight over who owned the original recipe. The main point of contention appears to have been the correct deployment of apricot jam. The bakery spreads it only under the chocolate icing that tops the chocolate sponge gâteau. The hotel, which won the right to name its cake the original Sachertorte, also uses apricot jam to sandwich the layers together.

Apricot & Cinnamon: *See Cinnamon & Apricot, page 216*
Apricot & Cumin: *See Cumin & Apricot, page 83*

Apricot & Ginger: Sweet apricot and hot ginger pair successfully in spicy chutneys, sauces for pork or a stuffing for duck. It's also worth considering their sweet applications, say in a soufflé, cake or biscuit. Parisian tea salon Ladurée offers apricot and ginger macaroons, as well as strawberry and poppy, orange and saffron, and jasmine and mango. But macaroons remind me of Brad Pitt. They're undeniably good-looking and have an appealing rough edge, yet I can't muster up any desire for them.

Apricot & Goat's Cheese: *See Goat's Cheese & Apricot, page 55*

Apricot & Hard Cheese: Tomás Graves tells how Mahón, an unpasteurised cow's milk cheese imported to Majorca from Menorca, was traditionally eaten with fruit, the different fruits that came into season as the cheese ripened making ideal complements to each stage of its maturity. *Nispros* or 'loquats' (an orange-coloured fruit comparable in flavour to apple) came first, followed by apricots, grapes and figs. Younger, milder cheeses suited the acidity of earlier fruit, while the heavier sugar content of fruits consumed later in the year, like dried apricots, prunes and raisins, paired better with more mature, fuller-flavoured cheese.

Apricot & Lamb: *See Lamb & Apricot, page 50*
Apricot & Mango: *See Mango & Apricot, page 289*
Apricot & Mushroom: *See Mushroom & Apricot, page 75*

Apricot & Orange: Omelette Rothschild has been on the menu at London's Le Gavroche for 35 years. It's an apricot and Cointreau soufflé, essentially: sweet, velvety and not half as rich as its name suggests.

Apricot & Peach: Get along just fine, but arguably too alike to make an arresting combination. Both are creamy, floral and fruity, with a low note of almond. Peaches, however, are creamier and more complexly fruity, while apricot has the stronger floral, lavender notes.

Apricot & Pork: This combination got my vote on the 'sausage trail' at the yearly food festival in Ludlow, Shropshire. For a small fee, you can sample the efforts of half a dozen local butchers, marking down your score on a sheet soon spotted with mustard and grease. The town smells like scout camp, its streets filled with impromptu inspectors wearing abstracted expressions as they chew over the merits of each banger. In the end, the salty, fatty porkiness of a sausage cut through with the sharp sweetness of apricot edged it over a crumbly number made with pork from that 'It-pig', the Gloucester Old Spot, and given gentle hints of eucalyptus from the sage.

Apricot & Raspberry: *See Raspberry & Apricot, page 337*

Apricot & Rose: Elizabeth David recommends baking rather than stewing to get the most flavour out of dried apricots. Soak if necessary and then bake in a lidded dish, with just enough water to cover, for an hour at 180°C/Gas Mark 4. David says this gives them a roasted, smoky flavour. Try this with the addition of a few drops of musky rosewater, which makes for a frankly erotic combination. Eat on the banks of the Nile.

Apricot & Rosemary: *See Rosemary & Apricot, page 317*

Apricot & Vanilla: Most apricots get sweeter *and* sourer when dried, which is what makes them such lovely snacks – the *bien-pensant* alternative to Haribo Tangfastics. But the sharpness and fizz is down to the sulphur dioxide that's used to preserve the bright orange colour. It halts the natural oxidation process in the fruit, which left to its own devices would give you a far sweeter – and browner – result, as in the famous Hunza apricot. These have to be soaked and cooked but it's worth it for their intensely honeyed, toffee flavour. They're exquisite with vanilla, so serve with good homemade custard or posh ice cream. Can't get Hunzas? Not in the mood to make custard? Some say sharon fruit has a sweet apricot-vanilla flavour.

Peach

The peach's affinity for dairy products extends beyond cream to the bolder flavour of blue cheese. Peach also works well with the rich oiliness of nuts – coconut and almond are particularly harmonious. The flavour of peach is complexly fruity, combining a range of tropical and drupe fruits, including raspberry. Nectarine is not particularly different in flavour terms, but a creative flavourist can add a fuzzy character to synthesised peach to distinguish it from its smooth-skinned relative.

Peach & Almond: *See Almond & Peach, page 244*
Peach & Apricot: *See Apricot & Peach, page 282*

Peach & Blackberry: When cooked, late-summer peaches are rich enough to suit the heavier, spicier flavours of autumn, like blackberry. Combine them in a cobbler – a baked fruit pudding with a scone-like topping arranged like paving stones over the fruit. A crumble with aspirations, in other words. Peel, stone and slice 4 peaches and mix them with a couple of handfuls of black-berries in a baking dish. Sprinkle over 3 tbsp sugar and dot with a little butter. Place 200g plain flour, 4 tsp sugar, 1 tsp baking powder and 60g butter in a food processor and pulse until you have a mixture that resembles bread-crumbs. Add 60ml milk and a lightly beaten egg through the feed tube. Pulse until the mixture becomes a dough. Remove it and knead briefly. Roll it out to a thickness of 1cm, cut out as many 4–5cm discs as you can and lay them over the fruit. Bake at 200°C/Gas Mark 6 for about 30 minutes. The blackberries will bring a spiciness of their own, but including 1 tsp ground allspice (or mixed spice) in the dough will take it even deeper.

Peach & Blueberry: More American than apple pie. Pair them in a cobbler (see Peach & Blackberry, page 283) or a tart. White-fleshed peaches tend to be very sweet and less acidic than yellow-fleshed varieties. They're also often more perfumed, with delicate hints of jasmine and tea, which is a sublime match for the floral but astringent blueberry.

Peach & Blue Cheese: *See Blue Cheese & Peach, page 63*

Peach & Cherry: All that's left, other than a crusty roll, by the time the fun starts in *Le déjeuner sur l'herbe*. What exactly Manet was depicting has been variously interpreted, but my guess is that the naked woman on the left had been deep in conversation with the two men until the hungry artist interrupted to ask if there was any cheese or ham, or perhaps a little celeriac remoulade, left. This would go some way to explaining the slightly aggressive blankness of her expression – a blankness at once designed to disguise her embarrassment at having polished off the nice bits and to face down Manet for clearly having turned up late. The guy in the middle is keeping out of it. The woman in the background is looking for that bottle of rosé they put in the river to chill.

Peach & Clove: *See Clove & Peach, page 220*

Peach & Grape: Occasionally you'll come across a peach or nectarine with distinctly vinous flavours. Conversely, peach is a frequent flavour note in wines, especially Chardonnays, Rieslings, Semillons and the Italian sparkling wine Prosecco. The pair are most famously combined in the Bellini, signature cocktail at Harry's Bar in Venice. By the way, elsewhere in Venice, in a bar in Campo Santa Margherita, you might try a *spritz al bitter*, which classically combines Prosecco, mineral water and Campari. After your first couple of sips, when you're wondering if you can take any more bitterness, a dish of green olives arrives and proves that you can.

Peach & Mango: *See Mango & Peach, page 291*

Peach & Orange: A little orange will make peach flavour more vivid, as in a Fuzzy Navel, which pairs orange juice with peach schnapps.

Peach & Prosciutto: *See Prosciutto & Peach, page 173*
Peach & Raspberry: *See Raspberry & Peach, page 338*

Peach & Strawberry: Which is cream's best friend, peach or strawberry? Both contain dairy flavours that give them a natural affinity for cream. Either of them stirred into whipped cream will make a simple and delicious dessert. Peach and strawberry make a lovely layered vacherin – see Coffee & Blackcurrant, page 19, using fresh fruit in place of the ices.

Peach & Vanilla: As a society lady at the turn of the twentieth century, you were nobody until you'd had a peach-based dessert named after you. For the actress Sarah Bernhardt, Escoffier created *pêches aiglon*, peaches poached in vanilla syrup, served on vanilla ice cream and topped with crystallised violets and spun sugar. The actress and singer, Blanche d'Antigny, who was the model for Zola's *Nana*, got *coupe d'Antigny*, half a peach poached in vanilla syrup, on alpine strawberry ice cream, topped with rich unpasteurised cream. Princess Alexandra, wife of Edward VII, was immortalised in peeled peaches with kirsch and maraschino cherries – not unlike the Empress Eugénie, whose eponymous dessert was further garnished with wild strawberries and served with a champagne sabayon. Quite who inspired the *coupe Vénus* – a *Carry-On* confection of peach halves suggestively topped with cherries – history fails to record. See also Raspberry & Peach, page 338.

Coconut

Like other nuts, coconut has a mild, milky, fruity flavour when fresh but becomes more boldly flavoured when toasted or baked, taking on a creamy, nutty sweetness. In common with sweet almond, it has a flavour notably compatible with others, both sweet and savoury. Coconut milk is simply made with grated coconut flesh and water, yet the canned brands can be surprisingly variable, especially in sugar content. The Thai brand Chaokoh has a good reputation for flavour, a low sugar content, and is particularly suitable for savoury dishes. Coconut cream, separate from the milk, is also widely available, as are coconut milk powder, desiccated or flaked coconut (both sweetened and unsweetened), coconut flour, extract, essence and water, and the coconut-flavoured rum, Malibu.

Coconut & Almond: *See Almond & Coconut, page 243*

Coconut & Anchovy: In Southeast Asian cooking, adding fish sauce to coconut milk is like giving your stew or curry a central nervous system. The two are also paired in one of Malaysia's favourite dishes, *nasi lemak* – creamy coconut rice served with *ikan bilis* (small dried anchovies), cucumber, peanuts, boiled egg and a spicy sauce. Like its paler-flavoured cousin, kedgeree, it's most often eaten at breakfast time.

Coconut & Anise: *See Anise & Coconut, page 182*

Coconut & Banana: *Kluay buat chii,* bananas stewed in coconut milk, is a popular sweet treat in Thailand. The name means 'bananas ordaining as nuns' – Thai nuns wear white robes and have their heads and eyebrows shaved during ordination. Dissolve 100g sugar in 400ml coconut milk, add a pinch of salt and 4 bananas cut into bite-sized pieces, and simmer until warmed through.

Coconut & Basil: *See Basil & Coconut, page 213*
Coconut & Beef: *See Beef & Coconut, page 44*

Coconut & Beetroot: Give beetroot a much-needed holiday from its traditional northern European flavour affinities by pairing it with a hot-country ingredient like coconut. Like many root vegetables, beets can be combined with coconut milk in a soup, but an even more tantalising idea comes from chef-restaurateur Cyrus Todiwala, who stuffs samosas with diced beetroot and grated fresh coconut, seasoned with mustard seeds, curry leaf, cumin and chilli, with a little potato to bind.

Coconut & Cardamom: Not to be trusted. In Indian rice puddings and *barfi*, a fudge-like sweet, the complex flavour of cardamom, with its hints of citrus and eucalyptus, throws a veil of sophistication over the childish sweetness of coconut. You come round, uncrossing your eyes, realising quite how much fat, sugar and white carbohydrate this delicious combination has hoodwinked you into ingesting.

Coconut & Carrot: *See Carrot & Coconut, page 228*

Coconut & Cherry: Back in the 1980s, a chocolate bar called Cabana came and went. Coconut studded with glacé cherries, topped with caramel and covered in milk chocolate. So sweet it made your teeth throb in unison, as if you'd strayed too close to the speakers at a disco. Coconut, like cherry and almond, is a drupe (or stone) fruit, and amongst its dominant creamy, nutty notes you can detect some fruitiness. Cherry, also fruity and nutty, is a particularly good match, and both work very well with chocolate. Judge for yourself with my cover version. I make them in a silicone mould divided into the ideal bar shapes, 8cm x 3cm x 2cm. Thoroughly beat an egg with 50g sugar, then stir in 125g desiccated coconut and about 15 quartered glacé cherries. Press this mixture into 10 bar shapes and bake for 15 minutes at 180°C/Gas Mark 4. Leave to cool while you make a toffee by melting 30g sugar, 30g butter and 2 tsp golden syrup in 100ml condensed milk over a low heat. Turn up the heat, bring to the boil and cook for 4–5 minutes, by which time the mixture will have turned a caramel colour. Allow to cool for a minute, then spread it over the coconut bars while they're still in their moulds. Once cool, cover with chocolate – milk if you want to be authentic.

Coconut & Chicken: When the Canadian composer Colin McPhee went to Bali in the 1940s to write about the island's music, he kept records of daily life there, taking particular interest in the meals prepared by a woman called Madé, who cooked for him regularly. After barbecuing chicken over coals, she would shred it, then pound it with grated coconut to allow the nut's oils to mingle with the meat. To this she added another pounded mixture of onions, ginger, red pepper, spice and fish paste cooked in coconut oil, before pouring over thick coconut milk and then lime juice. Madé insisted that the meal, served with rice, should be eaten with the hands, because they contributed to the flavour of the food. Cutlery, with its chill and metallic taint, would only get in the way.

Coconut & Chilli: *See Chilli & Coconut, page 208*
Coconut & Chocolate: *See Chocolate & Coconut, page 15*

Coconut & Cinnamon: A popular combination in Cuba, where they're combined in a rice pudding called *arroz con coco* and in *coco quemado*, which is similar to *flan*, the baked custard pudding so popular in Spain. To make *coco quemado*, put a cinnamon stick, 2 cloves, 125ml water and 150ml double cream in a saucepan and scald. Set aside for 5 minutes to infuse, then add 150ml coconut milk and 3 tbsp brown sugar. Stir over a low heat until the sugar has melted. Beat 2 eggs and 1 yolk together and gradually whisk the milk mixture into them. Strain through a fine sieve and divide it between 4 ramekins. Place them in a roasting tin of hot water and bake at 160°C/Gas Mark 3 for 45 minutes. Eat hot or cold.

Coconut & Coriander Leaf: *See Coriander Leaf & Coconut, page 194*
Coconut & Dill: *See Dill & Coconut, page 189*
Coconut & Egg: *See Egg & Coconut, page 134*

Coconut & Lemon: Coconut gets a refreshingly citric lift from lemongrass. Even if it lacks the sharp acidity of lemon, the vivid citrus-floral character of lemongrass lightens the weighty fattiness of coconut. The lemoniness comes from citral, a combination of two compounds that exists at a low level in the essential oil of lemon and dominates that of lemongrass. Lemon verbena and lemon myrtle also contain high levels of citral and are sometimes used as substitutes for lemongrass. Kaffir limes, native to Southeast Asia, have a flavour and aroma closer to lemon than ordinary limes, due to the potent citrus-herbal character of their constituent compound, citronellal. You might also detect a slight flavour of pears, and a leathery, waxy quality consonant with its famous glossy leaves. Kaffir lime zest has a similar flavour and is sometimes added to curry pastes, as is the small amount of pungent, perfumed, sour juice. Lemon balm can be used as a substitute for kaffir lime leaves, as it contains comparably high levels of citronellal. Both lemongrass and kaffir lime partner with coconut for curries, seafood broths and delicately spiced chicken. And don't overlook their sweet applications – they make great panna cotta and ice cream, or you can infuse coconut milk with lemongrass and use it for the recipe in Mango & Coconut, page 290.

Coconut & Lime: *See Lime & Coconut, page 301*
Coconut & Mango: *See Mango & Coconut, page 290*
Coconut & Peanut: *See Peanut & Coconut, page 24*

Coconut & Pineapple: Don't knock the piña colada. Naff it may be, but it's based on a real flavour affinity. Split a ripe pineapple in half, put your nose to the flesh and inhale, and you'll detect strong rum and coconut notes. Piña coladas are particularly delicious made with pineapple juice, white rum, ice and the fresh water and jelly of a green (immature) coconut. The jelly nut's viscosity and coconut-custard-like flavour make the more commonly used coconut cream or milk redundant.

Coconut & Pork: *See Pork & Coconut, page 34*

Coconut & Raspberry: The madeleine of my childhood was a sponge cake in the shape of an inverted flowerpot, coated in raspberry jam, rolled in coconut and topped with a glacé cherry. Try dissolving *that* in a cup of linden-flower tea. It's an idea worth adapting for simple vanilla fairy cakes if you're fed up of sickly pompadours of frosting. Warm some seedless raspberry jam and spread it on top of the cakes with a teaspoon, stopping just short of the edges – it's quite easy to make a neat circle if your cakes aren't too risen. Sprinkle with desiccated coconut.

Coconut & Shellfish: *See Shellfish & Coconut, page 141*
Coconut & Smoked Fish: *See Smoked Fish & Coconut, page 165*
Coconut & Strawberry: *See Strawberry & Coconut, page 262*

Coconut & Vanilla: You're walking along the South West Coast Path in Devon, hair finned by the breeze, buoyed by the sense that when the air smells this good you could live on it, when a coconut cream pie crashes into your consciousness. You sniff around suspiciously. It's the gorse. However unfriendly the yellow-flowered thatch of thorns might look, it radiates deep wafts of coconut and vanilla custard. I like my coconut cream pie topped with vanilla whipped cream and toasted coconut shavings that smell like hot, sweet, butter-coated popcorn.

Coconut & White Chocolate: *See White Chocolate & Coconut, page 352*

Coconut & White Fish: White fish and coconut are combined in the famous curries of Thailand and the *laksa* dishes of Malaysia. Less well-known are *amok*, one of Cambodia's national dishes, which consists of fish cooked in fragrant coconut milk and parcelled up in banana leaf, and *molee*, a Keralan Christian speciality in which fish is rubbed with turmeric and salt, then cooked in a coconut gravy with curry leaves, garlic, chilli and onions that have first been fried in coconut oil.

Mango

Mangoes, the fruit of a tropical evergreen tree, generally taste sweet and have fruity, creamy and floral flavours, often with a hint of resin. There are, however, many cultivars and producing countries and, depending on its origins and level of ripeness, your mango might equally taste like a stringy tinned peach soused in turpentine as a sleek fruit steeped in Gewürztraminer and vanilla cream. Mangoes make a harmonious match with other fruity, spicy and creamy ingredients, but care must be taken for the flavour not to dominate. The classic partner is fruity, spicy, bold-flavoured lime: the two make a simple dessert. *Amchoor* is a mango powder prized in Indian cooking for the sourness it lends to dishes.

Mango & Apple: Crisp, sour green apples remind mango of its youth. Shredded green papaya or mango provides the spicy Thai salad *som tam* with its satisfying crunch, but if you can't get your hands on either of those, use a Granny Smith apple instead. They're a little more porous than green mango, and you'll need to get some lime juice on it sharpish to arrest the browning, but it's a good enough substitute not to deny yourself a treat that, aside from its fresh crunchiness, holds the four main elements of Thai cuisine in perfect balance: chilli heat, sweetness (from the sugar – traditionally palm), sourness (from the lime) and the saltiness brought by funky fish sauce. When I first discovered how easy *som tam* was to make, I got through a bottle of fish sauce faster than an unwatched kid gets through ketchup. Halve, blanch and cool a handful of green beans. Make the dressing in Lime & Anchovy, page 300. Crush a few tablespoons of peanuts. Core and coarsely grate a couple of Granny Smiths. Halve about 10 cherry tomatoes. Put the grated apple into a bowl and toss with lime juice to prevent browning. Add all the other ingredients, mix in the dressing and serve immediately. Ripe mango and apple, for their part, get along famously. Mango is definitely the older sibling, dominating apple if unchecked, but held in balance they make a mouthwateringly sweet-sour juice, apple's freshness enfolded by the deep, heady creaminess of mango.

Mango & Apricot: These are characteristic notes in the ice wine made at Niagara-on-the-Lake in Ontario. The manner of production is incredibly romantic (though presumably less so for the grape pickers). The grapes are left on the vine through the autumn and into deep winter, when they're harvested at sub-zero temperatures, often by moonlight. The frozen grapes are pressed and, because their sugar and flavour-imparting compounds have a lower freezing point than their inherent water, the highly concentrated juice can be separated from the water and skins. The resulting wine is both sweet and pingingly acidic, with pronounced fruit. Noble-rotted Rieslings can also fetch up mango and apricot, and have their own romance, grown in vineyards steeped in mist on the banks of the Rhine.

Mango & Avocado: *See Avocado & Mango, page 200*
Mango & Cardamom: *See Cardamom & Mango, page 315*

Mango & Chilli: In Southeast Asian and Mexican cuisine, green mango is served dipped in a mixture of equal parts caster sugar and salt pounded with red chilli. Sometimes the fruit is dipped in lime juice before the salt mix. You'll adore this if you liked mouthwateringly sharp sherbet as a child. Try the same dip with tangy apple, pineapple or guava.

Mango & Coconut: An important part of ripe-mango flavour comes from the luscious lactones that murmur of coconut at the back of your palate. Coconut sticky rice and mango is sold all over Thailand, from market stalls and shacks by the side of the road. To make it at home, soak 175g glutinous rice for at least a few hours, if not overnight. Drain it, line a steamer with muslin and steam the rice for 20–25 minutes, until it's cooked. Meanwhile, you can get on with dissolving sugar and salt into coconut milk over a low heat. Start out with roughly 2 tbsp sugar, a couple of pinches of salt and 250ml coconut milk. Put the cooked rice in a bowl, let it cool a little, then gradually feed it the coconut milk until it can't hold any more. Peel and slice a mango, taking care not to reduce it to mush, and serve it on the side of the rice, finishing the dish with a scattering of black sesame seeds, if you have them.

Mango & Coriander Leaf: Mango has a great affinity for coriander leaf, sharing pine, citrus and floral notes, and the two are frequently paired in Asian and Mexican dishes. It's striking, given how polarising their flavours can be, to reflect how popular mango and coriander have become in the last ten years. Coriander is now the best-selling herb in the UK, even if many people find its flavour 'soapy' or (conversely) 'dirty'. Chef and writer Julia Child thought it had a dead taste; others detect a nylon, doll's-hair quality. Mango can have a resinous turpentine flavour, and in fact naturally contains trace amounts of kerosene. See also Cumin & Oily Fish, page 84.

Mango & Cumin: Like mango and coriander, a combination common to India and Mexico. In India, green mango might be stirred into a cumin-scented dhal. A Mexican salsa of black beans, red onion and mango benefits from a pinch of earthy cumin. Rasoi Vineet Bhatia, an upscale Indian restaurant in Chelsea, London, sometimes includes a mango and cumin lassi with coconut and fudge ice cream on its menu, for which it just might be worth reversing the order of your meal.

Mango & Ginger: *See Ginger & Mango, page 311*

Mango & Lime: Fresh lime squeezed on ripe mango is one of the world's greatest food pairings. They're both pugnacious flavours, although lime's slightly harsh, medicinal qualities are offset by the floral notes it shares with mango. Lemon, milder than lime, with sweeter rose and fruit notes, can't take mango to the same heights.

Mango & Mint: *See Mint & Mango, page 331*

Mango & Orange: Both mango and orange have citrus and floral characters, but when mixed they're subordinated to mango's complex blend of fruity resin and evergreen flavours. It's as if the orange was never there.

Mango & Peach: Both turn up as flavour descriptors for Chardonnay, at least in Europe and North America. Jeannie Cho Lee, Korea's first Master of Wine, throws an interesting light on both the cross-cultural difficulties of communicating flavour and the possibilities for considering it differently. In Asia, the reference points for Chardonnay might include pomelo, dried mango, egg custard and *wakame* seaweed, the latter used to describe more austere, mineral-style wines.

Mango & Pineapple: Preside over a library of fruit flavours. Over the full range of cultivars, mangoes might have notes of peach, pineapple, tangerine, banana, watermelon, pear, blackcurrant, guava, apricot, green apple, cherry, fig, sweet grapefruit, red grape, ripe melon, plum, lemon zest or passion fruit. The flavour of pineapple can recall strawberry, orange, peach, apple, banana, raspberry, jackfruit and pear.

Mango & Rhubarb: *See Rhubarb & Mango, page 255*

Mango & Shellfish: A delightfully natural partnership. Mango imparts the freshening citrus notes that go so well with shellfish, but also has hints of coconut that harmonise with the nuttiness of prawns and scallops. Thread some marinated prawns on skewers and grill or barbecue them for the few minutes they take to go orangey-pink, turning once. Serve with a neat heap of shiny mango salsa. See also Avocado & Mango, page 200.

Mango & White Fish: *See White Fish & Mango, page 148*

CITRUSSY

Orange

Grapefruit

Lime

Lemon

Ginger

Cardamom

Orange

All citrus fruits lead double lives, the flavour of their juice being quite different from that of the peel. In the manufacture of juice and other orange products, once the juice has been pressed from the ripe fruit, the peel is pressed separately to extract the aromatic liquid from its oil glands. Another oil, of a different character again, is distilled as a by-product when the juice is concentrated. These oils are used in soft drinks, or blended back into orange juice to improve the flavour without recourse to synthesised additives. All freshly squeezed fruit juice deteriorates pretty rapidly, so it's always best to squeeze it on demand. Of all citrus fruits, orange is by far the most popular, especially when the term extends, as it does in this chapter, to mandarins, satsumas, blood and bitter oranges, as well as the dominant sweet orange. Its breadth of flavour characteristics ensures that orange is highly compatible with other flavours. Sweet orange has the fruitiest flavour of all citrics, containing hints of mango and pineapple among its layers of generic citrus flavours, along with mild hints of spice and herb. Mandarins share the pleasing sweet-sourness of sweet orange, although the zest has a more noticeable herbal accent. Blood oranges usually add a berry, specifically raspberry, note to the sweetness. The zest of bitter oranges, such as Sevilles, has a stronger, waxy flavour with a hint of lavender. With the addition of plenty of sugar, their extremes of bitterness and sourness are what make marmalade so full-flavoured and interesting. Bitter oranges are also used in most orange-flavoured liqueurs, including Cointreau, Grand Marnier and Curaçao, and orange-flower water is made from their blossoms. Dried orange peel, for use as a flavouring, can be bought in Chinese and Middle Eastern supermarkets.

Orange & Almond: Claudia Roden's legendary orange and almond cake is unusual in that it calls for pretty much every part of the orange save the pips: the zest, with all its oil glands, the pith, the segment membranes and the vesicles – those wondrous juice-containing structures that look like tiny eye droppers. It's this thorough exhaustion of the fruit's possibilities that gives the cake its deeply musky, spicy character, redolent of marmalade but without the sticky sweetness. The almond contributes the dense texture that makes the cake equally at home on the pudding plate as on the afternoon tea plate, especially if served with cream or a compote. In a nutshell, you boil 2 oranges in water for nearly 2 hours, until completely soft. Once cool, quarter them, discard the pips and process the oranges to a pulp. Beat 6 eggs in a large bowl, then mix in 250g ground almonds, 250g sugar, 1 tsp baking powder and the orange pulp. Pour into a greased and lined, deep, round 23cm cake tin. Bake at 190°C/Gas Mark 5 for an hour. Between you and me, the oranges can be microwaved in a few minutes if you're short of time.

Orange & Anise: *See Anise & Orange, page 184*
Orange & Apple: *See Apple & Orange, page 271*
Orange & Apricot: *See Apricot & Orange, page 282*

Orange & Asparagus: Gangly asparagus might seem an unlikely match for voluptuous orange but it works. *Sauce maltaise*, a hollandaise flavoured with blood oranges, was created especially for asparagus. Boil 100ml blood orange juice until reduced to about 2 tbsp, then add the zest of 1 orange and simmer for 1 minute. Stir into a hollandaise made with 4 egg yolks and serve immediately.

Orange & Bacon: A marmalade-glazed ham is a thing of wonder. Use a marmalade that's made with plenty of Seville oranges; if it's too sugar-heavy, you're in danger of making ham with jam, which will please no one but Dr Seuss. Seville orange marmalade has a deep, bitter tang that will counter the gammon's saltiness. Eating this is only part of the fun. Rubbing a whole jar of marmalade into a large joint of meat is a rare sensual pleasure.

Orange & Beef: A bouquet garni of pared orange zest, bay leaf, thyme and parsley is often recommended for slow-cooked beef dishes, such as Elizabeth David's beef and wine stew with black olives. In case you need *two* good reasons to try it, Fiona Beckett writes that dried orange peel used in this way enhances the richness of medium-bodied red wines.

Orange & Beetroot: At The Fat Duck, Heston Blumenthal teases diners with an orange-coloured jelly that has the flavour of beetroot and a crimson jelly with the flavour of orange. The beetroot jelly is made with golden-coloured beets and the orange one with dark red blood oranges. The waiters playfully suggest you start with the orange one.

Orange & Carrot: *See Carrot & Orange, page 229*

Orange & Chilli: Rick Bayless describes a ripe, orange habanero chilli as having an aroma of passion fruit, apricot, orange blossom and herb, with a noticeable piquancy. The flavour is similar to the aroma, with added notes of sweet, tangy tangerine. You may be able to detect these notes in the teacup of tears you will have shed trying this most fearsomely fiery of peppers. Fruit flavours are often detectable in dried chillies too, and not just habanero: prune and raisin are commonly cited. If habanero's too hot, infuse olive oil over a low heat for about half an hour with a strip of orange peel and a couple of dried chillies. Strain off the peel and chillies and drizzle the oil over fish.

Orange & Chocolate: Both orange zest and orange-flower water have been used to flavour chocolate since at least the seventeenth century. The combination of orange and chocolate has endured where other once-common flavourings, like black pepper and anise, have faded into obscurity. Surprising, then, that Terry's famous Chocolate Orange was originally an apple. Launched in 1926, the apple proved so popular that an orange version was launched four years later. When both went back into production after the war, orange quickly overtook apple in popularity and the latter was discontinued in 1954. The Chocolate Orange finally grew up in 1975 when the dark chocolate version was introduced, its bitter astringency complementing the sweet muskiness of orange oil far better than frumpy, facetious milk.

Orange & Cinnamon: *See Cinnamon & Orange, page 218*

Orange & Clove: In *The Size of Thoughts*, Nicholson Baker comments on the sensuous pleasure of writing on an eraser with a ballpoint pen. I get a comparable kick studding a firm orange with cloves. Some use these as pomanders, but I let them bob around like limpet mines in a sea of mulled wine. The fresh citrus and smoky spice can give the dullest grog a spark.

Orange & Coffee: *See Coffee & Orange, page 21*
Orange & Coriander Leaf: *See Coriander Leaf & Orange, page 196*

Orange & Coriander Seed: Look at a coriander seed close up. It could be a peeled mandarin from the kitchen table in a doll's house. Bite it and you'll find it has an orange flavour too; like marmalade or Seville orange peel with a cedar background. Serve orange segments in a syrup flavoured with coriander seed for a layered orange flavour (and an update on the classic oranges in caramel), or explore coriander's spicy orange character by pairing it with some of the fruit's classic flavour affinities, such as cinnamon, duck, lemon or cranberry.

Orange & Fig: *See Fig & Orange, page 341*
Orange & Ginger: S*ee Ginger & Orange, page 311*
Orange & Grapefruit: *See Grapefruit & Orange, page 298*

Orange & Hard Cheese: Cheese with all sorts of fruits – grapes, apples, pears, quince – is, of course, completely uncontroversial, as are citrus fruits on cheesecake, yet Cheddar with marmalade is apt to raise eyebrows. But think about a rich, salty, mature Cheddar and how delicious it might be cut through by the bittersweetness of marmalade – there's a real balance of flavour there. For a sandwich, try grating the cheese and using a fine-cut marmalade, as thick hyphens of orange might prove too dominant. Walnut bread would be excellent. Alternatively make 'jam' tarts using marmalade mixed with grated Cheddar. Fill little cheese pastry tarts and bake at 220°C/ Gas Mark 7 for about 15 minutes, taking special care not to burn them.

Orange & Juniper: *See Juniper & Orange, page 324*

Orange & Lemon: St Clement, the patron saint of designated drivers, lends his name to this mix of orange juice and bitter lemon. Bitter lemon's bitterness comes not only from lemon but from quinine, the colourless, odourless alkaloid that puts tonic water in such agreeable ill temper. The adult palate can generally take only so many sweet drinks before tiring of them. This is less of a problem with alcoholic drinks, which generally have a balancing bitterness to them. Orange and lemon zest (or the harder-core mixed peel) are also used to flavour, and balance the sweetness of, puddings and cakes. The Meyer lemon is a lemon-orange hybrid, with a pronounced floral nose and flavour. It's low in acid, so is seen as a sort of sweet lemon, as Sevilles are sour oranges – see Orange & White Fish, page 297.

Orange & Lime: *See Lime & Orange, page 302*
Orange & Mango: *See Mango & Orange, page 291*
Orange & Melon: *See Melon & Orange, page 280*
Orange & Mint: *See Mint & Orange, page 331*

Orange & Olive: *La Cucina Futurista* was published in 1932 by the poet, Marinetti, after he'd spent a few years travelling around Europe organising banquets that featured wild flavour pairings and recipes with titles like Excited Pig, Elasticake, Steel Chicken and Piquant Airport. My favourite is called Aerofood. While the sound of an aeroplane motor and something suitable by Bach plays loudly from the kitchen, the diner is served, from the right, a plate of kumquats, black olives and fennel. Rectangles of silk, sandpaper and velvet are served from the left and the diner must eat with the right hand while simultaneously stroking these with the left. Meanwhile the waiter spritzes the nape of the diner's neck with a carnation perfume. Carnations have a rose-clove fragrance – try Santa Maria Novella's Garofano. The plane might prove trickier to source.

Orange & Onion: *See Onion & Orange, page 110*
Orange & Peach: *See Peach & Orange, page 284*

Orange & Pineapple: All the *joie de vivre* of a Hawaiian shirt without the stigma of wearing one. Pineapple blinds you to orange's dark side – the bitterness, the complexity, the just-detectable whiff of sulphur. The two share tangerine, fruity, green flavours, and pineapple juice is sometimes added to orange juice to give it a more natural orange flavour.

Orange & Rhubarb: Orange zest and rhubarb are often paired, especially in crumble, but not in my kitchen. I find the neediness of super-sour rhubarb and the belligerence of orange zest pull in different directions; the flavour equivalent of patting your head and rubbing your stomach. Even when rhubarb is cooked in milder orange juice, which doesn't have the pushy bitterness of zest, my palate can detect neither harmony nor pleasing contrast.

Orange & Rose: Orange-flower water and rosewater are often treated as interchangeable in recipes. Unsurprisingly, floral notes are dominant in both, but there's a citrus lick to orange-flower water, which is extracted from the blossoms of the bitter (Seville) orange tree. Good flower waters are made in Iran, while in the Lebanon an artisan company called Mymouné uses traditional distillation methods and no artificial ingredients. The key for both is to use them by the drop, not the teaspoon, so they bring a mysterious background note to the dish, like a shimmer from a zither, not the thudding of the drum. They're traditionally used in North African cooking in lamb and chicken tagines and all sorts of almond puddings and cakes; in France to flavour madeleines; and to add a floral note to fruit juices (especially orange) and grated carrot salads. See also Cinnamon & Orange, page 218.

Orange & Rosemary: *See Rosemary & Orange, page 319*

Orange & Saffron: Citrus flavours pair well with saffron. Orange and saffron turn up in Mediterranean fish stews and North African tagines but also make a great couple in cakes and biscuits. Soak a pinch of saffron in a tablespoon of warm milk and add it to a Victoria sponge cake mixture. Sandwich together with marmalade. Very Moorish.

Orange & Strawberry: Strawberries Romanoff was created for Tsar Alexander I by the legendary chef Marie-Antoine Carême. It's a sparkling combination. Hull some strawberries, marinate them in a 50:50 mixture of orange juice and orange liqueur, then stir through some crème Chantilly – see Vanilla & Raspberry, page 349.

Orange & Thyme: *See Thyme & Orange, page 327*
Orange & Vanilla: *See Vanilla & Orange, page 349*

Orange & Walnut: Use the walnuts and clementine in the toe of your Christmas stocking to make a relish with cranberries or a salad with bitter green leaves, or mix them with thick yogurt and a whirl of maple syrup for breakfast on Boxing Day.

Orange & Watercress: Tick the sweet, sour and bitter boxes. Add something salty (olives, perhaps) for a perfect salad. Good with duck. See also Apple & Walnut, page 272.

Orange & White Fish: Until the eighteenth century, oranges were used with fish much as lemons are today. At that time most oranges were sour Sevilles, as opposed to the sweet varieties that have dominated the market more recently. For an authentic eighteenth-century experience when Sevilles are hard to come by, a mixture of two sweet oranges to one lemon is an effective substitute, even if the aromatic quality isn't quite the same. In a similar vein, Mark Hix adds a little bitter-orange-flavoured Curaçao to his sole Véronique. As for sweet oranges, Alan Davidson notes their great affinity with a firm, strong-flavoured fish called *mérou* (grouper), and gives a recipe for a sauce made with 40g each of butter and flour whisked with 280ml meat stock/bouillon, 140ml orange juice and a pinch of salt. *Sauce maltaise*, flavoured with blood orange, is often paired with firm white fish – see Orange & Asparagus, page 294.

Grapefruit

The lumbering old uncle of the citrus family. Grapefruit shares the generic citrus flavours and some of the tropical fruitiness of orange, alongside a more pronounced herbal, woody flavour, but what really sets it apart is its musky, sulphurous character. Can work well with typical citrus-family partners such as seafood, but has a particular affinity for ingredients that share its bitter streak, like blue cheese and green leaves. Ruby grapefruits tend to be sweeter than yellow ones.

Grapefruit & Avocado: This combination is a modern classic in a salad with lobster, plump prawns or fresh crab. A café in Montpellier calls this *salade fraîcheur* and serves it with a shot glass of gazpacho on the side. On a witheringly hot afternoon, it was enough to rehydrate the body and the soul. The brightness of the flavours is one thing, but there's also pleasure in feeling the soft butteriness of avocado against the grapefruit's vesicles, tautly rippled like wet sand after the tide's gone out.

Grapefruit & Blue Cheese: *See Blue Cheese & Grapefruit, page 63*
Grapefruit & Cinnamon: *See Cinnamon & Grapefruit, page 217*
Grapefruit & Juniper: *See Juniper & Grapefruit, page 324*

Grapefruit & Orange: Grapefruit is a hybrid of sweet orange and pomelo, the large, yellow-green citrus fruit that looks like a bloated pear. It is, of course, far closer in flavour and appearance to the pomelo, but shares, among other things, orange's affinity for Campari. Both make refreshing (and variably bitter) sorbets paired with Campari, but the respective effects they have on the drink are more easily understood in the highball glass. Orange juice is the way in, the stabilisers on the frightening bike ride into Campari territory, helping to suppress its weird herbal notes and bitterness so stringent that your brain, at least on the first few attempts, flicks into alert mode at the influx of toxicity. Grapefruit, on the other hand, is pretty bitter itself, with its own extraordinary, herbal-fruity notes, and mixed with Campari makes a gloriously complex drink.

Grapefruit & Pineapple: *See Pineapple & Grapefruit, page 267*
Grapefruit & Pork: *See Pork & Grapefruit, page 36*

Grapefruit & Shellfish: The main identifying flavour compounds in grapefruit are nootkatone, mercaptan and naringin, which sound like the sort of user names you'd find on a web forum debating the relative merits of *Deep Space Nine* and *Star Trek: Voyager*. Appropriately enough, perhaps, as of all the citrus family grapefruit surely has the most alien flavour. Nootkatone, the most important (i.e. 'grapefruity') compound, has a warm, woody character that is present but suppressed in other citrus fruits by their more dominant compounds. Grapefruit mercaptan, which is primarily responsible for the smell of grapefruit and lends a musky, tropical top note to the flavour, has one of the lowest aroma thresholds known to science. That is, it's so potent that it can be detected in extremely minute quantities – 0.0001 parts per billion, to be exact. Grapefruit's odd, standoffish flavour has earned it a special place in *haute cuisine*; at Les Jumeaux, the Parisian restaurant run by the Gillaizeau twins, scallops are served with a split pea purée and pink grapefruit sauce; at Chez Jean, they're sautéed with chanterelle mushrooms, Chinese noodles and slices of pink grapefruit. More recently the vogue for grapefruit has been challenged by the yuzu, a small, wrinkled fruit big in Japan. Yuzu has a lemon-lime flavour, with hints of tangerine, grapefruit and pine, and is prized primarily for its aromatic peel, although the juice is used too. A very rough substitute can be made with equal parts lime and grapefruit juice. At Jean Georges in New York, your waiter might spray your plate of scallops with a spritz of yuzu juice. Don't hit him.

Grapefruit & Watercress: Share a strong minerality and bitterness that set off full-flavoured, fatty proteins. Blue cheese would be the obvious choice – especially if it's sweet, salty Roquefort, with its own underlying mineral quality. Remove any oversized stalks before tossing the leaves with skinless grapefruit segments and crumbling over the cheese. Maybe add some walnuts, too. Duck would be excellent in place of the cheese.

Lime

The hardest, sharpest member of the citrus family. Oil made from lime peel is strong and spicy, with pine, lilac and eucalyptus notes. Much of what is produced is used for flavouring cola. Lime juice is notably acidic, which accounts for its palate-cleansing qualities, and can seem quite salty squeezed on a salsa. Its sourness and bitterness work wonders set against a correspondingly determined sweetness – caramel in cola, for instance, butternut squash, or condensed milk in a key lime pie. The cultivar most widely available in the UK is the Persian lime, of which the citron and key lime are thought to be the parents. Key limes are smaller, thicker-skinned and, unlike most Persian limes, have pips. They're said to have a distinct flavour but, having hauled a bag home from the US to make an authentic key lime pie, I couldn't detect much difference. Lime flavour is also contributed by musky dried limes (whole or ground), spicy lime pickle, lime marmalade and lime cordial. For kaffir lime, see Coconut & Lemon, page 287.

Lime & Anchovy: Meet in a Thai salad dressing of lime juice and fish sauce – or in *nuoc cham*, the Vietnamese dipping sauce served with spring or summer rolls. Everything you love about fish plus citrus, cubed. Even with a lighter fish sauce, lime will always be the underdog, trying to shine a light on fish sauce's dark thoughts and failing beautifully. Proportions really are a matter of taste, and balance with the other flavours in your recipe. I pound 2 garlic cloves with 1 chilli, then add 2 tbsp lime juice, 2 tbsp fish sauce and a pinch of sugar. Addictively delicious on a homemade *som tam* salad – see Mango & Apple, page 289. Vegetarians can buy a 'fish sauce' made with soy beans. See also Pineapple & Anchovy, page 265.

Lime & Avocado: *See Avocado & Lime, page 199*

Lime & Basil: You can grow this combination yourself by hunting down lime basil seeds – they're fairly widely available. In Thailand, where they have basil varieties coming out of their ears, lime basil is most frequently used with fish.

Lime & Beef: Lime is sour, sweet, a little bitter, used in some cultures as a salt substitute, and above all intensely flavoured, with a strong hint of tropical fruit. Beef steps up to the plate, answering lime's acidity with a metallic tang of its own. The dressing in Lime & Anchovy, above, is often served with seared beef on a salad with lots of chilli, in a dish known as 'weeping tiger'. In Vietnam, lime wedges are served with beef *pho*, and as part of a dipping sauce for 'shaking beef', marinated in garlic and soy and served in lettuce leaves.

Lime & Butternut Squash: The heavy sweetness of butternut squash welcomes some interference from sharp, spicy lime. Pair them in a chowder, roast chunks of squash in a combination of olive oil and lime juice, or try tempura pumpkin with a soy-lime-sesame dipping sauce. For a Thai take on the combination, simmer chunks of pumpkin or squash in spiced-up coconut milk. When they're cooked through, stir in a mixture of lime juice, fish sauce and palm sugar. See also Butternut Squash & Bacon, page 230.

Lime & Chicken: *See Chicken & Lime, page 29*

Lime & Chilli: Diego Rivera and Frida Kahlo. This turbulent twosome brings fervour to a vast range of Mexican dishes, including *chapulines* – grasshoppers fried in lime juice and chilli powder and eaten as a snack. For those without the inclination, or patience, to catch grasshoppers, peanuts in their skin are served the same way, as are fried plantain, corn on the cob, watermelon, barbecued prawns and Doritos. Happily for chilli-lime addicts, the seasoning can be bought pre-mixed by the canister, so you can put it on your cornflakes if you like. In India, lime and chilli are paired in lime pickle (the best thing since marmalade in a cheese sandwich – see Orange & Hard Cheese, page 295). Finally, should you find the sweetness of bottled chilli sauce a little cloying, it can be freshened up with a squeeze of lime to make a versatile dipping sauce.

Lime & Chocolate: *See Chocolate & Lime, page 16*

Lime & Cinnamon: These are cornerstones of cola flavour, in which it's fairly common for cinnamon to appear in the form of cassia, a related spice with a harsher, more strongly flavoured profile and a good match for lime's own pugnacious qualities. Vanilla is another of cola's typical ingredients, alongside caramel, nutmeg, orange, lemon, coriander, and coca-leaf extract. I combine lime and cinnamon in a sorbet. Make a simple syrup by gently heating 200g vanilla sugar and several sticks of cassia (or cinnamon) in 250ml water until the sugar has dissolved. Bring to a simmer, then cool. Keep in the fridge until the cinnamon has imparted a strong flavour to the syrup, then strain. Juice 3 limes, strain and add to 200ml of the cinnamon syrup with 2 tsp lemon juice and 125ml water. Chill until very cold, then freeze according to your usual method. Serve in a caramel basket to extend the deconstructed cola theme.

Lime & Coconut: Combined with the tropical drowsiness of coconut, lime is the niggling intimation that you should get out of the hammock and exert yourself. Lime frosting on a coconut cake needs a knife-edge intensity to set off the sleepy sweetness. A grating of fresh coconut and a squeeze of lime can make a pineapple seem sweeter and juicier – as they do with fish, cooked or raw: they're paired in a popular ceviche (see Lime & White Fish, page 303). In India, strips of fresh coconut are mixed with lime juice, crushed garlic and chillies and served with curry.

Lime & Coriander Leaf: *See Coriander Leaf & Lime, page 196*

Lime & Cumin: Quite a power struggle. Let them fight over barbecued meat, roasted corn or tomato salsa. Or add mint to make *jal jeera*, a cooling drink popular in India, in which pounded roasted cumin seeds are mixed with pounded mint, salt, lime juice and water.

Lime & Ginger: *See Ginger & Lime, page 311*
Lime & Lemon: *See Lemon & Lime, page 306*
Lime & Mango: *See Mango & Lime, page 291*

Lime & Mint: Cubans take mint and lime and add rum to make mojitos, the ubiquitous cocktail of the last decade. What's the secret of its success? My theory is that the sour lime and refreshing mint come together with the kick of rum and the sugar rush to create something that sits at the crossroads of amphetamine and aromatherapy. Put 1 tbsp caster sugar in a highball glass with 2–3 tbsp lime juice. Add a leafy sprig of mint and fill to about a third full with soda water. Muddle to dissolve the sugar and release the essential oils in the mint. Add 50ml Havana Club and a handful of ice cubes. Listen to their seismic creak. Stir, then garnish with more mint and a straw. If strong enough, the mojito will produce a pleasurably painful perceptual sharpening, like putting on glasses when you're already wearing contact lenses. Or try a lime sorbet served with a shot of rum and garnished with mint leaves.

Lime & Oily Fish: *See Oily Fish & Lime, page 158*

Lime & Orange: These two intertwine to create a taut support for tequila in the high-wire act that is the margarita, the most popular mixed drink in the US. A good margarita holds its extremes of sweetness, sourness, bitterness and salt in thrillingly tenuous balance. It should make you gasp and stretch your eyes. Some don't care for the salt, feeling that a good tequila has a salinity of its own, but I can't resist it. The salt emphasises the sweet-sourness, and has the teasing effect of keeping you thirsty while you're drinking.

Lime & Peanut: *See Peanut & Lime, page 25*
Lime & Shellfish: *See Shellfish & Lime, page 143*

Lime & Tomato: Sangrita, a popular drink in Mexico, is made with tomato, lime and orange juice with a dash of chilli. It's sipped alternately with tequila. Some ditch the orange juice, making it a liquid form of my favourite basic salsa. Chopped tomatoes with lime juice have enough complexity of flavour to count as a salsa on their own. Try half a lime squeezed over 2 diced tomatoes and see just how salty and mouth-filling it tastes. Add a few drops of chilli sauce and a little chopped onion for extra piquancy. Serve with a handful of tortilla chips.

Lime & Watermelon: *See Watermelon & Lime, page 250*

Lime & White Fish: Nothing says you're on first-name terms with your fishmonger like serving a ceviche. Strips of raw fish are cured in lime (or lemon) juice and commonly mixed with chopped onion, bell pepper, chilli and coriander. Once the fish has had a chance to 'cook' in the lime juice, coconut milk might be added for a creamier result. In Ecuador, ceviche is often served with roasted corn kernels or popcorn; in Peru, sweet potato is a more typical accompaniment. Ceviche is said to have come about when the Spanish brought the Arabic notion of cooking with fruit to South America. As a culinary version of Chinese whispers, one couldn't hope for a more surprising outcome.

Lemon

Lemon zest contains a compound called citral that is immediately recognisable as lemony. Aromatic notes of rose, lavender and pine are also present, as is a slight herbaceousness; all these are released when you grate lemon zest. The juice has a clean, fresh flavour, dominated by citric acid. It can be used in moderation to give an unidentifiable lift to a dish, or in greater quantities to lend a definite lemon flavour. Lemon is highly combinable and adaptable: in sweet or savoury dishes, as a seasoning or star ingredient, in everything from apéritifs to petits fours. Pull it to extremes in a sweet lemon tart, sour lemon confectionery, bitter-lemon soft drinks and Middle Eastern salted preserved lemons. Lemon flavour is also dominant in the Italian liqueur limoncello, in lemon curd and in the exquisite lemon-sherbet sweets that smell like lemon myrtle. For more about lemon-flavoured herbs, see Coconut & Lemon, page 287.

Lemon & Almond: *See Almond & Lemon, page 243*
Lemon & Anchovy: *See Anchovy & Lemon, page 163*
Lemon & Anise: *See Anise & Lemon, page 183*

Lemon & Asparagus: In their book *Urban Italian*, Andrew Carmellini and Gwen Hyman enthuse about this partnership, noting how in a risotto 'the lemon cuts through the richness of the dish, opens up the asparagus flavour, and keeps things fresh'. What I love about their recipe is its good housekeeping. Nothing is wasted: the woody bottom inch of the stalks is used to flavour the stock, their middle sections are cooked, puréed and stirred into the rice just as it's ready, while the tips are blanched and added whole to finish. It reminds me of *risi e bisi* – see Pea & Hard Cheese, page 203.

Lemon & Basil: As suggestive of summer as a bucket and spade. Combine their mood-lifting citrus and liquorice flavours in a simple pasta. A *relatively* simple pasta: I once witnessed four Italian men argue for an hour over the exact means of preparing this properly. To serve two, cook 200g spaghetti until *al dente*. Meanwhile, heat 2 tbsp olive oil in a small pan and soften a finely chopped shallot in it. Add 2 tbsp white wine and simmer for a few minutes before adding the juice and zest of an unwaxed lemon. Season and turn the heat down. When the pasta is ready, drain it and stir in the lemon sauce with a couple of handfuls of grated Parmesan, a small handful of torn basil leaves and 2 tsp butter.

Lemon & Beef: Big in Italy, where the lemons are legendary. They squeeze them on bresaola, the salt-cured, air-dried beef fillet served in gossamer slices like Parma ham. It's silky, gamy and sometimes has a musty flavour. Raw beef, sliced a little thicker than bresaola, is called carpaccio, and gets the same lemon treatment. In Florence, it's not unusual to serve *bistecca alla fiorentina* – hefty slabs of T-bone steak seared over wood or charcoal – with a lemon wedge, which not only lifts the beef flavour but arbitrates between it and the local Chianti. Some say lemon makes an inferior Chianti taste fruitier and less, um, rough.

Lemon & Blueberry: Poor blueberry. Its pretty, floral notes are masked by the blurt of sour juice it emits when bitten. Similarly, the acidity of lemon detracts from its floral perfume. But a problem shared is a problem halved: with the redemptive sweetness of sugar or honey, both flavours get the chance to shine, and make a heady, perfumed combination in cakes and puddings.

Lemon & Broccoli: *See Broccoli & Lemon, page 126*
Lemon & Caper: *See Caper & Lemon, page 102*
Lemon & Caviar: *See Caviar & Lemon, page 154*

Lemon & Chicken: If the world was organised the way it might be, you could plot how lemon-chickeny a dish was on the Lemicken scale. A soft Thai chicken broth delicately scented with lemongrass – a 2. At 4, chicken rubbed with lemon, then roasted with a lemon in the cavity. A roast chicken baguette with tangy lemon mayonnaise – 5. A thick, spicy, slow-cooked Moroccan tagine made with chicken thighs and preserved lemons – 9. A 10 is the battered fried chicken with vivid yellow sauce that I am too ashamed to order in Western Chinese restaurants.

Lemon & Chilli: *See Chilli & Lemon, page 209*

Lemon & Chocolate: Not an easy combination to pull off, but when it works it can be sublime. I dream of sinking a long spoon into alternate layers of aromatic, zingy lemon custard and dark chocolate ganache, striped like a bumblebee in a tall glass. Joel Robuchon's take on the pair is to serve lemon-scented madeleines with little pots of chocolate.

Lemon & Coconut: *See Coconut & Lemon, page 287*

Lemon & Coriander Leaf: This recipe spreads faster than gossip. I know because I gave it to somebody, who gave it to somebody else, who then made it for me and asked if I'd like to have the recipe. The cheek, I thought, before I remembered I got it from a supermarket recipe card. It originally called for cod, but I've yet to find a white fish that's not woken up by the combination of lemon and coriander. Combine 100g breadcrumbs with the zest of a lemon, a fistful of finely chopped coriander (use the thin parts of the stalk too), 50g melted butter, a pinch of chilli flakes, salt and pepper. Pat the mixture down on 4 skinned fillets of white fish lined up on a greased baking tray. Bake for 20–25 minutes at 200°C/Gas Mark 6 if you're using a fish of a cod-like texture, or adjust accordingly.

Lemon & Coriander Seed: *See Coriander Seed & Lemon, page 346*
Lemon & Cumin: *See Cumin & Lemon, page 84*

Lemon & Dill: The citrus character of dill is created by d-limonene, a compound it shares with lemon, although it's not necessarily lemony. Some detect orange or generically citrussy notes. The knee-jerk reaction is to use lemon and dill for fish, but in Greece, where the partnership is extremely popular, lemon and dill are used far more widely: with lamb, with vegetables, and mixed into rice with onion and pine nuts to serve with feta. The combination is valued for its freshening effect and its ability to emphasise the sweetness of other ingredients.

Lemon & Egg: *See Egg & Lemon, page 134*

Lemon & Ginger: Fresh ginger is commonly described as zesty or citrussy and makes a very harmonious match for lemon. Lemon sauce is an established partner for ginger puddings, lemon icing is good on ginger cakes and the two combine in a hot toddy whose deliciousness may unfortunately pass you by when you're most in need of one. Being clogged up is a good, if unwelcome, demonstration of how much your nose contributes to flavour recognition. The taste receptors in your tongue detect sweetness, saltiness, bitterness, sourness and 'umami', or savouriness, but it's your olfactory nerve endings that detect the subtler differences between the lemony flavour in ginger and the lemony flavour in lemon. Try this toddy while your olfactory bulb is in full working order. Put a 5mm piece of fresh ginger in a glass with the juice of ¼ lemon, 1–2 tsp honey and 1 tbsp whisky, rum or eau de vie. Top up with boiling water, stir and leave to infuse until it's cool enough to drink.

Lemon & Globe Artichoke: *See Globe Artichoke & Lemon, page 128*

Lemon & Goat's Cheese: A citric character is inherent in many goat's cheeses, including the award-winning Cerney from Gloucestershire and the cute Innes Button from Staffordshire. Juliet Harbutt writes that Innes Button 'dissolves on the palate, leaving a trail of almonds, wild honey, lemon, white wine and tangerine', which, as pushing buttons goes, pushes mine.

Lemon & Juniper: *See Juniper & Lemon, page 324*

Lemon & Lamb: Succulent preserved lemons are slow-cooked with lamb in a Moroccan tagine. Sharp lemon is cooked with fatty lamb in Greece. Brown a 1.5kg joint in olive oil with garlic and then braise in a tightly covered pot with the juice of a couple of lemons and some oregano. If it begins to run dry, add a little water, but not too much: the point is to serve the lamb in slices with its concentrated, lemon-spiked juices. Traditionally the lamb is served well cooked rather than rare, with roast potatoes, rice or white beans.

Lemon & Lime: Cockney rhyming slang for crime (as in, *It was the lemon of the century, mate*). And all too appropriately: lime will bludgeon lemon to death given half a chance. Lemon and lime are, of course, from the same family, and their juices have a lot of flavour elements in common, but lime has an overpowering spicy pine and lilac character – meaning that lemon juice is useful for diluting lime juice, but you can't expect to taste both fruits unless you use the zest. The lemony, rosy, herbal characters are far more apparent in the peel.

Lemon & Mint: *See Mint & Lemon, page 331*
Lemon & Oily Fish: *See Oily Fish & Lemon, page 158*

Lemon & Olive: In Morocco, thick, silky slices of preserved lemon and army-fatigue green olives combine to make chicken interesting. At once bitter, bold and tangy, they bring a welcome counterpoint to the sweetness of tagines or fruity couscous dishes. They might also be paired in a salsa served with goat's cheese tart or in a salad to accompany oily fish.

Lemon & Orange: *See Orange & Lemon, page 296*
Lemon & Oyster: *See Oyster & Lemon, page 152*

Lemon & Parsley: A simple, freshening, unobtrusive couple, always keen to lend a hand in the professional kitchen, either in the form of *beurre maître d'hotel* (a compound of butter and parsley) or in the preparation known as *à la meunière*, wherein fish, usually sole, is dipped in flour, fried in clarified butter, then served with brown butter, lemon juice and chopped parsley. See also Parsley & Garlic, page 192.

Lemon & Potato: I once saw a chef berate a cookery show contestant for pairing these two. Maybe the way they were combined wasn't terribly appetising, but to claim that potato and lemon can't work together would baffle the Greeks, who often include potatoes in lemon-sauced dishes. In India, roughly mashed potato is mixed with lemon juice, breadcrumbs, coriander and chilli, formed into pancakes, then deep-fried and served as a snack with chutney and yogurt. New potatoes might be dressed with lemon-infused olive oil or a lemon-laced vinaigrette. Mashed potato with lemon and black pepper can be very good with fish. And Mrs Leyel gave a recipe for lemon cream pie, made by mixing a grated potato, the zest and juice of a lemon, a cup of sugar and a cup of water, then baking it in a double crust.

Lemon & Rose: *See Rose & Lemon, page 343*

Lemon & Rosemary: Lemon tart is classically served with crème fraîche, which has a slight sourness that works well with the sweetened, yet still sour-at-heart lemon curd. But the best partner I've ever tasted for a frisky lemon tart was rosemary ice cream. After much experimentation with steeping rosemary in cream or milk, which works but requires a bit of preparation in advance, I now use rosemary essence from The Hop Farm in Kent. Beat 2 egg yolks with 50g caster sugar and 2 tsp cornflour until smooth. Scald 275ml whipping cream, remove from the heat and beat in 2 tsp liquid glucose. Gradually add the cream mixture to the egg mixture and whisk together before returning all to the pan and heating, stirring constantly, to a custard thickness. Remove, pour into a clean bowl and cover the surface of the custard with cling film. Leave to cool, stir in about 20 drops of rosemary essence, then chill in the fridge before freezing.

Lemon & Saffron: Work like a couple of holiday reps to keep paella's orgy of disparate ingredients in order – chicken, rabbit, snails, green beans, bell peppers, mussels, prawns, butterbeans, globe artichokes, rice. The saffron suffuses the rice to sound a faint but consistent background note. With a flamenco dancer's contemptuous flick of the wrist, squeeze lemon over the entire dish before serving. This way, some mouthfuls are alive with citrus zing, others with a quieter, relieving sweetness. It's this balance of tastes that makes paella so dangerously easy to eat in vaster quantities than more monotonous meals, which must explain why Spanish cookshops sells paella pans as big as the satellite dishes on Goonhilly Downs.

Lemon & Shellfish: *See Shellfish & Lemon, page 142*
Lemon & Smoked Fish: *See Smoked Fish & Lemon, page 166*

Lemon & Thyme: So popular it comes in at least three strengths. For maximum impact, combine chopped thyme with the zest and juice of a lemon – excellent with fish, lamb or chicken, or as a dressing for fried artichokes. Then there's soft-leaved lemon thyme, which furnishes a full but beautifully soft lemon top-note with a herbal murmur underneath, obviously delicious anywhere that lemon and thyme might work in a gentler form. Subtlest of all is the flavour of Meyer lemons, thought to be a hybrid of lemon and mandarin, with a trace of the latter's mild thyme flavour and a sweeter, less acidic freshness than the true *citron limon*. The pairing of lemon and thyme is becoming quite common in sweet foods; I've recently seen them combined in recipes for lemon drizzle cake, a cheesecake and an ice cream. See also Orange & Lemon, page 296.

Lemon & Tomato: *See Tomato & Lemon, page 260*
Lemon & White Chocolate: *See White Chocolate & Lemon, page 352*
Lemon & White Fish: *See White Fish & Lemon, page 147*

Ginger

Native to Southeast Asia but now widely cultivated, ginger varies considerably in flavour depending on where it is grown. In general, fresh ginger is lemony, woody and earthy, with a kick of heat. Jamaican ginger grown in Jamaica is known for its fine quality. Jamaican ginger grown in Nigeria and Sierra Leone is characterised by its richness, pungency and a camphorous element that particularly distinguishes it from the more lemony varieties and betrays its relation to cardamom. Australian ginger is said to be the lemoniest, as of all varieties it contains the most lemon-flavoured citral in its oil. Popular the world over as both a sweet and a savoury ingredient, ginger is available fresh, dried, ground, glacé, pickled, preserved in syrup, juiced and in both soft and alcoholic drinks.

Ginger & Almond: *See Almond & Ginger, page 243*
Ginger & Apricot: *See Apricot & Ginger, page 282*
Ginger & Aubergine: *See Aubergine & Ginger, page 82*

Ginger & Beef: Beef loves tangy flavours, and you'll find it paired with ginger in Thai and Chinese stir-fries and in the crunchy, battered ginger beef created by two Chinese sisters in Calgary, where it's become something of a local speciality. A more unusual instance of the pairing is in crushed gingernut biscuit crusts for beef croquettes and escalopes.

Ginger & Butternut Squash: In most recipes butternut squash and pumpkin can be substituted for one another – say, in pumpkin pie where, once the spices and sugar have been added, few people would be able to spot the difference. Pumpkin pie spice is a blend of ginger, cinnamon, clove, nutmeg and allspice. The same ingredients make up a popular English blend now rather drily called 'mixed spice'. It used to be called pudding spice, which was a far better name, not only because it's more evocative but because it avoids confusion with allspice, which is a different thing altogether. As an aside, allspice is not a blend but a single spice, which looks like a black peppercorn and has a flavour dominated by eugenol, the compound that gives clove its flavour. It's called allspice because it also contains notes of cinnamon and nutmeg. See also Butternut Squash & Rosemary, page 231.

Ginger & Cabbage: Stir-fried with cabbage, fresh ginger compensates for the crisp spiciness cabbage loses when cooked. Spring greens are particularly good cooked this way, as they have dense leaves that don't get so messy and flaccid when heated, and a robust, bittersweet, zesty flavour.

Ginger & Cardamom: Cardamom is a member of the ginger family, a relationship that is more detectable to the nose and mouth than the eye. Both have warming properties with a distinct citric note. In India they're renowned for their beneficial effects on the digestion, and are commonly paired in a drink called *panakam*, made by dissolving jaggery (unrefined sugar) in hot water with dried ginger and ground cardamom, then straining and leaving to cool. I use this combination for *inji jamun*, a variation on the classic *gulab jamun* – see Rose & Cardamom, page 342 – flavouring the little caky *jamuns* with cardamom as standard, but substituting my own ginger syrup for the usual rose. Make the *jamuns* by putting 125g milk powder, 6 tbsp plain flour, 1 tsp baking powder, 1 tsp ground cardamom and 20g butter, cut into pieces, in a food processor, pulsing to combine, then adding water a tablespoon at a time until it becomes a silky dough. Shape into about 18 balls the size of lychees. Slowly dissolve 400g sugar in 650ml water with 4 or 5 thick slices of bruised fresh ginger. Deep-fry the *jamuns* in hot oil a few at a time, turning the heat down to medium once they're in the oil to allow them to brown slowly. Remove and drain on kitchen paper before submerging in the ginger syrup. Leave to cool and soak up the syrup, overnight if possible. Remove the ginger slices and serve chilled or at room temperature.

Ginger & Chilli: Chilli shows ginger what heat is, which is why manufacturers sometimes add a little to ginger ale to give it that extra kick. Chilli and ginger are paired in the sauce that goes with Hainanese chicken rice, originally from Hainan Province off the south coast of China but massively popular in Malaysia, Taiwan and Singapore, where the locals have pretty much adopted it as their national dish, and have dedicated several restaurant chains to it. As it's so popular, you might want to give it a whirl. The sauce is simply fresh chilli pounded with fresh ginger and garlic, sometimes loosened with a little vinegar, lime juice or stock. The chicken is poached whole in salted water with ginger and spring onion. The rice should be cooked with some fat from the cavity in the chicken and the water it was cooked in, now a fragrant stock. The bird is served in pieces at room temperature, drizzled with soy and sesame oil, with the ginger and chilli dipping sauce on the side. Sounds easy, but the skill is in arranging the skinless chicken neatly on the serving dish, almost as if you're trying to reassemble it.

Ginger & Chocolate: Bite into a piece of decent chocolate-covered stem ginger and the snap of dark chocolate should give way to a sugary rasp as your teeth sink into the nap of the ginger's juicy fibres. The dark chocolate's bitter complexity and its cool, almost menthol quality provide the perfect contrast to the ginger's sweet heat. I pair them in a florentine-style biscuit. It's not as pretty as the jewellery-box variegation of glacé fruits but it's far and away more flavourful. Melt 15g unsalted butter in a saucepan over a low heat. Add 40g caster sugar, 2 tsp plain flour and 2 tbsp double cream, and bring slowly to the boil. Simmer for 1 minute, then stir in 50g chopped glacé ginger and 50g flaked almonds, and remove from the heat. When it has cooled to room temperature, place teaspoonfuls of the mixture on lined baking sheets, pat them down and shape them into neat rounds. Make sure to keep the blobs a few cm apart to prevent them fusing into one sticky agglomeration in the oven. Bake at 190°C/Gas Mark 5 for about 12 minutes. Give them a few moments to harden, then transfer to a cooling rack. Melt 75g quality dark chocolate and paint it over the smooth side of the florentines, scoring wiggly lines into the warm chocolate with a fork.

Ginger & Cinnamon: The heart and soul of the gingerbread man. Historically the dough was bolstered by honey and pepper; these days it's likely to be molasses and a pinch of clove. To make a gingerbread-flavoured syrup for coffee, add 2 cinnamon sticks and 1 tsp vanilla extract to the syrup in Ginger & Cardamom, page 309.

Ginger & Clove: *See Clove & Ginger, page 220*
Ginger & Coffee: *See Coffee & Ginger, page 21*

Ginger & Egg: In China, 'century eggs' are made by plastering raw hen or duck eggs in a muddy mixture of lime, salt, pine ash and water, then storing them for weeks (or longer) in an earthenware jar or buried in the earth. When the shell is peeled off, the white will have set and turned an amber colour, like cold tea jelly, and the yolk a dark grey-green. They have a sulphurous odour and a pungent ammonia flavour, and are served with slices of pickled ginger as a casual snack. The English preserved egg is boiled, peeled and pickled in vinegar and is commonly sold in chip shops and pubs. In the pub, a tradition persists of burying the pickled egg in a packet of scrunched-up crisps (a good barman will do this for you). Salt and vinegar crisps are the typical flavour used, but Worcestershire sauce, with its sweet and sour spiciness, is a superior choice.

Ginger & Garlic: *See Garlic & Ginger, page 113*
Ginger & Lemon: *See Lemon & Ginger, page 305*

Ginger & Lime: A Moscow Mule combines vodka, lime and ginger beer; it can be a lame donkey made with ginger ale. A few drops of Angostura nails a shoe of metallic bitterness to its cumulative kick. Ginger beer is hotter, fuller flavoured and cloudy, whereas ginger ale is a clean, amber colour, with a subtler flavour that mixes well with dark spirits such as rum and whiskey (the types with an 'e': North American or Irish).

Ginger & Mango: Mango ginger, or zedoary, is related to neither plant, although, like ginger, it's a rhizome. Native to India and Indonesia, it has a taste that's bitter at first, then sweet, then sour, with a musky, aromatic flavour reminiscent of green mango. It's predominantly used in pickles and curries. As to ginger *and* mango, they combine in a crème brûlée just as nicely as they do with shellfish, and the chef Jean-Georges Vongerichten marries them with foie gras in one of his signature dishes.

Ginger & Melon: *See Melon & Ginger, page 280*

Ginger & Mint: Ginger mint has a flavour similar to peppermint, with the slightest hint of ginger. Candies and sodas flavoured with ginger *and* mint are popular in America, and a sprig of fresh mint or a slug of mint syrup can pep up insipid ginger ale in the summer.

Ginger & Oily Fish: The pickled ginger, or *gari*, that comes with *nigiri* (fish on rice) and sashimi is there to freshen the palate, ensuring you appreciate the fine flavours of each different fresh fish. For the same reason, purists prefer to eat their sushi with chopsticks because the fingers (which are perfectly acceptable to use) might transfer the flavour of one fish to another. If you are going to dip your *nigiri* in soy, dip it fish-side down, ensuring you get only a light seasoning of sauce and positioning the *nigiri* so that the fish meets your tongue, so you taste it more. Dip it rice-side down and your soy-drenched *nigiri* will almost certainly fall apart before it reaches your mouth. In better sushi restaurants the chef will in any case have absolved you of the decision by seasoning his *nigiri* with a soy-based sauce and wasabi as he sees fit. Dipping in extra soy and wasabi will be frowned upon. It's also considered bad form to pop the ginger in your mouth *with* the sushi or scarf it as an appetiser, so do it only when you're sure nobody's looking.

Ginger & Onion: *See Onion & Ginger, page 109*

Ginger & Orange: Both spicy and citrussy. In Finland, ground Seville orange powder is used with cinnamon, clove and ginger in a spice mix for gingerbread. Try this sticky ginger and orange cake. Cream 170g butter with

150g light muscovado sugar until pale and fluffy. Beat in 2 eggs, one at a time. Grate the zest of a large orange into the mix and sift over 170g self-raising flour, 1 tsp baking powder and a pinch of salt, before carefully folding them in. Add 3 tbsp milk and 4 finely chopped nuggets of preserved ginger. Transfer to a greased and lined round 18cm cake tin, smooth the surface and bake at 180°C/Gas Mark 4 for 40–50 minutes. Glaze with melted marmalade – 125ml should be enough – and leave to cool.

Ginger & Pork: Brought together in a simple Japanese dish called *shogayaki* (fried ginger). *Shogayaki* can also be made with (amongst other things) beef or squid, but it's most popular by far with pork, which is what you'll get unless the menu indicates otherwise. Marinate 200g thinly sliced pork fillet in 2 tbsp finely grated fresh ginger, 2 tbsp soy sauce and 2 tbsp mirin for 15 minutes. Working quickly, fry the drained pork in vegetable oil and divide between two plates. Tip the marinade into the pan and heat through before pouring it over the pork. Serve with rice and a bowl of miso.

Ginger & Rhubarb: The combination of ginger and rhubarb came about because it was considered to be good for the bowels, which may go some way to explaining why they're still paired when to my mind the two flavours seem a little annoyed with each other. Chef Jason Atherton serves them pickled with a pressed foie gras and smoked eel terrine and a ginger brioche. Delia Smith combines cooked rhubarb with orange jelly made with ginger beer instead of the usual water. And Andrew Pern, chef-patron of The Star Inn, near Helmsley in North Yorkshire, gives a recipe for rhubarb-ripple ice cream with ginger parkin, which you can eat at the Inn if you can't be bothered to make it yourself.

Ginger & Tomato: For a piquant, gingery tomato sauce, Mrs Beeton suggests cooking about a kilo of ripe tomatoes in an earthenware dish at 120°C/Gas Mark ½ for 4–5 hours. Let them cool to room temperature, remove the skins and mix the pulp with any juice left in the roasting dish. Add 2 tsp powdered ginger, 2 tsp salt, the cloves of 1 whole garlic bulb, finely chopped, 2 tbsp vinegar and a pinch of cayenne. Pour into bottles and store somewhere cool. It can be eaten immediately but the flavours improve noticeably after a few weeks. It will taste even better if you've powdered your own ginger: simply grate some fresh on to a baking sheet and leave to dry for 3–4 days, less if outside on a run of sunny days. Keep the dried gratings in a jar and whiz in a spice grinder when needed. You can leave the skin on for an earthier, nuttier flavour, or peel if you like it lighter.

Ginger & Vanilla: Add a scoop of vanilla ice cream to ginger ale in place of the usual cola and you'll have what's known as a Boston Cooler. See also Ginger & Cinnamon, page 310.

Ginger & White Fish: The citrus notes in fresh ginger make it an obvious partner for fish. Donna Hay recommends lining the bottom of a bamboo steamer with slices of ginger to impart their flavour to steamed fish. As a garnish for other dishes, she suggests a tangle of deep-fried shredded ginger. See also Onion & Ginger, page 109.

Cardamom

Open a jar of cardamom pods and you might be reminded of a vapour rub or sinus-clearing stick. Like bay leaves and rosemary, cardamom contains clear notes of camphor and eucalyptus. As a member of the ginger family, it also has a citrus, floral quality; depending on their country of origin, cardamoms are likely to be stronger in eucalyptus or floral-citrus flavours. Whichever dominates, those fresh notes are good for cutting through fattiness, especially with ingredients that let the spice's complexity of flavour shine – e.g. cream, chocolate, nuts or buttery rice.

Cardamom & Almond: The Nordic countries take a disproportionate amount of the world's cardamom crop and sprinkle it liberally in their cakes, buns and pastries. Finnish *pulla* is a cardamom-spiced plaited sweet bread, Norwegian *goro* is a thin, crisp, cardamom-flavoured wafer that looks like the cover of an old bible. *Fattigman* is made with the same dough but shaped with a special cutting tool and deep-fried. On Shrove Tuesday in Sweden, they make a cardamom-scented bun called a *semla*, whose top is lopped off and its scooped-out centre filled with almond paste and a blob of cream. The bun's top is then replaced and dusted with sugar. Non-bakers will find them seasonally available in Ikea.

Cardamom & Apricot: Cardamom and apricot are paired in cakes such as apricot Danish pastries, in crumbles and in jams. Dried apricots, poached in syrup with cardamom, are a speciality of Kashmir. Or try this apricot tart with a luxurious cardamom *crème pâtissière*. Whisk 50g caster sugar with 3 egg yolks. Continue whisking while you add 20g each of plain flour and cornflour. Scald 300ml milk with 3 bruised cardamoms and ½ tsp vanilla extract. Remove the pods and gradually stir the milk into the egg mixture. Transfer the lot to a pan and bring to the boil until large bubbles break on the surface. Lower the heat and cook for about 5 minutes, until very thick. Cool and use to fill a cooked 23cm sweet pastry case. Top with about 15 poached, peeled apricot halves and glaze with apricot jam.

Cardamom & Bacon: Black cardamoms are closely related to green ones. They share their warm aromatic flavour but are stronger, a little bitterer, and are roasted over a fire to dry them out, giving them a smoky flavour, like a green cardamom after a Laphroaig bender. Add a few pods to a stew or soup to impart a flavour subtly reminiscent of bacon.

Cardamom & Banana: Banana and cardamom combine in a soothing raita. Some slice the banana but I like to mash a couple of not particularly ripe ones and mix them with ¼ tsp ground cardamom, a pinch of dried chilli and 150–250g yogurt, depending on the looseness demanded by the main dish (a robustly hot, tangy lamb curry makes an excellent partner).

Cardamom & Carrot: See Carrot & Cardamom, page 227
Cardamom & Chocolate: See Chocolate & Cardamom, page 14

Cardamom & Cinnamon: Like Krishna and his mortal consort, Radha, legendary lovers. Together they add a sweet, aromatic note to Indian and Pakistani milk desserts. I combine them in a chai-like hot drink that gives cocoa a run for its money. Pour a mug of milk into a pan with a stick of cinnamon and 2 or 3 crushed cardamom pods and slowly bring to the boil. Remove from the heat, strain back into the mug, then add sugar to taste. You could let this cool and use it to make a fragrant banana milkshake.

Cardamom & Coconut: See Coconut & Cardamom, page 286
Cardamom & Coffee: See Coffee & Cardamom, page 20

Cardamom & Coriander Seed: Both spices have distinct citrus notes. If you find cardamom too camphorous for a sweet recipe, 'dilute' it by crushing it with a little coriander seed. The coriander's pretty, floral quality plays harmoniously to cardamom's sweeter side.

Cardamom & Ginger: See Ginger & Cardamom, page 309

Cardamom & Lamb: In Kashmir, cardamom is used to enrich lamb meatballs in a dish called *goshtaba*, for which small pieces of meat are painstakingly pounded with suet, resulting in a super-soft mixture likened to the texture of cashmere. Less time-consuming is *elaichi gosht*, a combination of lamb with an unusually large amount of cardamom. This is Madhur Jaffrey's recipe. Heat 3 tbsp oil in a large pan and add 2 tbsp finely ground cardamom (grind the pods up with the seeds if you can't be bothered to shell them; they add a little fibre to the sauce). Stir once and add 900g cubed shoulder of lamb. Continue stirring over a high heat for 2 minutes, then add 2 chopped tomatoes and a small, finely chopped red onion. Stir for another 3 minutes, then add 1½ tsp garam masala, 1 tbsp tomato paste, 1½ tsp salt and 625ml water. Simmer with the lid on for 1–1½ hours and add a very generous grinding of black pepper before serving with bread or rice.

Cardamom & Mango: Very popular in India. Cardamom's brightness combined with the sourness of yogurt can rescue overripe mango in a lassi. Blend the flesh of 1 mango with 250g yogurt, 125ml milk, a pinch of ground cardamom and an ice cube or two. Taste for cardamom levels and sweeten with sugar, honey or the rather inauthentic maple syrup, which has a pleasing affinity for the resinous whiff in mango.

Cardamom & Pear: *See Pear & Cardamom, page 274*
Cardamom & Rose: *See Rose & Cardamom, page 342*

Cardamom & Saffron: Saffron shares cardamom's yen for all things lush and creamy, and nicely complements its lemon character. Pair them in ice cream, custard and cakes, or use a little of each in savoury rice dishes.

Cardamom & Vanilla: *See Vanilla & Cardamom, page 348*
Cardamom & White Chocolate: *See White Chocolate & Cardamom, page 351*

BRAMBLE & HEDGE

Rosemary

Sage

Juniper

Thyme

Mint

Blackcurrant

Blackberry

Rosemary

Rosemary has a eucalyptus character akin to sage, although it contains more pine and floral notes and is sweeter. There are many varieties of rosemary. Among those particularly commended for their flavour are Tuscan Blue, which has a gentle, lemon-pine aroma, Spice Island, which has hints of clove and nutmeg, and Sissinghurst Blue, which has a pronounced smoky character that begs to be thrown on the barbecue. Rosemary tastes fine when it's dried carefully, but it does take on the typically hay-like flavour of dried herbs, and noticeably loses the complexity of fresh. It is a classic partner for lamb and goat's cheese, but also makes some excellent matches in sweet dishes with chocolate, oranges and lemons.

Rosemary & Almond: *See Almond & Rosemary, page 245*
Rosemary & Anchovy: *See Anchovy & Rosemary, page 163*

Rosemary & Apricot: *Ma'mool*, a plump, stuffed sweetmeat found all over the Middle East and North Africa, usually contains a mix of dates and nuts spiced with cinnamon. The crumbly pastry gives a pleasing contrast to the rich, chewy filling, which can be made with all manner of dried fruit and nut combinations. When dried, apricots lose some of their fruity, lavender aroma and can become rather sour. Rosemary, reminiscent of lavender, restores some of their subtle perfume. Tip 225g plain flour into a food processor, add 110g unsalted butter, cut in 1cm cubes, and whiz into crumbs. Little by little, add 1 tbsp rosewater and 3–4 tbsp milk until a dough forms. Set aside in the fridge. Put 120g chopped dried apricots in a pan with 100g chopped mixed nuts, 1 tbsp finely chopped rosemary, 50g sugar and 4 tbsp water. Cook over a medium heat until the water has evaporated, then stir in 75g ground almonds and make sure all is well combined. When the mixture has cooled a little, divide the dough into 20 and roll each piece into a ball. Indent with your thumb to create a bowl and fill with the apricot mixture, easing the pastry over it until it's no longer visible. Place them on a greased baking tray and flatten a little with the tines of a fork. Bake for 20 minutes at 160°C/Gas Mark 3. Once cool, sprinkle with icing sugar.

Rosemary & Butternut Squash: *See Butternut Squash & Rosemary, page 231*
Rosemary & Chestnut: *See Chestnut & Rosemary, page 233*

Rosemary & Chocolate: A backdrop of dark chocolate shows off rosemary's cool, evergreen flavours. If this recalls the lovely combination of Chocolate & Cardamom (see page 14), that's because the dominant flavour compound in both rosemary and cardamom is cineole, common to bay leaf too (think how all three make great milk-based desserts). Cineole has woody, eucalyptus, slightly minty notes. In rosemary, these are joined by peppery, camphorous characters, while cardamom takes it in a more citrussy, floral direction – you might say chocolate with rosemary is a wintry alternative to chocolate and cardamom. This recipe for 'Little Pots of Chocolate and Rosemary Cream' was conceived by the chef David Wilson. In a heavy-based stainless-steel pan, mix 250g caster sugar with 250ml dry white wine and the juice of ½ lemon. Heat gently until the sugar has dissolved, stirring occasionally. Stir in 600ml double cream and cook gently, stirring constantly, until thickened. Add 1 stem of rosemary (or 1 tsp dried rosemary) and 165g grated dark chocolate. Bring to the boil, stirring until the chocolate has dissolved, then lower the heat and simmer for 20 minutes, until the mixture is dark and thick. Cool, strain into 8 little pots (or even 10, it's very rich), cover and refrigerate before serving.

Rosemary & Garlic: *See Garlic & Rosemary, page 114*
Rosemary & Goat's Cheese: *See Goat's Cheese & Rosemary, page 58*
Rosemary & Grape: *See Grape & Rosemary, page 253*
Rosemary & Hazelnut: *See Hazelnut & Rosemary, page 240*

Rosemary & Lamb: The bittersweet, sap-green flavour of rosemary alleviates the fattiness of lamb, while its pine-fresh, eucalyptus notes can freshen the meat's gamier qualities. This might explain why rosemary really comes into its own with fatty cuts or older/well-hung lamb. The Italians pair even the youngest lamb with rosemary, including *abbacchio*, the weeks-old, milk-fed lamb that's roasted whole at Easter. Ground lamb seasoned with rosemary can make good sausages and a rich sauce for tossing with thick ribbons of pasta. American chef Douglas Rodriguez has been known to serve minced lamb and rosemary-seared lamb tenderloin on flatbreads with raisins, pine nuts and goat's cheese.

Rosemary & Lemon: *See Lemon & Rosemary, page 307*

Rosemary & Mushroom: At Alinea in Chicago, Grant Achatz makes a *matsutake* mushroom cake and *matsutake* caramel, served with a cube each of rosemary and sherry vinegar jelly, a sprinkling of pine nut salt and a mastic cream. It's an autumnal combination with strong notes of evergreen. Rosemary is an evergreen shrub, as is *Pistacio lentiscus*, of which mastic is the aromatic resin, used amongst other things as a popular flavouring for chewing gum in Greece. Pine nuts: self-explanatory. The highly prized *matsutake* doesn't have an evergreen flavour but grows under pine trees in Japan; its name translates as 'pine mushroom'. It has a strong aroma, with a distinct cinnamon note, although the flavour is less remarkable. In Japan the mushrooms are gathered, grilled in the open air over pine fires and eaten with soy sauce. See also Beef & Mushroom, page 46.

Rosemary & Oily Fish: When strident rosemary meets rambunctious oily fish such as sardines and mackerel, they knock the hard edges off each other and become, if not exactly refined, then certainly an enchanting couple. Finely chop some rosemary and parsley, then combine them with bread-crumbs and a little grated Parmesan. Spoon this stuffing into your gutted fish, grill them and serve with lemon.

Rosemary & Olive: *See Olive & Rosemary, page 177*

Rosemary & Onion: *Socca*, the toasty, nutty chickpea bread (or pancake, depending on which way you look at it) sold at the old market in Nice, is called *farinata* once you cross the Italian border into Liguria, where it's often served scattered with finely chopped rosemary and onion. The *socceurs* or *farinatistas* or whatever they're called have special hot plates for cooking, so it's hard to achieve quite the same results at home. No matter: it's still a treat. Whisk together 200g chickpea flour (also called gram flour in Indian shops), 300ml hand-hot water, 2 tsp salt and 3 tbsp olive oil and set aside for a few hours. Paint a heavy-based, ovenproof 25cm round (or 20–23cm square) tin with a good amount of olive oil. Heat the tin in the oven at 220°C/Gas Mark 7, then remove and thinly cover it with half the batter. Put it back in the oven for 10–15 minutes: best to keep an eye on it in case it starts to burn. Remove and scatter with very finely chopped rosemary and onion. Eat the first warm while you're making the second.

Rosemary & Orange: Orange blossoms became a popular wedding symbol in the nineteenth century, when they were used to decorate cakes, incorporated into bouquets, or their likenesses embroidered on the bride's veil. They signified good luck, innocence, happiness and fertility. Rosemary has had nuptial associations for even longer. Anne of Cleves wore some in her hair at her wedding to Henry VIII, and less grand congregations carried it to signify fidelity and remembrance. Orange blossom and rosemary make a happy couple themselves. The chef Allegra McEvedy gives a recipe for an orange-flavoured cake of ground cashews and semolina, sprinkled (once baked) with orange-flower water and topped with a rosemary-flavoured syrup. A cake to make for a friend fresh back from honeymoon, to signify that she has no more dress fittings.

Rosemary & Pea: *See Pea & Rosemary, page 204*

Rosemary & Pork: There's a great little *osteria* called Il Cinghiale Bianco in Florence. Cross the Ponte Vecchio from the north side of the river, slaloming the Senegalese handbag-hawkers, turn immediately right and it's down the Borgo San Iacopo on your left. (Turn left off the bridge and you'll find a fantastic drinking club off its head with flowers and collections of filthy drawings on the tables. But that's for another book.) Have the *arista al forno con* *patate*, magically tender roast pork in a tangy, caramely gravy with roast rose-maried potatoes, the rosemary infusing the meal with a Florentine headiness to give you Stendhal syndrome before you've so much as entered a church. Scrub Stendhal syndrome: it'll give you Stockholm syndrome. You'd happily never leave. *Porchetta*, from Lazio, further south, is boned pork stuffed with rosemary, garlic and (maybe) fennel and roasted on a spit. It's particularly associated with fairs, where slices are sold sandwiched in chewy white bread, sometimes with broccoli.

Rosemary & Potato: *See Potato & Rosemary, page 92*

Rosemary & Rhubarb: Recreating a restaurant dish at home, says Helen Rennie at culinate.com, is like piecing together a jigsaw puzzle. At Rendezvous, Steve Johnson's restaurant in Massachusetts, Rennie ate a raw rhubarb, dried apricot and dried cranberry compote, but was stuck at first as to how to reconstruct it. The key, it transpired, was to marinate the fruit in honey and rosemary for a couple of days. The flavour of rosemary works well with the sharp, fruity flavours of orange and lemon, and it's easy to see how that would apply to rhubarb too.

Rosemary & Watermelon: Rosemary is the barbecuer's faithful friend. Remove the needles by stroking the stalk against their angle of incline and you have a natural, flavour-imparting skewer for cubed meat. Or scent the smoke by throwing a handful of sprigs on to the coals when your meat or veg is nearly cooked. The American food writer Mark Bittman suggests grilling watermelon steaks with rosemary. Cut 5cm-thick 'steaks' (including the rind) from a small watermelon. With the tines of a fork, flick out as many seeds as you can without ruining the flesh. Brush the steaks with a mixture of 4 tbsp olive oil, 1 tbsp finely chopped rosemary, salt and pepper, then barbecue for 5 minutes on each side. Serve with lemon wedges. These make a very good accompaniment to barbecued pork.

Sage

A rugged herb, not to all tastes: some find it too strong, too bitter, or are put off by the medicinal associations of its camphorous-eucalyptus flavour. Fresh sage has lighter, more lemony notes, but loses these when dried, taking on a stronger, musty hay character. Fresh or dried, sage has a particular affinity for dense, sweet-savoury foods that benefit from its pronounced flavour and bitter finish – butternut squash, white beans, cooked onions, pork and chicken.

Sage & Anchovy: *See Anchovy & Sage, page 163*

Sage & Apple: Sage is rich and domineering, slamming its tankard down and demanding the company of weighty meat dishes. You might think brisk, fruity apple would bestow some freshness on the partnership but it doesn't. Sage is so doggedly sagey that, for all apple's efforts, a musty darkness prevails. Still, it's a lovely cold-weather combination: use it to furnish poultry with a deep, satisfying stuffing or make a pork stew with sage and apple dumplings. To make the dumplings, put 175g self-raising flour in a bowl with 75g suet, 8–10 finely chopped sage leaves and 1 peeled, cored and finely diced small cooking apple. Gradually mix in enough cold water to make a sticky but still workable dough. Shape it into dumplings with a pair of serving spoons, as you would quenelles. Drop them on to a stew, cover and simmer for 15–20 minutes. Eat in a dank dining room, silent but for the tick-tock of a grandfather clock.

Sage & Bacon: A friend was holding a cook-off. On the night, the competitors assembled in her kitchen; we chopped, blended, blanched and julienned. Some time later we were joined by a harried man who smoothed out a scribbled recipe, busied himself for about five minutes, slid a dish into the oven and disappeared into the party with a glass of wine. Of course, he won. And I peeled his recipe off the work surface as a consolation prize. It turned out to be an adapted version of Delia Smith's baked pancetta, leek and sage risotto. The oven method might not result in total textural authenticity but it does mean you get to hang out with your guests (or the clearly swayable judges at an informal cookery competition that's only supposed to be a bit of fun). Here's how *he* made it. Find a pan that's big enough to hold all the ingredients and can go straight from the hob to the oven. Warm some olive oil in it and cook a 200g packet of smoked bacon lardons with a fairly finely chopped onion until soft. Add 175g risotto rice and stir to coat the grains in the oil, then add 75ml white wine, 500ml stock, 2 tsp chopped sage and some seasoning. Bring to a simmer and transfer to a 150°C/Gas Mark 2 oven. Bake for 20 minutes, remove from the oven, stir in 2 tbsp grated Parmesan and put back in the oven for 15 minutes. Sprinkle over 50g grated Parmesan and serve.

Sage & Blue Cheese: *See Blue Cheese & Sage, page 63*

Sage & Butternut Squash: Try butternut squash raw. It's like French-kissing a scarecrow: straw and damp vegetables. Cooking brings out its sweeter, softer nature, unless it's partnered with sage. Sage's assertive flavour rubs off on the squash, revealing its meaty, virile side – so much so that a sworn carnivore might be won round to this pairing. The Chez Panisse café combines them on a pizza with Asiago cheese, while Russ Parsons gives a recipe for a butternut squash risotto garnished with fried sage leaves and toasted walnuts.

Sage & Chicken: *See Chicken & Sage, page 31*

Sage & Egg: Sage is happy in the company of all the classic English-breakfast ingredients but this Turkish-inspired recipe from the Australian chef Neil Perry puts an exciting twist on the pairing of egg and sage. Crush 1 clove of garlic with 1 tsp salt and mix into 90g Greek yogurt with some freshly ground pepper. Set aside and put 4 eggs on to poach. While the eggs are cooking, heat 100g unsalted butter in a pan, add 16 sage leaves and cook until the sage is crisp and the butter browned. Spoon a dollop of yogurt on to each plate, top with a poached egg, season with salt, pepper and a pinch of chilli powder and finish by drizzling over the butter. Perry suggests some chopped fresh chilli on the side. You can always fry the eggs, if you prefer.

Sage & Hard Cheese: *See Hard Cheese & Sage, page 69*
Sage & Juniper: *See Juniper & Sage, page 325*

Sage & Liver: A legendary flavour affiliation. Liver gives the fresh pine and cedar notes in sage their due, offsetting the sanguinary flavour shared by both ingredients. But pause a moment to consider their textures. I can't make a chicken liver and sage bruschetta without first brushing the moleskin leaves against my cheek. Cooked liver sometimes takes on a similarly suede-like quality, and together the ingredients make me think of rugged country clothing and damp valleys, or taking a bite of Ted Hughes.

Sage & Onion: *See Onion & Sage, page 110*
Sage & Pineapple: *See Pineapple & Sage, page 267*

Sage & Pork: Elizabeth David disliked sage, describing it as having an over-powering dried-blood flavour. The English, she claimed, had become accustomed to the herb through its common pairing with goose and duck, especially in the form of sage and onion stuffing. These days, most English people are more likely to associate the flavour of sage with pork, as it's so often used in sausages. In Italy a pork loin might be cooked slowly in sage- and lemon-scented milk. I've made this at home but, far from my flavour memory transporting me to the rusty-red rooftops and shadowy porticoes of Bologna, the ineradicable sausage association yanks me straight back to the cheerless breakfast room of a lochside B&B in Scotland, scraping at my plate in the deafening silence.

Sage & Prosciutto: Salty prosciutto is one of the few ingredients capable of teasing out the fun side of serious sage. In *saltimbocca* (Italian for 'jumps in the mouth'), a slice of prosciutto is laid over a flour-dipped escalope of veal, turkey, pork, chicken or even a fillet of flatfish such as plaice, and a brooch of sage is pinned through both with a cocktail stick. Cook quickly on both sides – sage-side first to flavour the butter. Keep warm while you deglaze the pan with something to match the meat – marsala with veal or chicken, fish stock or white wine with plaice, etc.

Sage & Tomato: In Italy, sage is used to season tomato-based dishes like *fagioli all'uccelletto* ('beans little-bird style') – cannellini beans simply cooked with tomato and sage. According to Pellegrino Artusi, the same ingredients were traditionally used to cook the eponymous little birds. The Zuni Café in San Francisco makes a sage pesto, giving the herb a little time in warm olive oil before pounding it with more olive oil, garlic, walnuts and Parmesan. They strongly recommend serving it with grilled or roasted tomato dishes.

Juniper

The flavours of a country estate: juniper is the principal flavouring in gin and is frequently paired with game. While bitter ingredients are commonly balanced with their sweet opposing numbers, juniper is often paired with other bitter flavours such as blackcurrant, tonic water, grapefruit and rare meat. The berries need to be crushed in order to release their thick evergreen flavour.

Juniper & Beef: *See Beef & Juniper, page 45*
Juniper & Blackcurrant: *See Blackcurrant & Juniper, page 333*

Juniper & Cabbage: These come together most famously in *choucroute garnie*, a sort of carnivore's lucky dip where the prizes are rich, meaty treats: wobbly chunks of pork belly, upright frankfurters, a pale and sinister *boudin blanc*, smoked knee, pickled hock, brined thigh. But the sauerkraut is much more than plastic hay. I love the slender ribbons of pale, barrel-fermented cabbage, scented with the balsamic fragrance of juniper. Its sharpness is what stops the sweet fattiness of the meat overpowering the dish: a cynic in a roomful of corpulent bores.

Juniper & Grapefruit: Kingsley Amis recalls enjoying a cocktail called Salty Dog on a trip to Nashville, Tennessee. Dip the rim of a glass in water, then salt, carefully pour in one part gin to two parts fresh grapefruit juice, add ice and stir. Amis calls gin and tonic 'suspect' and 'a rather unworthy, mawkish drink, best left to women, youngsters and whisky distillers'. He considers gin and water a superior combination, not least because drunk without ice and with just a splash of Malvern water, it will give you a chance to taste the botanical flavourings unimpaired and appreciate the difference between the brands. He also approves of gin with ginger beer and plenty of ice, 'one of the great long drinks of our time'.

Juniper & Hard Cheese: Pecorino ginepro, popular in Italy, is a semi-hard ewe's milk cheese soaked in juniper and balsamic vinegar. It's nutty and tangy, as you'd expect from a pecorino, and the flavour of the juniper works well with the gaminess of the cheese.

Juniper & Lemon: Juniper lords it over the other aromatics that lend gin its characteristic mix of flavours – coriander, angelica, anise, fennel seeds, cardamom and orange, amongst others. Lemon can be one of the more discernible secondary flavours, but then juniper itself has citrussy-lemon notes to it. Which is why, in turn, lemon is such a classic partner for gin – floated in a G&T, juiced in a Tom Collins, in a classic Gin Fizz (with sugar, soda and ice), or in the mixer, bitter lemon, whose bitterness comes, as with tonic water, from quinine.

Juniper & Olive: Flying is tough on the body. After a *lot* of Twiglets, a handful of olives, a Bloody Mary, a very small sandwich, two boxes of crunchy snacks of no known national provenance, a glass of champagne, a suspiciously smooth pâté with bread roll, a glass of red, a salad of explosively tough cherry tomatoes, a beef bourguignon whose accompaniment of boiled carrots and mashed potato serves only to emphasise the meat's weird insubstantiality, as if it came from the ghost of a cow, another glass of red, a horrible chocolate mousse, a Bailey's, a doll's-house selection of crackers with silicone cheese, a port (nice), two coffees (not), a snack pack of Jaffa Cakes, a three-quarter-flight selection of sandwich slices, a truly disgraceful cup of tea, a scone with raspberry jam and cream, and, to de-pop the ears on descent, a Fox's Glacier Fruit gone misshapen at the bottom of my handbag, I often feel a little brackish arriving at JFK. No better cure for this than a dirty martini. They're like regular martinis, except with brine from the olive jar added; the murky, salty oiliness of the brine brings the gin's aromatics alive. And boy, do they give you an appetite.

Juniper & Orange: Gin and orange may have slipped quietly out of fashion but this hardy, wintry pair still finds plenty to do on the plate. They're often used to season strong-flavoured meats such as venison and duck, but have an affinity for other bold, bitter ingredients such as cabbage, chicory and dark chocolate. La Sambresse, from the Brootcoorens Brewery in Belgium, is a beer flavoured with bitter orange peel and juniper.

Juniper & Pork: Juniper's bold freshness cuts through fat. Juniper and pork are classically paired in pâtés and terrines, but you don't have to go to great lengths to enjoy this combination. Elizabeth David recommends mixing crushed dried berries with chopped fennel bulb, salt, olive oil and garlic as a seasoning for pork chops.

Juniper & Prosciutto: *See Prosciutto & Juniper, page 172*
Juniper & Rhubarb: *See Rhubarb & Juniper, page 255*

Juniper & Sage: Juniper has a hint of that evergreen aroma, oily but fresh, that clears your sinuses when walking through coniferous forests. The juniper berry is, in fact, the only edible spice from a conifer. Sage also has notes of pine, cedar, pepper and eucalyptus; paired with juniper, it makes an excellent stuffing for duck. Try 125g fresh breadcrumbs mixed with 2 tbsp chopped sage, 10 crushed juniper berries and some cooked, chopped onion. Season and add a little lemon or orange zest.

Thyme

This chapter, although primarily concerned with the common thyme, *Thymus vulgaris*, also covers some other cultivars, such as lemon thyme and orange thyme. Common thyme is the type you brush past on the mountain trails and coastal paths of the Mediterranean; strong, with a sweet, herbaceous warmth that can tip into smokiness or a medicinal quality. For me, thyme is the essence of the word herbal – almost neutrally so – and forms the backbone of a bouquet garni or *herbes de Provence*. Its bittersweet, aromatic flavour flourishes in slow-cooked tomato sauces, braised meat dishes and bean stews. It also brings a tantalising hint of lush pasture to dairy, and increasingly turns up in sweet dishes.

Thyme & Bacon: *See Bacon & Thyme, page 170*

Thyme & Beef: Delia Smith says she always adds a little thyme to her beef stews. Don't worry if you don't have any fresh to hand – dried can be even better. Thyme is one of the few herbs whose flavour intensifies when dried, in the best cases taking on a distinctly spicy, smoky character that complements its herbal perfume, bringing welcome layers of flavour to a rich meat dish. Orange thyme and caraway thyme are good with roast beef too.

Thyme & Chicken: *See Chicken & Thyme, page 31*

Thyme & Chocolate: New best friends. Thomas Keller serves them together at The French Laundry in California's Napa Valley and at Per Se in New York, where, before your eyes, dark lids of chocolate are sprinkled with Maldon sea salt, then anointed with hot olive oil, which melts through the chocolate to reveal the thyme ice cream underneath. At Taillevent, the Parisian restaurant where Keller once worked, they have been known to serve thyme ice cream with a *moelleux au chocolat* (molten chocolate cake), which is somewhat easier to reproduce at home. Taste the thyme custard before its second heating and I think you have a clue as to why this pair seems to work so well. The thyme makes the cream taste as if it came farm-fresh from the churn, more pasture than pasteurised, and the dark chocolate like the freshest milk chocolate in the mouth. To make thyme ice cream, put about 10 leafy thyme sprigs in a pan with 275ml full-cream milk, scald, then leave to cool. Cover and steep overnight in the fridge. The following day, scald the milk and thyme again, then strain. In a bowl, beat 4 egg yolks with 90g caster sugar, then slowly pour the warm, thyme-infused milk on to that mixture, stirring all the time. Transfer to a clean pan and stir over a low heat, without letting it boil, until the mixture is thick enough to coat the back of the spoon. Strain through a fine sieve, stir in 300ml double cream, then cool and freeze in the usual way while you get on with making the cakes. You can't go wrong with Galton Blackiston's recipe for melting chocolate puddings, passed on by Delia Smith in several of her books and on her website.

Thyme & Cinnamon: *See Cinnamon & Thyme, page 219*
Thyme & Garlic: *See Garlic & Thyme, page 114*

Thyme & Goat's Cheese: Flavouring cheese with thyme can be traced back to Roman times. The natural thyme flavour in milk from animals that had fed on the herb must have acted as a serving suggestion. Roves des Garrigues, made from the raw milk of the Rove goat in Provence, has a thyme flavour, as do some Greek fetas and Fleur du Maquis, a sheep's cheese from Corsica. (Both *garrigue* and *maquis* roughly translate as 'scrubland', which gives you an idea of the sort of thorny, scented stuff these goats have nibbled on.) Bees are crazy for thyme, and thyme honey is highly prized in Greece for its unique, assertive flavour. How perfect that would be drizzled over the cheese.

Thyme & Lamb: A classic combination, even if rosemary and mint have a more famous relationship with lamb. In *Papilles et Molécules* ('taste buds and molecules'), François Chartier, a sommelier from Quebec, analyses food at the molecular level in order to arrive at wine pairings. He notes that thymol is key to the flavour of thyme as well as a constituent of lamb, and that there are red wines from the southern Languedoc in France that share that flavour note and would therefore make an exceptional pairing.

Thyme & Lemon: *See Lemon & Thyme, page 307*
Thyme & Mushroom: *See Mushroom & Thyme, page 80*
Thyme & Oily Fish: *See Oily Fish & Thyme, page 159*

Thyme & Olive: These two eke out an existence on the stony, parched soil of the Mediterranean. The feral, fragrant character of thyme contrasts beautifully with heavy, complex olive, sombre as a Greek church bell at noon.

Thyme & Onion: Thyme adds both depth and freshness to a creamy onion soup. Roughly chop 3 or 4 onions and sweat them in a little butter and oil, with a few sprigs of thyme, until really soft but not brown. Add 500ml vegetable or chicken stock and 250ml milk. Season, then bring to the boil and simmer for about 15 minutes. Leave to cool slightly, discard the thyme, liquidise and reheat to serve. Add a swirl of cream and some tiny thyme leaves if the spirit takes you.

Thyme & Orange: Thymol, the compound responsible for thyme's distinctive flavour, is also what distinguishes mandarin from other members of the orange family. Inhale the spritz as you're peeling a mandarin and you'll detect a beautiful herbal quality amid the citric zing. Orange and thyme are paired together far less than lemon and thyme but when they are, they often turn up with gamy poultry such as guinea fowl or turkey. The flavours of thyme and orange also occur naturally in orange balsam thyme, which can be hard to find but has a perfumed, musky orange-peel flavour that's popular in West Indian cookery and used to be a standard seasoning for beef. I refer readers who *do* have orange thyme, a 45kg turtle, some truffles and, I imagine, a pot the size of a lifeboat, to a gargantuan footnote in Daniel Defoe's *Robinson Crusoe*, which will enlighten you on how to cook them together.

Thyme & Pork: Weatherproof, thankfully. On a trip to the Dordogne it rained all morning, most of the afternoon and torrentially for a large part of the night. When it did let up, it was only for the clouds to accumulate fat raindrops of laughter to weep the moment anyone tiptoed towards the barbecue. Optimistically I had planned to cook garlicky pork sausages and thyme-fried onions to stuff into French bread smeared with Dijon mustard. Royally rained off, I put Plan B into action. Swaddled in layers of shapeless walking clothes, I braved the cold, dank kitchen, attached the gas to the cooker and went through a box and a half of soggy matches trying to light the blasted thing. Once I had, I found a cast-iron pot, cleared it of spiders, and put in oil, the sausages, some roughly sliced onions and a jar of sinister-looking beans. From the overgrown garden I plucked a sprig of thyme, vivid green from its soaking, and threw it in the pot with salt, pepper and a long slug of wine. Putting it in the oven, with a prayer to the presiding spirit of butane, I went to sit by the fire that my husband had made from a stack of tatty paperbacks about idealistic English people making an ultimately rewarding hash of moving to France or Tuscany, called things like *Stumbling on Artichokes* or *Nothing Toulouse*. I peeled off a few layers of GoreTex and fleece. Gradually the smell of pork, thyme and garlic displaced the fungal reek of long-empty holiday home. Beans have an amplifying effect on the aroma and flavours of food. It started to feel just a little homely. Of course you'd be completely glorifying my dish to call it a cassoulet, but then you'd be glorifying my five days in France to call it a holiday.

Thyme & Shellfish: Thyme can be a little boisterous for delicate shellfish, which is more at ease in the company of basil or tarragon. In robust shellfish stews (or Manhattan and New England chowders), however, it furnishes a deliciously spicy, minty-herbal background note. This simple dish will give you a taster. Soften ½ chopped onion in olive oil, then add a tin of drained, rinsed cannellini beans and a stem of fresh thyme. Season and leave to simmer very gently while you fry some prawns in butter and garlic. Remove the herb from the beans and serve them in a neat heap with the prawns on top.

Thyme & Tomato: Thyme with tomato is a sort of tomato-and-oregano-lite. Thyme's flavour comes from a phenolic compound called thymol, which tastes like a softer, friendlier version of carvacrol, the main flavour compound in oregano. Oregano's secondary flavour compound is thymol, thyme's carvacrol, so they have a lot in common. Clearly they can be paired with similar flavours – lamb, goat's cheese and garlic, although oregano turns up less frequently in sweet dishes (that said, chef Claude Bosi serves a chilled soup of Jaffa orange and yogurt with oregano ice cream). And it's said that American servicemen, returning home after the Second World War with a taste for pizza made with oregano, created a market for the cultivated herb – until the mid-twentieth century it was grown on only a small scale in the US.

Thyme & White Fish: *See White Fish & Thyme, page 149*

Mint

Mint is moody. Turns black when you chop it with a knife. In the UK, spearmint is paired with summer produce such as new potatoes, soft fruits, baby carrots and peas, and if you're not careful their delicate flavours can be overwhelmed by its sweet melancholy. Mint really cheers up when it's partnered with strong flavours, as in a richly beefy Vietnamese *pho*, or chargrilled lamb kebabs, feta cheese or dark chocolate. In the Middle East peppermint is sometimes combined with lemon verbena to make a soothing tea. The different flavour of peppermint is attributable in part to its cooling menthol content. Peppermint is grown predominantly for its essential oil, used in confectionery, ice cream, dental products and the mint-flavoured liqueur, crème de menthe.

Mint & Anise: *See Anise & Mint, page 183*
Mint & Asparagus: *See Asparagus & Mint, page 130*
Mint & Avocado: *See Avocado & Mint, page 200*
Mint & Basil: *See Basil & Mint, page 215*

Mint & Beef: A journalist for *Le Parisien* recently wrote that, as a nation who served boiled beef with mint, the British had no right to comment on anything to do with agricultural policy. On the coach trip of international cuisine, we Brits, so the journalist implied, were the hapless child whose mother had packed him egg sandwiches, while the rest of Europe gagged into their satchels. Leaving aside that we eat our mint with roast lamb, not boiled beef, he might have noted that the Vietnamese eat mint with beef, in their fragrant soups, salads and spring rolls; and that during their Festival of the Holy Spirit, the Portuguese share a communal meal of slowly simmered, spicy beef broth, poured over a thick slice of bread, a chunk of beef, and cabbage garnished with a sprig of mint.

Mint & Blackcurrant: Deep, dark and herbal, this combination has a whiff of one of those cough medicines you actually quite like. Combine them for a blackcurrant and mint turnover. Place a heaped tablespoon of blackcurrant jam and some torn mint leaves on a 10cm square of puff pastry. Moisten the edges with milk, fold the pastry in half on the diagonal and press the edges together to seal. Make a couple of small slits in the top with a knife, then brush with milk and sprinkle with sugar if you fancy that. Bake at 220°C/Gas Mark 7 for 12–15 minutes. Don't be tempted to add more jam; it will only escape from the pastry and burn.

Mint & Black Pudding: *See Black Pudding & Mint, page 39*
Mint & Chilli: *See Chilli & Mint, page 209*

Mint & Chocolate: Hell is a milk-chocolate mint crisp. The kind whose flecks of mouthwash-flavoured grit the manufacturers hope we'll be too drunk, after dinner, to spit back into the foil. Fudgy, saccharine milk chocolate meets sinus-widening menthol: I've had more appetising things collect in my dishwasher filter. Mint with bitter dark chocolate, on the other hand, you can feed me till my teeth ache. It was around Christmas 1978 that I realised the potency of the After Eight mint as a symbol of infinity. First, it was *always* after eight, if you thought about it. Second, there was the subtle, if not occult, clue embedded in the name: After 8 ... After ∞. What came after ∞? Nothing. *Exactly.* Then there was the wafer-thin mint itself. First the delicate snap of dark chocolate, bitter as plum skin. Then soft fondant so sweet your ears start straining back, until the peppermint invades your nasal passages like an inhalation, not so much refreshing your palate as dry-cleaning it, and leaving you fidgety for your next hit of chocolate before you've tongued the last trace of fondant from the roof of your mouth. All seemed powerful arguments for *never stopping eating*. And the packaging smells so good. The crisp foil of a Bendicks chocolate mint isn't a patch on the After Eight's musky black envelope. I could imagine tearing them open, like those fold-out samples you get in magazines, and smearing a hint of Rowntree's No. 8 behind each ear.

Mint & Cinnamon: *See Cinnamon & Mint, page 218*

Mint & Coriander Leaf: Coriander can be slightly soapy, which in combination with max-fresh mint might savour more of the bathroom than the kitchen. Counter this by adding them to a pounded mixture of shallots and chilli to make a garden-bright sambal. Loosen the mixture with lime juice or coconut milk. A sambal is essentially a relish, popular in Southeast Asia, and so is used to accompany rice or noodle dishes, simply cooked fish or meat, or spread into sandwiches. In some sambals the ingredients are pounded into a paste; others might have grated fruit or vegetables added, especially pineapple, carrot or cucumber.

Mint & Cucumber: *See Cucumber & Mint, page 187*
Mint & Cumin: *See Cumin & Mint, page 84*
Mint & Dill: *See Dill & Mint, page 190*
Mint & Fig: *See Fig & Mint, page 341*

Mint & Garlic: Mortal enemies in the breath wars. French chefs keep them apart, whereas their Turkish counterparts stir dried mint and garlic into thick, salted yogurt to serve with roast vegetables. Mint and garlic also feature in this unusual red lentil dhal from Madhur Jaffrey. Cook 2 crushed garlic cloves in 2 tbsp vegetable oil or ghee with ¾ tsp cayenne pepper. When the garlic starts to sizzle, add 185g red lentils, ½ tsp turmeric and 750ml water. Stir, bring to the boil, then simmer until the lentils are tender. Add 3–4 tbsp chopped mint, 3–4 sliced green chillies and 1 tsp salt. Simmer gently while you fry 2 more sliced garlic cloves in 2 tsp vegetable oil until golden. Add these to the lentils, stir and cook, covered, for a minute or two more. See also Globe Artichoke & Mint, page 128.

Mint & Ginger: *See Ginger & Mint, page 311*
Mint & Globe Artichoke: *See Globe Artichoke & Mint, page 128*
Mint & Goat's Cheese: *See Goat's Cheese & Mint, page 57*
Mint & Lamb: *See Lamb & Mint, page 51*

Mint & Lemon: Lacking peppermint's menthol wintriness, spearmint is the warmer, sweeter variant, and will seem even more so in contrast to bitter or sour flavours. Try some in homemade lemonade. Pare the zest off in long strips from at least 2 of 4 lemons, avoiding as much of the white pith as possible. Add to a pan with 200g sugar and 200ml water and bring to a simmer, stirring until the sugar melts. Remove from the heat and give the lemon zest a bit of a bash to release its oils. Juice the 4 lemons into a pitcher. When the sugar syrup has completely cooled, strain, then mix it with the lemon juice. Add water (sparkling or still) to taste. Add sprigs of mint and allow to infuse a little before serving.

Mint & Lime: *See Lime & Mint, page 302*

Mint & Mango: Combine in a fruity raita to serve with a chickpea curry, in a couscous, or with crab in a shredded Vietnamese-style salad. But as a match for mango, mint can't hold a candle to lime – unless, of course, you're in an Indian restaurant with a stack of hot poppadoms and a carousel of pickles. A shard of poppadom with a blob of mango chutney and minty raita is, in this rare case, far superior to the mango chutney/lime pickle combination.

Mint & Melon: *See Melon & Mint, page 280*
Mint & Mushroom: *See Mushroom & Mint, page 78*
Mint & Oily Fish: *See Oily Fish & Mint, page 158*
Mint & Onion: *See Onion & Mint, page 109*

Mint & Orange: How can people possibly enjoy this combination? Have they never drunk orange juice after cleaning their teeth?

Mint & Parsley: *See Parsley & Mint, page 192*

Mint & Pea: Pea with mint tastes like England in June. The pea's flavour is as bright and simple as sunshine, which mint overcasts with its own damp, gloomy take on summer.

Mint & Peanut: Mint jelly, or torn-up mint leaves, is sometimes paired with peanut butter in sandwiches. Try it before you decry it. If you're familiar with the chopped mint and roasted peanut garnish served with many Vietnamese dishes, you'll be able to imagine how successful this can be. The Kiwi chef Peter Gordon combines them in a lime-marinated cucumber salad, which, thoroughly drained, might be exceptionally good with peanut butter in a French-bread sandwich, *bánh-mì* style. See Cucumber & Carrot, page 186, for more on these wonderful Vietnamese snacks.

Mint & Potato: Might turn up in a ravioli in Rome. Mint-flavour potato snacks are popular in India, too, and are sweet and mellow in comparison to many flavours of British crisp. Closer to home, Irish chef Darina Allen adds chopped mint to a potato soup before blending it and garnishing with cream and more mint. But new potatoes simmered with mint and tossed in butter are hard to beat, as noted by George Orwell in his essay *In Defence of English Cooking*, in which he proclaims their superiority to the fried potato dishes traditional in most other countries.

Mint & Raspberry: *See Raspberry & Mint, page 338*
Mint & Strawberry: *See Strawberry & Mint, page 263*

Mint & Watermelon: For a gorgeous variation on the mojito, make a mint syrup by dissolving 200g sugar in 250ml water over a low heat. Add roughly 20 torn mint leaves (you need to tear them to release their oil) and leave to steep until the syrup has a pleasing mintiness, then strain and chill. Liquidise some watermelon flesh, sieve it and pour into a highball glass with a few tablespoons of the syrup, a slug of white rum and some ice.

Blackcurrant

An evocative combination of fruity, herbal and musky flavours, with a sour taste. Blackcurrants have a distinct hedgerow aroma – the gorgeous, heady fragrance of country lanes on late-summer evenings. To make them properly palatable, sugar or honey must be added in increments in order to reach the optimal sweet spot. Like all dark berries, blackcurrant loves apple, but to see what an exciting flavour it can be, it has to be tried with other bold flavours, such as juniper, peanut and coffee.

Blackcurrant & Almond: Sarah Raven gives a recipe for blackcurrant and almond cake that's as good for pudding as for afternoon tea. If the volume of blackcurrants seems conservative, that's because their flavour is so intense – it would be counterproductive to use more. The nuts are given a boost by almond extract, which gives the cake a marzipan-like flavour. Cream 200g butter with the same amount of caster sugar. When the mixture has gone pale, add 3 eggs, one at a time, beating in well. Fold in 200g ground almonds and 1 tsp almond extract. Put the mixture in a greased and lined 25cm loose-bottomed tin and scatter over 200g blackcurrants. Cook for 30 minutes at 180°C/Gas Mark 4 until golden and firm to the touch. Sift some icing sugar over before serving with cream, crème fraîche or Greek yogurt.

Blackcurrant & Anise: In the days before the drinks industry thought of sugaring hard booze with cordial and flogging it to teenagers, we had to do the work ourselves. We added lime to lager, orange to gin, lemonade to port and blackcurrant to absolutely everything: lager and black, cider and black, Guinness and black, bitter and black. (We would have added it to white wine, as we'd heard the French did, in *kir*, and to red in the less famous *communard*, or *cardinale* – which is not so offputting an idea when you think of the black-currant notes in Cabernet Sauvignon and Pinot Noir. But wine wasn't sold much in pubs back then.) If you wanted blackcurrant in something daintier than beer, you'd order a Pernod and black, which tasted like those black-currant sweets you sucked until the fruity coating cracked and – a little disturbingly, as in a dream of broken teeth – gave access to the soft, slightly salty liquorice centre. I relive this combination by pairing a tangy black-currant sorbet with pastis ice cream. For the pastis ice cream, combine 250ml double cream, 250ml milk, 4 egg yolks and 150g caster sugar in a heavy-bottomed saucepan. Cook over a low heat, stirring constantly, until the custard is thicker than cream. Strain the custard immediately into a bowl and stir for a minute or so. When cool, chill in the fridge until good and cold. Add 3 tbsp Pernod or Ricard and freeze according to your usual method. For the blackcurrant sorbet, put 325ml water and 200g caster sugar in a pan and heat gently, stirring now and then, until the sugar has dissolved. Add 450g black-currants and cook gently, covered, for about 5 minutes. Remove from the heat, cool and pass through a fine sieve. Chill, then freeze in the usual way.

Blackcurrant & Chocolate: *See Chocolate & Blackcurrant, page 14*
Blackcurrant & Coffee: *See Coffee & Blackcurrant, page 19*

Blackcurrant & Juniper: Blackcurrant and juniper are both powerfully flavoured northern European berries, typically paired to make a sauce for dark game meats. They also make a good flavoured jelly to serve with dark meat and mature hard cheese. Or you can infuse gin with blackcurrants and sugar for a potent liqueur. On a softer note, Lindt makes a milk chocolate bar filled with chocolate mousse and a blackcurrant and juniper jelly.

Blackcurrant & Mint: *See Mint & Blackcurrant, page 329*

Blackcurrant & Peanut: I was expecting a degree of culture shock when I went to live in America, but what really caught me off-guard were the peanut butter and jelly sandwiches – not *per se*, but because they were made with grape and sometimes even strawberry jam. Who were they kidding, not using black-currant? And who was I, a Limey, to complain? Smuckers, manufacturers of America's market-leading Jif peanut butter, claims the PB&J dates from the Second World War, when GIs were supplied with both products in their rations. In the absence of actual butter, you can see why the peanut variety caught on. After the war, the popularity of the sandwich skyrocketed but, without wanting to turn my nose up at something almost as American as apple pie, I couldn't see how sweet strawberry or grape could have been thought a better partner for fatty, salty peanut butter than the sharp and complex blackcurrant. I didn't know that blackcurrants were, in fact, rarely eaten in the States. At the turn of the twentieth century it was discovered that the blackcurrant plant, *Ribes negrum*, was a vector for a disease that affected the white pine tree, which was vital to the booming construction industry. Growing blackcurrants became a crime under federal law, and although enforcement of the ban has since been shifted to state jurisdiction, only a few states have lifted it. So the flavour is much less familiar to the US than the European palate. Where our purple sweets are almost always blackcurrant flavour, American purple candies are grape – specifically Concord grape, derived from a species native to North America. Although blackcurrant and Concord grape are easily distinguishable as flavours, both share a 'catty' quality in common with Sauvignon Blanc, gooseberries and green tea.

Blackcurrant & Soft Cheese: *See Soft Cheese & Blackcurrant, page 71*

Blackberry

Shop-bought or cultivated blackberries, tall as beehive hairdos, bright as spit-and-polished toecaps, may sometimes be pleasantly sweet but they never, ever have the countervailing intensity of sharpness, mustiness and deep spice that comes of growing in the wild. There are hundreds of different strains of wild blackberry, and a berry picked in one spot may taste quite different from another a few feet away. Look for notes of rose, mint, cedar and clove beyond the generic berry flavours. Some even have a shimmer of tropical fruit. Come August, when there should be plenty to choose from, treat the hedgerows like free-sample ladies, and once you've found a juicy, full-flavoured strain, denude the bush until your ice-cream carton is full. Black, shiny fruit won't be as sweet as those that have reached the matt blue-black of full ripeness, but then again, they're less likely, having retained their bulbous resistance, to dissolve in your grasp like a teenager's handshake. Although blackberries can add a fruity, spicy flavour to sweet vanilla cakes or sauces for game, they have an overriding affinity for apple – so much so they could almost be monogamous.

Blackberry & Almond: *See Almond & Blackberry, page 242*
Blackberry & Apple: *See Apple & Blackberry, page 269*

Blackberry & Beef: Blackberry sauce is often served with duck and venison but can be used on beef and other meats too. Aside from providing a pleasing tartness, the herbaceous, slightly spicy flavour of blackberry complements the meat's natural sweetness.

Blackberry & Goat's Cheese: *See Goat's Cheese & Blackberry, page 55*
Blackberry & Peach: *See Peach & Blackberry, page 283*

Blackberry & Raspberry: From the same genus, blackberry and raspberry share some flavour characteristics, but differ most clearly in blackberry's muskiness and tendency towards delicious cedarwood notes. To confuse matters, there are such things as black raspberries and red blackberries. A sure-fire way of telling one species from the other is whether or not the core of the fruit stays inside the berry when picked – raspberries come away clean, leaving that characteristic cavity, which I used to love peering into as a child; blackberries retain their woody flower base. Then there are the many raspberry-blackberry crosses. Loganberry, the oldest, is thought to have been an accident. In California in the late 1880s, the lawyer and horticulturist James Harvey Logan, attempting to cross two American varieties of blackberry, accidentally planted them next to an old European raspberry cultivar and the two species got friendly. Like many unplanned offspring, loganberry has had its identity crises, and is given to sourness. But it's more suited to cooking than the raspberry. Further hybrids include the tayberry, tummelberry and boysenberry, which, even more conflicted about its parentage, contains unmistakable strawberry notes.

Blackberry & Vanilla: *See Vanilla & Blackberry, page 348*

Blackberry & White Chocolate: Put a small bar of white chocolate in your pocket the next time you go blackberrying on a sunny, late-summer afternoon. When your carrier bag has begun to leak crimson juice, find a warm tussock and carefully unwrap the chocolate, which should have melted by then. Select a handful of your best berries, check them for bugs and dip them in the chocolate, safe in the knowledge that even if you were to eat the whole bag you could always pick some more.

FLORAL FRUITY

Raspberry

Fig

Rose

Blueberry

Coriander Seed

Vanilla

White Chocolate

Raspberry

Raspberries have a sweet-sour taste and a fruity, floral (especially violet), leafy flavour; their seeds contribute a warm, woody note. When ripe, they have an intense, perfumed quality and a sweetness that hints at raspberry jam. The ubiquity of raspberry flavour can blind one to its loveliness, but there are few more delightful starts to the day than a spread of good raspberry jam on buttered toast. Raspberry flavour mixes harmoniously with other sweet-sour fruits such as apricot, blackberry and pineapple, as well as some of the lighter herbal flavours. Like strawberries, raspberries have some inherent dairy notes, which make them especially delicious with cream, yogurt and soft cheeses.

Raspberry & Almond: Raspberry really benefits from a partnership with the soft, sweet flavour of almond. The nut planes down the fruit's sharper corners but never gets in the way of its sublime flavour. Try them together in an almond panna cotta with raspberry sauce or in a Bakewell tart with a good depth of jam, made as follows. Line a 20cm tart tin with sweet pastry and spread about 3 tbsp jam over the base. Cream together 100g butter and 125g caster sugar, then gradually mix in 3 beaten eggs. Add 1 tsp almond extract and 150g ground almonds. Carefully spread this mixture over the jam and bake for about 35 minutes at 200°C/Gas Mark 6, sprinkling 1 tbsp flaked almonds over the top of the tart 15 minutes before the cooking time is up. If you're using bought jam, Wilkin & Son's Tiptree Raspberry (especially the Tiny Tip variety, which contains more fruit than Sweet Tip) captures the fruit's flavour in a way that'll make you weak at the knees. Tiptree also makes a seedless jam, which is good news if you prefer not to spend all day digging out your molars with a fingernail, but it lacks the woody contribution that the seed makes to the overall flavour, which partners so nicely with the almond.

Raspberry & Apricot: Both members of the extended *Rosaceae* family, these two are renowned for their finely perfumed flavours that teeter between sweet and sour. Apricot is a drupe fruit – i.e. it's fleshy, with a seed-containing stone inside. A raspberry is an aggregation of drupelets, each tiny sphere an individual fruit containing its own dinky stone. If you can get your hands on raspberries and apricots in season, at their peak of perfumed sweetness, I can recommend nothing better than to arrange them in a bowl together and serve them at room temperature. Mediocre fruit can be redeemed by baking it, throwing the raspberries in five minutes before the apricots are cooked. Or you could make this very pretty rustic tart. Roll out some bought puff pastry to about 5mm thick, cut out a 23cm round and place on a baking sheet lined with baking parchment. Scatter 1cm-thick slices of apricot over the pastry, leaving a 1cm margin around the edge, then dot raspberries over and sprinkle with a tablespoon or two of caster sugar. Bake at 200°C/Gas Mark 6 for about 25 minutes, until the pastry is browned. Remove and glaze with some sieved warmed apricot jam. Cool slightly and serve with a little cream or vanilla ice cream.

Raspberry & Basil: Sophie Grigson recommends the partnership of basil and raspberry. She pairs them in an ice cream or suggests that you macerate some torn-up leaves with raspberries, sugar and either a shot of gin or a small squeeze of lemon or lime juice.

Raspberry & Blackberry: *See Blackberry & Raspberry, page 335*
Raspberry & Chocolate: *See Chocolate & Raspberry, page 17*
Raspberry & Coconut: *See Coconut & Raspberry, page 288*

Raspberry & Fig: Raspberry and fig is a harmonious combination, and 'berry jam' is one of the common flavour descriptors for good figs (notably the famed Violette de Bordeaux cultivar), as is honey, after which many figs are named: Autumn Honey, Italian Honey and the slightly less evocative Peter's Honey. The Zuni Café's Judy Rodgers writes that her favourite dessert is figs dipped in buttermilk, then flour, deep-fried in groundnut oil and served with whipped cream, raspberries and lavender honey.

Raspberry & Goat's Cheese: *See Goat's Cheese & Raspberry, page 58*

Raspberry & Hazelnut: Walking the Dolomites in September, you'll be able to pick enough of both to make a hazelnut cake and the raspberry filling to go in it. Austrian Linzertorte, one of the oldest cake recipes recorded (in 1696), combines hazelnut (or sometimes almond) pastry with a thick filling of jam (often raspberry, but apricot and plum are used too) and a lederhosen criss-cross of pastry on top.

Raspberry & Mint: Michel Roux recommends serving berries with a mint-flavoured *crème anglaise* (otherwise known as custard). Raspberry and mint will also make a fine dressing, especially on a goat's cheese salad – use a tablespoon each of raspberry vinegar and freshly squeezed lemon juice to 4 tbsp extra virgin olive oil. Shake with salt, pepper and 1 tbsp chopped mint until well mixed.

Raspberry & Peach: The great French chef Auguste Escoffier created the Peach Melba for Dame Nellie Melba, the Australian opera singer. Apparently the idea came to him as he was writing out the recipe for *pêches cardinal au coulis de framboise*, which the great diva had requested. Peach Melba is virtually the same thing – peaches with a raspberry sauce and a scattering of fresh almonds, if they're in season – but with added vanilla ice cream. See also Peach & Vanilla, page 285.

Raspberry & Pineapple: Barratt's Fruit Salads, one of the greatest achievements in the field of penny sweets, combine the flavours of raspberry and pineapple. James Beard wrote about the two fruits' remarkable affinity for each other. As an American born in 1903, he's unlikely ever to have tried a Fruit Salad but he may well have drunk a 'Queen's Favorite' soda – a mixture of pineapple, raspberry and vanilla. The combination also lies at the heart of a French martini, which is made with Chambord, a liqueur containing black raspberries, herbs and honey. Put 40ml vodka, 20ml Chambord and 30ml pineapple juice in a cocktail shaker with ice, shake, then strain into a cold martini glass.

Raspberry & Strawberry: *See Strawberry & Raspberry, page 264*
Raspberry & Vanilla: *See Vanilla & Raspberry, page 349*

Raspberry & White Chocolate: Naturally sour raspberries are a great match for the sweet dairy flavour of white chocolate. The Ivy's Scandinavian Iced Berries with Hot White Chocolate Sauce pairs small berries, not long out of the freezer, with a warm sauce of white chocolate melted with double cream. The contrasts in taste and temperature are delightful and, its sweetness moderated by the cream, the white chocolate serves to emphasise the berries' sharpness and perfumed flavour rather than, as is so often the case with this pairing, swamping them.

Fig

Fresh figs are sweet, with a light berry flavour overshadowed by the heady perfume that develops when they are properly ripe. They're very difficult to transport at this stage, so for optimal flavour you need either to live near a reliable source or to grow them yourself. Dried figs take on a much more forceful personality, with a bumped-up sweet-sour balance akin to dried apricots. Some dried figs have a sugary, fermented character, sumptuous as fortified wine; others are nuttier. I find thicker-skinned, brown dried figs can have a medicinal quality. Both fresh and dried figs are very compatible with sweet spices and with fatty, salty ingredients like blue cheese and prosciutto.

Fig & Almond: Although wasps are too impatient to wait for it, the honey-like drop of nectar at the eye of a fig indicates that it's ripe and ready to eat. It might also serve as a reminder that the honey flavour of figs is a match for almonds; they make for a light, nougat-like combination. If you can't get fresh figs, or the wasps have ruined them all, buy some dried and make the justly famous Spanish *pan de higo*, a sort of dense cake in which figs are ground with spices, seeds and almonds. It's served in slices with Manchego cheese.

Fig & Anise: Anise seeds go off like tiny liquorice fireworks when paired with sweet, sticky ingredients such as dried figs. Roughly chop 4 or 5 dark dried figs and mix into a tub of cream cheese with a teaspoon of crushed anise seeds and a pinch of salt. Serve on the dark, fibrous crackers you get in health-food stores.

Fig & Blue Cheese: *See Blue Cheese & Fig, page 62*

Fig & Chocolate: Some fans of dried figs claim they taste like chocolate. Which sounds a bit like wishful thinking to me. While the best dried figs do enjoy a tantalising and impressive range of sweet flavours – black treacle, maple syrup, any number of honeys, maybe a little salted caramel – they're not really the sort of flavours you find in chocolate. The only notes I can perceive in common are the sharp, red-berry flavours identifiable in ripe figs and some cocoa-rich dark chocolate. In the sweet 'salami' made by Seggiano in Calabria, chocolate is combined with almonds, apple, pear and lots of dried *dottato* figs, known for their glorious flavour and lack of graininess. If you can get your hands on some, eat it as you might real salami, between slices of white bread. Elsewhere in Calabria, Italian confectioners Nicola Colavolpe make a fig and chocolate panettone with a sugared hazelnut crust; back home, a trip to a good Italian deli should furnish a wooden box of figs, stuffed with walnut, orange and lime zest and covered in dark chocolate. Spain's contribution is *rabitos royale*, tiny, chocolate-covered figs filled with brandy and chocolate ganache, while in Seattle a company called The Greek Gods makes a fig and chocolate ice cream.

Fig & Cinnamon: *See Cinnamon & Fig, page 217*

Fig & Goat's Cheese: Split ripe, vinous figs and fill each one with a teaspoon of goat's cheese. Press them back together and bake at 180°C/Gas Mark 4 for 10–15 minutes. Eat with your fingers when just cool enough. Some like to wrap a little prosciutto around the fig. Chef Eric Ripert's take on this trio is a goat's cheese parfait and bacon ice cream, served with roasted fig and hazelnut in a red wine caramel.

Fig & Hard Cheese: *See Hard Cheese & Fig, page 67*
Fig & Hazelnut: *See Hazelnut & Fig, page 239*

Fig & Liver: The ancient Roman precursor to foie gras was called *iecur ficatum*, from *iecur*, meaning liver, and *ficatum*, derived from *ficus*, referring to the figs with which the birds were fed. Many modern European languages have thus erroneously taken *ficatum* as the root of their words for liver – *fegato* in Italian, *higado* in Spanish, *fígado* in Portuguese. (The English word is derived from the West Saxon, *libban*, meaning to live, denoting the serious-ness with which hard-drinking northern Europeans take the organ.) These days, foie gras geese are fed with a corn and fat preparation and the figs turn up only at the end, in the form of an accompanying compote or chutney.

Fig & Mint: Giorgio Locatelli recommends serving figs with a little mint sorbet and some chopped mint. If you're in Greece or Turkey in late summer, when you tire of plucking warm, ripe figs off the tree and slurping them down like sweet oysters, serve them sliced with your best balsamic and a little fresh mint, or combine them in a salad with feta or grilled halloumi.

Fig & Orange: The pomologist Edward Bunyard described dried figs as pungent and cloying, dismissing them as fit only 'for youthful palates'. There's no denying they are phenomenally sugary but, in their defence, they have a complexity that ensures the sweetness is never monotonous. Orange is often paired with fig, as the acidity of one tempers the sweetness of the other, and they're seasonal partners too. Before Christmas, I make these fig and orange bars to serve with mulled wine. Simmer 250g chopped dried figs in orange juice with the zest of 1 orange for about 20 minutes, until soft. Stir in 1 tbsp butter, turn off the heat and set aside. In a food processor pulse together 75g self-raising flour, 75g sugar, ¼ tsp bicarbonate of soda and a pinch of salt. Add 100g cold butter, cut into 1cm cubes, and pulse until the mixture has a breadcrumb texture. Stir in 100g rolled oats. Pat down half this mixture in a buttered 20cm round tin, spoon over the fig mixture (which should be chopped or given a quick whiz in the food processor first) and then spoon the other half of the dry mix on top. Bake at 190°C/Gas Mark 5 for 30 minutes, until the topping has turned light brown.

Fig & Prosciutto: *See Prosciutto & Fig, page 172*
Fig & Raspberry: *See Raspberry & Fig, page 338*
Fig & Soft Cheese: *See Soft Cheese & Fig, page 72*

Fig & Vanilla: *Tempus fugit.* One day we'll all have dentures and, for all its boozy, floral perfume, this seed-riddled twosome will seem as attractive as a poke in the eye with a breadstick. Enjoy them while you can, in fig and vanilla jam, ice cream or crumbly *ma'mool* – make the recipe in Rosemary & Apricot, page 317, using vanilla instead of rosewater in the dough and a fig fruit filling without the rosemary.

Fig & Walnut: Dried figs and walnuts are combined in any number of biscuits, but I think the idea, recounted by Jane Grigson, of opening up a fresh fig, putting a whole shelled walnut inside it and pinching it back together before leaving it to dry in the sun, sounds much more romantic. In Provence they call this *nougat du pauvre* – poor man's nougat.

Rose

O rose, thou art sickly. So much sugar is needed to balance its natural astringency that the addition of rose can often result in a cloying sweetness. And its floral muskiness, unless you're careful, can recall nothing so much as being pressed to your auntie's perfumed cleavage. Rose needs balancing with bitter ingredients, such as chocolate, coffee and citrus zest, or bitter-edged spices like clove. Alternatively, use rosewater in very modest amounts for an unfathomable background note, like you might vanilla. Most rose is used in the form of rosewater, but dried rose petals and rose jam can be bought in Middle Eastern supermarkets. Crystallised rose petals, which are used mainly for cake decorations, are sold in posh delis. Fresh rose petals from your garden can be used as an ingredient if they have not been sprayed with unappetising chemicals; a list of suitable species is given in *The Oxford Companion to Food*, edited by Alan Davidson.

Rose & Almond: *See Almond & Rose, page 244*

Rose & Apple: A few drops of rosewater give apple juice an exotic edge. Add two fingers of vanilla vodka to make what shall henceforth be known as a Scheherazade.

Rose & Apricot: *See Apricot & Rose, page 283*

Rose & Cardamom: Indian *gulab jamun* competes with other syrup-soaked lovelies such as baklava, *loukades* and the rum baba for the title of sweetest dessert in the world. It consists of deep-fried balls of a dough made primarily with milk and shaped to the size of a fruit called the *jamun*. They're typically flavoured with cardamom: either a few seeds are placed at their centre or the dough has the ground spice mixed into it. Gulab means rose, which is the flavour of the syrup in which the balls are steeped. There's a recipe for my ginger syrup version in Ginger & Cardamom, page 309.

Rose & Chicken: *See Chicken & Rose, page 30*

Rose & Chocolate: The bitterness of dark chocolate is a better match than milk for sweet rose flavour, even if my lifelong love of Fry's Turkish Delight suggests otherwise. How exotic it was to bite through thick, creamy milk chocolate and sink my teeth into rose-flavoured jelly. 'Full of Eastern Promise' might have been stretching it a bit, especially as the bar was made in a suburb of Bristol, but I didn't care. On TV, a dark-haired beauty wearing too much eye make-up had only to bite into the bar to be swept on to a white Arab stallion by a chisel-jawed sheikh. I'm still partial, although just as likely these days to indulge my love of this combination by making rose ice cream with milk chocolate pieces. In a heavy-bottomed pan, gently heat 250ml double cream and 250ml milk with 4 egg yolks and 150g sugar. Stir until the mixture has thickened, then strain into a bowl and stir for a minute or two longer. Cool, chill and stir in 2 tsp rosewater. Check the strength, adding a few drops until you have the right level of rosiness, bearing in mind that the freezing process will knock it back somewhat. Freeze in an ice-cream machine, adding a handful of chocolate chips after the custard has been churned but when it is still soft, before it goes into the freezer.

Rose & Coffee: *See Coffee & Rose, page 21*
Rose & Cucumber: *See Cucumber & Rose, page 187*

Rose & Lemon: Nestle side by side in boxes of Turkish delight, so thoroughly dusted with white cornflour and sugar that you have to hold them up to the light to know which flavour is which. To the palate, they seem to come from very different places on the flavour spectrum, although they both contain the essential oils geraniol, nerol and citronellol. Try to imagine lemon without the citric wince and you can detect its delicately perfumed, floral notes. Rose and lemon are also paired in a Persian dish called *faludeh*, one of the earliest recorded frozen desserts, dating from at least 400 BC. Ice would be brought down from the mountains and added to very fine noodles, usually flavoured with rose syrup and lemon juice.

Rose & Melon: *See Melon & Rose, page 280*
Rose & Orange: *See Orange & Rose, page 297*

Rose & Saffron: Mashti Malone's is a legendary ice-cream joint in Los Angeles, owned by a couple of Iranian brothers. Almost all their ices are made with rosewater. Quite a narrow business proposition, you might think, but in many Middle Eastern cuisines rose is as ubiquitous and versatile a flavour as vanilla. Mashti's signature ice cream pairs rose with cream chips – whole pieces of frozen cream – while other varieties include a magical rosewater saffron with pistachio. Create a similar effect by freezing 150ml double cream in a thin layer for a couple of hours, then breaking it into tiny pieces and stirring them into homemade ice cream.

Blueberry

Blueberries get on my wick. It's not entirely their fault. It's just that all this stuff about antioxidants and phytochemicals gives them an air of piety only increased by that little flared crown they have at the top that looks like the collar of a choirboy's cassock. Plus the white bloom on their skin reminds me of the leprous pallor of an old, sad Kit Kat (although it's supposed to be a sign that the berries haven't been handled too much). The flavour of blueberry is largely in its skin, so the smaller the better. If they're a little lacklustre, lure them from the path of virtue by cooking them with sugar and unlocking their aromatic potential.

Blueberry & Almond: *See Almond & Blueberry, page 242*
Blueberry & Apple: *See Apple & Blueberry, page 269*

Blueberry & Blue Cheese: Blueberries have a sharpness that makes them especially good paired with blue cheese in salads. Warren Geraghty, the chef at West in Vancouver, serves a disc of cinnamon-buttered toasted brioche under a baked blue-cheese cheesecake, topped with blueberries simmered in port, vanilla and brown sugar.

Blueberry & Cinnamon: Cooking blueberries brings out their flavour: add some cinnamon for extra improvement. Marion Cunningham suggests dipping warm blueberry muffins into melted butter, then cinnamon sugar.

Blueberry & Coriander Seed: *See Coriander Seed & Blueberry, page 345*
Blueberry & Lemon: *See Lemon & Blueberry, page 304*

Blueberry & Mushroom: Fruit and mushroom is a common and well-liked pairing in the north of Italy. Chef Marc Vetri pairs porcini and blueberries in a lasagne, and is judicious with the berries; the diner should come across a little burst of blueberry only here and there. The fruit flavour contrasts with the mushrooms' meatiness. Blueberry and mushroom risotto, usually made with beef stock, is another popular dish.

Blueberry & Peach: *See Peach & Blueberry, page 284*

Blueberry & Vanilla: Good blueberry flavour should have a floral top note and a creamy, fruity finish. Dear old vanilla, friend to all, picks up on this quality and combines with blueberry flavour in the fruit's most redemptive recipe, a blueberry and vanilla cake. Put 175g softened butter, 175g caster sugar, 3 large eggs, 225g self-raising flour, 1 tsp baking powder, 3 tbsp milk and 2 tsp vanilla extract in a bowl and beat with an electric mixer for 2–3 minutes or until well combined. Fold in 125g blueberries. Tip the mixture into a greased and lined deep, round 23cm cake tin and bake at 180°C/Gas Mark 4 for 45 minutes or until well risen and golden brown. Cool for 10 minutes, then remove from the tin and leave to cool completely. Beat 200g cream cheese with 100g icing sugar and 5 tbsp soured cream. Spread this over the cake and scatter 125g blueberries on top.

Coriander Seed

Coriander seeds have a delicious citrus and balsamic character, not unlike a nice version of those scented wooden balls some people keep in their underwear drawers. They lend a startlingly pretty flavour used as the sole aromatic in sweet biscuits or to offset the bitterness of wine when you mull it – after all, their flavour recalls the classic mulling combination of orange, cinnamon and clove. Coriander seeds bring a fragrant, feminine touch to curry powder blends and pastes and to mixed pickling spices. They're also one of the key botanicals in gin. A spare peppermill filled with roasted coriander seeds could easily get you hooked.

Coriander Seed & Apple: When the floral perfume of coriander seeds is mixed with sharp, fruity apple, the result is quite apricot-like and especially delightful. Try them paired in an ice cream. Peel, core and chop 500g sharp apples (e.g. Granny Smiths) and put them in a pan with 2 tbsp lemon juice and 75g sugar. Cook gently, covered, until soft. Beat in 2 tsp lavender jelly and 1 tsp freshly ground, lightly toasted coriander seeds, then leave to cool. Whip 300ml whipping cream until fairly thick and fold into the apple mix. Freeze in the usual way. Use redcurrant jelly if you don't have lavender, but lavender and coriander seed have very harmonious flavours.

Coriander Seed & Blueberry: Coriander seeds can contain up to 85 per cent linalool, a flavour compound with a woody, floral, slightly citrus quality that's a key component of synthesised blueberry flavour. Freshly ground, they can lend a fragrant background note to your home-baked blueberry muffins. Or be more adventurous, like the Ottolenghi deli in London, and make a couscous salad with bell pepper, red onion, wild blueberries, pink peppercorns and coriander seed.

Coriander Seed & Cardamom: *See Cardamom & Coriander Seed, page 314*

Coriander Seed & Coffee: Morocco is both a major grower and user of coriander. The seeds are used to flavour espresso-style coffee, adding a floral (rose, lavender) and citrus quality. Try adding 1 tsp coriander seed to 6 tbsp coffee beans before grinding and take it from there.

Coriander Seed & Coriander Leaf: Concentrate hard and you can detect a hint of coriander-leaf flavour in quiet, reliable coriander seed; on the whole they're very different and about as substitutable for each other as sprigs of spearmint are for Tic Tacs.

Coriander Seed & Cumin: *See Cumin & Coriander Seed, page 83*

Coriander Seed & Garlic: Beauty and the Beast. Coriander seed is such a gentle, pretty flavour that seeing it mixed with lots of garlic, with no more than a dressing of salt and the oil they were softened in, is like catching the head girl in a tattoo parlour. Nonetheless, this seasoning mixture, called *taklia*, is popular in Egypt and Turkey. Soften 3 sliced garlic cloves in some olive oil or butter and pound in a mortar with 1 tsp coriander seeds, a few pinches of salt and (optionally) a pinch of cayenne. Use in spinach or lentil soups or to flavour cream cheese.

Coriander Seed & Goat's Cheese: Spice experts detect notable differences between the egg-shaped coriander seed of India, which is sweeter, with a creamy quality, and the spicier round seed common to Europe and Morocco. Both have the floral, citrus quality that makes coriander seed a good match for goat's cheese.

Coriander Seed & Lemon: Harold McGee describes coriander seed as lemony and floral. Others find the citric note more reminiscent of orange. Whichever you think, the seeds pair effectively with lemon. They're often used together to marinate olives and they also work very well with fish. In the nineteenth century they were frequently joined by cinnamon as a seasoning combination for almond milk or cream puddings. Mrs Lee gives a recipe for a drink called citronelle ratafia. Combine 2 litres of brandy with the rinds of a dozen lemons, 28g coriander seed, 10g bruised cinnamon and a sugar syrup made of 900g sugar dissolved in 700ml water. Leave it for a month, presumably somewhere dark, then strain and bottle.

Coriander Seed & Olive: *See Olive & Coriander Seed, page 176*
Coriander Seed & Orange: *See Orange & Coriander Seed, page 295*

Coriander Seed & Pork: Coriander seed is an unsung hero of the flavouring world. In combination with other aromatics, it's used in curries, ketchup and pickles; pork products such as frankfurters, mortadella, French sausages and boudin noir; and has a rare starring role in *afelia*, a pork stew popular in Cyprus and Greece. Making *afelia* is the perfect way to get to know this spice. Marinate 1kg cubed pork tenderloin in 250ml red wine, 2 tbsp crushed coriander seeds and some salt and pepper for 4–24 hours. Drain the meat, reserving the marinade, pat dry, then dredge the pieces in plenty of flour. Brown in olive oil, then add the marinade to the pan with enough water to cover the meat. Cover and cook for 45–60 minutes, removing the lid towards the end of cooking if the sauce needs reducing. Prepare yourself for a waft of what will smell like meat stewed in mulled wine.

Vanilla

A universally popular fragrance and flavour. Vanilla is an orchid whose seed pods are fermented and cured to produce the flavouring. It's native to Mexico but is now grown in Tahiti, Madagascar and Indonesia. Tahitian vanilla is highly prized for its fruity, spicy character, described by some as specifically redolent of cherry and anise. Madagascan vanilla is the type most of us are familiar with; Mexican is spicier, richer and earthier. The Incas used vanilla to flavour chocolate, and this was its exclusive culinary role until Hugh Morgan, Elizabeth I's apothecary, began to advocate its wider application. It's still, of course, vital to the manufacture of most chocolate, but is also the world's favourite flavour of ice cream, an increasingly popular addition to savoury dishes, and works beautifully as a background flavour in desserts and liqueurs. Pods tend to give the purest flavour but vanilla extract, powder and lovely seedy pastes are all very workable too. Natural vanilla is expensive, reflecting the labour that goes into its production, and to meet the enormous demand created by the manufacture of cakes, biscuits, ice cream, confectionery and soft and alcoholic drinks, a synthetic form is produced in far greater quantities than vanilla itself – in fact 97 per cent of vanilla flavouring consumed is synthetic. Vanillin, the main constituent of vanilla essence and extract, is the character impact compound for vanilla and was first isolated in 1858. In 1874 it became one of the first flavours to be synthesised, using material from coniferous trees. Today vanillin is extracted from clove oil, waste material from the paper and wood-pulp industry and petrochemical products. There are many who wouldn't dream of using vanilla essence, but in blind tests conducted by the American magazine *Cook's Illustrated*, the panel of cooks and baking experts was unable to detect much difference in custards and sponge cakes made with a range of extracts and essences. While the custard made with vanilla essence was judged to be marginally inferior, the experts preferred the fake stuff for cakes – largely on the grounds of its greater strength of flavour, probably attributable to a higher proportion of vanillin per millilitre than in the extract.

Vanilla & Anise: *See Anise & Vanilla, page 185*

Vanilla & Apple: It's well known that vanilla ice cream – or good vanilla-flavoured custard – goes down a treat with apple pie or crumble. But how about grinding vanilla sugar into a fine powder and shaking it over hot, crisp apple fritters? Sift 100g plain flour with a pinch of salt, make a well in the centre and drop an egg into it. Beat well and gradually add a mixture of 100ml milk and 3 tbsp iced water to make a smooth, not too runny batter. Leave in the fridge while you peel and core 3 or 4 apples and slice them into

1cm rings. Dip in the batter, making sure they're thoroughly covered, then fry in 3–4cm oil for about 1 minute on each side. Serve sprinkled with the ground vanilla sugar. Cider can be used instead of the milk.

Vanilla & Apricot: *See Apricot & Vanilla, page 283*
Vanilla & Banana: *See Banana & Vanilla, page 279*

Vanilla & Blackberry: Spend a late-summer afternoon picking blackberries. Get home while it's still light. Wash and gently stew your berries with sugar, stopping short of making them perfectly sweet. Cool, strain and, as the air turns blue, serve with vanilla ice cream. A little honeycomb crumbled over each makes a great garnish.

Vanilla & Blueberry: *See Blueberry & Vanilla, page 344*

Vanilla & Cardamom: Second and third to saffron in the spice price stakes. Luxurious paired in a *crème pâtissière* for a fruit-topped tart (see Cardamom & Apricot, page 313) or in an ice cream, where their sweet, spicy, floral flavours come together very prettily. Many chefs prefer Tahitian vanilla for this sort of recipe, as it's sweeter and fruitier than the Madagascan and Mexican varieties. It also contains less of the usually dominant flavour compound, vanillin, and more floral notes.

Vanilla & Cherry: *See Cherry & Vanilla, page 248*
Vanilla & Chestnut: *See Chestnut & Vanilla, page 234*

Vanilla & Chocolate: Both native to Mexico, where the practice of flavouring chocolate with vanilla dates back to Aztec times. Today, most bars of chocolate are flavoured with vanilla in some way. The Californian chocolatiers Scharffen Berger grind whole vanilla pods with their cocoa nibs in accordance with founder John Scharffenberger's belief that chocolate is much enhanced by vanilla. At the other end of the scale, cheap chocolate is often flavoured with an overwhelming amount of vanilla essence to compensate for its lack of cocoa flavour. If you're curious as to what chocolate tastes like *without* vanilla, try the bars made by the French chocolatier Bonnat. See also White Chocolate & Chocolate, page 352.

Vanilla & Clove: Vanilla and clove, or 'baking spice' flavours, are commonly transferred to wine courtesy of the vanillin and eugenol naturally present in the wooden casks used for ageing. French oak, with its tight grain, is said to contain these subtler flavours, whereas larger-grained American oak, especially when toasted, has more pronounced coconut and herbaceous notes – see Dill & Coconut, page 189. At the time of writing, a new 300-bottle French oak barrel costs about $700, whereas one made of American oak comes in at roughly half that. To save costs, winemakers sometimes slot new staves into older barrels whose flavour has worn out, or, even more economically, drop wood chips in nets, like giant teabags, into the vast stainless steel tanks in which many modern wines are stored. Many drinkers say the chips impart the sort of one-dimensional vanilla character found in certain sickly Chardonnays, but even high-end winemakers are resorting to, or partially incorporating, this cost-cutting measure.

Vanilla & Coconut: *See Coconut & Vanilla, page 288*

Vanilla & Coffee: Spill a fresh espresso over some good vanilla ice cream. Italians call this *affogato*, which a waggish waiter in Rome once told me comes from 'Affogato tie my shoelaces.' Accident or not, the combination works. The protein in dairy binds to the tannins in coffee, making it less bitter and easier on the palate, although it does dampen the flavour a little too.

Vanilla & Egg: *See Egg & Vanilla, page 137*
Vanilla & Fig: *See Fig & Vanilla, page 341*
Vanilla & Ginger: *See Ginger & Vanilla, page 312*
Vanilla & Hazelnut: *See Hazelnut & Vanilla, page 240*

Vanilla & Nutmeg: Elizabeth David says the flavour of fresh bay leaves is reminiscent of nutmeg and vanilla, and notes how well they work in sweet cream. These days it's not unusual to find a bay leaf panna cotta on the menus of smart restaurants. Nutmeg and vanilla come together to make a heady, almost hyper-perfumed sweetness that's particularly irresistible in homemade custard tarts. Forget frou-frou macaroons and pretty cupcakes: custard tarts are deep, honest and intoxicating.

Vanilla & Orange: Vanilla and orange meet Stateside in the form of the legendary Creamsicle, the American version of what the Brits call a Mivvi. Both consist of vanilla ice cream on a stick, clad in fruit-flavoured ice. You might like to try the more adult combination of vanilla panna cotta with chilled orange segments, or seek out a bottle of Fiori di Sicilia essence, which adds a pronounced floral, orange and vanilla character to meringues and cakes like panettone.

Vanilla & Peach: *See Peach & Vanilla, page 285*
Vanilla & Peanut: *See Peanut & Vanilla, page 25*
Vanilla & Pineapple: *See Pineapple & Vanilla, page 268*

Vanilla & Raspberry: Around the age of six, I was always badgering my mother to buy Arctic Roll. I loved the ship-in-a-bottle impossibility of a cylinder of raspberry-jam-encircled ice cream enclosed in vanilla sponge *seemingly without a seam*. How *had* Birds Eye done it? Was it a section of a single, vast Arctic Roll, the length of the trans-Ural pipeline, piped full of ice cream by forces of unimaginable scale? And how come you could defrost it without the ice cream leaking out or the sponge turning soggy? These days, I like to tell myself I've outgrown my taste for elaborate confections, in favour of very simple, *very* expensive ingredients, simply prepared – fresh raspberries, say, their violet-scented elegance enhanced by a little Chantilly cream, prepared with icing sugar and vanilla extract and nothing else. And then my husband took me to La Cuisine de Joel Robuchon in Covent Garden and I ordered Le Sucre for dessert. Le Sucre is an iridescent, semi-transparent Christmas bauble of sugar, inflated in much the same way a glass-blower breathes sphericality into brandy balloons, filled with mascarpone and raspberry mousse and steadied on the plate by a ring of pink meringue flecked with gold leaf, on a coulis of mixed berries sprinkled with pistachio dust, next to a perfect quenelle of vanilla ice cream. And I thought, sod simplicity, as I shattered the bauble with the back of my spoon. *This* is how to eat.

Vanilla & Rhubarb: *See Rhubarb & Vanilla, page 256*

Vanilla & Shellfish: A combination to be approached with great trepidation. It's undoubtedly terrific in the hands of French *nouvelle cuisine* pioneer Alain Senderens, who's credited with pairing the two in the first place. He's said to have developed his dish of lobster in vanilla *beurre blanc* to complement the fine white Burgundies in the cellar of the restaurant where he was cooking at the time; the vanilla in the sauce matched the buttery, sweet, toasted caramel imparted to the wine after ageing in oak barrels.

Vanilla & Strawberry: *See Strawberry & Vanilla, page 264*

Vanilla & Tomato: When used in moderation, Mexican vanilla, which has a spicy quality, draws out a similar spiciness in tomato-based dishes, while taking the edge off the acidity. Some recommend a touch of Mexican vanilla in a tomatoey chilli con carne, but a bolder cook might pair just the two in a soup. Claude Bosi at Hibiscus, in London, takes them in a sweet direction in a dish with fragments of frozen raspberries.

Vanilla & Walnut: *See Walnut & Vanilla, page 237*

White Chocolate

White chocolate is made with cocoa butter, milk, sugar and vanilla, and it's the variation in the quantity and quality of these four ingredients that accounts for what difference exists between the various bars you can buy. Vanilla is almost always by far the strongest flavour. A prominent chocolatier tells me that the possibilities for varying the flavour of white chocolate are so limited that no quality brand would offer more than one pure white chocolate bar in its product range. Cocoa butter has a strong taste but it's not necessarily that pleasant, and nearly all chocolate manufacturers deodorise the butter in their products, even if, like pasteurisation, the process suppresses some of the good flavours too. Lightly roasting the beans can get around the problem. That said, Venezuelan chocolate makers El Rey don't deodorise, and their bar made with 34 per cent cocoa butter is often said to be the best-tasting on the market. It's less sweet than most white chocolate, and more potently chocolatey. Green and Black's white chocolate is shot through with lots of vanilla seeds and tastes like a sweet but luxurious vanilla ice cream, with hints of strawberry and apricot brandy that recall how white chocolate can benefit from sour balancing flavours.

White Chocolate & Almond: White chocolate is so sweet because it lacks the cocoa solids that give milk and especially dark chocolate their balancing bitterness. Almonds, especially roasted, can diffuse its sweetness, as Nestlé may have had in mind when it included them in North America's first white chocolate bar, launched in the 1940s. Combine them yourself and you can both increase the nut content and use your preferred white chocolate. Roast 150g blanched almonds in the oven at 180°C/Gas Mark 4 for 8–10 minutes, until lightly browned, then set aside. Line a baking tray with baking parchment. Put 200g white chocolate in a bowl set over (but not touching) a pan of simmering water. When it's completely melted, stir in the nuts, then spread the mixture over the baking parchment. Bear in mind that you'll be breaking it into chunky pieces, so don't spread it too thin. Let it cool a little, then chill until set. In the US this is known as bark. You could throw some dried sour cherries in too, to give your bark some bite.

White Chocolate & Blackberry: *See Blackberry & White Chocolate, page 335*

White Chocolate & Cardamom: Rococo sells a white chocolate bar infused with cardamom. The combination reminds me of sweet, spicy, milky Indian desserts like *kheer* and *kulfi*, lovely and sort of suffocating at the same time.

White Chocolate & Caviar: *See Caviar & White Chocolate, page 154*

White Chocolate & Chocolate: Nearly all chocolate bars, dark, milk and white, are flavoured with some form of vanilla; cheap ones heavily so to make up for the essential lack of chocolatiness. Vanilla is white chocolate's primary flavour. Which makes me think that when a decent dark or milk chocolate is combined with white (in a dark chocolate truffle, say, with a white chocolate coating), thereby upping its vanilla content while diluting its cocoa solids, the darker chocolate is essentially being cheapened. It's like adding a blended whisky to your single malt.

White Chocolate & Coconut: Go ahead, make a coconut cake and give it an icing of thick white chocolate. But be warned, it's like being buried alive in frosting. Raspberries might be your St Bernard.

White Chocolate & Coffee: To me, the combination of coffee and the rich dairy flavour of white chocolate can be a little too redolent of fudgy *café au lait* made with UHT milk, as it sometimes is in France. UHT is cooked at a high temperature, causing a Maillard reaction in which sweet caramel characteristics, absent from fresh milk, are created. The white chocolate/coffee combination is at its best, I think, in Café Tasse's Blanc Café bar, which contains ground coffee beans that give a pronounced bitter contrast to the white chocolate.

White Chocolate & Lemon: Good white chocolate, like Pierre Marcolini or Venchi's Bianco, often has a natural lemon character. Pair white chocolate and lemon in a cake, like Rose Beranbaum's lemon-laced white chocolate cake filled with rich lemon curd and topped with a creamy white chocolate and lemon curd buttercream. She calls it Woody's Lemon Luxury Layer Cake; a mouthful in every sense.

White Chocolate & Olive: *See Olive & White Chocolate, page 177*

White Chocolate & Pineapple: White chocolate is a firm friend of red berry fruits but it also works well with tropical ones. Think how notes of pineapple and passion fruit complement vanilla in an oak-aged Chardonnay. Heady stuff, mind: you wouldn't want too much of it.

White Chocolate & Raspberry: *See Raspberry & White Chocolate, page 339*

White Chocolate & Saffron: Artisan du Chocolat makes an elegant pink-gold bar of saffron-flavoured white chocolate. It says the white chocolate brings out the hay flavour of saffron. I'd add that the honeyed vanilla flavour of white chocolate shines a light on saffron's floral complexity.

White Chocolate & Strawberry: *See Strawberry & White Chocolate, page 264*

Bibliography

Achatz, Grant. *Alinea*. Ten Speed Press, 2008. See pages 255, 318.

Acton, Eliza. *Modern Cookery for Private Families*. Longman, Brown, Green & Longmans, 1845. See page 145.

Allen, Darina. *Darina Allen's Ballymaloe Cookery Course*. Kyle Cathie, 2001. See page 332.

Allen, Gary. *The Herbalist in the Kitchen*. University of Illinois, 2007. See page 180.

Amis, Kingsley. *Everyday Drinking*. Bloomsbury, 2008. See page 324.

Ansel, David. *The Soup Peddler's Slow and Difficult Soups: Recipes and Reveries*. Ten Speed Press, 2005. See page 83.

Apicius. *Cookery and Dining in Imperial Rome*. Edited and translated by J. Dommers Vehling. Dover, 1977. See pages 114, 141.

Arndt, Alice. *Seasoning Savvy*. Haworth Herbal Press, 1999. See page 18.

Artusi, Pellegrino. *The Art of Eating Well* (1891). Translated by Kyle M. Phillips III. Random House, 1996. See pages 86, 173, 202, 253, 323.

Audot, Louis Eustache. *French Domestic Cookery*. Harper & Brothers, 1846. See page 87.

Baljekar, Mridula. *Real Fast Indian Food*. Metro, 2000. See page 41.

Bayless, Rick. *Rick Bayless's Mexican Kitchen*. Scribner, 1996. See pages 15, 56, 199, 294.

Beard, James. *Theory & Practice of Good Cooking*. Knopf, 1977. See pages 168, 339.

Beeton, Isabella. *Mrs Beeton's Book of Household Management*. S. O. Beeton, 1861. See pages 118, 312.

Beranbaum, Rose. *Rose's Heavenly Cakes*. Wiley, 2009. See page 352.

Bittman, Mark. *How to Cook Everything Vegetarian*. Wiley, 2007. See pages 68, 256, 320.

Blumenthal, Heston. *The Big Fat Duck Cookbook*. Bloomsbury, 2008. See pages 122, 154, 155, 177, 257, 263, 294.

Boswell, James. *A Journey to the Western Islands of Scotland*. J. Pope, 1775. See page 188.

Brillat-Savarin, J. A., & Simpson, L. Francis. *The Handbook of Dining*. Longman, Brown, Green, Longmans & Roberts, 1859. See pages 29, 116.

Bunyard, Edward A. *The Anatomy of Dessert*. Dulau & Co., 1929. See pages 233, 248, 341.

Burbidge, F. W. *The Gardens of the Sun*. John Murray, 1880. See page 63.

Burnett, John. *Plenty and Want: A Social History of Food in England from 1815 to the Present Day*. Nelson, 1966. See page 256.

Byrne, Aiden. *Made in Great Britain*. New Holland, 2008. See page 184.

Campion, Charles. *Fifty Recipes to Stake Your Life On*. Timewell Press, 2004. See page 109.

Cannas, Pulina & Francesconi. *Dairy Goats Feeding & Nutrition*. CABI, 2008. See page 55.

Carême, Marie-Antoine. *L'Art de la Cuisine*. 1833. See page 149.

Carluccio, Antonio. *The Complete Mushroom Book*. Quadrille, 2003. See page 78.

Carmellini, Andrew, & Hyman, Gwen. *Urban Italian*. Bloomsbury, 2008. See page 303.

Castelvetro, Giacomo. *The Fruit, Herbs and Vegetables of Italy* (1614). Translated by Gillian Riley. Viking, 1989. See page 128.

Chartier, François. *Papilles et Molécules*. La Presse, 2009. See page 326.

Chiba, Machiko. *Japanese Dishes for Wine Lovers*. Kodansha International, 2005. See page 124.

Christian, Glynn. *How to Cook Without Recipes*. Portico, 2008. See page 84.

Clark, Sam & Sam. *The Moro Cookbook.* Ebury, 2001. See page 39.

Clifford, Sue, & King, Angela. *The Apple Source Book: Particular Uses for Diverse Apples.* Hodder & Stoughton, 2007. See page 270.

Coates, Peter. *Salmon.* Reaktion, 2006. See page 159.

Cook's Illustrated (www.cooksillustrated.com). See pages 175, 347.

Corrigan, Richard. *The Clatter of Forks and Spoons.* Fourth Estate, 2008. See pages 105, 255.

Cunningham, Marion. *The Breakfast Book.* Knopf, 1987. See page 344.

David, Elizabeth. *A Book of Mediterranean Food.* Lehmann, 1950. See page 93.

David, Elizabeth. *An Omelette and a Glass of Wine.* Penguin, 1986. See pages 260, 283.

David, Elizabeth. *French Provincial Cooking.* Michael Joseph, 1960. See pages 155, 156, 177, 244, 294.

David, Elizabeth. *Italian Food.* Macdonald, 1954. See pages 44, 46, 82, 149, 172, 322, 349.

David, Elizabeth. *Spices, Salt and Aromatics in the English Kitchen.* Penguin, 1970. See pages 270, 325.

Davidson, Alan & Jane. *Dumas on Food.* Folio Society, 1978. See pages 17, 233, 280.

Davidson, Alan. *Mediterranean Seafood.* Penguin, 1972. See page 298.

Davidson, Alan. *North Atlantic Seafood.* Macmillan, 1979. See pages 148, 157.

Davidson, Alan. *The Oxford Companion to Food.* OUP, 1999. See page 134.

de Rovira Sr, Dolf. *Dictionary of Flavors.* Wiley Blackwell, 2008. See page 267.

del Conte, Anna. *The Classic Food of Northern Italy.* Pavilion, 1995. See page 281.

Dolby, Richard. *The Cook's Dictionary and Housekeeper's Directory.* H. Colburn & R. Bentley, 1830. See page 115.

Douglas, Norman. *Venus in the Kitchen.* Heinemann, 1952. See page 36.

Dumas, Alexandre. See Davidson, Alan & Jane.

Dunlop, Fuchsia. *Shark's Fin and Sichuan Pepper.* Ebury, 2008. See pages 51, 109.

Esquire Handbook for Hosts. Edited by P. Howarth. Thorsons, 1999. See page 151.

Farley, John. *The London Art of Cookery.* Fielding, 1783. See page 142.

Fearnley-Whittingstall, Hugh. *River Cottage Every Day.* Bloomsbury, 2009. See page 132.

Fearnley-Whittingstall, Hugh, & Fisher, Nick. *The River Cottage Fish Book.* Bloomsbury, 2007. See pages 139, 148, 166, 248.

Fearnley-Whittingstall, Hugh. *The River Cottage Meat Book.* Hodder & Stoughton, 2004. See pages 121, 168.

Field, Eugene. *The Writings in Prose and Verse of Eugene Field.* C. Scribner's Sons, 1896. See page 270.

Fisher, M. F. K. *Consider the Oyster.* Duell, Sloan & Pearce, 1941. See page 152.

Floyd, Keith. *Floyd on Britain and Ireland.* BBC, 1988. See page 102.

Gill, A. A. *The Ivy: The Restaurant and its Recipes.* Hodder & Stoughton, 1997. See pages 116, 339.

Gladwin, Peter. *The City of London Cook Book.* Accent, 2006. See page 31.

Glass, Leonie. *Fine Cheese.* Duncan Petersen, 2005. See page 65.

Glasse, Hannah. *The Art of Cookery Made Plain and Easy.* 1747. See pages 51, 96, 145, 156, 158, 163.

Graham, Peter. *Classic Cheese Cookery.* Penguin, 1988. See pages 61, 274.

Graves, Tomás. *Bread and Oil: Majorcan Culture's Last Stand.* Prospect, 2001. See page 282.

Grigson, Jane. *English Food.* Macmillan, 1974.

Grigson, Jane. *Fish Cookery.* Penguin, 1975. See page 144.

Grigson, Jane. *Jane Grigson's Fruit Book.* Michael Joseph, 1982. See pages 249, 272, 341.

Grigson, Jane. *Jane Grigson's Vegetable Book.* Michael Joseph, 1978. See pages 131, 266.

Grigson, Sophie. *Sophie Grigson's Herbs.* BBC, 1999. See page 338.

Harbutt, Juliet. *Cheese: A Complete Guide to over 300 Cheeses of Distinction.* Mitchell Beazley, 1999. See page 306.

Hay, Donna. *Flavours.* Murdoch, 2000. See page 313.

Hay, Donna. *Marie Claire Cooking.* Murdoch, 1997. See page 183.

Henderson, Fergus, & Gellatly, Justin Piers. *Beyond Nose to Tail.* Bloomsbury, 2007. See pages 41, 48.

Henderson, Fergus. *Nose to Tail Eating.* Macmillan, 1999. See pages 47, 134.

Hieatt, Constance B., Hosington, Brenda, & Butler, Sharon. *Pleyn Delit: Medieval Cookery for Modern Cooks.* University of Toronto, 1996. See page 143.

Hill, Tony. *The Spice Lover's Guide to Herbs and Spices.* Wiley, 2005. See page 218.

Hirsch, Dr Alan. *Scentsational Sex.* Element, 1998. See pages 186, 231.

Hollingworth, H. L., & Poffenberger, A. D. *The Sense of Taste.* Moffat Yard & Co., 1917. See page 30.

Hom, Ken. *A Taste of China.* Pavilion, 1990. See page 113.

Hooper, Edward James. *Western Fruit Book.* Moore, Wilstach, Keys & Co., 1857. See page 268.

Hopkinson, Simon, & Bareham, Lindsey. *Roast Chicken and Other Stories.* Ebury, 1994. See page 89.

Hopkinson, Simon, & Bareham, Lindsey. *The Prawn Cocktail Years.* Macmillan, 1997. See page 200.

Jaffrey, Madhur. *Madhur Jaffrey's Quick and Easy Indian Cookery.* BBC, 1993. See page 314.

Jaffrey, Madhur. *Madhur Jaffrey's Ultimate Curry Bible.* Ebury, 2003. See page 330.

James, Kenneth. *Escoffier: The King of Chefs.* Continuum, 2002. See page 285.

Kamp, David. *The United States of Arugula.* Broadway, 2006. See page 156.

Kapoor, Sybil. *Taste: A New Way to Cook.* Mitchell Beazley, 2003. See pages 84, 165.

Katzen, Mollie. *Still Life with Menu Cookbook.* Ten Speed Press, 1994. See page 135.

Kaufelt, Rob, & Thorpe, Liz. *The Murray's Cheese Handbook.* Broadway, 2006. See page 57.

Keller, Thomas. *The French Laundry Cookbook.* Workman, 1999. See pages 21, 154.

Kennedy, Diana. *Recipes from the Regional Cooks of Mexico.* Harper & Row, 1978. See page 199.

Kitchen, Leanne. *Grower's Market: Cooking with Seasonal Produce.* Murdoch, 2006. See page 266.

Lanchester, John. *The Debt to Pleasure.* Picador, 1996. See page 6.

Lang, Jenifer Harvey. *Tastings.* Crown, 1986. See page 64.

Larkcom, Joy. *Oriental Vegetables.* John Murray, 1991. See page 125.

Lawson, Nigella. *Forever Summer.* Chatto & Windus, 2002. See page 23.

Lawson, Nigella. *How to be a Domestic Goddess.* Chatto & Windus, 2000. See page 247.

Lawson, Nigella. *How to Eat.* Chatto & Windus, 1998. See page 70.

Levene, Peter. *Aphrodisiacs.* Blandford, 1985. See page 131.

Lewis, Elisha Jarrett. *The American Sportsman.* Lippincott, Grambo & Co., 1855. See page 222.

Leyel, Mrs C. F., & Hartley, Miss O. *The Gentle Art of Cookery*. Chatto & Windus, 1925.
See page 307.

Locatelli, Giorgio. *Made in Italy*. Fourth Estate, 2006. See pages 80, 94, 234, 257, 277, 341.

Luard, Elisabeth. *Truffles*. Frances Lincoln, 2006. See page 116.

Maarse, H. *Volatile Compounds in Foods and Beverages*. CRC Press, 1991.

Mabey, Richard. *The Full English Cassoulet*. Chatto & Windus, 2008. See page 76.

Marinetti. *The Futurist Cookbook* (1932). Translated by Suzanne Brill. Trefoil, 1989.
See page 296.

Marsili, Ray. *Sensory-Directed Flavor Analysis*. CRC Press, 2006. See page 46.

McGee, Harold. *McGee on Food and Cooking*. Hodder & Stoughton, 2004. See pages 31,
88, 105, 145, 154, 171, 172, 183, 191, 196, 279, 346.

Michelson, Patricia. *The Cheese Room*. Michael Joseph, 2001. See page 237.

Miller, Mark, with McLauchlan, Andrew. *Flavored Breads*. Ten Speed Press, 1996. See
page 101.

Miller, Mark. *Coyote Café*. Ten Speed Press, 2002. See page 184.

Ojakangas, Beatrice A. *Scandinavian Feasts*. University of Minnesota, 2001. See page 163.

Oliver, Jamie. *Jamie's Dinners*. Michael Joseph, 2004. See page 277.

Olney, Richard. *The French Menu Cookbook*. Collins, 1975. See pages 29, 114, 268.

Parsons, Russ. *How to Pick a Peach*. Houghton Mifflin Harcourt, 2007. See pages 185, 322.

Paston-Williams, Sara. *The National Trust Book of Traditional Puddings*. David & Charles,
1983. See page 271.

Pern, Andrew. *Black Pudding and Foie Gras*. Face, 2008. See pages 39, 312.

Perry, Neil. *The Food I Love*. Murdoch, 2005. See page 322.

Phillips, Henry. *History of Cultivated Vegetables*. Henry Colburn & Co., 1822. See page 148.

Plath, Sylvia. *The Bell Jar*. Heinemann, 1963. See page 27.

Pomés, Leopold. *Teoria i pràctica del pa amb tomàquet*. Tusquets, 1985. See page 259.

Puck, Wolfgang (www.wolfgangpuck.com). See page 165.

Puck, Wolfgang. *Wolfgang Puck's Modern French Cooking for the American Kitchen*.
Houghton Mifflin, 1981. See page 153.

Purner, John F. *The $100 Hamburger: A Guide to Pilots' Favorite Fly-in Restaurants*.
McGraw-Hill, 1998. See page 66.

Raven, Sarah. *Sarah Raven's Garden Cookbook*. Bloomsbury, 2007. See page 332.

Reboux, Paul. *Book of New French Cooking*. Translated by Elizabeth Lucas Thornton.
Butterworth, 1927. See page 229.

Renowden, Gareth. *The Truffle Book*. Limestone Hills, 2005. See page 116.

Robuchon, Joel. *The Complete Robuchon*. Grub Street, 2008. See page 305.

Roden, Claudia. *A New Book of Middle Eastern Food*. Penguin, 1985. See page 293.

Roden, Claudia. *The Book of Jewish Food*. Viking, 1997. See page 51.

Rodgers, Judy. *The Zuni Café Cookbook*. Norton, 2002. See pages 171, 173, 323, 338.

Rose, Evelyn. *The New Complete International Jewish Cookbook*. Robson, 2004. See page 82.

Rosengarten, David. *Taste*. Random House, 1998. See pages 124, 154, 157, 179.

Round, Jeremy. *The Independent Cook*. Barrie & Jenkins, 1988. See page 253.

Roux, Michel. *Eggs*. Quadrille, 2005. See pages 72, 338.

Saint-Ange, Madame E. *La Bonne Cuisine de Madame E. Saint-Ange*. Translated by
Paul Aratow. Ten Speed Press, 2005. See page 232.

Saulnier, Louis. *Le Répertoire de La Cuisine*. Barron's Educational Series, 1914.

Saveur Editors. *Saveur Cooks Authentic Italian*. Chronicle, 2008. See page 198.

Schehr, Lawrence R., & Weiss, Allen S. *French Food: on the table, on the page, and in French Culture.* Routledge, 2001. See page 149.

The Silver Spoon. Phaidon, 2005. See page 129.

Slater, Nigel. *Real Fast Food.* Michael Joseph, 1992. See pages 157, 271.

Smith, Delia (www.deliaonline.com). See pages 312, 321, 326.

Smith, Delia. *Delia's How to Cook Book One.* BBC, 1998. See page 224.

Smith, Delia. *Delia Smith's Complete Cookery Course.* BBC, 1982. See page 183.

Smith, Delia. *Delia Smith's Summer Collection.* BBC, 1993. See page 258.

Smith, Delia. *Delia Smith's Winter Collection.* BBC, 1995. See page 247.

Tan, Christopher. *Slurp: Soups to Lap Up and Love.* Marshall Cavendish, 2007. See page 13.

Thompson, David. *Thai Food.* Pavilion, 2002. See pages 22, 77, 165.

Toussaint-Samat, Maguelonne. *A History of Food.* Blackwell, 1992. See page 117.

Uhlemann, Karl. *Uhlemann's Chef's Companion.* Eyre & Spottiswoode, 1953. See page 86.

Vetri, Marc, & Joachim, David. *Il Viaggio di Vetri: A Culinary Journey.* Ten Speed Press, 2008. See page 344.

Waltuck, David, & Friedman, Andrew. *Chanterelle: The Story and Recipes of a Restaurant Classic.* Taunton, 2008. See page 130.

Weinzweig, Ari. *Zingerman's Guide to Good Eating.* Houghton Mifflin Harcourt, 2003. See page 175.

Weiss, E. A. *Spice Crops.* CABI, 2002. See page 55.

Wells, Patricia. *Bistro Cooking.* Kyle Cathie, 1989. See page 157.

Wells, Patricia. *Patricia Wells at Home in Provence.* Scribner, 1996. See page 21.

White, Florence. *Good Things in England.* Jonathan Cape, 1932. See page 159.

Willan, Anne. *Reader's Digest Complete Guide to Cookery.* Dorling Kindersley, 1989. See page 179.

Wolfert, Paula. *The Slow Mediterranean Kitchen.* Wiley, 2003. See page 254.

Wright, John. *Flavor Creation.* Allured, 2004.

Wright, John. *Mushrooms: River Cottage Handbook No.1.* Bloomsbury, 2007. See page 81.

Wybauw, Jean-Pierre. *Fine Chocolates: Great Experience.* Lannoo, 2006. See page 184.

Zieglar, Herta. *Flavourings: Production, composition, applications.* Wiley-VCH, 2007.

Other

Buttery, Ron G.; Takeoka, Gary R.; Naim, Michael; Rabinowich, Haim; & Nam, Youngla. *Analysis of Furaneol in Tomato Using Dynamic Headspace Sampling with Sodium Sulfate.* J. Agric. Food Chem., 2001, 49 (9) pp.4349–51. See page 261.

Claps, S.; Sepe, L.; Morone, G.; & Fedele, V. *Differenziazione sensoriale del latte e della caciotta caprina in rapporto al contenuto d'erba della razione.* In: *Proceedings of I formaggi d'alpeggio e loro tracciabilità.* Agenzia Lucana per lo Sviluppo-Associazione Nazionale Formaggi Sotto il Cielo, 2001, pp.191–9. See page 55.

Kurobayashi, Yoshiko; Katsumi, Yuko; Fujita, Akira; Morimitsu, Yasujiro; & Kubota, Kikue. *Flavor Enhancement of Chicken Broth from Boiled Celery Constituents.* J. Agric. Food. Chem., 2008, 56 (2) pp.512–16. See page 96.

Simons, Christopher T.; O'Mahony, Michael; & Carstens E. UC Davis. *Taste Suppression Following Lingual Capsaicin Pre-treatment in Humans.* Chemical Senses, 2002, 27 (4) pp.353–365. See page 210.

Recipe Index

General Index

B

baba ghanoush (aubergine dish), 81
Babbo restaurant, New York, 52
baby bella mushrooms, 77
bacalao (salt cod), 204
Baci, 16
bacon, 167–70
The Baghdad Cookery Book, 50
Bahia, 141
Baker, Nicholson, 295
Bakewell tart, 244, 337
baklava, 342
Bali, 287
Baljekar, Mridula, 41
balsamic vinegar, 257, 281, 324
Baltic countries, 87, 157
bananas, 277–9
Bangalore, 245
banoffee pie, 278
banon goat's cheese, 55
Baptiste mango, 249
Barcelona, 113
Bareham, Lindsey, 89, 200
barfi (confectionery), 286
Barratt's Fruit Salads, 339
basil, 213–15
Basque Country, 156, 206
bastilla pie, 243
Batali, Mario, 52, 183
bay leaves, 255, 313, 317, 349
Bayless, Rick, 15, 56–7, 199, 294
Bayonne, 171
Beacon restaurant, New York, 230
Beard, James, 168, 339
Béarnaise sauce, 50, 52, 130, 182, 257
Beaufort cheese, 239
Beaujolais wine, 72
béchamel sauce, 193
Beckett, Fiona, 294

Bedouins, 20
beech mushrooms, 81
beef, 42–8
beef bourguignon, 43
beef-on-weck sandwich, 45
beef penang, 44
beef rendang, 44
beef tartare, 44–5
beef Wellington, 45, 79
Beenleigh Blue cheese, 61, 64
beer, 233, 325, 333
bees, 273
Beeton, Mrs, 118, 236, 312
beetroot, 85–8
Belazu, 175
Belgium, 93, 325
bell peppers, 205–6
Bellini cocktail, 284
Bellow, Saul, 45
Beluga caviar, 153
Ben and Jerry's, 247
Bendicks chocolates, 330
Bennett, Alan, 249
benzaldehyde, 241, 247
Benzi, François, 154–5
Berenbaum, Rose, 352
Berkswell cheese, 64, 68
Bernhardt, Sarah, 285
beurre blanc, 350
beurre maître d'hôtel, 306
beurre noir, 241
beurre noisette, 240–1
Bibendum, London, 258
biff à la Lindström (beef dish), 102
Birds Eye, 349–50
bird's eye chillies, 28
Biron, David, 266
biryani, 180
biscotti, 181, 183
bistecca alla fiorentina (steak), 304
Bistro Moderne, New York, 117
bitter lemon, 324

bitter oranges, 293
Bittman, Mark, 68, 256, 320
blackberries, 334–5
blackcurrants, 332–4
Black Forest gâteau, 247
Blackiston, Galton, 326
black pudding, 38–40, 269
Bleu de Termignon, 61
blini, 154, 165
bloaters, 164
blood
 black pudding, 38–40
 in liver, 41
blood oranges, 110, 293, 294, 298
Bloody Mary, 96, 261
BLT, 258
blueberries, 343–4
blue cheese, 61–4
Blue Elephant restaurants, 44
Blumenthal, Heston, 7, 122–3, 154–5, 177, 240, 257, 263, 294
'Boiled Beef and Carrots', 43
Boletus edulis, 79
Bolivia, 22, 24
Bologna, 323
bolognese sauce, 223
Bonnat, 348
boquerones (anchovies), 161
borage, 185, 263
Bordeaux, 153
Bordeaux wine, 88
Bornholm, 87
borscht, 86, 87, 105
Bosi, Claude, 328, 350
Boston Cooler, 312
bottarga, 171
boudin blanc, 323
boudin noir, 38, 346
bouillabaisse, 42, 91, 147, 149, 180
Boulud, Daniel, 117, 130
bouquet garni, 325

fish
  oily fish, 155–9
  smoked fish, 164–6
  white fish, 145–50
fish and chips, 148–9
fishcakes, 101, 166, 188
Fisher, M. F. K., 152
Fisher, Nick, 166
fish pie, 144, 147
fish sauce, 161, 207, 265,
  285, 300
Fitzgerald, F. Scott, 277
five-spice powder, 216
flan (baked custard
  pudding), 287
flaó (goat's cheese
  pudding), 57
flatbread, 194, 195
Fleur du Maquis cheese,
  326
Flinn, Anthony, 122
Florence, 86, 304, 3
  19–20
florentines, 310
flounder, 145, 150
flower waters, 297
Floyd, Keith, 102
fluffernutter sandwiches,
  25
focaccia, 177
foie gras, 39, 48, 116, 117,
  129, 140, 184, 311, 312,
  340–1
fontina cheese, 274
fools, 58
Forman, H. & Son, 87,
  165
Foudjou (potted goat's
  cheese), 57
Fourme d'Ambert cheese,
  61, 63
Fowlers Forest Dairy, 69
fragola uva grape, 253
France
  almonds, 244
  beetroots, 86
  blue cheeses, 61

boudin noir, 38
cauliflower, 123
cherries, 248
choucroute garnie, 33
fish, 145–6, 147, 156
flower waters, 297
globe artichokes,
  128–9
goat's cheeses, 55, 57
ham, 169
hard cheeses, 65
melons, 280, 281
mint, 330
olives, 174, 175
omelettes, 132–3
parsley, 191–2
peas, 202, 203
potato dishes, 94
shellfish, 79
strawberries, 263, 264
thyme, 327–8
washed-rind cheeses,
  59–60
watercress, 99, 100
Franche-Comté, 60
Frangelico, 238, 240
frangipane, 239
frankfurters, 33, 37, 323,
  346
The French Laundry,
  Napa Valley, 326
French onion soup, 68
Fribourg, 60
Friese Nagelkaas cheese,
  67
Friesland, 67
frites, 93
frittata, 132
fritters, 77, 201, 281,
  347–8
From Russia With Love,
  109
fruitcake, 67
Fry's Turkish Delight,
  342
Fuerteventura, 56
Fuzzy Navel, 284

G

gado gado, 24, 92
Gagnaire, Pierre, 59
gajar halwar (carrot and
  milk dessert), 227
gala pie, 35
Galia melons, 279
Galicia, 65
Galician cabbage, 89
Galliano, 181, 184, 185
gallic acid, 220
Galvin at Windows,
  London, 85
game, 323, 333, 334
gamjatang (soup), 37
gammon, 118, 167, 191,
  294
ganache, 304–5
garden cress, 100
Gardner, Ava, 153–4
Garfunkel, Art, 269
gari (pickled ginger), 311
garlic, 111–15
garum, 161
Gaskell, Elizabeth, 91
Gaston's, Arkansas, 66
Le Gavroche, London,
  282
gazpacho, 250, 259, 298
gefilte fish, 105
Gein, Ed, 271
gelo di melone (watermelon
  soup), 249
Gentleman's Relish, 161
Georgia, 32, 234
Geraghty, Warren, 344
Gerard, John, 45
Germany
  cheeses, 68
  Himmel und Erde, 40
  horseradish, 45
  lovage, 95
  potato crisps, 90
  Rotwurst, 38
  Rouladen, 43
  Spätlese wine, 62
  Gewürztraminer wine, 85

gherkins, 185, 188
Gianduja, 16
Gidleigh Park, Devon, 204
Gill, A. A., 116
Gillaizeau twins, 299
gin, 187–8, 206, 255, 323, 324, 333, 338, 345
ginger, 308–13
ginger ale, 311, 312
ginger beer, 311, 312, 324
ginger mint, 311
Giono, Jean, 244
gjetost (cheese), 56
glacé cherries, 249, 286
Gladwin, Peter, 31
Glamorgan sausages, 68
Glass, Leonie, 65
Glasse, Hannah, 51–2, 96, 145, 156, 158, 163
globe artichokes, 127–9
Gloucester Old Spot pigs, 272, 282
glutamic acid, 145, 257
glycine, 145
gnocchi, 68, 69, 93, 94, 180
Goa, 28
goat, 45
goat's cheese, 55–8
gold leaf, 46
Goo Goo Cluster, 17
Goodfellas, 33
goose, 31, 121, 187, 233, 322
goose barnacles, 93
gooseberries, 155, 255, 334
goose eggs, 132
goose fat, 177
Gordon, Peter, 133, 332
Gorgonzola, 61, 62, 63, 76, 206
goro (cardamom-flavoured wafers), 313
gorse, 288
gosht aloo (lamb and potato), 91
goshtaba (lamb meatballs), 314

Gouda, 237
Gourmet Burger Kitchen chain, 133
Graham, Peter, 61, 274
Grand Marnier, 293
graniol, 343
Granny Smith apples, 22
Grant, William & Sons, 188
grapefruit, 298–9
grapes, 251–3
grasshoppers, 301
gravadlax, 157
Graves, Tomás, 282
grayling, 155, 159
grazalema (goat's cheese), 57
Greece
  avgolémono, 134–5
  capers, 103
  celery and lamb, 96
  coriander seed, 346
  dill, 190
  figs, 341
  fish, 161
  lemons, 305, 306, 307
  olives, 176
  skordalia, 90, 103, 115
  tomatoes, 260
Greek Gods, 340
Greek salad, 58, 176
Green and Black's, 67, 351
gremolata, 192
Griffith, Melanie, 20
Grifola frondosa, 29
Grigson, Jane, 131, 144, 249, 266, 272, 341
Grigson, Sophie, 338
grillade des mariniers (beef and onions), 46
griottes (Morello cherries), 51
Gruyère, 28, 64, 68, 69, 78, 123, 142, 147
guacamole, 194, 195, 200
guaiacol, 164
guinea fowl, 327

Guinness, 333
gulab jamun, 280–1, 309, 342
gull's eggs, 132, 133
gumbo, 140, 153
Gyngell, Skye, 279
gyudon (steak and onions), 46

H
habanero chillies, 208, 209, 294
haddock, 147, 148, 164, 165, 166, 193
haggis, 53, 93
Hainan Province, 309
Hainanese chicken rice, 309–10
Haiti, 249
halibut, 147
halloumi cheese, 55, 57, 341
ham, 167, 168, 169, 171–4, 191–2, 294
Hamburg, 43
Hangtown fry, 152
Hanoi, 146
Harbutt, Juliet, 306
hard cheese, 64–70
hare, 38, 75
harissa, 84
Harry's Bar, Venice, 284
Harvey Wallbanger, 184
Hawaii, 158, 170, 173
Hay, Donna, 183, 313
Hazan, Marcella, 46
hazelnuts, 238–41
Hazlewood, Lee, 199
Heathcote, Paul, 17
Heine, Heinrich, 265
Heinz tomato ketchup, 93
hen of the woods, 29
Henderson, Fergus, 41, 48, 134
Hendrick's Gin, 187–8
Henry VIII, King, 319

L

laab pla (fish and mint), 158
labskaus, 43, 102
lactones, 290
Ladurée, Paris, 282
Laetiporus sulphureus, 29
lager, 333
Lagrein grape, 19
Laguiole cheese, 69
laksa (noodle soup), 28, 288
lamb, 49–53
lamb's lettuce, 240, 252
lamb's liver, 40, 42
Lancashire hotpot, 91
Lancaster lemon tart, 244
Lanchester, John, 6
land cress, 101
Lang, Jenifer Harvey, 64
Langen, Germany, 96
langostinos, 93
langoustines, 143, 159
Langres cheese, 59–60
Languedoc, 236, 326
lanttulaatikko (swede and nutmeg), 121
Laos, 146, 189
Laphroaig, 314
lard, 33
Larkcom, Joy, 125
lasagne, 344
lassi, 84, 291, 315
Latin America, 136
lavender, 231–2, 255, 345
La Vera valley, 210
Lawson, Nigella, 23, 25, 70, 247
Lazio, 127, 320
Le Stanc, Dominique, 66
Lear, Edward, 203
Leary, Denis, 168–9
Lebanon, 73, 195, 234, 297
Lee, Jeannie Cho, 291
Lee, Mrs, 346
leeks, 29, 39, 76, 107, 110, 114, 169

Leith, Prue, 262
lemon, 303–8
lemon balm, 287
lemon myrtle, 287
lemon thyme, 308, 325
lemon verbena, 287, 329
lemonade, 331
lemongrass, 287–8, 304
lenthionine, 77
lentils, 170, 204, 330–1
Lersch, Martin, 63
Levene, Peter, 131
Lewis, Elisha Jarrett, 222
Leyel, Mrs, 307
Liguria, 319
Limburger cheese, 68
lime, 300–3
lime basil, 300
limoncello, 303
linalool, 345
Lincolnshire Poacher cheese, 64, 68, 69
Lindt, 333
linguine alle vongole, 261
Linzertorte, 338
Liptauer cheese, 102
liquorice, 155, 175, 179, 181, 183, 186, 277, 333
Lisbon, 193
Lithuania, 86
Livarot cheese, 59, 60
liver, 40–2, 169, 340
Liverpool, 43
lobscouse, 43
lobster, 93, 97, 101, 117, 129, 132, 139, 140, 144–5, 155, 170, 223, 227, 232, 298, 350
lobster Thermidor, 142
Locatelli, Giorgio, 80–1, 94, 234–5, 257, 277, 341
Logan, James Harvey, 335
loganberries, 335
lollies, 249
lop yuk (Chinese bacon), 167
loquats, 282

Los Angeles, 156, 165, 343
Louis XIV, King of France, 123
Louisiana, 128, 140, 153
loukades, 342
loukenkas sausages, 153
lovage, 95, 235
lox, 73, 111
Luard, Elisabeth, 116
Ludlow, 282
Lukins, Sheila, 165
Lynch, David, 20
Lyons, 46, 116

M

Mabey, Richard, 76
macadamia nuts, 249
macaroni cheese, 222
macaroons, 282
Macau, 144
McDonald's, 133, 147, 189
mace, 221, 223
McEvedy, Allegra, 319
McGee, Harold, 31, 88, 105, 145, 154, 171, 172, 183, 191, 196, 279, 346
mackerel, 78, 105, 155, 157, 158, 159, 161, 163, 164, 193, 255, 319
McLauchlan, Andrew, 101
McPhee, Colin, 287
Madagascan vanilla, 347, 348
Madeira wines, 236
madeleines, 297, 305
mafe (West African stew), 24, 25
Maggi stock cubes, 95
Mahón cheese, 64, 65, 282
maids of honour, 243–4
La Maison du Chocolat, 182
Majorca, 282
Majorero cheese, 56
makrillsopa, 157
Malaysia
coconut, 132, 285

red cabbage, 270
red flannel hash, 43, 102
red mullet, 78, 155, 159
red mullet liver, 42
red snapper, 148
Redzepi, René, 154
Reese's Peanut Butter
  Cups, 17
Reid, Robert, 29
rempeyek kacang (peanut
  snack), 24
Rendezvous,
  Massachusetts, 320
Rennie, Helen, 320
Renowden, Gareth, 116
Rhine valley, 290
Rhône-Alps, 140
rhubarb, 254–6
Ridge Lytton Springs, 190
Riesling, 124, 284, 290
rillettes, 187
Rioja wine, 93
Ripert, Eric, 340
risi e bisi, 203, 303
risotto, 76, 87, 105, 122–3,
  124, 143, 166, 179, 201,
  303, 321, 322, 344
Ritz Hotel, London, 100
Robuchon, Joel, 153, 162,
  305, 350
rocket, 99, 163
Rococo, 351
Roden, Claudia, 51, 293
Rodgers, Judy, 171, 173,
  338
Rodriguez, Douglas, 318
Rogue Creamery, Oregon,
  167
Rogue River Blue cheese,
  61
Rohmer, Éric, 253
Rolling Stones, 196, 270
Romagna, 86
Romanesco, 126
Romans
  asafoetida, 114
  cinnamon, 44

figs, 340
fish, 161
  thyme, 326
Rome, 128, 173, 332, 349
Romerijo restaurant, El
  Puerto de Santa María,
  93
romesco sauce, 207
Roquefort, 61, 64, 167,
  252, 299
rose, 342–3
Rose, Evelyn, 81
rosemary, 317–20
Rosengarten, David, 124,
  154, 157, 179
rosolje (fish and beetroot),
  87
Rosso, Julee, 165
rösti, 92, 148
rôtisseries, 30
Rotwurst (blood sausage),
  38
Rouen, 175
rouille, 42
roujiamo (hot meat
  sandwich), 34
Rouladen, 43
Round, Jeremy, 253
Roux, Michel, 72, 338
Roves des Garrigues
  goat's cheese, 326
Rovira, Dolf de, Sr, 267
Rowntree's, 330
rum, 265, 277, 285, 288,
  302, 311
rum baba, 342
Russ and Daughters, New
  York, 111
Russia
  borscht, 105
  caviar, 153
  kulebjaka, 78
  mushrooms, 77
  smoked salmon, 73
  sour cherries, 51
  walnuts, 234
Russian salad, 190

Russula xerampelina, 80
Ryan, Meg, 20

S
saag gosht (lamb and
  spinach), 195
Sachertorte, 281
safflower, 179
saffron, 179–81
sage, 321–3
Sage Derby cheese, 69
Saint-Ange, Madame E.,
  232
St John restaurant,
  London, 47
Saint Marcellin cheese, 73
sal ammoniac, 183
*salade frisée aux lardons et
  oeuf poché*, 168
salade niçoise, 157
Salers cheese, 65
salmon, 78, 101, 105, 132,
  155, 156, 157, 159, 174
salsas, 194, 197, 250, 290,
  302
salsify, 225
saltibarsciai (beetroot
  soup), 86
saltimbocca, 43, 323
salt pork, 225
Salty Dog, 324
samak quwarmah (fish and
  lime), 158
sambal belascan (shrimp
  paste and chilli), 141
sambals, 330
La Sambresse beer, 325
sambuca, 175, 181, 183,
  184, 279
samosas, 286
samphire, 141, 155–6
San Antonio, Texas, 43–4
San Daniele ham, 171, 172
San Marzano tomatoes,
  257
San Matteo, 21
Sancerre, 131

Pairings Index

Clove 270
Coriander Seed 345
Hard Cheese 270
Hazelnut 271
Horseradish 271
Liver 41
Mango 289
Nutmeg 221
Orange 271
Peanut 22
Pear 271
Pineapple 265
Pork 272
Rose 342
Sage 321
Shellfish 272
Soft Cheese 70
Vanilla 347
Walnut 272
Washed-rind Cheese 59

Apricot 281–3
Almond 241
Cardamom 313
Chocolate 281
Cinnamon 216
Cumin 83
Ginger 282
Goat's Cheese 55
Hard Cheese 282
Lamb 50
Mango 289
Mushroom 75
Orange 282
Peach 282
Pork 282
Raspberry 337
Rose 283
Rosemary 317
Vanilla 283

Asparagus 130–1
Almond 241
Anise 130
Egg 132
Hard Cheese 65
Lemon 303

Mint 130
Mushroom 130
Oily Fish 155
Orange 294
Pea 201
Peanut 131
Potato 131
Prosciutto 171
Shellfish 139
Truffle 131
White Fish 145

Aubergine 81–2
Bell Pepper 81
Chilli 81
Garlic 82
Ginger 82
Lamb 50
Nutmeg 82
Prosciutto 171
Soft Cheese 82
Tomato 257
Walnut 234

Avocado 198–201
Bacon 198
Blue Cheese 61
Chicken 27
Chilli 198
Chocolate 198
Coffee 199
Coriander Leaf 194
Cucumber 199
Dill 189
Grape 252
Grapefruit 298
Hazelnut 199
Lime 199
Mango 200
Mint 200
Nutmeg 221
Oily Fish 156
Pineapple 265
Shellfish 200
Soft Cheese 200
Strawberry 262
Tomato 201

Bacon 167–70
Anise 167
Apple 167
Avocado 198
Banana 277
Beef 42
Bell Pepper 205
Black Pudding 38
Blue Cheese 167
Broccoli 125
Butternut Squash 230
Cabbage 118
Cardamom 313
Chicken 168
Chilli 207
Chocolate 13
Clove 168
Egg 168
Globe Artichoke 127
Hard Cheese 169
Horseradish 104
Liver 41
Mushroom 75
Onion 169
Orange 294
Oyster 150
Parsley 191
Parsnip 169
Pea 170
Pineapple 170
Pork 33
Potato 88
Sage 321
Shellfish 170
Thyme 170
Tomato 258
Truffle 115
Washed-rind Cheese 59
White Fish 146

Banana 277–9
Almond 277
Anise 277
Bacon 277
Cardamom 314
Caviar 153
Cherry 277

Cherry 286
Chicken 287
Chilli 208
Chocolate 15
Cinnamon 287
Coriander Leaf 194
Dill 189
Egg 134
Lemon 287
Lime 301
Mango 290
Peanut 24
Pineapple 288
Pork 34
Raspberry 288
Shellfish 141
Smoked Fish 165
Strawberry 262
Vanilla 288
White Chocolate 352
White Fish 288

Coffee 19–22
Almond 19
Avocado 199
Banana 278
Beef 19
Blackcurrant 19
Cardamom 20
Cherry 20
Chocolate 20
Cinnamon 20
Clove 220
Coriander Seed 345
Ginger 21
Goat's Cheese 56
Hazelnut 21
Orange 21
Rose 21
Vanilla 349
Walnut 22
White Chocolate 352

Coriander Leaf 194–8
Avocado 194
Chicken 28
Chilli 208

Coconut 194
Coriander Seed 345
Cumin 195
Garlic 195
Goat's Cheese 56
Lamb 195
Lemon 305
Lime 196
Mango 290
Mint 330
Orange 196
Parsley 196
Peanut 197
Pineapple 266
Pork 34
Potato 197
Shellfish 141
Tomato 197
Watermelon 250
White Fish 197

Coriander Seed 345–6
Apple 345
Blueberry 345
Cardamom 314
Coffee 345
Coriander Leaf 345
Cumin 83
Garlic 346
Goat's Cheese 346
Lemon 346
Olive 176
Orange 295
Pork 346

Cucumber 185–8
Anise 186
Avocado 199
Caper 102
Carrot 186
Cumin 84
Dill 186
Garlic 113
Goat's Cheese 187
Melon 279
Mint 187
Oily Fish 156

Onion 108
Peanut 24
Pork 187
Rhubarb 254
Rose 187
Shellfish 188
Strawberry 263
Tomato 259
Watermelon 250
White Fish 188

Cumin 83–5
Apricot 83
Beetroot 83
Carrot 228
Cauliflower 83
Coriander Leaf 195
Coriander Seed 83
Cucumber 84
Egg 134
Lamb 51
Lemon 84
Lime 302
Mango 290
Mint 84
Oily Fish 84
Pork 35
Potato 85
Shellfish 141
Washed-rind Cheese 85

Dill 189–91
Avocado 189
Beef 189
Beetroot 86
Coconut 189
Cucumber 186
Egg 134
Lamb 190
Lemon 305
Mint 190
Mushroom 77
Oily Fish 157
Pea 190
Pork 190
Potato 191
Shellfish 191

Acknowledgments

Thank you to my husband, Nat, for the time he dedicated to this book when he had his own to get on with.

I am very grateful to my editor Richard Atkinson for his invaluable help in getting the text and the look of the book just right. Also to Peter Dawson, Polly Napper, Natalie Hunt, Xa Shaw Stewart, Katie Bond, Emma O'Bryen, Penelope Beech, David Foy and all the lovely people I've met at Bloomsbury for taking such great care over and showing such enthusiasm for this project.

The same goes for my agent Zoe Waldie at Rogers, Coleridge & White, without whose encouragement and advocacy this book might never have made it past the idea stage.

Thanks also to James Lever, William Fiennes, Joanna Bamford, Todd Bridge at La Cave à Fromage, Lucy Thomas at Innocent Drinks, Nicola Franklin at O.W. Loeb & Co. Wines, Carol Brys and Marie Wright at International Flavors and Fragrances Inc., Pete Brown, Kate Johns, John Lowery, and every relative, friend, chef, deli owner, cooking fanatic and taxi driver who shared their knowledge and opinions on the subject of flavour pairings with me over the last three years.

Niki Segnit had not so much as peeled a potato until her early twenties when, almost by accident, she discovered that she loved cooking. Much as she enjoys haute cuisine, she's not likely to attempt to reproduce it at home, preferring to experiment with recipes from domestic kitchens abroad. Her background is in marketing, specialising in food and drink, and she has worked with many famous brands of confectionery, snacks, baby foods, condiments, dairy products, hard liquors and soft drinks. She lives in central London with her husband.

Extracts from *The Debt to Pleasure* by John Lanchester, Pan Macmillan, London © 1996 John Lanchester. Extracts from *The Bell Jar* by Sylvia Plath, reprinted by permission of Faber and Faber Ltd © 1963 The Estate of Sylvia Plath. Extracts from *Venus in the Kitchen* by Norman Douglas, Bloomsbury Publishing, reprinted by permission of The Society of Authors as the Literary Representative of the Estate of Norman Douglas. Extracts from *How to Eat* by Nigella Lawson, published by Chatto & Windus, reprinted by permission of the Random House Group Ltd and by permission of John Wiley & Sons, Inc. © 1998 Nigella Lawson. Every effort has been made to trace the copyright owner of *The Book of New French Cooking* by Paul Reboux. Extracts from *French Provincial Cooking* by Elizabeth David, published by Michael Joseph, reprinted by permission of the Estate of Elizabeth David. Excerpts from *Everyday Drinking* by Kingsley Amis, Bloomsbury Publishing © 2008 The Literary Estate of Sir Kingsley Amis.

First published in Great Britain in 2010

Copyright © 2010 by Niki Segnit

The moral right of the author has been asserted.

Bloomsbury Publishing Plc, 36 Soho Square, London W1D 3QY
Bloomsbury Publishing, London, New York and Berlin

A CIP catalogue record for this book is available from the British Library.

ISBN 978 0 7475 9977 7

10 9 8 7 6 5 4

Designed by Peter Dawson, www.gradedesign.com
General Index by Hilary Bird

Printed in Great Britain by Clays Limited, St Ives plc

All papers used by Bloomsbury Publishing are natural, recyclable products made from wood grown in well-managed forests. The manufacturing processes conform to the environmental regulations of the country of origin.

Mixed Sources
Product group from well-managed forests and other controlled sources
www.fsc.org Cert no. SGS-COC-2061
© 1996 Forest Stewardship Council
FSC

www.bloomsbury.com/nikisegnit

THE *flavour* THESAURUS

White Chocolate
Vanilla
Coriander Seed
Blueberry
Rose
Fig
Raspberry
Blackberry
Blackcurrant
Mint
Thyme
Juniper
Sage
Rosemary
Cardamom
Ginger
Lemon
Lime
Grapefruit
Orange
Mango
Coconut
Peach
Apricot
Melon
Banana
Pear
Apple
Pineapple
Strawberry
Tomato
Rhubarb
Grape
Watermelon
Cherry
Almond
Hazelnut
Walnut
Chestnut
Butternut Squash
Carrot
Parsnip
Nutmeg
Clove
Cinnamon
Basil
Chilli
Bell Pepper
Pea

Floral Fruity

Bramble & Hedge

Creamy Fruity

Fresh Fruity

Woodland

Spicy